Pre-publication REVIEWS, COMMENTARIES, EVALUATIONS . . .

"This book offers a comprehensive, yet practical approach for therapists seeking to explore spiritual issues with a wide range of clients utilizing varied treatment modalities. It balances theory with practical application of activities to promote spiritual exploration and reflection. The contributors clarify the distinction between religion and spirituality in a manner that allows practitioners to address spiritual issues both within and outside the context of traditional religious practice.

The contributors' emphasis upon respect for the values and beliefs of clients demonstrates a strong ethical commitment to personal and professional boundaries with regard to spirituality and religion. They recognize the diversity of spiritual expression and perspective as well as religious practice. I found myself particularly appreciative of their focus on partnership in the development of the therapeutic alliance that runs throughout the book. Spirituality and religion are viewed in a positive light as resources of potentially untapped strength which can be mobilized toward the promotion of healing organized in a consistent manner that is user-friendly. The chapters offer tailored activities and focused interventions from a wide range of theoretical perspectives designed to address the spiritual needs of a varied diagnostic client population at different points in the life cycle."

—Alexander Tartaglia, MA, MDiv, DMin
Associate Dean, School of Allied Health Professions,
Virginia Commonwealth University

"Spirituality is usually a vague concept that is seldom formally taught in professional psychotherapy training programs. If treatment is to be meaningful it would seem important to tailor treatment to the clients' spiritual beliefs. This book makes such interventions possible. There are many valuable and practical tools in this gem of a book."

—Jon Carlson, PsyD, EdD, ABPP
Distinguished Professor,
Governors State University

"This is a book-set I want to own for myself. The size of the books reflects the exponential growth of interest in recent years in spirituality in the counseling and psychotherapy fields. Spirituality in these books is represented in diverse, even conflicting perspectives. It is unlikely that the reader will not appreciate chapters that are gems to him or her, while disagreeing strongly with others. That is the strength of these two books. The varied approaches to incorporating spirituality into therapy offer a broad sampling of practical applications, but also serve as a rich reference resource."

—Harry J. Aponte, MSW, LCSW, LMFT
Clinical Associate Professor,
The Couple & Family Therapy Program,
Drexel University

"These two books contain some of the most important readings in the last several years in the area of spirituality and therapy. These excellent works move beyond the theoretical and biblical discussions that have dominated the literature toward the practical application of incorporating spirituality into the therapy room, and clients' lives. The interventions are theoretically and spiritually sound, while also being readable and useful. I strongly recommend these books for beginning and advanced-level therapists."

—Joseph L. Wetchler, PhD
Professor and Director,
Marriage and Family Therapy Program,
Purdue University, Calumet

"This diverse collection of practical and theoretical chapters on the use of spirituality in counseling is modestly called a *Therapist's Notebook*, but may be more accurately described as an encyclopedia of resources for clinicians, educators, and spiritual directors on the critical confluence of psyche, spirit, mind, and soul. The chapters contain a wealth of ideas for utilizing the spiritual and religious strengths of clients as well as necessary guidelines and cautions about respect for individual difference. The clinical handouts and bibliographies alone make it a valuable handbook. There are also important discussions of interest to both the practitioner and researcher."

—**James Higginbotham, PhD**
Assistant Professor of Pastoral Care and Counseling,
Earlham School of Religion

"This book offers an entirely unique exploration of lived spirituality by combining depth and clarity without sacrificing either. The editors succeed in offering a text that remains grounded in the concrete dilemmas of life and practice, thereby evoking the complex emotional impact of how we each grapple with questions of spirit. The book will be especially useful for pastoral educators and counselors, clergy, as well as both secular and religious psychotherapists and psychologists who are seeking to find ethical ways to respond to their clients' spiritual and religious concerns. The book includes highly practical chapters on couples work, working with shame, using film and humor in sessions, and working with specific minority populations. A highlight of the presentation is how complex ideas are introduced, and then quickly set within therapeutic sessions through clinical vignettes so that it is immediately apparent how each topic might be usefully explored with one's own clients. Each chapter concludes with a selection of essential resources, including handouts for therapist self-exploration and exercises for clients to use within and outside of sessions. The exercises further enhance the applicability of spiritual questions to everyday contexts while challenging more superficial understandings of life's problems. They will also prove invaluable in the classroom as tools for giving trainees an embodied experience of the felt quality of the spiritual domain. This book consistently offers a deeply respectful and human approach to these complex issues by avoiding pathological language and instead emphasizing that as therapists, we also grapple with ultimate questions of meaning and values."

—**Greg Madison, ADEP, AdvDipCPsychol, PhD**
Coordinator of MA in Pastoral Psychology
and Counseling, St. Stephens College,
Edmonton Alberta; Visiting Lecturer,
School of Psychotherapy and Counseling
at Regents College, London, United Kingdom

The Therapist's Notebook for Integrating Spirituality in Counseling
Homework, Handouts, and Activities for Use in Psychotherapy

HAWORTH *Practical Practice in Mental Health*
Lorna L. Hecker, PhD
Senior Editor

101 Interventions in Family Therapy edited by Thorana S. Nelson and Terry S. Trepper

101 More Interventions in Family Therapy edited by Thorana S. Nelson and Terry S. Trepper

The Practical Practice of Marriage and Family Therapy: Things My Training Supervisor Never Told Me by Mark Odell and Charles E. Campbell

The Therapist's Notebook for Families: Solution-Oriented Exercises for Working with Parents, Children, and Adolescents by Bob Bertolino and Gary Schultheis

Collaborative Practice in Psychology and Therapy edited by David A. Paré and Glenn Larner

The Therapist's Notebook for Children and Adolescents: Homework, Handouts, and Activities for Use in Psychotherapy edited by Catherine Ford Sori and Lorna L. Hecker

The Therapist's Notebook for Lesbian, Gay, and Bisexual Clients: Homework, Handouts, and Activities for Use in Psychotherapy by Joy S. Whitman and Cynthia J. Boyd

A Guide to Self-Help Workbooks for Mental Health Clinicians and Researchers by Luciano L'Abate

Workbooks in Prevention, Psychotherapy, and Rehabilitation: A Resource for Clinicians and Researchers edited by Luciano L'Abate

The Psychotherapist as Parent Coordinator in High-Conflict Divorce: Strategies and Techniques by Susan M. Boyan and Ann Marie Termini

The Couple and Family Therapist's Notebook: Homework, Handouts, and Activities for Use in Marital and Family Therapy by Katherine A. Milewski Hertlein, Dawn Viers, and Associates

The Therapist's Notebook for Integrating Spirituality in Counseling: Homework, Handouts, and Activities for Use in Psychotherapy edited by Karen B. Helmeke and Catherine Ford Sori

The Therapist's Notebook for Integrating Spirituality in Counseling II: More Homework, Handouts, and Activities for Use in Psychotherapy edited by Karen B. Helmeke and Catherine Ford Sori

Interactive Art Therapy: "No Talent Required" Projects by Linda L. Simmons

Therapy's Best: Practical Advice and Gems of Wisdom from Twenty Accomplished Counselors and Therapists by Howard Rosenthal

The Christian Therapist's Notebook: Homework, Handouts, and Activities for Use in Christian Counseling by Philip J. Henry, Lori Marie Figueroa, and David R. Miller

The Therapist's Notebook for Integrating Spirituality in Counseling
Homework, Handouts, and Activities for Use in Psychotherapy

Karen B. Helmeke, PhD
Catherine Ford Sori, PhD
Editors

Routledge
Taylor & Francis Group
New York   London

First published by
The Haworth Press, Inc.
10 Alice Street
Binghamton, N Y 13904-1580

This edition published 2011 by Routledge

Routledge
Taylor & Francis Group
711 Third Avenue
New York, NY 10017

Routledge
Taylor & Francis Group
27 Church Road, Hove
East Sussex BN3 2FA

PUBLISHER'S NOTE
The development, preparation, and publication of this work has been undertaken with great care. However, the Publisher, employees, editors, and agents of The Haworth Press are not responsible for any errors contained herein or for consequences that may ensue from use of materials or information contained in this work. The Haworth Press is committed to the dissemination of ideas and information according to the highest standards of intellectual freedom and the free exchange of ideas. Statements made and opinions expressed in this publication do not necessarily reflect the views of the Publisher, Directors, management, or staff of The Haworth Press, Inc., or an endorsement by them.

Identities and circumstances of individuals discussed in this book have been changed to protect confidentiality.

Scripture quotations marked (NIV) are taken from the HOLY BIBLE, NEW INTERNATIONAL VERSION®. NIV®. Copyright © 1973, 1978, 1984 by International Bible Society. Used by permission of Zondervan. All rights reserved.

Scripture taken from the NEW AMERICAN STANDARD BIBLE®, Copyright © 1960, 1962, 1963, 1968, 1971, 1972, 1973, 1975, 1977, 1995 by The Lockman Foundation. Used by permission.

New Revised Standard Version Bible, copyright 1989, Division of Christian Education of the National Council of the Churches of Christ in the United States of America. Used by permission. All rights reserved.

Scripture quotations marked "NKJV" are taken from the New King James Version®. Copyright © 1982 by Thomas Nelson, Inc. Used by permission. All rights reserved.

Cover design by Lora Wiggins.

Library of Congress Cataloging-in-Publication Data

The therapist's notebook for integrating spirituality in counseling : homework, handouts, and activities for use in psychotherapy / Karen B. Helmeke, Catherine Ford Sori, editors.
    p. cm.
Includes bibliographical references and index.
ISBN-13: 978-0-7890-3257-7 (set : soft : alk. paper)
ISBN-10: 0-7890-3257-0 (set : soft : alk. paper)
ISBN-13: 978-0-7890-2991-1 (book 1 : soft : alk. paper)
ISBN-10: 0-7890-2991-X (book 1 : soft : alk. paper)
[etc.]
    1. Psychotherapy—Religious aspects—Problems, exercises, etc. 2 Psychotherapy patients—Religious life—Problems, exercises, etc. 3. Spirituality—Problems, exercises, etc.
    [DNLM: 1. Psychotherapy. 2. Spirituality. WM 420 T3983 2006] I. Helmeke, Karen B. II. Sori, Catherine Ford.

RC489.S676T439 2006
616.89'14—dc22

                                                                                                    2005033491

To my husband, Gary, whose faith continues to draw me toward him, and to our daughters, Amanda and Ella, whose joy in life and discovery of God renew and inspire my own faith, with all my love.

Karen B. Helmeke

My spiritual lineage—past, present, and future:
my Grandma Kate and Grandma Bess
my parents, Marvin and Elnora Ford,
and my late sister, Cynthia Lori, and her sons, Jeremy and Joel; and Uncle Albert
my husband John and our children,
Jessica C. Roberson and Heather Paul,
Marissa Sori, Marlene Dickson, Al Sori, Ann Campagna, and Paul Sori,
and all our grandchildren:
Cameron, Alexis, and Lyric; Cassandra, Rick, Alec;
Rachel, Jonathan, Victoria; Brendan, Elizabeth, Ethan;
Ann Marie, John, Alfredo; Deandra, Lauryn, Marin, and Baby Paul!

Catherine Ford Sori

And together, we dedicate this book to God.

CONTENTS

ABOUT THE EDITORS

Karen B. Helmeke, PhD, MDiv, is an Adjunct Associate Professor of Family and Consumer Sciences at Western Michigan University in Kalamazoo, Michigan, and maintains a small private practice in marriage and family therapy in Portage, Michigan. She formerly served on the faculty at Christian Theological Seminary in Indianapolis, Indiana, where she taught in the accredited marriage and family therapy program. She has several published works in the areas of couples therapy, qualitative research, training and supervision issues, and spirituality. She has also presented her work at AAMFT conferences on spirituality and multicultural issues in training. Dr. Helmeke is on the editorial boards of the *Journal of Marital and Family Therapy,* the *Journal of Feminist Family Therapy,* and the *Journal of Couple & Relationship Therapy.*

Catherine Ford Sori, PhD, is a University Professor in the Division of Psychology and Counseling at Governors State University in University Park, Illinois, and Associate Faculty at the Chicago Center for Family Health. Dr. Sori is frequently invited to present on topics pertaining to children, families, illness, bereavement, and family play therapy. She has written numerous journal articles and book chapters. Recent publications include "Training Family Therapists to Work with Children and Families: A Modified Delphi Study" (with Douglas Sprenkle, PhD) in the *Journal of Marital and Family Therapy* and *The Therapist's Notebook for Children and Adolescents: Homework, Handouts, and Activities for Use in Psychotherapy* (co-edited with Lorna L. Hecker, PhD).

Contributors

Bernard J. Baca, PhD, LCSW, specializes exclusively in IMAGO Relationship Couple's therapy, and has conducted national workshops on couple's therapy, clinical treatment of sex offenders, and object relations theory and technique. Dr. Baca was awarded a doctorate in clinical psychology from the Union Institute and two master's degrees in clinical psychology and social work from Central Michigan University and University of Wisconsin–Madison respectively. He is a member of the editorial board of the *Journal of Imago Relationship Therapy* and cochair of the research committee for the Association of Imago Therapists. Dr. Baca has been in private practice for twenty-two years in both Indiana and Santa Fe, New Mexico. He is a certified couple's IMAGO therapist and couple's workshop presenter and was trained by both Dr. Harville Hendrix and Dr. Pat Love, both nationally recognized authors and clinicians specializing in couple's therapy. In addition, Dr. Baca consults with other professionals and assists them in case consultation as well as supervising graduate clinical students at Christian Theological Seminary in Indianapolis, Indiana.

Adriana Balaguer Dunn, PhD, received her PhD in clinical psychology from the University of Denver. Dr. Dunn is an associate professor in the Department of Professional Psychology and Family Therapy at Seton Hall University. She has been teaching in the master's, postmaster's, and doctoral programs in marriage and family therapy. She is a clinical member of the AAMFT, an AAMFT approved supervisor, and a member of the APA, Division 43 Family Psychology. Dr. Dunn conducts research in the areas of spirituality and family therapy and of early relationship development in Latino couples. She has presented at AAMFT conferences on spirituality focused genograms, on working with Latino couples and on cultural competency in family therapy.

Judith K. Balswick, EdD, recently retired, was a senior professor at Fuller Theological Seminary, School of Psychology, Department of Marital and Family Therapy. She is a licensed marriage and family therapist in California, an AAMFT approved supervisor, and a CAMFT certified supervisor. She has publications in the areas of Christian perspectives on the family, parenting, sexuality, leaving home, life ties, family pain, and the dual-earner marriage. She is a frequent speaker at conferences on marriage, family, parenting, and relationship issues. She has taught classes in gender and human sexuality, family therapy, building strong families in the church, and supervision. Her specialties are family enrichment, interpersonal relationships, and group therapy.

Nancee Biank, MSW, LCSW, is the director of Children and Family Services at Wellness House, Hinsdale, Illinois, a nonprofit organization that offers psychosocial support to cancer patients and their families. Nancee developed the groundbreaking Family Matters Program for children who have a parent with cancer. She was recently invited to present this model to an international audience at the seventh World Congress of Psycho-oncology in Copenhagen, Denmark, and is currently working with Catherine Ford Sori on a book for families titled *Tell Them*

That We Know . . . Children's Responses to Illness and Loss. Nancee is also in private practice and is cofounder of Partners in Transition in Hinsdale, Illinois. She trained at the Institute for Psychoanalysis, Child, and Adolescent Therapy Program, University of Illinois, Jane Adams College of Social Work in Chicago; and also with Judith Wallerstein. Nancee lives with her husband, Vincent, in Hinsdale and enjoys spending time with her children and granddaughter.

Edward R. Canda, PhD, is a professor and director of the PhD program in social work at the University of Kansas. He is also a courtesy professor of religious studies and a member of the Center for East Asian Studies. Dr. Canda has more than 100 publications and 100 presentations, most addressing connections between spirituality, cultural diversity, and social work. Two of his recent books are *Spiritual Diversity in Social Work Practice* (with Leola Dyrud Furman) and *Transpersonal Perspectives on Spirituality in Social Work* (edited with Elizabeth Smith, The Haworth Press). He has an MA in religious studies and MSW and PhD degrees in social work.

Aaron H. Carlstrom, PhD, is a therapist at the Kansas State University Counseling Services, where he is the diversity coordinator. He holds a bachelor's degree in psychology from Marquette University, and a master's degree in community counseling and PhD in counseling psychology from the University of Wisconsin–Milwaukee. His clinical and research interests include the areas of multicultural counseling, career development, and biofeedback training. Specifically, he is interested in the integration of the development of both multicultural and career competencies of college students, finding meaningful and significant work, and the role of openness to growth-enhancing experiences in both multicultural and career development.

Stephen E. Craig, PhD, LPC, LLP, is an assistant professor and coordinator, MA Community Counseling Program, in the Department of Counselor Education and Counseling Psychology at Western Michigan University. He obtained a PhD at the University of North Texas and is a licensed professional counselor (LPC) and doctoral-limited licensed psychologist (LLP) in Michigan. Dr. Craig's interests revolve primarily around social interest development in adolescents; Adlerian psychological principles; and counselor supervision. He has published in nationally refereed journals, published a book chapter related to closure issues in family counseling, presented at state, regional, and national conferences, and completed his doctoral dissertation research on a structural equation model of contributing factors to adolescent social interest development. He recently served as co-president of the Michigan Association for Counselor Education and Supervision (MACES), and holds additional memberships in the American Counseling Association (ACA); the Association for Counselor Education and Supervision (ACES); North Central Association for Counselor Education and Supervision; the Michigan Counseling Association; and the Kalamazoo Counseling Association.

Gene Deegan, PsyD, is a consultant and consumer-provider in Lawrence, Kansas. He is the former program manager for consumer led-research and training, in the Office for Adult Mental Health Research of the University of Kansas School of Social Welfare. He has a doctorate in Clinical Psychology from Rutgers University and has done research at Rutgers and Kansas University on the role of spirituality in mental health. He has given many workshops and presentations on this topic.

Lonnie E. Duncan, PhD, is an assistant professor in the Department of Counselor Education and Counseling Psychology at Western Michigan University. He is married and has two children. His research and clinical interests are in urban mental health issues, religion and spirituality, statistics and research, supervision and training, and African-American mental health. His clinical work expands fifteen years where he has worked in University Counseling Centers as well as community mental health agencies. He is co-founder of Compassionate Care Counseling where he provides consultation and direct service to various agencies on ways to their delivery of mental health services to urban youths and their families.

Monika Eichler, LMSW, has worked over the past decade exploring how mind-body-spirit practices affect overall health and well-being. Her practice experiences include case management and psychotherapy. She currently conducts research on best practices in community support services at the Office of Mental Health Research and Training at Kansas University. In addition, she is a founding member of a Waldorf initiative, Prairie Moon School, in Lawrence, Kansas, as well as an assistant professor at Holos University Graduate Seminary, based out of Springfield, Missouri.

Marvin L. Ford has had a long and distinguished career with the federal government in the Internal Revenue Service. For more than a decade, Ford was lead instructor for various IRS schools, teaching both basic and advanced courses for tax auditors and revenue agents. He has been IRS spokesman in Northern Indiana since 1968, appearing on TV and radio, as well as speaking to professional groups and at business and retirement seminars. For many years Ford taught a variety of business and tax classes at Purdue University Calumet. He co-authored and edited the texts used in forty-two states for annual tax seminars. He taught at those sponsored in Indiana by Purdue University for many years. Ford also co-authored the Indiana University coursebook, and taught at their schools throughout the state. In addition to more than sixteen IRS awards and commendations, Ford was nominated Federal Technical Employee of the year for 1990, and was nominated for the 1992 Presidential Volunteer Action Award. Purdue University presented him an award in 1999 for his long-time service in working on the coursebook, planning and instructing its seminars. In 2002, Quality for Indiana Taxpayers named Ford tax professional of the year. A sought-after speaker, Marvin Ford is well known for his keen sense of humor and quick wit. He is married to Elnora, and is the father of one of the editors, Catherine Ford Sori.

Terry D. Hargrave, PhD, is a professor of counseling at West Texas A&M University in Canyon, Texas. He is the author of numerous professional articles and six books including *Families and Forgiveness: Healing Wounds in the Intergenerational Family* and *Forgiving the Devil: Restoring Relationships in Damaging Families.* He is founder and president of Amarillo Family Institute, Inc., where he specializes in the treatment of aging families, reconciliation in violent and damaging families, grief, and marital therapy.

Joseph J. Horak, MTS, PhD, is CEO of Horak Family and Psychological Services, PC and president of C.A.S.E. Worldwide, a firm that consults to family-owned businesses, family foundations, and businesses undergoing mergers and acquisitions. Another of his specialties is to help families establish philanthropic vehicles, and he recently published on this topic. He is a member of the APA and a clinical member and approved supervisor with AAMFT. He is chair of the Michigan licensing board for Marriage and Family Therapy, a past president of the Michigan Association for Marriage and Family Therapy and chair of the AAMFT Ethics Committee. Dr. Horak has held adjunct faculty appointments at Wayne State University, Western Michigan University, and Western Theological Seminary, and was a guest lecturer at the Russian Academy of Sciences, Institute for Psychology in Moscow.

Karen Horneffer, PhD, received her PhD in clinical and community psychology from the University of Illinois, as well as her yoga teacher certification from Kripalu. She is director of the Holistic Health Care Program at Western Michigan University in Kalamazoo, Michigan, and has special interests in mind-body-spirit approaches to health care and education. Karen has published several articles and chapters, including two which appear in Vass et al. (2001) *Seeds of Awakening: Cultivating and Sustaining the Inner Life.*

Peter J. Jankowski, PhD, holds a PhD degree in marriage and family therapy from Texas Tech University. He is currently an associate professor in the Department of Psychology at Bethel University, St. Paul, Minnesota. He is a licensed marriage and family therapist and AAMFT approved supervisor. His research and writing interests are in the areas of clinical decision-making, qualitative research methodology, peace psychology, and spirituality in psychotherapy.

J. Mark Killmer, MDiv, PsyD, LMFT, is a licensed marriage and family therapist and Presbyterian clergyperson currently serving as executive director of the Samaritan Counseling Center in Munster, Indiana. He also works as an adjunct professor for the marriage and family therapy master's program at Purdue University Calumet. Mark is a clinical member and an approved supervisor in AAMFT and a clinical member of the American Association of Christian Counselors (AACC). Clinical specialties include conflict resolution, recovery from affairs, acting-out adolescents, forgiveness, and the integration of spirituality in therapy. Mark has presented at state and national AAMFT conferences on the use of forgiveness. He has published an article on the treatment of anxiety disorders with devout Christian clients.

Anita Berardi Maher, MA, PhD, LMFT, is an associate professor of marriage and family therapy in the Graduate Department of Counseling at George Fox University in Portland, Oregon. She received her MA in marriage and family therapy from Azusa Pacific University; an MA in theology from the School of Theology at Fuller Theological Seminary; and her PhD in marriage and family therapy from the School of Psychology at Fuller Theological Seminary. She is a licensed marriage and family therapist and an AAMFT approved supervisor. She has also maintained a private practice for the past fifteen years and offers her volunteer services to the community and the American Red Cross as a trauma response specialist. She is active with the AAMFT, having served as both secretary and president of the Oregon Division.

Philip M. Mamalakis, PhD, has recently taken a position at Holy Cross Greek Orthodox School of Theology in Brookline, Massachusetts, as assistant professor of pastoral care. He has a MDiv from Holy Cross and a PhD from Purdue University. He has published and presented on fatherhood, interfaith marriages, forgiveness, couples therapy, and working with couples going through divorce. He served as the divorce services coordinator at Families First in Missoula, Montana, where he taught parent education, counseled couples, and wrote a monthly parenting column for a local magazine. He is married with five children.

Robert F. Massey, PhD, is a professor in the Department of Professional Psychology and Family Therapy, and director of PhD, EdS, and MA/EdS in marriage and family programs at Seton Hall University, New Jersey. He is a clinical member of the AAMFT and an AAMFT approved supervisor. Dr. Massey conducts research in the areas of spirituality and personality factors in couple relationships, and has presented his work at regional, national, and international conferences.

Lori McKinney, PhD, is a former university professor at Governors State University in Illinois. She completed her PhD in social psychology at the University of Illinois in Chicago. Dr. McKinney's research includes work on intentional forgetting and repressive coping styles. She is actively involved in mentoring Christian women using both biblical and psychological principles. She currently resides in Colorado, where she is founding a ministry.

Rand Michael, DMin, is an associate professor and clinical director of marriage and family therapy at George Fox University in Portland, Oregon. He is a clinical member and approved supervisor for the AAMFT. His teaching and counseling specialties consist of couple therapy; transitions; interpersonal communication; spirituality and mental/relationship health well-being; and international clinical training, consulting, service, and mental health. His current writing project is a book with the working title *Couple Therapy: Marriage Enrichment and Change.*

Robert R. Powell, MA, LPC, has been the executive director of Florence Crittenton Services for the past six years. Florence Crittenton Services specializes in counseling at-risk youth and their families. Prior to Florence Crittenton Services, Bob has counseled youth for over twenty years. He is completing his doctorate in counselor education at Western Michigan University in Kalamazoo, Michigan. He obtained his master's in guidance and counseling from Wayne State University in 1991. His clinical specialties are in child and adolescent counseling. He has been providing supervision to counselors that specialize in youth for over fifteen years as well.

Paul E. Priester, PhD, is an assistant professor at the University of Wisconsin–Milwaukee. His PhD is in counseling psychology from Loyola University, Chicago, and his master's degree is in rehabilitation counseling from the University of Iowa. He also received specialized training in substance abuse from Marycrest University, the psychology of religion from the University of Iowa, pastoral counseling from Loyola University, Chicago, and hypnotherapy training with Erica Fromm at the University of Chicago. His clinical specialties include: the role of spiritual development in recovery from addictions; 12-step recovery process; integrating spirituality into the psychotherapy process; culturally sensitive treatment of religious minorities (especially Muslims, Conservative Christians, and Orthodox Jews); and Islam-based models of psychotherapy. He has several publications in these areas as well.

Jessica C. Roberson is a student at the International Academy of Design and Technology, an artist, and a musician whose passion is playing gospel and praise and worship music. One of her hobbies is compiling examples of religious jokes, which she eagerly shares with others. She is the mother of three children (who share her joy in music), and resides in Lansing, Illinois. Jessica Roberson is Catherine Ford Sori's daughter.

Shermie L. Schafer, MDiv, STM, LMFT, LCSW, was trained by Drs. Harville Hendrix and Pat Love in Imago Therapy for Couples and Singles, in 1992 and 1993. She has been doing psychotherapy for twenty-five years, and maintains a small private practice. She serves as supervisor in the counseling training program at Christian Theological Seminary in Indianapolis. She has also served as a parish minister, a hospital chaplain, a university instructor, a grant project director, and a health care provider. Her most recent publications include a book chapter titled "Return to the Dance: The Power of Ritual in Ordinary Lives" in *Women and Religious Ritual,* and a book chapter titled "Healing Ritual for Victims of Abuse" in *When Love Is Not Enough* (with Rabbi Sandy Sasso).

Richard S. Shaw, DMFT, is an associate professor of marriage and family therapy in the graduate department of counseling at George Fox University in Portland, Oregon. He is a marriage and family therapist trained in theology, psychology, and marriage and family therapy. He holds a doctorate in marriage and family therapy and a master's degree in integration leadership from Fuller Theological Seminary. He specializes and practices as a marriage and family therapist part time with individuals, couples, and families in the areas of depression, anxiety, marital issues, shame, and grace, and integration of psychotherapy and faith issues. Richard is married to Karen and has two children. They reside in Wilsonville, Oregon.

Julie A. States, PhD, CAC, is a staff psychologist with the Center for Counseling and Psychological Services at Penn State University and also maintains a private psychotherapy practice in State College, Pennsylvania. She holds a doctorate in counseling psychology and has conducted research on spirituality in the recovery process from alcoholism. Dr. States is a licensed psychologist and a certified addiction counselor in Pennsylvania, and has many years of experience providing counseling and psychological services to individuals, couples, and groups. In addition to her clinical specialty in addiction, Dr. States is also interested in holistic counseling approaches that incorporate the physical, mental, emotional, and spiritual aspects of individuals.

She is an advanced certified practitioner of process acupressure, which is an integrative therapy approach combining traditional acupressure with psychological process skills.

Karen Swanson, EdD, is Director for the Institute for Prison Ministries at the Wheaton College, Wheaton, Illinois. She has completed a certificate in correctional chaplaincy from Taylor University, Upland, Illinois, and is a regular volunteer with the Life Learning Program, a correctional ministry program in the Cook County Jail, Chicago. She is the executive director of Life House Ministries, a Christ-centered reentry program for ex-offenders, and is the director of Women's Ministry at Fox Valley Church in West Dundee, Illinois. One research area of interest has been the faith and moral development in a faith-based correctional education program. She has also written *Enhancing the Physical Education Pre-Service Curriculum: Implementing Service-Learning.*

Marsha Vaughn, PhD, is an associate professor of psychology at Judson College in Elgin, Illinois. She completed a chaplain residency (ACPE-accredited) at Covenant Hospital in Lubbock, Texas, and is on the advisory board for Grace Community Christian Healthcare in Carpentersville, Illinois. She is a licensed marriage and family therapist and AAMFT approved supervisor. Her clinical interests are spirituality and chronic illness and community development. One area of research interest has been grounded theory of language and therapist influence in marriage and family therapy.

Sharilyn Wells, is the former director of Project Acceptance in Lawrence, Kansas, one of the older consumer-run organizations for persons with mental illness. She was the vice president of the homeless coalition in Lawrence, Kansas, and she has been involved in advocacy efforts for the mentally ill. Ms. Wells was involved in developing a spirituality training workshop with Kansas University for mental health professionals and consumers, has given state workshops on spirituality and recovery, and actively participates in her spirituality group.

Phyllis L. White, MDiv, has been an ordained pastor for twenty-six years, having received her degree from Garrett-Evangelical Theological Seminary. She is currently completing a MA in counseling (marriage and family therapy track) at Governors State University where she is the co-coordinator of the Counseling Lab. She is a member of Chi Sigma Iota and the American Counseling Association.

Gwendolyn J. Williams, PhD, is currently an associate professor and program chair in Special Education at Florida A&M University. She has numerous publications in her professional areas of interest, which include community transitions, family, school and community partnerships, mental retardation, multiple impairments, behavior management, and assistive technology. She is the editor/developer of the online journal, *Journal of Multiculturalism in Education.* She teaches both undergraduate and graduate level courses. Dr. Williams has developed and taught online graduate and undergraduate courses in special education. She is a behavior management consultant and a public speaker on multicultural issues. Dr. Williams advocates for children with disabilities at the local, state, and national levels. She received her doctoral degree from Florida State University in Special Education and Community Transitions.

Foreword

Karen Helmeke and Catherine Sori have produced an invaluable resource on an underdeveloped theme—how to incorporate spirituality into the work of therapists who work in secular settings. In my 33 years as a credentialed marriage and family therapist (MFT), one of the most dramatic changes has been the relatively recent willingness of the field to address this dimension of life that was largely taboo until the 90s. Before this book, however, we lacked specific guidance on how to do this integration.

Our field has always been comfortable with the social and psychological dimensions of humankind. Eventually therapists started paying more attention to the biological aspect of personhood. This book witnesses to the growing interest in a fourth dimension. We are biological-psychological-social-*and spiritual* beings. Many of our clients already viewed themselves this way—it just took us a long time to catch up. As the editors point out, therapists were not reticent because of their secularism, but they did not know how to incorporate this fourth dimension without compromising their professionalism or imposing their views. Here is where this book shines.

In this carefully edited and extraordinarily rich book, the chapters move from the general to the more specific. Early chapters focus on therapist preparation for this work and address issues like spiritual self-care, ethical use of spiritual materials, and disclosure. The editors are serious that integrating spirituality demands sensitivity. The book then moves to assessment independent of specific interventions. The next two sections are on couples therapy and specific technique related to engaging topics like shame and humor. The final section includes chapters on very specific techniques related to traditional spiritual practices like use of scripture and prayer.

The work is exceptionally well-integrated for an edited book. First, all chapters follow a similar outline. Second, the typical bane of most edited books—uneven writing—is absent. This is a great tribute to the editors' skills and their insistence that authors re-write and re-write again. Third, there are several charts that cross reference contributions by topics, techniques, populations, assessments, and professional development. Finally the personal spirit of the two editors—who I personally know embody the kind of spiritual sensitivity they hope to engender in their readers—permeates this warm and wise book.

Even as a seasoned clinician, I found this book to be a veritable feast that whetted my appetite for more. I am delighted that the editors have already prepared another book—a second course for this rich offering. I invite the reader to join me at the table.

Douglas H. Sprenkle
Professor of Marriage and Family Therapy
Purdue University

Preface

Many clinicians, although quite spiritual or religious themselves, hesitate to invite spirituality into the therapy room, perhaps out of respect for the client, perhaps because they do not want to impose their own beliefs on their clients, or perhaps because they would like to entertain these significant topics, but are not sure of their own competence in integrating matters of religion and spirituality into the realm of psychotherapy. In one clinical study of marriage and family therapists, although 95 percent of the therapists considered themselves to be spiritual, only 48 percent of them said they were comfortable using very general spiritual interventions in therapy and only 17 percent were comfortable with specific religious interventions (Carlson, Kirkpatrick, Hecker, & Killmer, 2002). Very few of the respondents in the study had received training in spirituality; only 14 percent reported that spirituality had been emphasized in their training. The authors hypothesize that this lack of education may be related to therapists' discomfort in addressing and integrating spirituality in therapy. Although there have been many calls in recent years to integrate spirituality and religion into therapy, there have been relatively few practical guidelines about how to go about doing so. It is our hope that the exercises contained within this book will provide some ideas and guidance of how this could be done, and spur on further creative avenues for including spirituality and religion in therapy, potentially one of our clients' most considerable assets, resources, and sources of strength and inspiration. We have edited this book with you, the reader, in mind, hoping to make this book as practical and useful as possible.

Although this book is about integrating spirituality in counseling, the book also addresses both the spirituality and the religion of clients. In part, this is because so many Americans identify themselves as religious. According to a recent Gallup poll (1999), 60 percent of the respondents said that religion in very important to them, while another 30 percent said that religion is fairly important to them. A great deal of overlap can occur between the two; although spirituality sometimes is something quite separate from organized religion, many times it is experienced within formal religious structures. On the other hand, although "religion" and "spirituality" are often intertwined, and are often used interchangeably, some important differences are evident between the two, including how one understands oneself. In the same Gallup poll mentioned previously, when asked to describe their beliefs, 54 percent of the respondents said that they are religious, and 30 percent said that they are spiritual but not religious (they were not given the option of saying both spiritual and religious). We would like to note some of the distinctions between these two terms, as do many authors in their own chapters in this book, by providing the following definitions of religion and spirituality. According to Stander, Piercy, Mackinnon, & Helmeke (1994),

> Religion includes shared and generally institutionalized values and beliefs about God. It implies involvement in a religious community. Spirituality, on the other hand, is a more personal belief in and experience of a supreme being or the ultimate human condition. It includes an internal set of values and active investment in those values. Spirituality is also a sense of connection, a sense of meaning, and a sense of inner wholeness. (p. 39)

One clinical ramification of the distinctions between religion and spirituality relates to how these issues are addressed in therapy. In general, interventions that are more religious in nature require additional care that they be sensitively and ethically applied. Since religion involves institutions, and formalized beliefs and practices, clinicians need to exercise utmost respect in how they introduce, address, and use interventions related to religious issues. Precisely because clients' religious beliefs and expressions are so important to them, and because clinicians are in a more powerful position relative to clients, we urge clinicians to be aware of the influence they exert, especially when integrating more specific, religious interventions.

Organization of the Chapters

Each chapter of the book follows the same format. Following the title and name of the author(s), the reader will see what Type of Contribution the chapter describes: an activity that clinicians can use in session, a homework assignment they can give to clients, a handout that can be used, or some combination of the three. We have encouraged many authors to include handouts in their chapters so that you will have a summary of the instructions to use in session, or directions that you can give to a client to take home.

Next is a brief summary of the authors' Objectives for the chapter, followed by a Rationale for Use section. Many of the Rationale for Use sections are lengthier than those found in the books from the earlier *The Therapist's Notebook* series. This was intentional on our part, in recognition that there is not yet general agreement on whether and how spirituality should be integrated in therapy. The authors have been given more room to explain how and why their exercises can be utilized.

The Instructions section follows the Rationale for Use section. Here we have striven for clarity in describing how the exercises are to be conducted. "Explain it so that the readers will know how to do it" is a refrain that many of our authors have heard. We have supplemented the Instructions section with a Brief Vignette so that the readers have an opportunity to see how the exercise may be applied. Names of clients/people in the Brief Vignette section of the chapters have been altered, as have some of the background information and details, to protect clients' confidentiality. Suggestions for Follow-Up and Contraindications are then provided for further guidance on how to expand the content of the chapter. Then, three different types of reference sections have been included. First, the References section contains the full references for any book, chapter, article, etc., cited in the chapter. Second, a Professional Readings & Resources section includes additional resources that may be of use to the clinician. The third, Bibliotherapy Sources for the Client, contains suggested readings and materials, including videos and Web sites that clients may find helpful. It may turn out that the collection of materials and resources cited in these three sections throughout the book may prove to be one of the most useful resources for clinicians utilizing this book. It has been amazing to us to watch the growth of the list of spiritual and religious resources, and therapists are encouraged to borrow from these lists freely when needing some type of spiritual or religious resource.

Finally, many authors have included a Handout (or Handouts), which will be found at the end of the chapters. Again, some of these have been designed for the convenience of the counselor, to assist in conducting or explaining the exercise, while other handouts have been designed to be utilized by the client.

Organization of the Book

This book has been divided into two separate volumes. In book one, we have grouped the chapters according to their primary topic. The following are the five sections in the table of contents: Therapist Preparation and Professional Development; Assessment of Spirituality; Integrating Spirituality in Couples Therapy; Specific Techniques and/or Topics Used in Integrating Spirituality; and, Use of Scripture, Prayer, and Other Spiritual Practices.

Book two includes the following sections: Models of Therapy Used in Integrating Spirituality; Integrating Spirituality with Age-Specific Populations: Children, Adolescents, and the Elderly; Integrating Spirituality with Specific Multicultural Populations; and, Involving Spirituality when Dealing with Illness, Loss, and Trauma. Many of the chapters included in book one will assist the clinician in preparing to undertake the integration of spirituality in therapy prior to meeting with clients and in knowing how to initiate such integration with clients, such as through an assessment of clients' spirituality. Numerous examples of ways that spirituality can be incorporated into psychotherapy are included in the rest of book one and in book two.

Many of the chapters in both book could have been classified under other categories than the section outlined above, as they address more than one issue. In order to make the book as useful as possible for the reader, we are including two tables that will help the reader to find a topic, presenting problem, technique, or population that may be of interest, and that may not be evident from the title or section. Please see Tables P.1 and P.2 for this information. To illustrate how these two charts may be used, suppose a supervisor or faculty member is interested in using this book for training purposes. They could look on either chart under the column "Professional Development" to find chapters that deal with self-of-the-therapists issues, or could be adapted to use in this way, even if the chapter was written initially for use with a client. Please note that the topics, presenting problems, techniques, and populations listed in the chart are not meant to limit the readers' understanding of how the concepts and exercises in a chapter might be applied. We encourage readers to discover their own adaptations and applications of the interventions contained in both books.

The Need for Sensitive Application

Ever since the inclusion and incorporation of spirituality and religion began being more intensely discussed in the field of psychotherapy in the early 1990s, a constant concern that has been voiced in the literature is that therapists should exercise care to ensure that they are not imposing their religious beliefs and values onto their clients. Indeed, this concern is echoed in most, if not all, of the chapters in both volumes of this book. Many authors assert the ethical importance of respecting the values and beliefs of the client, not imposing the therapist's own beliefs on the client, making sure that therapists have had some kind of training in which their own spiritual and religious values, beliefs, and biases can be examined, and having some way of assessing clients' spiritual and religious beliefs as well as their interest and willingness to include their spirituality, prior to incorporating spirituality in therapy. As was just mentioned, some of the chapters have this as a more explicit focus, but this emphasis can be found in numerous chapters throughout both volumes. We endorse these concerns and suggest that the readers first examine themselves as described in several of the chapters, and then assess their clients' openness and readiness to incorporate spirituality in therapy prior to using any of the interventions described.

As the readers begin to use and adapt the ideas contained within the chapters of these two volumes, we encourage respectful and sensitive application of the exercises. The diversity of spiritual and religious beliefs and practices represented only begins to reflect the wide diversity of beliefs and practices of our clients. Some of these exercises may be appropriate for some clients, but not for others. Along those lines, one point we would like to emphasize regarding the diversity of beliefs and practices represented is that the inclusion of a chapter in either book does not mean that the author or authors of that chapter adhere to the beliefs and practices reflected in any other chapters of the book.

TABLE P. 1. *The Therapist's Notebook for Integrating Spirituality in Counseling:* Summary of chapters.

Chapters	Topics/presenting problems in vignette	Techniques	Specific population	Assessment	Professional development
1. Sori, Biank, and Helmeke	Therapists caring for spiritual self		Therapists	Therapists' spiritual self-care	Therapists' spiritual self-care
2. Maher (Incorporating)	Self-of-the-therapist issues	Self-reflection	Therapists	Therapists' spiritual assessment	Ethical use of spirituality
3. Powell and Craig	Disclosure statements		Therapists		Professional disclosure and ethics
4. Helmeke and White	Building a practice; Networking with clergy		Therapists and clergy		Collaborating with other professionals
5. Killmer (Spiritual Dialogues)	Anxiety	Spiritual dialogues	Devout clients	Assessing spirituality of client and therapist	Self-of-the-therapist reflection
6. Eichler, Deegan, Canda, and Wells	Grief resolution; Anxiety			Spiritual strengths and resources	Therapists' assessment of own spiritual strengths/resources
7. Balaguer Dunn and Massey	Depression; Interracial marriage	Spiritual genogram	Individuals, couples, and families	Family-of-origin influence on spirituality	Therapists' own spirituality genogram
8. Maher (Impact of Abuse)	Abuse; Depression; Spiritual identity; God images	Guided imagery		Clients' relational schemas	Therapists' relational schemas and God images
9. Hargrave and Williams	Forgiveness; Sexual abuse			Assessing stations of forgiveness	
10. Baca, Schafer, and Helmeke	Couple conflict/distance	Application of Imago Relationship therapy	Couples		
11. Michael	Couple conflict/career transitions	Mission statement	Couples and families		
12. Mamalakis	Couple emotional distance	Use of metaphor; biblical principles	Couples; Christian clients		
13. Shaw	Shame; self-esteem		Couples and individuals; Christian clients	Shame	
14. Horak (I am)	Shame; depression; anxiety	Silent reflection; empty chair		Clients' relationship with God	

TABLE P. 1 *(continued)*

Chapters	Topics/presenting problems in vignette	Techniques	Specific population	Assessment	Professional development
15. States	Recovery/addictions	Guided imagery			
16. Sori, Helmeke, Ford, and McFarrin	Stress	Using humor in therapy			
17. Priester and Carlstrom	Promoting forgiveness	Using films in therapy; use of metaphor and story			
18. Vaughn and Swanson	Illness and loss	Spiritual auto-biography/journaling			Therapists' own spiritual autobiography
19. Sori and McKinney	Negative thinking; anxiety; inadequacy	Use of scriptural affirmations; use of prayer; Q-Sort	Christian clients		
20. Balswick (Biblical Means)	Family therapy with adolescents; guilt/need for forgiveness; verbal abuse in marriage; family secrets in couples therapy	Use of biblical themes	Christian clients		Therapist-client relationship
21. Jankowski	Poor self-concept	Contemplative prayer; *lectio divina*			
22. Duncan	Distress and trauma; intimate relationships	Application of NTU psychotherapy	Christian clients; African-American clients		
23. Killmer (Spiritual practices)	Depression; anxiety	Individual: prayer, spiritual readings, and spiritual disciplines; communal spiritual practices	Christian clients		Therapists' use of spiritual practices
24. Horneffer	Stress; breakup of relationship; career decisions	Eastern tools; meditation; guided imagery			
25. Priester	Intimacy; career decisions	Use of the examen; use of discernment; rituals	Couples and families		

Note: The applications of concepts and exercises described in these chapters are not necessarily limited to the topics, presenting problems, techniques, and populations listed in this table. Therapists are encouraged to find their own applications for the interventions and ideas found in this book.

TABLE P. 2. *The Therapist's Notebook for Integrating Spirituality in Counseling II:* Summary of chapters.

Chapters	Topics/presenting problems in vignette	Techniques	Specific population	Assessment	Professional development
1. Bischof and Helmeke	Anxiety/depression; couples therapy	Exception questions			Solution-focused questions re: spiritual life
2. Ginter and Horneffer	Intimate relationships; inadequacy	Parts mapping; guided imagery		Internal parts	Mapping internal parts; experiencing being in Self
3. Balswick ("Cast")	Shame	Artwork; role-play; empty chair	Individuals, couples, families	Internal parts	Identifying resilient parts
4. Craig	Adolescents experiencing loss	Exploring early memories	Adolescents and adults; those experiencing life transitions	Influence of childhood memories on spirituality	Exploring early spiritual memories
5. Priester (Cognitive-behavioral)	Obsessive-compulsive disorder	Journaling	Couples and families		
6. Tuskenis and Sori	Poor attachment to God; spiritual coping styles; career transition; stress	Guided imagery		Attachment to God and spiritual coping	Styles of attachment to God and spiritual coping
7. Biank and Sori	Loss/death of a parent	Play techniques (music, art)	Children and parents		Coping with loss of parent
8. McAdams and Sweeney	Loss/death in the family	Play therapy techniques (sandtray)	Children		
9. Hoogestraat	Adolescent rebelliousness	Movies in therapy	Adolescents		
10. Hoogestraat and Hayunga	Adolescents familiar with technology	Use of metaphors	Adolescents	Adolescents' spiritual needs	
11. Wagenaar	Eating disorders		Adolescents and young adults		Therapists' perceptions of God's view of self
12. Helmeke	Loneliness; loss and grief; questions of loss of meaning and purpose	Life review	Elderly	Family-of-origin influence on spirituality	Conducting spiritual life review
13. Waller and Sori	Infidelity; depression; working with African-Americans' beliefs		African-American clients	Assessing African-American spiritual and religious orientation	Therapist spiritual and religious orientation

TABLE P. 2 *(continued)*

Chapters	Topics/presenting problems in vignette	Techniques	Specific population	Assessment	Professional development
14. Meyerstein (Spiritually sensitive)	Depression; couple conflict; Intermarriage		Jewish clients		
15. Prouty Lyness, Prouty, and Partridge	Saints; life transitions	Use of religious heritage; developing a sense of a spiritual family	Catholic clients		
16. McGrady and McDonnell	Spiritual health; Spiritual identity; anxiety	Circle of self; writing task	Lesbian and gay clients		Completing Circle of Self activity
17. MacDonald	Sexual identity; religious identity; depression	Spiritual journey mapping	Lesbian, gay, and bisexual clients	Sexual identity development; GLBT stances toward spirituality and religion	
18. Prest and Robinson	Illness (acute, chronic, terminal)	Circular, solution-focused, scaling, and reflexive questions; rituals	Ill clients and families		Coping with illness
19. Fahr	Chronic illness	Autoethnography (writing, art, music, photography)	Ill clients		Using autoethnography re: traumatic issue, event, or illness
20. Meyerstein (Psalms)	Illness	Use of Psalm clips	Ill clients		Coping with illness and loss
21. Horak (Deconstructing)	Image of God; clergy abuse	Timeline		Effects of parental figures on God images	Personal evolution of self; deconstructing experience of God
22. Meyerstein (Fetal Loss)	Fetal loss and infertility		Couples		
23. Distelberg and Helmeke	Miscarriage and infertility	Use of story	Couples and fathers	Effects of loss	
24. McDonnell, Cerridwen, and Carney	Caregivers; illness	Use of metaphor; storywriting; drawing	Caregivers		

Note: The applications of concepts and exercises described in these chapters are not necessarily limited to the topics, presenting problems, techniques, and populations listed in this table. Therapists are encouraged to find their own applications for the interventions and ideas found in this book.

Just as counselors and the clients with whom they work observe a wide array of spiritual and religious beliefs and practices, both counselors and clients have had a wide variety of spiritual and religious experiences, ranging from inspiring and uplifting to, unfortunately, traumatic and abusive. It is important for clinicians to acknowledge their own experiences, good or bad, and to recognize that their clients may have had vastly different reactions to spirituality and religion. Similarly, and also unfortunately, if not done thoughtfully, with careful preparation and sensitivity to clients, the attempt to integrate spirituality and/or religion into the therapeutic process could become an equally negative, traumatic experience for clients.

That being said, we believe that clients' spirituality, when incorporated in sensitive, respectful, and curious ways, can be a powerful influence for positive change in therapy. It is our hope that we provide in the following pages some templates that will demonstrate how such a sensitive and respectful incorporation of spirituality in counseling can be accomplished.

REFERENCES

Carlson, T., Kirkpatrick, D., Hecker, L., & Killmer, M. (2002). Religion, spirituality, and marriage and family therapy: A study of family therapists' beliefs about the appropriateness of addressing religious and spiritual issues in therapy. *American Journal of Family Therapy, 30*(2), 157-171.

Gallup, G. H. (1999). *Religion in America: 1999.* Princeton, NJ: The Gallup Organization.

Stander, V., Piercy, F., Mackinnon, D., & Helmeke, K. (1994). Spirituality, religion and family therapy: Competing or complementary worlds? *American Journal of Family Therapy, 22*(1), 27-41.

Acknowledgments

We found that the process of editing this book was certainly one that has shaped our own spiritual journeys. Not only did we get plenty of new ideas for integrating spirituality into our work with clients, but many were the times when we were the ones touched by what the authors wrote. We will be very pleased if you, the therapist, and your clients along with you, benefit from this book as we have. The process of editing has not been without its difficulties, however. At one point as we were getting bogged down, we decided we needed the distraction of humor, and so we collaborated on a chapter on religious humor. In the process, we felt a special resonance with the following story, which we would like to share with you:

> A book editor dies and goes to purgatory. St. Peter can't decide if she's been good or bad, so he decides to give her a choice between heaven and hell.
> First the editor is taken to visit hell, and her skin is burned by the flames. She watches as demons whip a group of people sitting hunched over in front of their word processors, leaving open, infested blisters visible on their backs.
> St. Peter then takes the editor to heaven, where her skin is burned by the flames. She watches as demons whip a group of people sitting hunched over in front of their word processors, leaving open, infested blisters on their backs.
> "My God!" the editor exclaims, "This looks just like hell!"
> "Oh, no," says St. Peter. "Here your work gets published."

As Walsh (1998) quotes her mother as saying, "Blessed are we who can laugh at ourselves, for we will never cease to be amused" (p. 67). And there have been innumerable times when all we could do was to laugh at ourselves, as we stumbled and fumbled our way to the finish line (otherwise known as the "dead"line).

Clearly, we would not have been able to do this without each other's strong support, or without the support of our loved ones. We would both like to acknowledge Froma Walsh, who has been a pioneer and a role model for integrating spirituality and psychotherapy. Individually, we each have many to acknowledge and thank.

First and foremost, I (KBH) thank my husband, Gary, for his patience with and understanding of my preoccupation and passion for this project, for the many contributions of his expertise, and for the many other ways he has supported and assisted me throughout this process, including many parenting responsibilities. He has been someone for me to count on. I also want to thank my two bright, beautiful young daughters, Amanda and Ella, who have brought a new understanding of the Divine into my life. I adore watching the igniting of a "Holy Spark" within each of them, and am constantly touched by their own spiritual reflections of how God is at work in them, in others, and in the world. Although they have not always showed enormous enthusiasm for my immersion in what Amanda refers to as "the book" (said with a sarcastic tone while making quotation marks with her fingers in the air), I do hope that someday they will be glad for what their mommy is doing. I also want to acknowledge my family of origin, and how important it was for me to grow up in a home where the importance of God's presence in our lives was recognized. I am so grateful to my parents, Waldo and Bonita Helmeke, and my sister, Judy, for modeling their faith through their religious involvement and through their daily acts of service to so many in their lives, and for sharing with me the significance of their faith. I am also grateful for the independent thinking of my two brothers, John and Joe, and appreciate the divergent spiritual paths they have each taken. I am also grateful for my parents' parents, and for the spiritual legacies my grandparents have passed on to me; even the stories of the faith of my maternal grandparents whom I have never met have exerted their own influence on me. My paternal grandma was one of the most spiritual persons I have ever known, and I would be overjoyed if someday I might reach a point in which my life reflects a bit of the generosity and kindness of her spirit. Finally, huge thanks to Kate, my co-editor. I do not know how I would have been able to complete this book without her, as it meant so much to me to have someone with whom to share the struggles and burdens, even the unforeseen ones such as the blizzard, when thirteen inches of snow descended in the one square mile where we decided to meet to work on the book! Kate's constant upbeat, positive attitude provided immense encouragement.

Thanks to my (CFS) family and friends for their prayers and tolerance over the past several months. Specifically, thanks to my steadfast husband, John, for all of his love, support, encouragement, and prayers—and for his computer expertise in doing Web searches and in fixing *many* computer glitches; and to my father and contributor, Marvin Ford, for all his prayers, faith in me, humor, read-throughs, and helpful edits (and for taking me to church all those years!); to my mother, Elnora, for her constant presence, support, and understanding; to my two beautiful daughters, Jessica Roberson, my older daughter and contributor, who helped so much with research and formatting; and my younger daughter, Heather Paul, for working to keep me organized and for her expert fitness advice. I am so grateful to my spiritual inheritance from my grandparents (especially Grandma Kate), and to my late sister, Cynthia, and to the generations ahead of me—my children and their children, who are continuing this spiritual legacy. (Cameron, Alexis, and Lyric—thanks for coming to play with me, and for sharing your prayers and beliefs about God!) I would also like to thank my wonderful friend Kathy Hazlett for her prayers, presence, and expert computer skills; and my tremendous contributors, Nancee Biank, Lori McKinney, Byron Waller, and Albert Tuskenis. All of you have blessed my life in so many ways! Special thanks also to my "Ladies Garden Club," Lorna and Anna, for making me take time out to simply play. And I thank Karen for inviting me to accompany her on this path of spiritual and professional growth, and for her incredible thoroughness, thoughtfulness, and dedication to make this book such an exceptional resource. Thanks for patience, humor, and enthusiasm! One of the things I value most from this experience is the deepening of our friendship, and the many shared moments we will always remember (from the blizzard to the hot tub editing!).

Both of us want to offer a big thanks to Lorna Hecker, the series editor, for her continual guidance, humor, and encouragement along the way, and the editors at The Haworth Press. We also want to thank each one of the contributors who have authored a chapter of this book, and to share how impressed, touched, and humbled we have been by the skillfulness and respect with which they have incorporated spirituality into their work. Thanks for their persistence in this long journey. Above all, we thank God for God's help, direction, sense of humor, and that—at last—"IT IS FINISHED!"

SECTION I:
THERAPIST PREPARATION
AND PROFESSIONAL DEVELOPMENT

Spiritual Self-Care of the Therapist

Catherine Ford Sori
Nancee Biank
Karen B. Helmeke

Type of Contribution: Activity, Handout, Homework

Objective

It is a privilege to share clients' journeys with them in therapy—being with them when they are at their most vulnerable, delighting in their courage and insight, and supporting them along their paths toward healing and growth. This privilege, however, is not one without its burdens and challenges. To be prepared to do the difficult work we do as clinicians and to ensure that we will not abuse this privilege, it is essential for counselors to tend to our own well-being, which for many includes our spiritual well-being. This chapter explores ideas to help therapists address our own spiritual self-care to enhance both our personal lives and our professional work with clients.

Rationale for Use

Virginia Satir once said that she would go with people into the scary places (Simon, 1992). Some clients may struggle with horrors from their past, horrors that often remain unspeakable until that moment in therapy when the unspeakable can be spoken. To create the kind of space in which these moments can occur requires a great deal from therapists. As therapists, we do not remain unaffected by our encounters with the pain that clients have experienced. Maintaining a professional distance does not mean that we do not end up caring about our clients and their problems, as we listen and respond to their stories. The demands of being a counselor often exact a toll from us. If we do not deal with our own issues as they are activated in therapy sessions, or as they arise through the ebb and flow of life, we may unknowingly embark on a path to spiritual depletion or burnout. Being able to assist clients in their journey toward health requires that we as counselors possess a level of personal well-being. The nature of our work demands that we address our well-being, and for many counselors, one significant way to increase personal well-being is to integrate issues of spiritual self-care. Utilizing our own spiritual resources is one avenue for strengthening our overall well-being.

Clinicians are also recognizing that one way to strengthen our clients' well-being is to tap into our clients' spiritual resources. For instance, in one clinical study involving marriage and family therapists, 96 percent of the participants agreed or strongly agreed that there is a relationship between spiritual health and mental health (Carlson, Kirkpatrick, Hecker, & Killmer, 2002). Yet to be able to utilize these resources in clients, therapists need to tend to their own spiritual needs as well. Some would even assert that therapists are not qualified to address spiritual issues in depth with clients unless they are actively pursuing their own personal spiritual path (Killmer, 2006a), which may or may not be grounded in a formal religion.

We suggest that if we as therapists are planning to address clients' spiritual or religious issues in therapy, if we are going to make use of our clients' spiritual resources to help put clients on a path toward wholeness and healing, then we need to attend to issues in our own spiritual paths that might present obstacles to our spiritual well-being. There are many possible ramifications of attempting to address clients' spirituality without attending to our own religious and spiritual issues:

1. We become reactive to clients' religion or spirituality, either because their religion or spirituality has or has not been what we have found to be helpful for ourselves.
2. Because of our own attitudes toward the importance of our own spirituality and religion, we fail to recognize when some aspects of clients' religion or spirituality have hindered their mental health.
3. We may fail to recognize how clients' spirituality can be a strength or resource that we can utilize in therapy, due to our own history of negative religious or spiritual experiences in our families or in religious institutions.
4. The boundaries between a client's experiences and our own become blurred because the client's religious and spiritual issues resonate with our own vulnerabilities and woundedness.
5. We fail to recognize how our beliefs about how and when change occurs in therapy are grounded in our spiritual and religious beliefs about human nature, sin, salvation, and the role and agency of God in the world, etc.
6. Because we have not examined and come to terms with issues from our past, including the struggle to find meaning in our losses, disappointments, difficulties, and suffering, our capacity to tolerate others' pain and uncertainties is curtailed.

One way we might come to terms with the issues in our past is to reflect on our memories of childhood experiences of spirituality and religion (see Craig, 2006), or our personal experiences of parental figures (Horak, 2006a, 2006b), and how those experiences, positive or negative, were instrumental in the formation of various spiritual beliefs, practices, and biases, as well as views of God, self, others, and the world. Since the focus of this chapter is on spiritual self-care, readers are referred to Maher (2006) and Eichler, Deegan, Canda, and Wells (2006) for further reading on assessing the therapists' own spiritual beliefs and self.

Spiritual self-care includes the need to examine our spiritual roots—where we came from, what beliefs we share with other family members past and present, and where and how we differ (see Helmeke, 2006; Vaughn & Swanson, 2006; Walsh, 1999). The authors suggest doing one's own spiritual genogram to facilitate this understanding (for discussions of spiritual genograms, see Balaguer Dunn & Massey, 2006; Frame, 2000; Hodge, 2001; Maher, 2006; as well as Roberts, 1999). It is also useful to examine spiritual rituals in our family of origin. Walsh (1999) suggests that therapists inquire about and encourage families to engage in spiritual rituals that have been meaningful to them in the past, as well as to create new rituals (such as the use of the examen as discussed in Priester, 2006). Examining spiritual rituals from our own family of origin and comparing them to our current spiritual rituals can also be a useful tool for therapists to bridge a connection between their spiritual roots and present practices. Reflecting upon which spiritual rituals or practices our family of origin engaged in concerning mealtimes, bedtimes, travel, Shabbat or Sunday observances, family life transitions, religious or other holidays, for instance, and what rituals our current family continues to engage in (Helmeke, 2006) can deepen our understanding of and sense of continuity with our spiritual and religious heritage. Walsh (1999) states, "Therapists and trainees benefit from deepening knowledge of their family traditions and reflection on their own spiritual journeys. . . . Such self-awareness increases comfort in tapping into clients' spirituality for healing and growth" (p. 50). A spiritual journey is a lifelong process that involves both exploration and growth (Walsh, 1999). Without such an awareness and attention to our own spiritual needs, we are crippled in our attempts to help clients utilize their spirituality as a path of resiliency and growth.

As we focus on our own spirituality and spiritual self-care, we strengthen the connection between our inner self (or soul), our God (or higher power), and others. Walsh (1999) states,

> As I've come to work less from my head and more from my soul, I know less than I used to but I trust more my leap of faith and believe it's made me a better therapist. . . . This deeper level of work is not only transformative for our clients but can be restorative for therapists. (pp. 49-50)

Effects of Neglecting Our Spiritual Self

Spiritual depletion occurs when our lives are out of balance, or as Barrett (1999) puts it, there is more output than input. This could occur due to overwork, lack of a strong support system, and a pileup of personal stressors or life crises (such as illness, loss, financial difficulties, family problems, etc.), all of which demand emotional and physical energy from us. When we are not regularly attending to our spiritual needs we have little reserve to buffer us when the storms of life appear. When these storms are coupled with too little time, focus, and energy to take care of our own emotional and spiritual needs (input), we may become spiritually depleted.

This can also occur if we work with an especially difficult population. Barrett (1999) describes the profound effect that working with trauma victims had on her spirit. She wrote:

> I had come to realize that I had been vicariously traumatized. I had not been damaged physically or sexually, and not by family members. Yet I had a damaged spirit. My happy, optimistic, energetic, divine spirit was gone. . . . I had found in my life that I was no longer moving toward this process of growth and creativity. I had lost many of my essential beliefs that had brought me to this profession and to my specialty in trauma. My view of the world had changed. I no longer believed that people were basically good. Rather, I had become afraid of the evil inclination. . . . I was no longer clear about the meaning of life. . . . I knew in my soul that it was a crisis of spirit . . . it was destroying me and my family. (pp. 196-197)

Barrett's Steps to Spiritual Self-Care

Barrett's recognition of her spiritual crisis led her to the realization that she needed to begin a path of spiritual renewal, not only for herself, but also so she could be more spiritually available to her clients. Barrett highlights three stages to spiritual renewal, which parallel the three-stage trauma model developed by Trepper and Barrett (1999). The following describes the three stages of the renewal process that Barrett utilized.

Create a context for change. Barrett's (1999) first stage is to create a context for change. This involves taking stock of what has hindered our spiritual growth and self-care. To do this, it is necessary to slow down, reflect, and ask for support from family and friends. Barrett suggests incorporating the following elements into spiritual self-care:

1. *Spiritual discipline* involves regulating ourselves to focus on and experience spiritual moments.
2. *Meditation* necessitates purposefully slowing down and blocking distractions as we reflect on what has deeper meaning in our lives.

3. *Connection to our self and others* calls for us to move away from spiritual isolation as we become aware of and express what is really important in life.
4. *Celebration of life*, including laughter (see also Sori, Helmeke, Ford, & McFarrin, 2006), can move us beyond ourselves.
5. *Support from others* who care for us and have a mutual focus offers a tangible sense of power.
6. *Rededication* involves stepping back to view the larger picture of "who we are and what we stand for" (p. 200).
7. *Acknowledgment of need* requires us to recognize and admit that we are vulnerable and are not able to control everything in our lives. By removing the denial of our needs, we gain the self-awareness necessary to move beyond obstacles that hinder our personal spiritual growth and self-care.

Recognizing patterns that constrain and learning new patterns that expand reality. Barrett's (1999) second stage is "challenging patterns and expanding realities" (p. 202). This involves recognizing the patterns that have harmed us, and beginning to incorporate activities that introduce positive energy into our lives. This may include beginning a ritual of meditation, as well as examining how to care for ourselves on all levels: the spiritual, physical, and relational. As Barrett emphasizes, "When I had been living a life that had ignored my spirit, most of my energy had been sapped. Using energy to replenish energy made more sense than using energy to deplete or maintain the status quo" (pp. 202-203). This stage then involves developing a plan of spiritual self-care that focuses on training oneself to be aware of one's spirit in the moment.

Consolidation. Consolidation is the third and final stage in Barrett's (1999) model. Although a spiritual journey is never ending, attitudes and behaviors involved in spiritual self-care can be consolidated every time they are practiced. This requires daily awareness and rehearsal so that this becomes a routine part of our life. When we care for our own spiritual needs we are not only modeling for our clients, but we are providing a buffer for ourselves for times of personal or professional stress or crisis.

Spiritual Self-Care Activities

Spiritual self-care is very personal and each of us must determine what nurtures our soul as we develop our own individualized plan of self-care. Several suggestions follow, but this discussion is by no means exhaustive.

Meditation. Meditation requires that we purposefully slow down and focus our energies on something restorative, such as a passage of scripture, a thought, or a saying, etc. This practice has several benefits. Meditation is believed to facilitate an integration or sense of wholeness, as well as a closer connection to others (Bell, 1998). Many of us encourage our clients to meditate. However, practicing meditation along with deep breathing exercises to reduce tension and anxiety, is not only beneficial to clients, but to those who work with them.

In addition, Walsh (1999) points out that meditating outside therapy can increase rapport with clients, and therapeutic effectiveness. Rosenthal (1990) suggests that personal meditation helps therapists to be more attentive and responsive to clients. This would allow them to maintain a calm focus, and to be more fully present, even when clients are experiencing great turmoil. The implication is that this would likely reduce the impact of secondary trauma many therapists experience, especially when working with clients in crisis, or who have experienced abuse or other serious trauma (see Barrett, 1999).

Prayer. While meditation suggests an inward focus, prayer involves directing our thoughts, requests, praise, and thanks outward—vertically (toward God or our higher power) and sometimes also horizontally, when we pray with and/or for others (see below, under Religious Coping

Activities). Many different types of prayer can be used, some of which have been suggested in this book. See Jankowski (2006) for examples of contemplative prayer, which combines the practices of silence and meditation. See Killmer (2006b) and Keating (1995) for discussions of centering prayer, which involves slowing the mind so that one can hear from God while sitting quietly and reflecting on a particular word (such as peace or joy).

Conducting a personal moral inventory. Part of taking care of ourselves spiritually is to take stock and assess how well we are living up to our own beliefs and values, including how we are conducting ourselves in significant relationships: "Am I being the son or daughter, the spouse or partner, the parent, the co-worker, the employer or employee, the neighbor that I believe God wants me to be and that I want to be?" Conducting a personal moral inventory involves a willingness to look at our own contributions to problems in our relationships, to be open and receptive to seeing what changes we need to make in ourselves and seeing how our actions affect others.

Just as with our physical self-care, we cannot change what we deny, such as that extra weight ("These pants must have shrunk in the wash") or chest pains ("It is probably just indigestion"); being open and willing to see those aspects of ourselves that need improvement is necessary in order for us to take care of ourselves spiritually.

Some religious groups build this practice of introspection into the yearly liturgical calendar. For example, many Christians, Catholics and Lutherans among them, observe Lent, through a variety of practices such as fasting and prayer. Lent is a forty-day period (excluding Sundays) prior to Easter, and is intended to be a period of penance and spiritual reflection, particularly reflection on the sufferings of Jesus prior to his death on Good Friday. Similarly, Jews observe a ten-day period beginning with Rosh Hashanah and ending with Yom Kippur, or Day of Atonement. This ten-day period, referred to as Days of Awe or Days of Repentance, is a time for introspection, culminating with Yom Kippur, one day out of the year set aside to atone for the sins of the past year and to demonstrate one's repentance to God. Both Lent and Yom Kippur are religious observances with accompanying rituals that allow us to look at what needs to be different in ourselves and in our lives.

Attachment to God and spiritual coping styles. For those who believe in God, it may be helpful to explore one's attachment to God. Tuskenis and Sori (2006) discuss how people experience God as an attachment figure (see Kirkpatrick, 1999, as well as Pargament, 1997; Richards & Bergin, 2004). In fact, Kirkpatrick and Shaver (1992) found that the same types of interpersonal attachment styles (secure, avoidant, and anxious-ambivalent) also describe how people are attached to God. Our attachment style to God determines how and when we turn to God for support and comfort in times of stress. Cole and Pargament (1999) have identified three spiritual coping styles that are particularly relevant to spiritual attachment, that reflect different ways of turning to God for support. They are the *collaborative, deferring,* and *self-directing* styles (Cole & Pargament, 1999). When we use a collaborative coping style we see God as a partner to help us make sense of and cope with difficult situations. Those who have a secure attachment to God often use this style. A deferring coping style is when we turn our problems or situation over to God, trusting him to work on our behalf, but is not associated with any particular attachment style. Research (Cole & Pargament, 1999) suggests when we are dealing with issues over which we have little control, (such as a serious illness), a deferring spiritual coping style may be beneficial. In fact, Dossey's (1993) review of medical research on the efficacy of prayer concluded that most effective prayers with a medical population were not prayers of petition, but prayers that deferred to the will of God. The self-directing spiritual coping style, used most often by those with avoidant spiritual attachment, is based on notions of God-given independence and responsibility; it consists of relying primarily on oneself, rather than God, in dealing with personal problems and stressful situations. Belavich and Pargament (2002) in their study of people who had a loved one facing surgery, found that pleading with God, begging God for a miracle, also helped participants to experience a sense of control through their contact with God. The benefits of spiritual coping appear to be more about having a positive, personal relationship with God and less about participating in organized religious activities (e.g., church attendance) (Belavich & Pargament, 2002; Pargament, 1997). It may be useful for therapists to examine the issue of attachment style to God and the spiritual coping styles they currently use. See Tuskenis and Sori (2006) for activities that may be adapted to enhance the therapist's own attachment to God and to expand one's existing repertoire of spiritual coping activities.

Religious coping activities. People often engage in numerous religious activities that also enhance their spiritual well-being. These include attending religious services, seeking sources of religious support, doing good deeds for others, reading the Bible or other religious or spiritual literature, keeping a spiritual journal, attending Bible studies or prayer groups, or praying with and for others. It is interesting to note that a study by Pargament, Ensing, Falgout, Olsen, Reilly, Van Haitsma, et al. (1990) found that the more general spiritual coping activities predicted positive outcomes more so than did more traditional, specifically religious predictors (e.g., church attendance or Bible reading).

Nature, movement, and the arts. Many report that they experience spiritual well-being when they are enjoying the world around them—walking in the woods, wandering through a rose garden, standing on a mountaintop, or perhaps viewing the vastness of the ocean. Others say they feel close to God (or their higher power) through movement, which might include dance, swimming, running, or other physical exercise.

Spiritual self-care may include attention to the physical environment (Barrett, 1999). Appreciation for the aesthetic aspects of our physical world, such as color, art, music, soothing sounds and scents, and comfortable, pleasant surroundings all may promote a sense of spiritual well-being. See Horneffer (2006) for a description of an activity that incorporates hatha yoga in therapy which therapists could also use themselves.

Spiritual self-care through care for others. O'Hanlon and Hexum (1990) tell the story about the classic case of Milton Erickson, who was asked to visit the aunt of one of his clients. She was depressed and all she ever did was to go to church, where she spoke to no one. Erickson stopped in to see her during a visit to Milwaukee, and noticed that the one sign of life in her house was three different colored African violets. Erickson told her he thought she was not being a good Christian, withholding from others this extraordinary gift she had with African violets, which are extremely difficult to grow, and told her she needed to send an African violet for every christening, engagement, wedding, illness, or death that occurred in her congregation. She took his words to heart and years later at her death was mourned as "The African Violet Queen of Milwaukee" by all of those who had been touched by her life. It can be vital to our spiritual well-being to live, not only for ourselves, but also for others.

It may seem ironic that one way of taking care of ourselves is to become involved in taking care of the needs of others. Although giving to others can leave us depleted, in many other ways giving of ourselves to others can be an incredible way to reenergize our souls. Getting outside of ourselves and our absorptions by serving the needs of others and investing ourselves in the plights of others can draw us into connection with the rest of humanity, and replenish our spiritual reserves.

Spending time with others and play. Regularly spending time with those who nurture us is vital to our spiritual self-care. We all need people with whom we can be ourselves, to whom we can turn to for prayer, encouragement, and/or support, who laugh as well as cry with us. Being connected to others is essential to our spiritual well-being. After the death last year of my (CFS) colleague and friend, Dr. Mary Smith Arnold, having my grandchildren over and playing with them the next day brought me tremendous spiritual comfort as I reflected on this loss. Nancee Biank often talks about the value of having one's own "circle of support"—people who we care about and who care for us, who will support us and nurture us in times of difficulty—which is essential for the therapist's own well-being.

In the next section we will discuss the steps to developing a personal spiritual self-care plan. Embarking on a journey of spiritual self-care requires a great deal of thoughtful reflection, as well as a willingness to examine oneself. Although we are suggesting that therapists create a plan for spiritual self-care, we do not intend this to be yet another obligation that therapists must do, because we have to or because it would be good for us. Rather, we intend for this exercise to be invitational in nature, to help the readers facilitate their assessment of what they are longing to have more of in their lives.

Instructions

The first step is to assess your current level of spiritual self-care, making note of your strengths and weaknesses. Indications that you are neglecting this area of your life might include not sleeping well, being short-tempered, crying, not eating or overeating, feeling empty, not enjoying life, feeling stressed or burdened, not doing the things that you used to do, or that you know would help you, feeling depressed, and feeling distant or disconnected from family, friends, or God.

The second step is to explore why this area of your life is being neglected. It might be useful to explore with a friend or in therapy why one's spiritual needs have been neglected, or perhaps crowded out by work, family demands, or just busyness. Then make a decision to improve the balance in your life to include time to care for your spiritual needs. Make use of the checklist in the handout (Therapist Spiritual Self-Care Checklist) at the end of this chapter to note any positive things you are doing, as well as to decide on additional activities you would like to incorporate into your spiritual self-care plan. It might be helpful to note things in the past that nurtured your soul that you are no longer doing, but that might be helpful to incorporate in the present. Next, develop a concrete plan for how and when you will begin. In deciding what you are going to do, select something that you are likely to follow through on. For example, you might decide to meditate or pray for ten minutes first thing in the morning, rather than an hour every morning. Go slow and start with one or two activities that will enhance your spiritual well-being. If it might be helpful to you, write down your plan and post it where you can see it as a daily reminder. It might also help to share your plan with someone else, as this accountability may provide additional motivation. Or you might make this commitment with someone else, a friend, a spouse, a family member, and both of you could work on your own plan, with the knowledge and support of the other. As your spiritual needs are likely to change over time, you might find it helpful to review and update your plan of spiritual self-care periodically.

Brief Vignettes

Catherine Ford Sori

My spiritual self-care involves seven areas: faith, family, fellowship, friends, family therapy, fun, and fitness. I will briefly touch on and give some examples for each of these areas. However, note that it is a constant struggle for me not to let work, the ringing telephone, or the busyness of life crowd these activities from my schedule. I must remind myself daily how important it is to care for my spiritual self, and that I as well as others will benefit from my spiritual growth and well-being.

Faith. As a Christian, I (CFS) believe that only two things in life are certain: change is constant and God never changes. My faith anchors me and my religious beliefs define who I am. In the past several years my life has gone through many ups and downs. Some of these were normal life cycle transitions, such as our last child leaving home, marriages, births, deaths, and coping with the declining health of aging family members. Others were sudden and unexpected, such as personal and family illnesses, divorce in the family, job changes, moving, crises with children and grandchildren, and increased job stress. When problems pile up it seems more difficult to utilize faith practices. I try to do certain activities regularly, which bolster and strengthen me, and that keep me grounded. These include giving God thanks, and praying collaboratively to ask God to guide me, give me wisdom, and be my partner as I make decisions and go about my daily life. Prayer also sometimes includes deferring to God when it appears I can do little to control or change a situation. In these cases I gain peace when I turn things over to him, and simply "let go and let God." When worry or stress threaten my peace I actively review scriptural promises (see Sori & McKinney, 2006) that apply to my situation. For example, in the process of editing this book and teaching an overload, I often rehearsed Isaiah 40:31, "But those who hope in the Lord will renew their strength. They will soar on wings like eagles; they will run and not grow weary, they will walk and not be faint" (NIV). (I even have a large eagle puppet perched next to my computer!)

Family. It is important for me to recognize the lineage of my faith, and I feel a special spiritual connection to my maternal grandmother, Grandma Kate. I remember practicing the piano feverishly so that I could play her favorite hymns when she visited, and I can still hear her sweet voice singing "The Old Rugged Cross." Many in my extended family (aunts, uncles, cousins) hold similar beliefs, which strengthens the connection I feel to them. My father, Marvin Ford, took my sister and me to church regularly, and I can also recall his off-key voice singing fervently beside me in church. Shared faith was a strong bond between my late sister, Cynthia, and myself, and it is important for me to me to keep this and her memory alive through sharing memories and family rituals (see Sori, 2003).

Today I am blessed to have children who have strong spiritual beliefs (some who are missionaries), and one major element in my spiritual self-care is being invested in the spiritual lives of my children and grandchildren. At holidays we have spiritual rituals that have been meaningful. In addition, each year I take my grandchildren to see *The Nutcracker* (a family tradition), and on Christmas Eve they put on costumes and dance to the music around the tree! This ritual connects us to our musical heritage (I come from a family of musicians), shared love of dance, and I experience tremendous joy in sharing these with the next generations. Being with our children and grandchildren and seeing the continuity of faith across another generation helps keep me spiritually alive. Praying for the next generation gives me a sense of where I have come from, where I am at, and how the present connects to the future.

Fellowship. Having people who share my beliefs, and to whom I can turn to for prayer and support (and who also turn to me) is a vital element in my self-care plan. In addition to my steadfast husband, John, who is always there to encourage and support me, a close friend and I try to pray daily for each other and for our families. Over the years we have been through many trials, tribulations, births, deaths, and celebrations. We have laughed together, cried together, and prayed together as we practiced "bearing one another's burdens" (see Galatians 6:2). It is so exciting to keep track of all the answered prayers we receive. When one of us is discouraged, the other is always there for encouragement. I am also blessed to have several other friends who are part of my spiritual support circle.

Friends. I was raised with a strong work ethic, and one of my weaknesses is a tendency to take on too much and to work to the point of exhaustion. Being with friends with whom I can laugh and play nourishes my soul. Having friends to talk with, who listen, and who are fun to be with is an important part of replenishing my spiritual self. My "Ladies Garden Club" meetings (which are a euphemism for sitting in a good friend's hot tub!) are times I am restored through laughter and fellowship—and mutual support and caring. Having numerous friends who share my various passions helps me feel connected in a special way.

Family therapy. The more I care for my own spirit, the more I can feel a special connection to clients, students, and colleagues. I have several colleagues and we pray for one another, for students, and for other colleagues. One benefit of writing this book has been to strengthen my spiritual connection to Karen, as well as my co-authors, in new and meaningful ways. This spiritual collaboration has been the best part of this project!

Fun. God made us to enjoy life, and one of my favorite scriptures is John 10:10 "I have come that they may have life, and have it to the full" (NIV). I had a playful and fun-filled childhood, but as an adult I must remind myself that play is essential for my well-being. One of my life's missions is to "spread the gospel" of incorporating play in therapy with children and families. But I must purposefully incorporate play in my own life.

One way to enjoy life is to realize a long-held dream, as expressed in Proverbs 13:12, "a longing fulfilled is a tree of life" (NIV). One peak spiritual experience of my life occurred when I was in New York with my late colleague, Dr. Mary Arnold. One of my lifelong dreams was to see the Statue of Liberty. Mary shared my love and respect for "Lady Liberty," and this meaningful experience elevated our connection to a deeper, spiritual level. Mary died a few weeks after this trip, and I treasure a photograph taken of us in front of the Statue of Liberty.

Fitness. This has been the newest addition to my spiritual self-care plan. After months of sitting at the computer while working on this book, I realized how depleted I was, and finally heeded the advice of family and friends about how exercise is an important part of spiritual self-care. I joined a fitness club, and have found a renewed bounce in my step and a zest and enthusiasm for life! Taking care of the physical body enhances my spiritual well-being.

As you can see, many of these areas of spiritual self-care overlap. And this is my current plan . . . for now. The key to spiritual well-being is to be ever vigilant, always keeping your finger on the pulse of your spiritual self, and remembering that others benefit from the time and energy you devote to addressing your own spiritual needs.

Nancee Biank

Because I routinely work with families involved with illness, death, and dying, there are elements of spiritual self-care that I call upon regularly—let's call them maintenance. Then there are other elements of spiritual self-care that get enacted during a particularly difficult time.

Maintenance involves exercise, listening to and playing music, being involved in a peer supervision group, and refueling with family time. Exercise is important physically for all the reasons that we already know including an increase in endorphins and more energy, to name a few, but personally, exercise defines my ability to be strong, to keep going when I want to quit, and my ability to focus. All of these things are needed when I am sitting with a family who is in the midst of chaos when losing a loved one. When I am exercising I can think of nothing else but the next weight to be lifted or the next step to be taken. When I am finished I am exhausted, but an exhaustion that screams "Look how capable you are! Look what you accomplished in just one hour!" the same motivation one sometimes needs in order to go into a session.

Music is the antithesis of exercise. It provides me with the joy, beauty, depth of spirit, and exhilaration that defines life and can only come from music. With music I can go to the mountains. I can go to Africa. I can revisit Beethoven and his "Ode to Joy," written as he was going deaf. If such beauty can be created out of one man's life, surely I can meet my next clients where they are.

Connecting with people of the same understanding without even having to talk is what peer supervision is all about. A chance to be, a chance to be understood, and a chance to give to others simultaneously validates my ability to continue my work. It also allows me other eyes and ears that can provide a foundation for my work when my thinking may be clouded.

Family. Family embodies refueling. It is a place where I can connect with generations that have lived through tragedy and joy and led as examples in both. It is where I am called to lead and teach future generations. Sharing a meal is communion with people who believe in one another and all give thanks to the same Higher Power for their existence. It is where differences can be addressed and resolved between courses, or continued for days, but they get resolved. How different is that from the work we do? To be able to turn to the people you love and say: "I need you to carry me today" is practice for helping a family find comfort and solace with one another, even in the heat of battle.

For darker days and deeper sessions, there is a message I found in a fortune cookie about five years ago that I have sitting on my desk: "God helps those who don't try to take over His work." To me, that fortune, which I was so lucky to receive, reminds me of my place. I am a conduit. I am never alone. I then draw on the prayer of St. Francis of Assisi: "Lord make me an instrument of your peace. . . ." With that I am reminded of the foundation that has preceded me for thousands of years. For generations there were counselors before me and for generations to come there will be more. For now I have been blessed to accompany a family on their journey. I remind myself that whatever happens in the session ahead is supposed to happen. With this in mind, I am able to go forward in peace and listen.

Karen Helmeke

In reflecting on how I take care of myself spiritually, three broad categories of self-care emerge: acceptance of limits, making connections, and nurturing both inward and outward spirituality. All of these help me to try to maintain some balance in my life, a key aspect of my spiritual self-care.

Acceptance of limits. Part of nurturing my spirituality is to accept that my spiritual needs, as well as abilities for and interests in expressing my spirituality, change at various points in my life. At times in my life I have felt very connected to God, and other times to be so is much more of a struggle. Some parts of my life have been more solitary and quiet, and others have been more communal and hectic. Each has placed its own limits and demands on my spirituality. Rather than berating myself for not being more than I could be at that particular time and place, part of my spiritual self-care has been learning to accept myself, and in that spirit of self-acceptance, finding ways to connect with God, myself, and others. The quest to deepen my spirituality then becomes a grace-filled invitation rather than one more obligation I will probably not fulfill.

I am currently in a very hectic family life stage, working and caring for two young children. In accepting that there are limitations to the amount of time, quiet, and energy that I possess, I become free to be a bit more creative about how I take care of spiritual self. I find I am more likely to make the most out of the small moments, using something similar to the mindfulness meditation described by Horneffer (2006). It has become important to make use of those mindful moments, breathing, relaxing, centering, and being mindful of God's presence and support as I go about my day. In those small moments, I often try to focus on what I am grateful for. I also try to focus on others and their needs and situations. Priester (2006) describes the use of the examen as a way to discern God's movement in our lives, and to seek direction in our lives. He discusses moments of consolation, those times during the day for which we feel the happiest and most grateful, when we feel the greatest sense of belongingness to oneself, God, others, and the universe, when we have given and received the most love. He also describes moments of desolation as those times during the day when we feel most disconnected, unhappy, least alive, etc. It has been helpful to consider questions such as these during those small moments throughout the day. The practice of making use of these small, mindful moments also helps me stay more attuned to my clients when I am with them.

In accepting the limits of my current situation, another way to attend to my spiritual self has been to find ways to incorporate spirituality into the life of our family. Once I was able to let go of thinking that there was a certain way to be "spiritual," I was able to discover that my own spirituality is intertwined with nurturing and observing my children's development, including their spiritual development. It has been an incredibly joyful experience to witness my children's budding theology; their questions and insights about God, life, and relationships often inspire and renew my own faith.

Making connections. Although spiritual self-care is seemingly a private endeavor, for me, it is about making connections, of various kinds. The following describe some of these connections.

1. *Making connections among all types of self-care.* I cannot take care of myself spiritually without taking care of myself physically, emotionally, relationally, and professionally. They are all integrally related to each other, so that I cannot take better care of myself spiritually without taking care of all aspects of myself. Just as "keeping in shape" physically has a positive effect on so many other parts of my life, "keeping in shape" spiritually also enhances other aspects of my self. When I do not take care of myself in any of these areas, the other areas become unbalanced as well.

2. *Making connection between past, present, and future.* Learning about my family's family-of-origin spiritual and religious practices and beliefs has allowed me to develop a sense of continuity with the past. Continuing rituals that were important in my family of origin and developing new rituals with my own family help me feel connected with the future. My life and faith today exists in large part because of the life and faith of my ancestors, and likewise, my husband and I will leave a spiritual legacy for our children and their children. One ritual of spiritual self-care that makes me feel very connected with my family of origin is a brief morning devotional time. My mother and sister and I all read the same devotional, with daily readings. My mother has often mentioned how important it is to her to know that we are all reflecting on similar themes throughout the day. Although my mother and sister live far away from me, this is a time for me to feel connected to them and their faith.

3. *Spiritual self-care in the context of community.* Although developing my own private, more inward spirituality is essential for my spiritual well-being, I am also aware that I need to be part of a community of faith. Thus, part of my spiritual care regimen involves participation in a local congregation, which provides me with a sense of belonging. That is where I feel connected to the larger community of believers.

4. *Finding ways that remind me of connectedness.* Spending time outdoors, enjoying the beauty of nature, and being moved by music and art are some of the ways that remind me that I am connected to something so much bigger than myself. Having a sense of the scope of the divine helps to keep my own problems, and those of others, in perspective. When my own efforts to facilitate change seem so negligible, it helps to be reminded that I may be one small part, but all of the small parts are connected to the whole and—to borrow from one of the foundational concepts of marriage and family therapy—the whole is greater than the sum of its parts. (Watzlawick, Beavin, & Jackson, 1967)

Nurturing both inward and outward spirituality. While part of nurturing my spirituality involves "feeding" myself through my own inward world of piety and prayer, another aspect also concerns my involvement in the world, with a focus on "feeding" others by attending to the needs of others. It is a paradox that I am fed by feeding others, that spending energy can renew energy, and trying to reserve energy can drain energy, but that has so often been my experience: self-care can involve care for others. At times those inward spiritual acts, designed to replenish, have left my spirit depleted. In contrast, investing my self, time, and energy in the welfare of others so often reenergizes my spirit. I have discovered that I need a balance between the inward and outward acts of spiritual self-care; my spiritual well-being suffers if I have too little of either.

This can, at times, be a difficult balance to try to achieve; it can be too easy to neglect either side of the spectrum. With many competing demands and needs, the tendency and desire to nurture others sometimes comes at the expense of taking care of self. In contrast, too much of a focus on my inner spiritual self leaves me insular and out of touch. Because I believe spirituality is in essence relational, being involved in the lives of others, and being engaged in acts of mercy and justice that benefit others is crucial to my spiritual self-care.

These two aspects of spirituality are mutually reciprocal, which is why a balance between both is so critical. For instance, times of biblical reflection renew the call to invest myself in social justice issues such as helping the hungry and the poor, as well as taking other actions to help others. However, when I am involved and active in service to others, I have an opportunity to be confronted with human faces and human needs, which provides me with a renewed clarity in the focus of my prayer and meditation. During moments of private reflection and confession, I can contemplate those aspects of myself that I think I need to work on, so that I can become a better person, mother, wife, friend, etc. Conversely, an outward focus, such as my work as a marriage and family therapist, renews my commitment to be a healthier person because I am inspired by the courage shown by clients willing to face their problems, risk self-examination, and make changes so that they can live a healthier life. If I neglect either the outward or inward focus of spirituality, my spiritual well-being suffers. A deepened involvement in either my inward or outward spirituality, however, enhances, informs, and enriches the other.

Suggestions for Follow-Up

As mentioned previously, spiritual self-care is a lifelong process. Plans need to be reviewed and modified when one's life circumstances change, or in times of personal crisis. However, one specific follow-up activity is to think of a catchy phrase, a quote, mantra, verse, or song to help you remember your plan so you feel focused and strengthened by your inner self.

Contraindications

As discussed earlier, therapists need to examine the ways in which their spiritual and/or religious beliefs and the expressions of those beliefs affect the conduct and process of therapy. This is especially true than when integrating clients' spirituality or religion in therapy. Just being more spiritual or religious will not benefit our clients if the way we choose to be spiritual or religious and the way we choose to express and/or integrate our spirituality in therapy is harmful to our clients. Developing a plan for enhancing our spiritual self-care is an opportunity to incorporate elements of self-care that have been out of balance or neglected in our lives, as well as an opportunity to evaluate elements of self-care for the ways in which they benefit the work we do with clients.

References

Balaguer Dunn, A., & Massey, R. F. (2006). The spirituality-focused genogram: A tool for exploring spirituality and the spiritual resources of individuals, couples, and families in context. In K. B. Helmeke & C. F. Sori (Eds.), *The therapist's notebook for integrating spirituality in counseling: Homework, handouts, and activities for use in psychotherapy* (pp. 77-87). Binghamton, NY: The Haworth Press.

Barrett, M. J. (1999). Healing from trauma: The quest for spirituality. In F. Walsh (Ed.), *Spiritual resources in family therapy* (pp. 193-208). New York: Guilford Press.

Belavich, G., & Pargament, K. I. (2002). The role of attachment in predicting spiritual coping with a loved one in surgery. *Journal of Adult Development, 9,* 13-29.

Bell, L. G. (1998). Start with meditation. In T. Nelson & T. Trepper (Eds.), *101 interventions in family therapy* (Vol. 2, pp. 52-56). Binghamton, NY: The Haworth Press.

Carlson, T. D., Kirkpatrick, D., Hecker, L., & Killmer, M. (2002). Religion, spirituality, and marriage and family therapy: A study of family therapists' beliefs about the appropriateness of addressing religious and spiritual issues in therapy. *American Journal of Family Therapy, 30,* 157-171.

Cole, B. S., & Pargament, K. I. (1999). Spiritual surrender: A paradoxical path to control. In W. R. Miller (Ed.), *Integrating spirituality into treatment: Resources for practitioners* (pp. 179-198). Washington, DC: American Psychological Association.

Craig, S. E. (2006). Exploration of adolescent and adult spirituality through early memories: An Adlerian psychological perspective. In K. B. Helmeke & C. F. Sori (Eds.), *The therapist's notebook for integrating spirituality in counseling II: More homework, handouts, and activities for use in psychotherapy* (pp. 27-35). Binghamton, NY: The Haworth Press.

Dossey, L. (1993). *Healing words: The power of prayer and the practice of medicine.* San Francisco: Harper.

Eichler, M., Deegan, G., Canda, E. R., & Wells, S. (2006). Using the strengths assessment to mobilize spiritual resources. In K. B. Helmeke & C. F. Sori (Eds.), *The therapist's notebook for integrating spirituality in counseling: Homework, handouts, and activities for use in psychotherapy* (pp. 69-76). Binghamton, NY: The Haworth Press.

Frame, M. W. (2000). The spiritual genogram in family therapy. *Journal of Marital and Family Therapy, 26*(2), 211-216.

Helmeke, K. B. (2006). "My spiritual life": Conducting a spiritual life review with the elderly. In K. B. Helmeke & C. F. Sori (Eds.), *The therapist's notebook for integrating spirituality in counseling II: More homework, handouts, and activities for use in psychotherapy* (pp. 115-126). Binghamton, NY: The Haworth Press.

Hodge, D. R. (2001). Spiritual genograms: A generational approach to assessing spirituality. *Families in Society, 82*(1), 35-48.

The Holy Bible, New International Version (1984). Grand Rapids, MI: Zondervan.

Horak, J. J. (2006a). Deconstructing God in relation to the reconstruction of self. In K. B. Helmeke & C. F. Sori (Eds.), *The therapist's notebook for integrating spirituality in counseling II: More homework, handouts, and activities for use in psychotherapy* (pp. 217-222). Binghamton, NY: The Haworth Press.

Horak, J. J. (2006b). I am not worthy: Shame and spirituality. In K. B. Helmeke & C. F. Sori (Eds.), *The therapist's notebook for integrating spirituality in counseling: Homework, handouts, and activities for use in psychotherapy* (pp. 167-173). Binghamton, NY: The Haworth Press.

Horneffer, K. (2006). Embracing emotional pain as a means of spiritual growth: Tools from the East. In K. B. Helmeke & C. F. Sori (Eds.) *The therapist's notebook for integrating spirituality in counseling: Homework, handouts, and activities for use in psychotherapy* (pp. 267-285). Binghamton, NY: The Haworth Press.

Jankowski, P. (2006). Facilitating change through contemplative prayer. In K. B. Helmeke & C. F. Sori (Eds.), *The therapist's notebook for integrating spirituality in counseling: Homework, handouts, and activities for use in psychotherapy* (pp. 241-249). Binghamton, NY: The Haworth Press.

Keating, T. (1995). *Open mind, open heart.* New York: The Continuum Publishing Company.

Killmer, J. M. (2006a). Conducting spiritual dialogues in therapy. In K. B. Helmeke & C. F. Sori (Eds.), *The therapist's notebook for integrating spirituality in counseling: Homework, handouts, and activities for use in psychotherapy* (pp. 55-67). Binghamton, NY: The Haworth Press.

Killmer, J. M. (2006b). The use of spiritual practices in conjunction with therapy with Christian examples. In K. B. Helmeke & C. F. Sori (Eds.), *The therapist's notebook for integrating spirituality in counseling: Homework, handouts, and activities for use in psychotherapy* (pp. 257-265). Binghamton, NY: The Haworth Press.

Kirkpatrick, L. A. (1999). Attachment and religious representations and behavior. In J. Cassidy & P. R. Shaver (Eds.), *Handbook of attachment: Theory, research, and clinical applications* (pp. 803-822). New York: Guilford Press.

Kirkpatrick, L. A., & Shaver, P. R. (1992). An attachment theoretical approach to romantic love and religious belief. *Personality and Social Psychology Bulletin, 18,* 266-275.

Maher, A. B. (2006). Incorporating spirituality into the therapeutic setting: Safeguarding ethical use of spirituality through therapist self-reflection. In K. B. Helmeke & C. F. Sori (Eds.), *The therapist's notebook for integrating spirituality in counseling: Homework, handouts, and activities for use in psychotherapy* (pp. 19-28). Binghamton, NY: The Haworth Press.

O'Hanlon, W. H., & Hexum, A. L. (1990). *An uncommon casebook: The complete clinical work of Milton H. Erickson.* New York: W. W. Norton.

Pargament, K. I. (1997). *The psychology of religion and coping.* New York: Guilford Press.

Pargament, K. I., Ensing, D. S., Falgout, K., Olsen, H., Reilly, B., van Haitsma, K., & Warren, R. (1990). God help me: (I.): Religious coping efforts as predictors of the outcomes to significant negative life events. *American Journal of Community Psychology, 18*(6), 793-824.

Priester, P.E. (2006). Integrating the discernment of spiritual guidance in family and couples therapy: Use of the examen. In K. B. Helmeke & C. F. Sori (Eds.), *The therapist's notebook for integrating spirituality in counseling: Homework, handouts, and activities for use in psychotherapy* (pp. 287-292). Binghamton, NY: The Haworth Press.

Richards, P. S., & Bergin, A. E. (2004). *Casebook for a spiritual strategy in counseling and psychotherapy.* Washington, DC: American Psychological Association.

Roberts, J. (1999). Heart and soul: Spirituality, religion, and rituals in family therapy training. In F. Walsh (Ed.), *Spiritual resources in family therapy* (pp. 256-271). New York: Guilford Press.

Rosenthal, J. (1990). The meditative therapist. *Family Therapy Networker, 14,* 38-41, 70-71.

Simon, R. (1992). Reaching out to life: An interview with Virginia Satir. In R. Simon's *One on one: Conversations with the shapers of family therapy* (pp. 167-172). Washington, DC: The Family Therapy Networker, and New York: Guilford Press.

Sori, C. F. (2003). Legacy of loss and "re-membering." *The Family Journal: Counseling and Therapy for Couples and Families, 11*(3), 306-308.

Sori, C. F., Helmeke, K. B., Ford, M. L., & McFarrin, J. C. (2006). Take two and call me in the morning: Using religious humor in therapy. In K. B. Helmeke & C. F. Sori (Eds.), *The therapist's notebook for integrating spirituality in counseling: Homework, handouts, and activities for use in psychotherapy* (pp. 183-199). Binghamton, NY: The Haworth Press.

Sori, C. F., & McKinney, L. (2006). Free at Last! Using scriptural affirmations to replace self-defeating thoughts. In K. B. Helmeke & C. F. Sori (Eds.), *The therapist's notebook for integrating spirituality in counseling: Homework, handouts, and activities for use in psychotherapy* (pp. 223-234). Binghamton, NY: The Haworth Press.

Trepper, T., & Barrett, M. J. (1990). *Systemic treatment of incest: A clinical handbook.* Bristol, PA: Taylor & Francis.

Tuskenis, A. D., & Sori, C. F. (2006). Enhancing reliance on God as a supportive attachment figure. In K. B. Helmeke & C. F. Sori (Eds.), *The therapist's notebook for integrating spirituality in counseling II: More homework, handouts, and activities for use in psychotherapy* (pp. 47-63). Binghamton, NY: The Haworth Press.

Vaughn, M., & Swanson, K. (2006). "Any life can be fascinating": Using spiritual autobiography as an adjunct to therapy. In K. B. Helmeke & C. F. Sori (Eds.), *The therapist's notebook for integrating spirituality in counseling: Homework, handouts, and activities for use in psychotherapy* (pp. 211-219). Binghamton, NY: The Haworth Press.

Walsh, F. (Ed.) (1999). *Spiritual resources in family therapy.* New York: Guilford Press.

Watzlawick, P., Beavin, J. H., & Jackson, D. D. (1967). *Pragmatics of human communication: A study of interactional patterns, pathologies, and paradoxes.* New York: W. W. Norton.

Professional Readings and Resources

Barrett, M. J. (1999). Healing from trauma: The quest for spirituality. In F. Walsh (Ed.), *Spiritual resources in family therapy* (pp. 193-208). New York: Guilford Press.

Roberts, J. (1999). Heart and soul: Spirituality, religion, and rituals in family therapy training. In F. Walsh (Ed.), *Spiritual resources in family therapy* (pp. 256-271). New York: Guilford Press.

Rosenthal, J. (1990). The meditative therapist. *Family Therapy Networker, 14,* 38-41, 70-71.

Tuskenis, A. D., & Sori, C. F. (2006). Enhancing reliance on God as a supportive attachment figure. In K. B. Helmeke & C. F. Sori (Eds.), *The therapist's notebook for integrating spirituality in counseling II: More homework, handouts, and activities for use in psychotherapy* (pp. 47-63). Binghamton, NY: The Haworth Press.

Walsh, F. (Ed.) (1999). *Spiritual resources in family therapy.* New York: Guilford Press.

Handout: Therapist Spiritual Self-Care Checklist

Write a narrative of the current aspects of your spiritual self-care. Then proceed through the following checklist, which is a partial list of activities that you already may be integrating into your spiritual self-care. Go through the list and check all you already do, and then check those you would like to add.

Spiritual Self-Care Activities	Currently Do	Want to Do or Do More Of
1. Go for a walk or exercise	☐	☐
2. Listen to or create music	☐	☐
3. Spend time with friends	☐	☐
4. Laugh and play	☐	☐
5. Read Bible or religious literature	☐	☐
6. Meditate or pray	☐	☐
7. Spend time with family	☐	☐
8. Enjoy art—creating or viewing it	☐	☐
9. Enjoy nature—go to the beach, forest, mountains, etc.	☐	☐
10. Play with or enjoy a pet	☐	☐
11. Attend religious services	☐	☐
12. Talk with clergy or therapist	☐	☐
13. Dance and/or sing	☐	☐
14. Worship	☐	☐
15. Pray with and/or for others	☐	☐
16. Work for the welfare of others	☐	☐
17. Feed the hungry, welcome the stranger, clothe the naked, take care of the sick, or visit those in prison	☐	☐
18. Make lists of positive things in life, answers to prayer, or keep a gratitude or spiritual journal	☐	☐
19. Participate in a community of faith	☐	☐
20. Recognize your family history of resiliency and spiritual beliefs; Share stories of strengths and/or religious beliefs from past generations	☐	☐
21. Volunteer, or give to others	☐	☐
22. Conduct a moral inventory of self	☐	☐
23. Participate in hobbies or sports	☐	☐
24. Others: _____	☐	☐

Sori, C. F., Biank, N., & Helmeke, K. B. (2006). Spiritual self-care of the therapist. In K. B. Helmeke & C. F. Sori (Eds.), *The therapist's notebook for integrating spirituality in counseling: Homework, handouts, and activities for use in psychotherapy* (pp. 3-18). Binghamton, NY: The Haworth Press.

2

Incorporating Spirituality into the Therapeutic Setting: Safeguarding Ethical Use of Spirituality Through Therapist Self-Reflection

Anita Berardi Maher

Type of Contribution: Homework for the therapist

Objective

As various mental health professions are increasingly open to incorporating the client's spirituality into the therapeutic process, therapists now more than ever feel greater freedom to discuss topics that heretofore may have been perceived as off limits. Yet, inviting discussion about a client's spirituality within the context of therapy is fraught with danger due in large part to the subjective nature of such a deeply personal, life changing, and in today's world, political aspect of human experience. This chapter invites the therapist to consider one's ethical obligations to the client before attempting to utilize a client's spirituality as a therapeutic tool. Specifically, the therapist is invited to engage in a self-examination process in which one's clinical and spiritual orientations are articulated as part of a process of safeguarding against a pejorative, reactive, and/or prescriptive use of spirituality in the therapeutic setting.

Rationale for Use

Given the power and complexities of spirituality, the potential exists for a therapist to compromise safe and effective treatment through its misuse. There are myriad reasons why using a client's spirituality as a therapeutic tool can threaten the mandate to do no harm. This chapter focuses on those issues uniquely related to the person of the therapist: How and/or why are we susceptible to losing clinical perspective? Spiritual identities not only uniquely shape our clients and hold immense power in their lives, but influence the therapist as well. It shapes how we view the world and ourselves within the various roles we enact as family members, friends, citizens, mental health professionals, and significant relational others in the lives of our clients.

The two central qualities of spirituality threatening its appropriate use in the clinical setting are its highly subjective and identity defining nature. How we understand ourselves as spiritual beings cuts to the core of how we understand ourselves as humans. The meaning and purpose we assign our lives, for many, are derived from our spiritual identities. Add to this the subjective nature of spiritual beliefs and it is easy to understand why religious interpretations and the lifestyle choices that emerge from those understandings can be quite polarized even among those of the same spiritual community. These qualities underlay all additional concerns raised in the following text.

The subjective experience of spiritual expression and its core defining function are intimately linked with one's geopolitical environment. Where and when we were born, our race, ethnic origins, and gender, the socioeconomics of our family of origin, our education, and the communities and families we surround ourselves with as adults all influence our understanding of ourselves as spiritual beings even as we attempt to have those aspects of our identity influenced by our faith orientation. Our spiritual interests and experiences draw us into like-minded communities, each with its own tide, its own agenda and sense of mission in the world (Neusner, 2003; Richards & Bergin, 2000; Smart, 1999). Today, many of us make quick evaluations—whether right or wrong—of a person's political opinions and lifestyle choices simply by identifying his or her spiritual orientation. Even more challenging, many of us may be prone to holding members of communities unlike our own in deep suspicion, creating divisions based on fear and prejudice.

Related to the influence place and time have on our spiritual identity, our understanding of ourselves as spiritual beings is influenced by internalized God images (Maher, 2006). These God images reflect our most significant attachment relationships (Brokaw & Edwards, 1994; Rizzuto, 1974; White, 1984). It is common for therapists to recognize the interconnections between formative relational experiences and career paths. Likewise, internalized God images also exert influence over our lifestyle and vocational choices. For many of us, there is a very intimate connection between our spiritual understandings and beliefs and why we chose the mental health profession.

While one's sense of spirituality shapes and resonates with one's worldview, it ultimately shapes and influences attitudes and behaviors. This intimate relationship between one's inner spiritual experience and outward social response has many permutations. We might be familiar with clients who hold us in deep suspicion when invitations to broaden perspectives are viewed as a challenge to their faith system. Likewise, many therapists believe that the values and goals of therapy are at odds with or do not fully address their mission in life derived from deep faith convictions. They feel personally obligated to redefine the therapeutic setting to adjust or accommodate those shortcomings. On the contrary, just as some clients make great strides in personal change due to deepening their connection with the values inherent in their faith system, likewise many deeply religious and/or spiritual therapists function most safely and effectively precisely as a result of reliance on their spiritual identities.

Finally, despite our profession's advancements in recommending safe and ethical guidelines regarding the use of spirituality in therapy (Chappelle, 2000; Doherty, 1995, 1999; Miller, 1999; Miller, 2002; Richards & Bergin, 1997; Sperry, 2001; Walsh, 1999), no universally accepted approach exists on how to proceed. Many clinical texts on incorporating spirituality into the therapeutic setting naturally reflect the subjective faith experience of the writer. These approaches evoke strong reactions as practitioners and either resonate with the spiritual orientation of the author or stand in opposition to the author's presentation. These subjective responses make it difficult for us to adopt the common wisdom contained in the material and then contextualize it to meet the needs of our clients.

Of focus here is the recognition that the therapist, like the client, enters the therapeutic environment with his or her own set of biases; our spiritual identities, and hence the spiritual communities in which we immerse ourselves, co-create a worldview, an understanding of ourselves and others, and ultimately a sense of purpose and mission in the world. And given the power of spiritual beliefs on the worldview of the therapist, how can we preserve the integrity of the therapeutic environment as greater credence is given to addressing spiritual issues in therapy?

Instructions

This chapter acknowledges two broad frameworks for accomplishing this task, yet focuses only on the latter. Although not addressed in this chapter, safe and ethical incorporation of spirituality into therapy requires affirmation of the core values of the mental health professions in order to remind ourselves of the purpose and limits of psychotherapy (Tjeltveit, 1999; Woody & Woody, 2001). By affirming the structure of the therapeutic environment, the stage is set to maximize the therapist's freedom to incorporate the client's spirituality into the therapeutic setting while differentiating between psychotherapy and spiritual formation/discipleship and/or religious mentoring. Additional resources to assist the reader in this process are offered in the Professional Readings & Resources section of this chapter.

The second step, and the one of focus here, requires the therapist to engage in one's own self examination and languaging process as a direct form of clinical accountability. Here, therapists are invited to engage in a process of clarifying what they do and why in the language of their profession, their faith community, and then in everyday, common, conversational language. This discipline is intended to not only increase one's own self awareness regarding the congruency or lack thereof between their core professional and spiritual identities, but to also practice what we teach our clients: to clarify who we are, what we are about as part of the process of identifying where we want to go. Therapists want to go in a direction directed by and respectful of the client. Knowing that the therapeutic relationship is never devoid of the therapist having—and owning—one's own values, this chapter explores a way we can own our spiritual identities without being prescriptive.

Therapist Self-Examination

Due to the subjective nature of spirituality and its tendency to tap into core identity issues, the following self-reflection process is recommended in preparation for utilizing a client's faith system in treatment. In the Brief Vignette section, aspects of this author's own self-exploration process are briefly summarized.

For each of the following five subheadings, write your responses in outline or narrative form. Many of your responses may change and/or deepen over time as a natural part of the reflection process. This exercise may also be beneficial to do within group supervision and/or within the context of peer supervision as hearing multiple perspectives also stirs deeper clarification of one's own thoughts.

Therapist spiritual history and current context. Conduct your own spiritual assessment to uncover personal beliefs, preferences, and biases. How were faith/religious issues practiced and/or talked about in your family of origin? What beliefs about God, a Divine Being and/or religion are overtly and covertly expressed within your current family? Explore the sociopolitical climate influencing religious belief and practice in the greater culture, and observe one's own personal responses. Refer to Maher (2006) in which a sample spiritual assessment is provided. Spiritual genogram and inventory instruments can be found in Frame (2000), Hodge (2001), Ingersoll (2001), and Lawrence (1997).

Language. Practice expressing your spiritual beliefs using ecumenical language to minimize the likelihood of imposing one's beliefs onto the client (Richards & Bergin, 1997). Although spiritual language can never be totally devoid of constructs predisposing assent to belief systems not universally shared, therapists can search for "generic" language describing the manifestations of their sense of the spiritual (Chappelle, 2000; Miller, 1999; Richards & Bergin, 1997). This is most important for therapists steeped in religious communities with its associated language systems and hence unfamiliar with how to verbalize human experience without using the terminology of their faith system.

Begin by responding in narrative form to the spiritual assessment questions located in Chapter 8 in this book. Specifically, in Handout Three at the end of the chapter, Client Handouts: Exploring Your Spiritual History: Then, Now, and in the Future, Exercise One: Your Past and Present Spiritual History, respond to question 2 under Current Spiritual Interests and question 1 under Exploring Life's Ultimate Meaning and Purpose. Those questions are summarized and added to as follows:

1. If you believe in God or a Divine Being, how would you describe the "character" of this entity? And how do you believe this spiritual being relates to you in times of struggle, sadness, pain, fear, and happiness?
2. How would you describe the purpose of your life (through the lens of your faith)? How have your spiritual and/or religious beliefs influenced these thoughts?
3. Additional question: How do you understand the nature of human beings, of good and evil, of struggle and triumph, through your spiritual/faith lens?

Once you have completed your responses, try to rewrite your answers by eliminating any spiritual terms or references that someone outside of your faith system would not understand. For now, let us assume they have a good grasp of English (or whatever language you are writing in) but are clueless in grasping theological and/or spiritual terminology. This is a difficult challenge for many, as the rewrite is often much lengthier than the original! This is the beginning of learning how to differentiate between allowing our faith to inform our life but not being languaged in a manner that imposes our religious doctrines on to our clients.

Theoretical synchrony. This section invites the therapist to explore the theoretical synchrony between one's theory of therapy and one's own spiritual beliefs about the nature of persons and what constitutes health and wholeness. First, write out your theory of therapy using the language (theories) of the social and behavioral sciences. The following is an abbreviated outline developed as part of a clinical exam I use with mental health intern students. While this exercise may require extended reflection (including a quick dash into your nearest theory texts), push yourself to identify what you do and why you do it using the language of your chosen profession. Many excellent textbooks summarizing the major psychotherapeutic approaches are available. Resources are also listed in the Professional Readings and Resources section of this chapter.

1. *General theory of therapy:* What brings people to therapy and how does it serve them? Describe the overall purpose and function of the therapeutic process, and of the therapist. What theorists and philosophical underpinnings influence your work?
2. *Nature of persons:* How do you understand human beings? What makes us tick, what do we need to function optimally? Logical areas to explore include descriptions of what constitutes healthy functioning; how is it achieved, maintained, and restored. What constitutes dysfunction or lack of health (or whatever clinical language you use); how does it occur and how is it maintained?
3. *Assessment:* What is the purpose and function of assessment? What processes do you use and why? How might these activities resonate or conflict with your philosophical beliefs as detailed in items 1 and 2 above?
4. *Treatment strategies:* Describe what you do in session (in broad strokes and specifically) and why. Does it resonate with your theoretical orientation as described above?

This last question is often intimidating for therapists who suddenly observe that what they do bears no resemblance to the techniques suggested by their theory or theories. What we often forget is that treatment strategies are the therapist's creative expression of one's theory in direct relationship with the client. What we do bears the unique fingerprints of our personal style, our clients' needs in the moment, and our worldview, our theoretical orientation, if you will. This question is asking you to identify the connection between your worldview and what you actually do, not check to see if you are using the theory's recommended techniques (that author's unique fingerprints).

Now compare your answers to the clinical reflection questions with your previous theological reflections. Where do you see synchrony and/or incongruencies? What significance might this have to you at this time?

Self-resource. The previous exercises invite the therapist to engage in a self-reflection process. This item emphasizes the importance of learning about belief systems other than one's own, including the beliefs of our clients, as well as members of our local and global communities. Refer to texts such as Richards and Bergin (2000), Smart (1999), Smith (1991), and Neusner (2003). Enroll in world religion courses or attend worship services of various faith orientations within your own community. This process broadens the therapist's perspective, enabling us to see how other faith communities understand God and themselves as spiritual beings.

Finally, learn about the various spiritual resources in your community. Inevitably, when spiritual issues are freely addressed in therapy, client needs will surface that extend beyond our scope of practice and competence as a therapist. At this juncture it is our obligation to invite clients to consult with spiritual resources within their faith community.

Isomorphism. Be aware of the potential isomorphism between the supervisor-supervisee, and the therapist-client systems in regard to one another's spiritual thoughts, experiences, and identities. It is easy for all levels of the therapeutic relationship to unknowingly act out distrust and/or (well-meaning) hidden agendas. Likewise, personal biases and fears may also discourage the supervisor and/or the therapist from embracing the role of spirituality in the emotional and relational health of each other and our clients. Comfort discussing such issues in the supervisory relationship allows the therapist to impart comfort in the therapeutic relationship. Ultimately, it is the client's process that is to be empowered using spirituality as a resource according to the client's wishes and perspective.

Take a few moments and reflect on your comfort level discussing your experience of spirituality with clinical peers, supervisors, and/or supervisees. What issues make such discussions possible or not advisable? What attitudes and/or biases in you might need to be tempered so you can become a "safe other" in conversations regarding one another's spiritual thoughts and experiences?

As therapists increasingly invite clients' spirituality to be present in treatment, the supervisory and consultation room will need to invite the same. The very issues that polarize entire nations can, and do, alienate therapeutic communities. By working on mutual respect and hearing of one another, we stand in opposition to this cultural phenomenon, modeling relational healing. This is the very heart of preparing ourselves to be safe and effective when incorporating our client's spirituality into the treatment process.

Brief Vignette

Therapist Application

Home base. As a therapist and educator, I have given much thought to exploring the various ways in which people understand themselves as spiritual beings. Often I have been intrigued by how a facet of human experience intended to provide identity, hope, direction, and meaning has also been for many a source of deep pain and confusion. Rather than being an avenue of relational healing, this dimension of human experience is often used as a weapon in assuming power and control over others, in deciding who is right, or good, or acceptable. Personally believing that therapists must tend—and do whether it is acknowledged or not—to the spiritual nature of a person's functioning, it is imperative that we guard against its misuse. These thoughts and values motivate me to engage in my own examination process.

Briefly summarizing my own spiritual genogram, I was born in the late 1950s to a first-generation Italian Catholic home in the Northeast. This sociocultural context and the relational dynamics of my home have influenced my internalized God images. The polarized religious views as expressed in today's public arena certainly stir internal responses that both reflect and influence my faith. But my spiritual life has also been shaped by my theological and psychological education, solidified yet ever evolving and brought to life in my most significant relationships with others inside and outside of my faith community.

Identifying basic values using inclusive language. In this section I offer a short summary of my own theological ponderings using a combination of ecumenical language infused with general everyday, yet slightly (I admit!) "therapeutic," language. It is followed by a paragraph briefly summarizing my clinical orientation in order to demonstrate the synchrony between my thoughts as expressed within these two communities.

Omitted from this vignette are two complementary works. The first one missing is a narrative providing greater detail regarding the nature of persons, of human struggle and what constitutes wholeness and health written in clinical language reflective of my theoretical orientation as a psychotherapist. The second narrative not included involves taking these same concepts and writing my response purely from the theological/religious language of my faith community as recommended in the Instructions section of this chapter.

Steeped in my Christian heritage, I believe that humans are relational by nature, reflecting the nature of the Divine. I understand the essence of human struggle to be a result of relational disconnection—with oneself, one another, creation, and hence with God. I view caring and just relationships as the necessary ingredients for spiritual survival often expressed through our biological, psychological, and social functioning. I experience therapy as a spiritual endeavor in that through the I-thou encounter of authentic relating, we are all impacted by one another, informed and changed, and in so doing experience the essence of being human (Buber, 1958). Although spirituality has many definitions (Becvar, 1997; Chappelle, 2000; Olson & Olson, 2000; Walsh, 1999) I experience it through embracing my humanness with full awareness and intention informed by values of love, care, honesty, and fairness authored by a Divine Being.

This spiritual orientation, expressed in ecumenical language, influences my approach to therapy. I was drawn to the marriage and family therapy profession for two reasons. One was the inclusiveness of system's thinking, the hallmark characteristic of this profession. It is an approach that incorporates an understanding of persons as embedded within a social ecology as well as an understanding of family and greater cultural systems as comprised of the individual. Second, a systemic approach embraces the concept that we are relational by nature, hence our health and well-being are informed and/or enhanced by our relationships with one another and within our own selves (Borszormenyi-Nagy & Krasner, 1986; Nichols, 1987; Papero, 1990; Schwartz, 1994). Today I find my clinical thinking also influenced by narrative therapy, a short-term yet comprehensive treatment approach in which the client's total experience is honored as new possibilities are explored (Freedman & Combs, 1996). In sum, my clinical orientation integrates attachment (Cassidy & Shaver, 1999), systems, and postmodern approaches.

As I contemplate how I understand my world through clinical, spiritual, and moral lenses (as detailed by Doherty, 1995; 1999) I see the synchrony. It is this "total package" that I bring into the therapy room.

Suggestions for Follow-Up

To successfully complete the therapist preparation process, the clinician may wish to enroll in a psychology and spirituality integration course. The reading resources listed for therapists are also recommended.

As you language your orientation from these multiple perspectives, begin where you feel most comfortable. Some may choose to first articulate their clinical orientation; others may find that ideas flow more naturally by writing or talking aloud using the language of their faith community; and still others may not be sure what language they are using; they just start expressing their thoughts about the topics being queried. Begin in whatever fashion is most productive for you. The more you strive to language your thoughts completely, the more you will be apt to dig into both professional and spiritual resources. Enjoy the work in progress that this exercise invites.

Contraindications

There are no contraindications for therapists engaging in their own self-exploration process. However, clinicians are advised to listen to their own internal dialogue concerning these issues. As with all issues touching core parts of our human experience, discussions related to spirituality and/or faith perspectives can open deep wounds and unleash powerful emotional responses. The therapist is advised to seek out clinical peers, supervisors, a personal therapist, and/or a spiritual mentor to process some of these responses.

Completion of the recommended self-reflection exercises may feel overwhelming for clinicians with no formal faith orientation or with little exposure to theories of therapy. For these therapists, bibliosources are provided in the Professional Readings and Resources and References sections. These texts offer insight into a variety of religious faiths and theories of therapy. Familiarizing yourself with divergent religious and therapeutic systems of thought may assist you in putting your own experience into words.

Caution is warranted when discussing the use of spirituality in supervision and group practices. In some counseling clinics, supervisors and administrators often fear that any discussion of spirituality in the therapeutic session might breach the separation of church versus state. However, some of these strong reactions reflect encounters with therapists who sought to convert clients or used spiritual interventions inappropriately. A hostile environment may exist in situations in which supervisors and/or colleagues are antagonistic to working with a client's religious orientation, exude overt disapproval of a colleague's religious orientation, or use spirituality within therapy in a dogmatic or prescriptive manner. In such situations, the therapist or supervisor may wish to recommend in-service training facilitated by an outside consultant to assist colleagues through a process of mutual understanding while also offering treatment guidelines for incorporating the client's spiritual interests in the therapy process.

References

Becvar, D. S. (1997). *Soul healing.* New York: Basic Books.

Borszormenyi-Nagy, I., & Krasner, B. (1986). *Between give and take.* New York: Brunner/ Mazel.

Brokaw, B. F., & Edwards, K. J. (1994). The relationship of God image to level of object relation's development. *Journal of Psychology and Theology, 22*(4), 352-371.

Buber, M. (1958). *I and thou* (2nd ed.). New York: Charles Scribner.

Cassidy, J., & Shaver, P. R. (1999). *Handbook of attachment.* New York: The Guilford Press.

Chappelle, W. (2000). A series of progressive legal and ethical decision-making steps for using Christian spiritual interventions in psychotherapy. *Journal of Psychology and Theology, 28*(1), 43-53.

Doherty, W. J. (1995). *Soul searching.* New York: Basic Books.

Doherty, W. J. (1999). Morality and spirituality in therapy. In F. Walsh (Ed.), *Spiritual resources in family therapy* (pp. 179-192). New York: Guilford Press.

Frame, M. W. (2000). The spiritual genogram in family therapy. *Journal of Marital and Family Therapy, 26*(2), 211-216.

Freedman, J., & Combs, G. (1996). *Narrative therapy.* New York: Norton.

Hodge, D. R. (2001). Spiritual genograms: A generational approach to assessing spirituality. *Families in Society, 82*(1), 35-48.

Ingersoll, R. E. (2001). The spiritual wellness inventory. In C. Faiver, R. E. Ingersoll, E. O'Brien, & C. McNally (Eds.), *Explorations in counseling and spirituality* (pp. 185-194). Belmont, CA: Brooks/Cole/Thomson Learning.

Lawrence, R. T. (1997). Measuring the image of God: The God Image Inventory and the God Image Scales. *Journal of Psychology and Theology, 25*(2), 214-226.

Maher, A. B. (2006). Impact of abuse on internalized God images: Spiritual assessment and treatment using guided imagery. In K. B. Helmeke & C. F. Sori (Eds.), *The therapist's notebook for integrating spirituality in counseling: Homework, handouts, and activities for use in psychotherapy* (pp. 89-112). Binghamton, NY: The Haworth Press.

Miller, G. (2002). *Incorporating spirituality in counseling and psychotherapy.* New York: Wiley.

Miller, W. R. (Ed.) (1999). *Integrating spirituality into treatment.* Washington, DC: American Psychological Association.

Neusner, J. (2003). *World religions in America: An introduction.* Louisville, KY: Westminster John Knox Press.

Nichols, M. P. (1987). *The self in the system.* New York: Brunner/Mazel.

Olson, D., & Olson, A. K. (2000). *Empowering couples.* Minneapolis, MN: Life Innovations, Inc.

Papero, D. V. (1990). *Bowen family systems theory.* Boston: Allyn and Bacon.

Richards, P. S., & Bergin, A. E. (1997). *A spiritual strategy for counseling and psychotherapy.* Washington, DC: American Psychological Association.

Richards, P. S., & Bergin, A. E. (2000). *Handbook of psychotherapy and religious diversity.* Washington, DC: American Psychological Association.

Rizzuto, A. M. (1974). Object relations and the formation of the image of God. *British Journal of Medical Psychology, 47*(1), 83-99.

Schwartz, R. C. (1994). *The internal family systems model.* New York: Guilford Press.

Smart, N. (1999). *Worldviews: Crosscultural exploration of human beliefs* (3rd ed.). Trenton, NJ: Prentice Hall.

Smith, H. (1991). *The world's religions: Our great wisdom traditions.* San Francisco: HarperSanFrancisco.

Sperry, L. (2001). *Spirituality in clinical practice: New dimensions in psychotherapy and counseling.* Philadelphia: Taylor and Francis.

Tjeltveit, A. C. (1999). *Ethics and values in psychotherapy.* New York: Routledge.

Walsh, F. (Ed.) (1999). *Spiritual resources in family therapy.* New York: Guilford Press.

White, S. A. (1984). Imago Dei and object relations theory: Implications for a model of human development. *Journal of Psychology and Theology, 12*(4), 286-293.

Woody, P. H., & Woody, J. D. (2001). *Ethics in marriage and family therapy.* Washington, DC: American Association of Marriage and Family Therapy.

Professional Readings and Resources

As with clients, given the diversity of spiritual and/or religious beliefs, caution is recommended when supervisors refer specific reading, video sources, or experiential activities related to this topic to supervisees. It is also recommended that supervisors invite supervisees to participate in recommending resources to aid in mutual resourcing and discussion of this topic.

Barnes, F. P. (2001). *Values and ethics in the practice of psychotherapy and counseling.* Philadelphia: Open University Press.

Becvar, D. S. (1997). *Soul healing.* New York: Basic Books.

Brokaw, B. F., & Edwards, K. J. (1994). The relationship of God image to level of object relation's development. *Journal of Psychology and Theology, 22*(4), 352-371.

Chappelle, W. (2000). A series of progressive legal and ethical decision-making steps for using Christian spiritual interventions in psychotherapy. *Journal of Psychology and Theology, 28*(1), 43-53.

Corey, G., Corey, M. S., & Callahan, D. (2002). *Issues and ethics in the helping professions.* Belmont, CA: Wadsworth Publishing.

Doherty, W. J. (1995). *Soul searching.* New York: Basic Books.

Fowler, V. (1981). *Stages of faith.* New York: HarperCollins.

Frame, M. W. (2000). The spiritual genogram in family therapy. *Journal of Marital and Family Therapy, 26*(2), 211-216.

Hodge, D. R. (2001). Spiritual genograms: A generational approach to assessing spirituality. *Families in Society, 82*(1), 35-48.

Ingersoll, R. E. (2001). The spiritual wellness inventory. In C. Faiver, R. E. Ingersoll, E. O'Brien, & C. McNally (Eds.), *Explorations in counseling and spirituality* (pp. 185-194). Belmont, CA: Thomson Learning.

Lawrence, R. T. (1997). Measuring the image of God: The God Image Inventory and the God Image Scales. *Journal of Psychology and Theology, 25*(2), 214-226.

Miller, G. (2002). *Incorporating spirituality in counseling and psychotherapy.* New York: Wiley.

Miller, W. R. (Ed.) (1999). *Integrating spirituality into treatment.* Washington, DC: American Psychological Association.

Neusner, J. (2003). *World religions in America: An introduction.* Louisville, KY: Westminster John Knox Press.

Nichols, M. P., & Schwartz, R. C. (1998). *Family therapy: Concepts and methods* (4th ed.). Boston: Allyn and Bacon.

Olson, D., & Olson, A. K. (2000). *Empowering couples.* Minneapolis, MN: Life Innovations, Inc.

Richards, P. S., & Bergin, A. E. (1997). *A spiritual strategy for counseling and psychotherapy.* Washington, DC: American Psychological Association.

Richards, P. S., & Bergin, A. E. (2000). *Handbook of psychotherapy and religious diversity.* Washington, DC: American Psychological Association.

Sharf, R. S. (2000). *Theories of psychotherapy and counseling* (2nd ed.). Belmont, CA: Wadsworth

Smart, N. (1999). *Worldviews: Crosscultural exploration of human beliefs* (3rd ed.). Trenton, NJ: Prentice Hall.

Smith, H. (1991). *The world's religions: Our great wisdom traditions.* San Francisco: HarperSanFrancisco.

Sperry, L. (2001). *Spirituality in clinical practice: New dimensions in psychotherapy and counseling.* Philadelphia: Taylor and Francis.

Tjeltveit, A. C. (1999). *Ethics and values in psychotherapy.* New York: Routledge.
Walsh, F. (Ed.) (1999). *Spiritual resources in family therapy.* New York: Guilford Press.
Woody, P. H., & Woody, J. D. (2001). *Ethics in marriage and family therapy.* Washington, DC: American Association of Marriage and Family Therapy.

Bibliotherapy Sources for the Client

This chapter addressed the needs of the therapist in preparation to incorporate the client's spiritual interests in treatment. Bibliosources for the therapist are listed under Professional Readings and Resources.

3

Spirituality and Professional Disclosure

Robert R. Powell
Stephen E. Craig

Type of Contribution: Handout

Objective

The purpose of this chapter is to provide therapists with examples of how to address spiritual issues in their professional disclosure statements. Emphasis is placed on the therapist's willingness to explore the client's spirituality and not necessarily on the therapist's own religious beliefs.

Rationale for Use

Corey, Corey, & Callanan (1998) suggest that one of the best ways to protect the interests of clients is to assist them in making informed choices about their therapy. To this aim, therapists are charged with the task of disclosing sufficient information about therapeutic process so that clients make a voluntary, informed decision to enter counseling. Although the purpose of informed consent and professional disclosure seems relatively simple, the method of implementation may vary considerably from therapist to therapist.

Few therapists would disagree that informed consent and professional disclosure are integral parts of the therapeutic process. However, many therapists disagree regarding the types of disclosure that are deemed important. As with Corey et al. (1998), the authors believe that the process of informed consent consists of a balancing act between disclosing too much to clients and disclosing too little. In addition to the basic dimensions of disclosure including the length and duration of sessions, session fees, and therapist's approach to counseling, the authors believe that many therapists who recognize spirituality as an important dimension to therapy should also disclose their willingness to explore such aspects with their clients.

Whether a therapist discloses religious opinions or intends to use spirituality within his or her treatment model is a debatable issue. Bergin, Payne, & Richards (1996) suggested that informed consent and an open agreement between client and therapist regarding the relevance of values and religious issues in the therapy transaction are foundational and crucial to an effective therapeutic alliance. Tan (1996) encourages therapists to include their stance on religious and spiritual issues in the informed consent process. Tan (1996) also indicates that the theoretical orientation and clinical preferences of the therapist with regard to religion play a crucial role in what treatment model is used and how explicitly religion is integrated into therapy.

Depending on the therapist's orientation, choosing to withhold information related to religious beliefs can be considered an effective intervention as well. According to Rizzuto (1996), psychoanalytic therapists should abstain from revealing religious affiliation, beliefs, or any other personal information. After all, psychoanalytically trained therapists generally try to foster the development of transference (Arlow, 2002), and therapists who fail to maintain a certain degree of neutrality may interfere in this process. Too much disclosure may hinder the development and subsequent working through of transference. The risk of collusion and avoidance is very high when it is known that the therapist is a religious person. The blurring of roles on the therapist's part diminishes the possibility of dynamic exploration of wishes and conflicts.

Even so, therapists must be careful to avoid unethical coercion of clients. Explicit integration of religion in clinical practice should be addressed in a clinically sensitive, ethically responsible, and professionally competent manner. By addressing this issue at intake, the therapist can assess the appropriateness with each client, and clients will be making a more informed decision of whether or not to enter therapy with this particular therapist.

Whether or not a therapist chooses to disclose his or her religious orientation is worthy of further discussion. If the therapist comes from a spiritual foundation, Jones (1996) believes that it is impossible to separate religious values when conducting therapy. Rather than committing themselves to impossible values of neutrality, therapists should instead recognize that they cannot intervene in the fundamental aspects of the client's life without getting deeply involved in moral and religious matters. It thus seems incumbent on therapists to press for greater explicitness within the therapeutic relationship. Perhaps disclosure on an as needed basis is a "middle of the road" solution. Often similar dynamics are present in the supervisor and counseling student relationship. Martinez & Baker (2000) investigated whether counselors in training made assumptions if their supervisors did not disclose their religious beliefs. They found that if supervisees did not know what their supervisors' religious beliefs were, they assumed that the supervisor held a personally unhelpful, antireligious attitude. However, as practitioners themselves, the preference of most supervisee's was that there should not be over disclosure of their religious faith to clients. Any inquiry would be dealt with in a "traditional" nondisclosing fashion.

Careful consideration of religious beliefs and intent to use spirituality in therapy is warranted for all therapists. If religious preferences are included in intake data, the opportunity for dialoguing is inevitable. Sperry (2000) cautions that the greater the degree and the level of incorporation of spiritual dimensions into psychiatric practice, the broader the range of implications and applications. If religion is to be a part of the therapeutic process, it is strongly recommended that there be informed consent, due to all the possibilities and clinical implications of this practice. Meador & Koenig (2000) indicate that a "patient-centered" approach, which includes adequate disclosure by the clinician of his or her particular religious worldview as it may influence the treatment, is advocated as a framework for maintaining a context of informed consent in the treatment process. Dauser, Hedstrom, & Croteau (1995) found that therapists who provide a comprehensive, personalized, written pre-therapy disclosure statement increase client autonomy and participation without risking harm to the client.

Whether the therapist has a religious orientation or not, if it is interwoven in the client's clinical issues then exploration is warranted. A therapist should be open and prepared to discuss religion regardless of his or her own spirituality. If it is assessed that religion plays an important role in the client's functioning, the therapist is ethically obligated to address this area of concern.

Instructions

According to Hedstrom & Dauser (1994), a complete professional disclosure statement should include the following eleven elements:

1. counseling process or techniques,
2. services provided and/or types of clients,
3. expectations and/or anticipated results and possible risks,
4. alternatives to counseling,

5. qualifications of counselor,
6. rights and limits of confidentiality,
7. length and frequency of sessions,
8. right to terminate counseling or description of rights if counseling is involuntary,
9. cost and method of payment,
10. identification of supervisor, and
11. identification of board of licensing. (Refer to Handout One: Professional Disclosure Guidelines.)

Therapists who choose to disclose their perspective on the role of spirituality in counseling should include beliefs and/or practices in the services provided and/or types of clients section of their disclosure statement.

When deciding if religious orientation should be included in the professional disclosure statement, the therapist should consider several factors:

1. how religion fits into their therapeutic approach,
2. how explicitly spirituality will be demonstrated, and
3. if religious views should be discussed at intake or if the subject is initiated by the client.

It is recommended that if a therapist chooses to disclose religious beliefs or intent to use spirituality in therapy, that it be disclosed during the initial session during the structuring process. Based on the level of the therapist's intent to utilize spirituality in the treatment process, the following sample statements are offered to include in the professional disclosure process (refer to Handout Two: Sample Professional Disclosure Statements of Intent to Utilize Spirituality):

- For a generic recognition of religion: "This therapist is committed to taking an unbiased approach regardless of age, race, gender, or religious affiliations."
- For acknowledgment of religious beliefs: "Although this therapist is a practicing (therapist can fit in their religion or denominational affiliation, e.g., Roman Catholic, Christian, Reformed Jew), religious beliefs are not the primary focus of the therapy approach and the therapist will only be addressing spirituality when requested."
- For an alternative acknowledgment of religious beliefs: "Although Christian (or insert other religious or denomination background) Counseling is not the foundation of this therapist's approach, faith and religion will be explored if the client so desires."
- For a strong statement of intent to bring spirituality into therapy: "This therapist is a practicing Christian (or insert other religious or denomination background) and will be using spirituality throughout the therapeutic process."

Brief Vignette

The following case illustration reflects a client who is struggling with several issues that are laden with religious connotation as offered by Sperry & Giblen (1996). Betty entered therapy with Brad, her ex-husband. She was forty-seven years old, a bright, hardworking divorced woman who came to therapy for assistance in coping with her ex-husband. She was a mother of six grown children, one of whom had been diagnosed with cancer only months after Betty separated from her husband. Her son died two years after the divorce, but not without an infinite number of prayers and heroic medical efforts by Betty. Betty was nonetheless blamed for her son's death by her ex-husband and her elderly parents, all of whom pointed to her marital separation as the catalyst for the son's illness. Betty's grief and rage were palpable, and her search for faith was passionate but filled with doubt and questioning.

Exploration of Betty's faith was inevitable. Betty's reliance on her faith and feelings of anger and guilt were prevalent. If the willingness to explore spiritual issues was addressed prior to the onset of therapy, the stage is set to delve into the spiritual implications that Betty may be struggling with. When prevalent, a therapist should explore a client's faith when the presenting problems have religious implications. The following statement was included within the therapist's Professional Disclosure Statement:

> This therapist acknowledges the importance of religion in an individual's life. Although Christian Counseling is not the foundation of this therapist approach, faith and religion will be explored if desired by the client.

A sample of potential dialogue with the therapist and Betty is as follows:

THERAPIST: Betty, it would seem that your faith is an important part of your life.

BETTY: Yes, it is!

THERAPIST: I would like to point out that in my disclosure statement I indicated that religion is not the primary focus of our work, but if this is an area of your life that you would find helpful to explore, as your therapist, I would be willing to do this with you. Is this an area that you would like to pursue with me?

BETTY: Thank you. Your support in my faith is refreshing.

Suggestions for Follow-Up

The handout provides a format for developing a professional disclosure statement that should mention religion or religious beliefs at some level. It is during the presentation and discussion of the professional disclosure statement that the therapist's explanation of religious beliefs and interpretations should occur. During the intake process, the client's religious beliefs would be addressed, including the exploration of implications this has within the therapeutic process. It would also be appropriate for ongoing discussion and a "checking in" throughout therapy to address the impact of spirituality on the client's therapeutic experience.

Contraindications

If religion is addressed during the review of the disclosure statement, perceptions of the therapist and therapeutic process are already being formed. Even if religion is not part of the therapeutic approach of the therapist and their beliefs are discussed during intake, the client may make false assumptions and become wary about the therapist's motivations. A clear understanding of the professional disclosure statement and the rationale for its use must be accomplished. Individuals can hold strong opinions in the areas of faith and religion. If the therapist is not clear or is not consistently checking in with the client's understanding of the therapist's intent, the therapeutic process could be undermined.

References

Arlow, J. (2002). Transference as defense. *American Psychoanalytic Association, 50*(4), 1139-1150.

Bergin, A., Payne, I. R., & Richards, P. S. (1996). Values in psychotherapy. In E. P. Shafranske (Ed.), *Religion and the clinical practice of psychology* (pp. 297-325). Washington, DC: American Psychological Association.

Corey, G., Corey, M. S., & Callanan, P. (1998). *Issues and ethics in the helping professions* (5th ed.). Pacific Grove, CA: Brooks/Cole Publishing.

Dauser, P., Hedstrom, S., & Croteau, J. (1995). Effects of disclosure of comprehensive pretherapy information on clients at a university counseling center. *Professional Psychology, Research and Practice, 26*(2), 190-195.

Haas, L. (1991). Hide-and-seek or show-and-tell? Emerging issues of informed consent. *Ethics and Behavior, 1,* 175-189.

Hedstrom, S., & Dauser, P. (1994). Written disclosure statements: Informed consent in action. *Journal of Michigan Counseling Association, 23*(1), 5-10.

Jones, S. (1996). A constructive relationship for religion with the science and profession of psychology: Perhaps the boldest model yet. In E. P. Shafranske (Ed.), *Religion and the clinical practice of psychology* (pp. 113-147). Washington, DC: American Psychological Association.

Martinez, S., & Baker, M. (2000). "Psychodynamic and religious?" Religiously committed psychodynamic counselors, in training and practice. *Counseling Psychology Quarterly, 13*(3), 259-264.

Meador, K., & Koenig, H. (2000). Spirituality and religion in psychiatric practice: Parameters and implications. *Psychiatric Annals, 30*(8), 525-532.

Rizzuto, A. (1996). Psychoanalytic treatment and the religious person. In E. P. Shafranske (Ed.), *Religion and the clinical practice of psychology* (pp. 409-431). Washington, DC: American Psychological Association.

Sperry, L. (2000). Spirituality and psychiatry: Incorporating the spiritual dimension into clinical practice. *Psychiatric Annals, 30*(8), 518-523.

Sperry, L., & Giblen, P. (1996). Marital and family therapy with religious persons. In E. P. Shafranske (Ed.), *Religion and the clinical practice of psychology* (pp. 511-532). Washington, DC: American Psychological Association.

Tan, S. (1996). Religion in clinical practice implicit and explicit integration. In E. P. Shafranske (Ed.), *Religion and the clinical practice of psychology* (pp. 365-387). Washington, DC: American Psychological Association.

Professional Readings and Resources

Nelson, A., & Wilson, W. (1984). The ethics of sharing religious faith in psychotherapy. *Journal of Psychology and Theology, 12,* 15-23.

Shafranske, E. (1990). Clinical psychologists' religious and spiritual orientations and their practice of psychotherapy. *Psychotherapy, 27,* 72-78.

Shafranske, E. (1996). *Religion and the clinical practice of psychology.* Washington, DC: American Psychological Association.

Tan, S. (1990). Explicit integration in Christian counseling (an interview). *The Christian Journal of Psychology and Counseling, 2,* 7-13.

Bibliotherapy Source for the Client

Tan, S., & Ortberg, J. (1995). *Coping with depression.* Grand Rapids, MI: Baker.

Handout One:
Professional Disclosure Guidelines
Eleven Elements of a Professional Disclosure Statement

1. *Counseling process or techniques:* This section contains information that describes the counselor's theoretical orientation in common language. By reading this section, the client should have a clear idea of what to expect in the counseling relationship. Typical resources utilized by the counselor should also be stated, such as homework assignments, tests, tape recordings, etc. This section may also include office practices, such as scheduling appointments and reaching the counselor outside office hours.

2. *Services provided and/or types of clients:* The counselor should describe any specialization in age level of persons seen in practice. The types of services provided (individual or group counseling, assessment, consultation, etc.) and the types of common presenting problems should be described. The counselor may wish to provide information about specific areas of expertise (eating disorders, drug and alcohol counseling, Christian Counseling, etc.).

3. *Expectation and/or anticipated results and possible risks:* It is recommended that counselors discuss possible risks and expectations/anticipated results together. In this way a client can have a more realistic understanding of the benefits and possible risks of counseling. Presented separately, the client may obtain an overly optimistic view, or conversely, be unduly frightened of possible negative effects. This section may also contain information about client and counselor roles.

4. *Alternatives to counseling:* The benefits and risks of alternatives to counseling should also be shared with clients. Examples of alternatives that might be identified include self-help books, peer self-help groups, and crisis intervention systems. The risk of allowing the condition to remain untreated might also be addressed. (Haas, 1991)

5. *Qualification of counselor:* The counselor may present information about education, experience, years in practice, professional licenses and certifications, and professional affiliations.

6. *Rights and limits of confidentiality, including third-party issues:* Clients are reminded that information they share will be kept confidential; however, there are limits to this protection. The limits need to be clearly specified and identified. For example, duty-to-protect issues should be described, including danger to self and/or others, and reporting related to suspected child abuse. Clients should be aware that the counselor may also share information with insurance companies, courts, or in the context of supervision.

7. *Length and frequency of sessions:* The counselor should describe typical practices.

8. *Right to terminate counseling, or description of rights if counseling is involuntary:* Clients should be informed that they may terminate counseling at any time. In cases in which counseling is involuntary, as with children or with persons who are court-ordered to participate, their rights regarding participation and limits to confidentiality should be shared. If there are consequences attendant to termination of involuntary counseling, these should be made known to the clients involved.

9. *Cost and method of payment:* The cost of counseling, as well as any additional services (such as testing, telephone calls, etc.), should be described in this section. If fees are on a sliding scale, the process of fee determination should be explained. How fees are to be collected (billing procedures, payment at each session, etc.) should also be addressed. Policies regarding insurance reimbursement should also be included.

10. *Identification of supervisor:* Counselors who are supervised should share with their clients the identity of their supervisor. If they participate in a peer consultation group, this information may also be shared. Assurance that identifiable data will not be revealed to other professionals should be included in the statement.

11. *Identification of board of licensing:* The name, address, and telephone number of the agency that regulates the practice of counseling should be provided. Clients should be informed as to why this information is given in the disclosure statement (e.g., if questions or concerns about the counselor or the counseling process cannot be resolved with the counselor, the client may contact the appropriate licensing body).

Powell, R. R., & Craig, S. E. (2006). Spirituality and professional disclosure. In K. B. Helmeke & C. F. Sori (Eds.), *The therapist's notebook for integrating spirituality in counseling: Homework, handouts, and activities for use in psychotherapy* (pp. 29-35). Binghamton, NY: The Haworth Press.

Handout Two:
Sample Professional Disclosure Statements of Intent to Utilize Spirituality

1. *For a generic recognition of religion:* "This therapist is committed to taking an unbiased approach regardless of age, race, gender, or religious affiliations."
2. *For acknowledgment of religious beliefs:* "Although this therapist is a practicing (therapist inserts his or her religious background or denominational affiliation here, e.g., Roman Catholic, Christian, Reformed Jew), religious beliefs are not the primary focus of the therapy approach and the therapist will only be addressing spirituality when requested."
3. *For an alternative acknowledgment of religious beliefs:* "Although (therapist inserts his or her religious background or denominational affiliation here) counseling is not the foundation of this therapist's approach, faith and religion will be explored if the client so desires."
4. *For a strong statement of intent to bring spirituality into therapy:* "This therapist is a practicing (therapist inserts his or her religious background or denominational affiliation here), and will be using spirituality throughout the therapeutic process."

Powell, R. R., & Craig, S. E. (2006). Spirituality and professional disclosure. In K. B. Helmeke & C. F. Sori (Eds.), *The therapist's notebook for integrating spirituality in counseling: Homework, handouts, and activities for use in psychotherapy* (pp. 29-35). Binghamton, NY: The Haworth Press.

– 4 –

Networking with Local Clergy:
A Resource for Building a Spiritual Referral Source

Karen B. Helmeke
Phyllis L. White

Type of Contribution: Activity, Handouts

Objective

The purpose of this chapter is to help counselors make positive connections to their local area clergy. Such positive connections can provide mutual benefits to both therapists and clergy. Suggestions as to how a counselor establishes a support network among area clergy are provided.

Rationale for Use

It is not unusual for clients to raise issues containing religious or spiritual overtones in therapy, just as it is not unusual for many therapists to experience some discomfort and uncertainty about how to proceed when clients do so (Helmeke & Bischof, 2002). Developing a base of "religion experts" or "spirituality experts" is one way that therapists can increase their own confidence and competence in dealing with the spiritual crises their clients may be facing. The local clergy can serve as authorities on religious and spiritual issues clinicians encounter in their work with clients, they can function as a support group for those counselors who are interested in spirituality, and they can be a source for referrals of clients who want spirituality included as an integral part of their therapy. Halford, Markman, Kline, & Stanley (2003) suggest that once counselors are known to clergy, those counselors may be able to establish referral networks, "as most clergy we know would be glad to refer couples to low-cost, culturally sensitive services, especially those featuring educational- and research-based interventions" (p. 398).

Fortunately, it is not just the therapists who stand to benefit from a therapist-clergy relationship. Clergy, in turn, who establish trusting relationships with area therapists have someone to whom they can turn with questions pertaining to mental health issues, for advice on working with specific individuals, couples, and families, and for help in knowing when a referral is in order. Just as it is beneficial for a counselor to have a source of referrals, it is also an asset for members of the clergy to have a reliable and trustworthy person to whom they can refer laypeople whose problems are beyond their expertise, interest, and abilities. Or, if not able to take the referrals, the therapist can serve as a referral source, providing the clergy with names of trusted counselors who specialize in various treatment issues. Such therapist-clergy collaborations hold the potential for a great deal of mutual reciprocity in meeting particular needs.

Historically, though, counselors and clergy have tended to view each other with some distrust. The need in the field of psychology to establish itself as a legitimate science has probably been a contributing factor for some of the reluctance to consider what role religion and spirituality might play in therapy (Helmeke & Bischof, 2002). Psychologists and other counselors were influenced by Freud's antagonism toward religion (Aponte, 1996), and from the onset of its development as a field, psychotherapy has often viewed religion with some mistrust or misgivings.

Fortunately, this tendency has been changing in recent years, as many of the fields of counseling have become interested and open to understanding the impact of the client's religion and spirituality on the process of psychotherapy, and have begun to view clients' religious and spiritual beliefs and practices as resources, strengths, and complements to the therapeutic process. Although in a national survey of mental health professions, some mental health groups' religious beliefs and practices were in stark contrast with those of the American public, there were two groups of mental health professionals, marriage and family therapists and clinical social workers, whose levels of religious interest were similar to those of the general public (Jensen & Bergin, 1988). For instance, 50 percent of marriage and family therapists said they attended religious services regularly, an even higher percentage than did the general public (40 percent). Weaver, Koenig, & Larson (1997) suggest that because of their levels of religious commitment, "marriage and family therapists may be better positioned than other mental health professionals to develop linkages with the religious community" (p. 16). Within all of the fields of counseling, those counselors whose own spirituality and religion are important to them make excellent candidates for clergy-counselor collaboration.

Just as some counselors historically have viewed religion and the religious with mistrust, some clergy distrust the work of counselors. There are clergy, particularly some of those who are theologically and politically conservative, who view much of the work counselors do as being too secular and humanistic, having no spiritual base at the least and as being particularly atheistic at the worst. Others may fear that counselors will ignore religious issues and beliefs, or worse, treat them as pathological (Larson et al., 1988). Counselors need to recognize and respect these misgivings. Clergy may not be familiar with the practices and philosophies of area counselors, and may not understand the differences in training among the variety of mental health professionals. They may be reluctant to send laity "outside the fold" for fear of not knowing what kind of counseling their parishioners may receive.

Yet many clergy feel overwhelmed by the number of members of their church, synagogue, temple, or mosque who approach them for help. Many individuals do not discriminate who they see depending on the severity of their problems. In one study, Larson et al. (1988) found that "clergy are as likely as mental health professionals to be sought out by individuals from the community who have serious psychiatric disorders" (p. 1068). Halford et al. (2003) report that couples with marital problems and couples who are divorcing are more likely to see a member of the clergy than a mental health professional. They advocate that collaboration between mental health professionals and clergy will improve mental health care. For instance, Halford et al. report that in the United States and Australia, the majority of divorcing couples, between an astounding 80 and 90 percent, have not consulted a mental health professional. Not only do many clergy feel as though they do not have the time to deal sufficiently with these problems, but many have only received limited training in counseling techniques and theories. They do not feel adequately prepared for treating some of the problems that come through their office doors. Others may just not enjoy this pastoral role, yet feel obligated to meet with those who come asking for help.

The possibilities for reciprocating needs between counselor and clergy are natural, when one considers the overlapping roles that therapy and religion assume and the overlapping mental health issues that clergy and counselors face on a regular basis. Stander, Piercy, MacKinnon, & Helmeke (1994) discuss several overlapping roles shared by religion and therapy: fostering a sense of perspective, giving meaning to life, providing rituals that transform and connect, providing social support networks, structuring society and setting ethical norms, giving an identity and heritage to its members, supporting families, facilitating positive change in individuals, looking out for the physical and emotional welfare of its members, and educating its members. Not only do religion and therapy serve these same functions, but often clergy and counselors both try to meet similar emotional and spiritual needs of their congregants. Both clergy and counselors see clients with very similar presenting problems, such as premarital counseling, loss and grief, dealing with the chronically or terminally ill, struggles with anxiety and depression, relationship problems, and sexual and physical abuse.

Clearly, joining forces seems a reasonable way for mutually meeting reciprocal needs. Counselors and clergy can collaborate with one another in a number of specific ways. Weaver et al. (1997) single out three primary areas: domestic violence, preventing child abuse, and working with the elderly. There are a number of other possible areas of counselor-clergy collaboration. Clergy regularly see couples for premarital therapy, as part of wedding preparation. Yet this is an area in which many mental health professionals have also received training. Clergy could refer premarital couples to a therapist who would be able to meet with the couples individually or as part of a group. Or, if clergy prefer to do this work themselves, counselors could provide them with information and resources on conducting premarital counseling, including information on pre-marital inventories such as PREPARE (Olson, Fournier, & Druckman, 1996), FOCCUS (Facilitating Open Couple Communication Understanding and Study, Markey & Micheletto, 1997), and RELATE (Relationship Evaluation, Holman, Busby, Doxey, Klein, & Loyer-Carlson, 1997), as well as other training that is available to clergy. Similarly, counselors can help clergy in their premarital work with couples who are remarrying by educating clergy about common issues that stepfamilies face, and by sharing tips on strengthening blended families.

Because most couples first turn to clergy for help with their relationship problems, counselors with training in marriage and family therapy can serve as consultants to clergy, providing training in relationship education (Halford et al., 2003). Weaver et al. (1997) cite several studies that show that people going to clergy for counseling bring problems primarily related to marriage and family issues, such as marital conflict, problems with adolescent children, and divorce. Or, as mentioned previously, counselors could establish themselves as someone to whom the clergy could refer or ask someone to ask for names of competent therapists in relationship issues.

Clergy frequently work with laity who are dealing with issues of loss and grief. Counselors could offer support groups within the local congregation dealing with issues of loss and grief, or clergy could refer members of their congregation to groups being offered by area counselors. Individual or group therapy could be offered for cancer survivors and their families, for divorcing couples, for children whose parents are divorcing, etc. Counselors could also offer to teach a program related to loss and grief as part of the adult education offerings in a church or synagogue.

Therapists can provide many other benefits for area clergy. Besides providing support groups for various issues, therapists can also offer further training directly to clergy. A counselor can lead an area clergy group in which clergy come together to learn more about counseling methods, theories, and techniques. For instance, area clergy can be invited to bring difficult marital cases to such a consultation group, and with the therapist in the role as facilitator, the clergy can brainstorm different treatment approaches. Weaver et al. (1997) state, "Clergy are often unprepared to recognize the family and mental health problems of persons who seek their help" (p. 18), and assert that clergy need training in clinical evaluative skills. They specifically list the following areas: divorce and separation, parenting problems, marital counseling, child or spouse abuse, counseling singles, sexual adjustment, remarriage/stepfamily, and premarital counseling. Weaver et al. also found that training clergy in referral skills is an area that is sorely needed, and point out how counselors can "provide an important service by offering guidance and training to clergy about how and when to make a referral" (p. 18).

Another type of training that counselors can provide for clergy is to offer a family-of-origin group, where clergy meet to discuss issues from their own families of origin, and to consider how these issues impact their work in their congregation or synagogue. In such a group, therapists trained in family systems can help clergy recognize similar systems dynamics at work in their congregation, and how to deal with some of the stresses that clergy experience in their congregations. A number of books discuss how this work could be conducted, three of the strongest being Edwin Friedman's (1985) *Generation to Generation: Family Process in Church and Synagogue;* Peter Steinke's (1993) *How Your Church Family Works: Understanding Congregations As Emotional Systems;* and Steinke's (1996) *Healthy Congregations: A Systems Approach.*

A number of other books address the emotional and psychological stress that clergy experience as they try to handle conflictual dilemmas in their congregations, such as *Antagonists in the Church* by Haugk (1988), *Clergy Killers: Guidance for Pastors and Congregations Under Attack* by Rediger (1997), and *Never Call Them Jerks: Healthy Responses to Difficult Behavior* (Boers, 1999). One other resource that is familiar to many clergy is The Alban Institute, a research and consulting organization that helps clergy address difficult issues in their congregations. The Web site for this organization is www.alban.org.

If there are not enough interested clergy to form a group, a therapist could provide some coaching in differentiated leadership in the congregation to an individual clergy member. By applying the skills and information that counselors have with working with families as systems to clergy's work in their own congregations, counselors can make themselves an invaluable resource to clergy.

Similarly, a counselor who has established a positive connection with area clergy can utilize the expertise of the clergy. A therapist could invite a member of the clergy to supervision groups, case study and presentation groups, or peer consultation groups, to teach about specific aspects of that clergy's faith background, such as doctrine, spiritual and worship practices, spiritual beliefs regarding God, the nature of humans, sin and forgiveness, salvation and the afterlife, morals and the existence of evil, beliefs about who Jesus was/is, etc. Clergy then become an important resource for understanding the nuances of various religious backgrounds, which can assist therapists in becoming more spiritually sensitive (Stander et al., 1994) to the impact of clients' religious and spiritual beliefs and practices on the process of therapy.

A mutually supportive relationship between a clergy member and a counselor could also become a resource for a counselor's own spiritual development. Counselors who might lack such spiritual support in their other professional networks can look to an area clergy member for spiritual guidance or direction. Regular meetings could become part of the spiritual self-care of the therapist.

Another way that clergy can be of benefit to therapists is their familiarity with the related field of pastoral counseling. Clergy may subscribe to journals related to pastoral counseling, such as *Journal of Pastoral Care, Journal of Pastoral Counseling, Journal of Psychology and Christianity, Journal of Psychology and Judaism, Pastoral Psychology,* and *Journal of Psychology and Theology,* or the clergy can point out ones most pertinent to the counselor. Some members of the clergy may belong to the American Association of Pastoral Counselors, one of the oldest and most respected organizations of its kind, whose journal dates back to the 1970s.

There are some basic elements of establishing effective collaborations between clergy and counselors. McMinn, Aikens, & Lish (2003) propose a two-tiered schema for working well with clergy. The first tier involves basic collaborative qualifications, while the second tier involves additional qualifications for more advanced collaborations. For basic collaborations, McMinn et al. found that clergy desired respect from the counselors, that is, being treated as a professional with training and expertise who has valuable input in working with the same clientele as the counselor. One other aspect of respect was for the counselor to view the collaboration as mutual, rather than one-way (e.g., only the clergy benefits from the collaboration). Another element of basic collaboration was the ability to maintain an ongoing relationship and the capacity to communicate, even through such simple steps as signing release forms so that counselors could obtain and share additional information with the clergy about the client. For more advanced collaboration, an awareness of religious spirituality and shared values were necessary.

The following section describes some additional steps that counselors can take to nurture and foster mutual relationships with area clergy.

Instructions

Prior to making initial contact and introducing themselves to area clergy, counselor can take preliminary action to prepare for their first meeting. These actions are described in the following text. Additional suggestions are also provided for how counselors can make their first contact with local clergy and how to proceed in the initial meeting.

How to Prepare

First, the counselor can become familiar with a number of different faith backgrounds, in order to determine which denominations or sects he or she is most likely to be compatible and to feel comfortable with. Clergy usually see a relationship with a counselor as an asset if that counselor has compatible beliefs, values, and practices, or at least is able to demonstrate an understanding and respect for other religious backgrounds. Counselors who have not already done so may want to take a class in comparative religion at a local college or university. Counselors can read current books on various religions, denominations, and movements, including books that emphasize some historical perspectives on different faith backgrounds. One can look up books related to general works on Western or Eastern religions, ones that focus on religion in America or specific themes in American religion, or ones on specific movements or churches (Mead & Hill, 2001). Two highly recommended books are *Bruce & Stan's Guide to Cults, Religions, and Spiritual Beliefs: A User-Friendly Approach* (Bickel & Jantz, 2002), and Mead and Hill's *Handbook of Denominations in the United States*. Mead and Hill's book includes denominations of Christian, Jewish, and Islam faiths, while Bickel and Jantz's book includes all three of those plus Hinduism, Buddhism, other Eastern philosophies, New Age spirituality, and more.

The Internet will also be a helpful source in learning about various religious backgrounds. Many denominations have their own official Web sites where one can find information on a denomination's headquarters, publications, denominational history and polity, issues facing the denomination, how the denominations view religious and spiritual education, and much more. Many denominational Web sites even have a suggested reading list. Counselors can get to denominational Web sites by typing the name of the denomination into a major search engine. Some Web sites use initials as addresses to their sites. For example, the United Methodist Web site is www.umc.org. (See Handout One: List of Denominational Web Sites, at the end of the chapter for a list of Web sites from some of the denominations of various faiths.)

Many denominations publish their own journals and newspapers, and these may be available online, by subscription, or through local congregations. These denominational materials will tell counselors what the current issues are for a particular denomination and thus for a particular clergy in the area.

Counselors will also want to be aware of the ordination requirements that individual clergy must meet. Some clergy must have a master of divinity degree while others do not have any educational requirements. For some denominations, this requires three years or more of graduate school. Most clergy go through a rigorous denominational process that involves education about their chosen career and psychological testing, along with interviewing with a denomination body. On the other hand, some of the nondenominational pastors are simply ordained by the local congregations when their call to ministry is recognized. In some denominations, clergy may be married while others require celibacy. Some denominations and movements ordain women, while others do not. Some require a number of courses in pastoral counseling, including basic counseling techniques and other clinical training. Much of this information can be acquired on a denomination's Web site.

Finally, once counselors have identified some religious denominations whose clergy they would be interested in contacting, counselors can find out more specific information about the area clergy and local congregations from those specific backgrounds. First, they can go online to see if any of the local churches/synagogues/temples have their own Web sites. These Web sites will tell where the building is located, when the congregations worships, what their mission statement is, and who is on the staff. The sites will probably include a calendar and newsletter. Some pastors even post their past sermons. Counselors should use a good search engine and enter the name of the congregation, and as there are hundreds of thousands of "First" churches, it is also helpful to enter the name of the denomination and the name of the community.

Initiating Contact with Clergy

Once the counselor has decided which members of the clergy he or she will contact, initial steps can be taken to meet with them. The counselor should contact the clergyperson by phone, letter, or e-mail. (Or, if a therapist is already a member of a local congregation, the therapist may want to begin by setting up a meeting with his or her own clergy.)

In this introduction, the counselor should be sure to use the proper form of address for the clergy of that particular denomination. For example, Catholic priests and many Episcopalian priests are called "Father." However, this may not be appropriate if the local Episcopalian priest is a woman. In that case, "Reverend" or "Pastor" may be a better choice.

One of the purposes of this initial contact is to allow the counselor to introduce himself or herself, share credentials, and speak about an interest in spirituality, including any specialized training the counselor has received and the counselor's own religious background. In this initial contact, the counselor can ask for a time to meet with the clergyperson, and perhaps invite the pastor or rabbi out for breakfast, lunch, or even a cup of coffee. For a sample letter from a counselor to a pastor see Handout Two: Sample Letter to Clergy at the end of the chapter.

Initial Meeting with the Clergy

One of the primary tasks to achieve in this first meeting is for counselors to share who they are personally as well as professionally. Counselors can repeat their credentials, being careful not to use too much professional jargon. They can inform the clergy what kind of training they have received, what licenses they hold, and what types of clients and problems they typically see. Included in this description can be a brief explanation of the type of mental health professional the counselor is, and how this might differ from other counseling professions. Any specialized training or areas of interest that the counselor has obtained that may be of particular relevance for clergy are also important items to discuss.

In order to share who they are personally, counselors will need to be ready to talk about their professional and spiritual journeys. Counselors should be ready to talk about which theories and methods they use in their practice, as well as their general philosophical approach to counseling. They should also be prepared to explain how they integrate spirituality into their work, and how they inform their clients about this integration. Counselors may want to bring a copy of their professional disclosure statement, which includes a brief disclosure of how he or she integrates spirituality in counseling (see Powell & Craig, 2006).

Counselors can prepare ahead of time a list of questions to ask during this first meeting. Asking pastors and rabbis how they became clergy and what drew them to this particular congregation can be a good way to begin. Counselors can ask specific questions about the congregation: its size, theology, special projects, etc. Clergy can be asked about what their most difficult counseling problems are, what types of cases they usually see, what types of cases they need the most help with, and what kinds of presenting problems they prefer to refer.

During this initial meeting, the counselor should invite the minister or rabbi to ask questions. It is likely that clergy will want to know something about the religious background and spiritual beliefs of the counselor, so counselors must be especially ready to talk about their faith and spirituality as it has developed over the years. If the counselor has had negative experiences with organized religion, he or she should reflect ahead of time what and how they want to share these experiences, including how they have integrated them in their work and how those experiences may have shaped the way they interact with clients concerning the topic of religion and spirituality. Other questions that counselors should be prepared to respond to in this initial meeting include the following:

- Do you attend church/synagogue/temple? Where?
- Why do you (or do you not) attend church/synagogue/temple?
- How do you see yourself as a spiritual person if you do not attend church/synagogue/temple or follow any known practice?
- How do you integrate your faith in your practice?
- Do you pray with clients?
- What do you believe about divorce/abortion/homosexuality/stem cell research/genetic testing (other similar topics)?
- What kinds of clients do you typically see?
- What specialized training or expertise do you have to offer my parishioners?
- Are you covered by insurance, and if so, what kind?
- What is your view on the use of medications?
- How available are you? How soon can you meet with someone after I refer them to you?
- What is your general approach and school of thought?
- How would you approach the following presenting problem? (Clergy may want to know specific examples of how counselors would handle various scenarios, e.g., a teenager who says she is pregnant or a couple who is thinking about getting a divorce.)

Clergy may also be interested in knowing what your expectations are for a working relationship with them. They may be interested in having a trusted counselor to whom they could refer their congregants, but are uncertain about the logistics of the arrangements. Some clergy may need to be reassured that the counselors understand themselves to be in a supporting role to the clergy, rather than attempting to take over the job of the clergy. Other clergy may be more than happy to have a reliable and trustworthy person to whom they can send people. Counselors also need to make sure that the clergyperson knows and understands the ethical constraints of confidentiality issues, and that if the clergyperson does refer someone, the counselor will not be able to acknowledge when or if a client has followed through on the referral. Also, the counselor would not be able to share information with the clergy member that was obtained from counseling sessions, unless appropriate release forms are filled out.

Finally, counselors should ask the clergymember with whom they are meeting whether they could be of assistance to them, or whether the counselor might be able to address any existing needs. These might be needs that the minister or rabbi has, such as someone to consult with on difficult cases, or these may be needs specific to the local congregation, such as the need for someone to lead an adult education class on some mental health topic, or someone to offer a support group on spiritual resources for caregivers. The clergy might also be aware of ways that a counselor could provide support to a group of area clergy.

Many communities have one or more local groups for area clergy, sometimes known as ministeriums or ministerial associations. The counselor may be able to provide some type of support services for this kind of ecumenical group, such as being a guest speaker or becoming an ongoing consultant to the group. For instance, counselors might present programs on mental health to the area clergy, including such topics as suicide, living with mental illness, or crisis intervention. Crisis intervention includes topics such as how to help the community after a disaster or trauma, how to be most helpful to those who are severely injured and to their families, how to help stroke victims, Parkinson patients, and Alzheimer's patients and their families, and how to help parents who have lost a child. After the counselor has presented to the clergy group, he or she might also offer to present similar workshops on various mental health issues to local congregations.

Another service is for a counselor to offer members of the group discounted rates for personal counseling sessions. Another offer to the clergy might be one or two free sessions of consultation for pastors or rabbis who are dealing with difficult pastoral care cases.

After learning about a local group of clergy in the area, the counselor can contact the presiding minister of the group to request permission to attend a meeting and introduce himself or herself. This can be an opportunity to build collaborative relationships with a number of area clergy, using some of the suggestions mentioned previously.

Brief Vignette

Vicki had recently opened a private counseling practice. She had introduced herself to other therapists in the area. None of them shared her interest in spirituality, especially its use in therapy. In order to have support in her own spiritual journey and as a way to introduce her practice, she called the local Chamber of Commerce to ask the name of the presiding clergyperson for the area clergy association. The chamber secretary thought that Pastor Cross of Brook Crossing United Church of Christ was the contact person. She also mentioned that not all of the clergy belonged to the association.

Prior to contacting Pastor Owens, Vicki went on the Internet to find out more about the United Church of Christ (UCC), and she found that Brook Crossing Church had its own Web site. Through these sources, she became familiar with the history of the UCC, its practices and beliefs, its requirements and process for ordination, and its stances on such controversial issues as abortion and homosexuality. Vicki copied many of the articles for further study. After looking at the denominational Web site, Vicki moved to the Brook Crossing Web site, where she read the church's mission statement and looked at their calendar of activities. She learned that Brook Crossing was an active congregation of 600. The church considered itself as liberal and progressive. They were involved in such activities as voter registration and Habitat for Humanity. They also worked with the underprivileged by providing food, clothing, and emergency money to those in need. The church also ran a preschool and an after-school care program which included tutoring for those who requested it. The congregation had two services, a traditional service on Sunday morning at 8:30 a.m. and a contemporary service at 10:30 a.m., with a coffee hour between the services. Sunday School was provided at both services. The congregation cooperated with the local Roman Catholic, Methodist, and Presbyterian churches to provide weekly Taize services on Wednesday evenings. (Taize is an international, ecumenical community founded in 1940 by Brother Rogers in Taize, France, whose prayers, songs, and liturgies have been used widely in churches across the world.) Brook Crossing also cooperated with the Methodists to provide youth activities for junior and senior highs on Wednesday evenings. Vicki again copied some of this information for further study. She then jotted down the pastors' names, church addresses, and phone numbers.

After finding out this information, Vicki wrote a letter of introduction to Pastor Owens (see Handout Two: Sample Letter to Clergy, at the end of the chapter). She included such things as where she went to school, when she got her degree, which licensing exams she had passed, memberships in professional organizations, and professional certification. For instance, she mentioned that she was a member of the state professional organization called Illinois Association for Marriage and Family Therapy, and the national professional organization called the American Counseling Association. She then stated that she was very interested in her own spirituality and in respecting and dealing with clients' faith stances and religions. She shared that she grew up as a United Methodist, and then became a Unitarian Universalist. Finally, she asked if she might call him later to set up a time to meet with him.

Vicki followed up on her letter to Pastor Owens with a phone call. Again she introduced herself as a counselor who was new to the area and mentioned her letter to him. After some small talk about the contents of her letter, she asked Pastor Owens if she could meet him for lunch. Pastor Owens agreed. They set a date. Vicki suggested that she pick up Pastor Cross at his church. He agreed and they said goodbye.

Vicki dressed professionally for her appointment with Pastor Owens. She arrived at the church about ten minutes before their appointment, and she introduced herself to the church secretary. When Pastor Owens was finished with his meeting, they drove to a local restaurant. During lunch, Vicki asked Pastor Owens about his congregation and their activities, as well as how he entered his profession, how he came to the congregation, and if he was enjoying his tenure in Lake City. Vicki willingly discussed her faith journey and explained how she grew up in a small-town Methodist congregation, but during college she worshiped at the closest church to her dormitory, which happened to be the College Avenue Unitarian Universalist (UU) Church. She turned to the pastor there when she began to question some of the things she had always believed as she moved more deeply into her studies in psychology and philosophy. She found that the pastor's openness and responsiveness to her questions helped her to think about what she believed. During her senior year, she transferred her membership to the UU church.

She also discussed why she chose counseling as a profession. She spoke of her approach toward counseling and clients, that she did not like to pathologize clients but preferred to work with their strengths, and that she viewed clients' spirituality as, potentially, one of the primary sources of strengths for clients. She also shared why she thought incorporating spirituality into counseling was important, and explained how she did this.

Vicki also asked Pastor Owens about his views on counseling, as well as what types of cases he dealt with most frequently. Upon hearing that he most frequently encountered relational problems with married or engaged couples, Vicki asked how comfortable he felt dealing with those cases. She then inquired as to whether and how she could be of help to him in dealing with relational problems. They talked about several premarital counseling programs. Vicki offered to get Pastor Owens information on the programs she liked best. She also mentioned that she would be willing to co-facilitate a premarital group with Pastor Owens if they agreed upon a program. He agreed to the idea, stating that she could work with any couples who had serious problems in her private practice. The conversation then turned to difficulties Pastor Owens had in working with married couples. Vicki offered to meet to discuss some of Pastor Owens's more difficult cases.

Vicki then asked Pastor Owens about the local ministerial association. She made the following inquiries:

- How often did they meet?
- What did they do at meetings?

- Did they have any special projects?
- Were there any problems that the group was facing?
- Were all the local pastors part of the group?
- Could she be of help in any way?

Finally, she asked Pastor Owens if he thought it might be possible for her to attend a meeting. Pastor Owens said that he thought attending a meeting would be an excellent idea and invited her to the next meeting as his guest.

Suggestions for Follow-Up

It will be important to continue to have contact with the clergy member with whom one is collaborating. More than just the initial contact, the counselor can check in with the pastor or rabbi at regular intervals, have monthly meetings, perhaps regularly attend the local ecumenical clergy group's meetings, or work collaboratively on an ongoing case. Nurturing and fostering the relationship will enhance the potential benefits of the basic collaboration for both clergy and counselors. For more advanced collaboration between clergy and psychotherapists, other possibilities for working together can emerge. For instance, those who have developed closer professional bonds may want to consider establishing a church-based counseling ministry, where counseling offices are located within the building of the church or temple. In some cases, the counseling ministry may be funded by the larger church or synagogue, or by a consortium of churches. For a description of such a counseling ministry, see Spriggs, Sloter, & Spriggs (2003).

Contraindications

As mentioned previously in this chapter, counselors should be sure to inform ministers and rabbis how issues of confidentiality need to be handled. Prior to discussing any cases with a member of the clergy, counselors should be sure to review the codes of ethics of their prospective mental health professions.

Another possible situation that may arise is whether one's own minister or rabbi requests counseling. Again, each counselor should check his or her own code of ethics for guidance, but in general, counselors should not see a minister or rabbi as a client if the counselor is a member of the clergy's congregation or if the counselor has established some other professional relationship with the clergy member. If the counselor has a question about the appropriateness of meeting with a particular clergyperson, then he or she should seek supervision.

References

Aponte, H. J. (1996). Political bias, moral values, and spirituality in the training of psychotherapists. *Bulletin of the Menninger Clinic, 60,* 488-502.

Bickel, B., & Jantz, S. (2002). *Bruce & Stan's guide to cults, religions, and spiritual beliefs: A user-friendly approach.* Eugene, OR: Harvest House Publishers.

Boers, P. (1999). *Never call them jerks: Healthy responses to difficult behavior.* Bethesda, MD: The Alban Institute.

Friedman, E. H. (1985). *Generation to generation: Family process in church and synagogue.* New York: Guilford Press.

Halford, W. K., Markman, H. J., Kline, G. H., & Stanley, S. M. (2003). Best practice in couple relationship education. *Journal of Marital and Family Therapy, 29,* 385-406.

Haugk, K. C. (1988). *Antagonists in the church: How to identify and deal with destructive conflict.* Minneapolis: Augsburg Publishing House.

Helmeke, K. B., & Bischof, G. H. (2002). Recognizing and raising spiritual and religious issues in therapy: Guidelines for the timid. *Journal of Family Psychotherapy, 13*(1/2), 195-214.

Holman, T. B., Busby, D. M., Doxey, C., Klein, D. M., & Loyer-Carlson, V. (1997). *The Relationship Evaluation (RELATE).* Provo, UT: RELATE Institute.

Jensen, J. P., & Bergin, A. E. (1988). Mental health values of professional therapists: A national interdisciplinary survey. *Professional Psychology: Research and Practice, 19,* 290-297.

Larson, D. B., Hohmann, A. A., Kessler, L. G., Meador, K. G., Boyd, J. H., & McSherry, E. (1988). The couch and the cloth: The need for linkage. *Hospital and Community Psychiatry, 39,* 1064-1069.

Markey, B., & Micheletto, M. (1997). *Instructor manual for FOCCUS.* Omaha, NE: Archdiocese of Omaha.

McMinn, M., Aikins, D. C., & Lish, R. A. (2003). Basic and advanced competence in collaborating with clergy. *Professional Psychology: Research & Practice, 34*(2), 197-202.

Mead, F. S., & Hill, S. S. (2001). *Handbook of denominations in the United States* (11th ed.). Nashville, TN: Abingdon Press.

Olson, D. H., Fournier, D. G., & Druckman, J. M. (1996). *PREPARE.* Minneapolis, MN: Life Innovations.

Powell, R. R., & Craig, S. E. (2006). Spirituality and professional disclosure. In K. B. Helmeke & C. F. Sori (Eds.), *The therapist's notebook for integrating spirituality in counseling: Homework, handouts, and activities for use in psychotherapy* (pp. 29-35). Binghamton, NY: The Haworth Press.

Rediger, G. L. (1997) *Clergy killers: Guidance for pastors and congregations under attack.* Louisville, KY: Westminster John Knox Press.

Spriggs, J. D., Sloter, E., & Spriggs, J. D. (2003). Counselor-clergy collaboration in a church-based counseling ministry. *Journal of Psychology & Christianity, 22*(4), 323-326.

Stander, V., Piercy, F. P., MacKinnon, D., & Helmeke, K. (1994). Spirituality, religion, and family therapy: Competing or complementary worlds: *The American Journal of Family Therapy, 22,* 27-41.

Steinke, P. L. (1993). *How your church family works: Understanding congregations as emotional systems.* Bethesda, MD: The Alban Institute.

Steinke, P. L. (1996). *Healthy congregations: A systems approach.* Bethesda, MD: The Alban Institute.

Weaver, A. J., Koenig, H. G., & Larson, D. B. (1997). Marriage and family therapists and the clergy: A need for clinical collaboration, training, and research. *Journal of Marital and Family Therapy, 23*(1), 13-25.

Professional Readings and Resources

www.alban.org: The Alban Institute.

www.academicinfo.net/religionindex.html: Offered by the University of Phoenix, this is a good gateway to lots of sites dealing with religion.

www.religion-online.org: A collection of more than 5,200 articles and chapters that explores many aspects of religion and spirituality.

www.virtualreligion.net/vri/

www.yahoo.com/r/rl: A search results page that lists many categories dealing with religion.

Bickel, B., & Jantz, S. (2002). *Bruce & Stan's guide to cults, religions, and spiritual beliefs: A user-friendly approach.* Eugene, OR: Harvest House Publishers.

Boers, P. (1999). *Never call them jerks: Healthy responses to difficult behavior.* Bethesda, MD: The Alban Institute.

Fowler, J. W. (1981). *Stages of faith.* New York: Harper & Row.

Friedman, E. H. (1985). *Generation to generation: Family process in church and synagogue.* New York: Guilford Press.

Haugk, K. C. (1988). *Antagonists in the church: How to identify and deal with destructive conflict.* Minneapolis: Augsburg Publishing House.

Mead, F. S., & Hill, S. S. (2001). *Handbook of denominations in the United States* (11th ed.). Nashville, TN: Abingdon Press.

Rediger, G. L. (1997). *Clergy killers: Guidance for pastors and congregations under attack.* Louisville, KY: Westminster John Knox Press.

Steinke, P. L. (1993). *How your church family works: Understanding congregations as emotional systems.* Bethesda, MD: The Alban Institute.

Steinke, P. L. (1996). *Healthy congregations: A systems approach.* Bethesda, MD: The Alban Institute.

**Handout One:
List of Denominational Web Sites**

Denomination	Official Web site and/or informational site[a]
CHRISTIANITY	
Baptist	
American Baptist Churches in the USA	www.abc-usa.org
National Baptist Convention of America	www.nbcamerica.net
National Missionary Baptist Convention of America	www.nmbca.com
Southern Baptist	www.sbc.net
Catholic Churches	
Roman Catholic Church	www.vatican.va
	www.catholic.org
	www.catholic.net
Christian Churches	
Disciples of Christ	www.disciples.org
Churches of Christ	www.church-of-christ.org
Congregational Churches	
United Church of Christ	www.ucc.org
Episcopal/Anglican Churches	
Episcopal Church	www.episcopalchurch.org
Fundamentalist/Bible Churches[b]	
Baptist Bible Fellowship International	www.bbfi.org
Lutheran	
Evangelical Lutheran Church in America	www.elca.org
Lutheran Church—Missouri Synod	www.lcms.org
Wisconsin Evangelical Lutheran Synod	www.wels.net
Methodist	
African Methodist Episcopal Church	www.ame-church.com
United Methodist Church	www.umc.org
The Free Methodist Church of North America	www.fmcna.org

Helmeke, K. B., & White, P. L. (2006). Networking with local clergy: A resource for building a spiritual referral source. In K. B. Helmeke & C. F. Sori (Eds.), *The therapist's notebook for integrating spirituality in counseling: Homework, handouts, and activities for use in psychotherapy* (pp. 37-52). Binghamton, NY: The Haworth Press.

**Handout One:
List of Denominational Web Sites** *(continued)*

Denomination	Official Web site and/or informational site[a]
Orthodox and Oriental Orthodox Church	
Greek Orthodox Archdiocese of North America	www.goach.org
Russian Orthodox Church	www.russian-orthodox-church.org
Pentecostal	
Assemblies of God, General Council of	www.ag.org
Church of God in Christ	www.cogic.org
Pentecostal Assemblies of the World	www.pawinc.org
Presbyterian	
Presbyterian Church (USA)	www.pcusa.org
Presbyterian Church in America	www.pcanet.org
Orthodox Presbyterian Church	www.opc.org
Reformed	
Reformed Church in America	www.rca.org
BLENDED	
Jehovah's Witnesses	
Jehovah's Witnesses	www.watchtower.org
Latter-Day Saints (Mormons)	
Church of Jesus Christ of Latter-Day Saints	www.ods.org
Unitarian Universalist Association	
Unitarian Universalist Church	www.uua.org
JUDAISM	
Conservative Judaism	
United Synagogue of Conservative Judaism	www.uscj.org
Orthodox Judaism	
The Orthodox Union	www.ou.org[a]
Reform Judaism	
Reform Judaism	www.rj.org

Helmeke, K. B., & White, P. L. (2006). Networking with local clergy: A resource for building a spiritual referral source. In K. B. Helmeke & C. F. Sori (Eds.), *The therapist's notebook for integrating spirituality in counseling: Homework, handouts, and activities for use in psychotherapy* (pp. 37-52). Binghamton, NY: The Haworth Press.

Handout One:
List of Denominational Web Sites *(continued)*

Denomination	Official Web site and/or informational site[a]
ISLAM	www.islamicity.org[a]
Islam	
Sunnism	
Shi'ism	www.shia.org[a]
Sufism	www.ias.org[a]
	www.sufism.org[a]
Nation of Islam	www.noi.org
EASTERN AND OTHER PHILOSOPHIES	
Hinduism	www.hindunet.org[a]
Buddhism	
Digital International Buddhist Organization	www.dibo.org[a]
	www.buddhism.org[a]
Jainism	www.jainism.org
Taoism	www.taopage.org[a]
Wicca	www.wicca.org

[a]Some religions are so loosely organized that they do not have "official" Web sites. However, there are organizations that support their mission and ministry. These sites are from those organizations.

[b]These churches tend to have more of a local governing structure, rather than having a traditional denominational structure, so no official Web site exists for many of the churches as a group.

Helmeke, K. B., & White, P. L. (2006). Networking with local clergy: A resource for building a spiritual referral source. In K. B. Helmeke & C. F. Sori (Eds.), *The therapist's notebook for integrating spirituality in counseling: Homework, handouts, and activities for use in psychotherapy* (pp. 37-52). Binghamton, NY: The Haworth Press.

Handout Two:
Sample Letter to Clergy

Rev. Daryll Owens
444 W. Brookside Lane
Lake City, Illinois 33333

Dear Reverend Owens,

I am a new counselor in the area. I am part of Catalyst, a group practice that works with women and families. Please permit me to introduce myself.

I am a marriage and family therapist who graduated from State University with a MEd in counseling. I passed the national exam and received my Illinois license in marriage and family therapy that same year. I am also a trained and certified infertility counselor, having taken advanced courses in infertility problems at ABC Training Institute, which is associated with the Best Hospital's Infertility Clinic. My undergraduate degree is from Private University. My major was in psychology. My minor was in philosophy.

In my practice, I see couples for premarital, marital, and infertility counseling. I also see families with problems as far ranging as difficulty following a job-related transfer, learning to live with a disabled child, coping with a chronic illness, or parental differences on child-rearing. I frequently work with blended families. Although I work with children, I do so only as part of a family group because I believe that most children's problems cannot be addressed without working with the family system.

I firmly believe that individual beliefs and faith stance are important to mental health. I respect those beliefs and try to incorporate them into my counseling whenever possible.

I hope to call you soon so that we can get to know each other and discover ways we might work together to help the people of Lake City.

Sincerely,

Vicki L. Avery, MS, LMFT

5555 S. Sylvan Way
Lake City, Illinois 33333
Phone and Fax Numbers: 777-555-2222

Helmeke, K. B., & White, P. L. (2006). Networking with local clergy: A resource for building a spiritual referral source. In K. B. Helmeke & C. F. Sori (Eds.), *The therapist's notebook for integrating spirituality in counseling: Homework, handouts, and activities for use in psychotherapy* (pp. 37-52). Binghamton, NY: The Haworth Press.

SECTION II:
ASSESSMENT OF SPIRITUALITY

5

Conducting Spiritual Dialogues in Therapy

J. Mark Killmer

Type of Contribution: Activity, Handout

Objective

A spiritual dialogue is an in-depth conversation in which client and therapist grapple with serious spiritual concerns such as meaning in life, moral responsibility, and/or ultimate values. Spiritual dialogues are used *within* therapy to engage spiritual perspectives that may aid or hinder the process of healing. In working with religious and/or spiritual clients, the author envisions the use of spiritual practices by clients *in conjunction with* therapy in addition to spiritual dialogues. These practices can activate spiritual resources to provide support and facilitate change. Using spiritual practices in conjunction with therapy is presented in Chapter 23 of this book (Killmer, 2006).

A spiritual dialogue is an open, honest, respectful, and differentiated conversation rooted in a trusting relationship. Client and therapist seek to understand the implications of clients' religious or spiritual perspectives for their current distress. A spiritual dialogue strives to identify and address key spiritual concerns, to discern religious or spiritual guidance, and/or to wrestle with how to respond to these religious or spiritual insights.

The primary objective of this chapter is to provide clinicians with a workable and adaptable model for integrating religion and spirituality into therapy. While openness to spirituality has increased dramatically in clinical circles, many therapists seem to struggle with how to integrate religion/spirituality in an effective manner. In one clinical study, approximately two-thirds of marriage and family therapists reported a willingness to include spirituality in therapy (Carlson, Kirkpatrick, Hecker, & Killmer, 2002). When compared to previous studies of clinicians, this percentage represented a significant increase. It was interesting to note, however, that 95 percent of the therapists in the study considered themselves to be spiritual persons. In addition, the same percentage saw a strong positive relationship between spirituality and mental health. This means, then, that nearly 30 percent of therapists with a very high regard for spirituality *chose not* to include it in therapy. When these therapists were asked about their comfort with specific spiritual and/or religious interventions, the percentages again dropped significantly, ranging from 17 percent for specific religious interventions to 48 percent in response to very general spiritual ones. A close study of their responses found therapists uncertain rather than rejecting of these interventions. These results point to the need for effective models to integrate spirituality into therapy.

A secondary objective of this chapter is to increase sensitivity of therapists to the spirituality of clients. Even when a therapist makes the decision *not* to include spirituality in therapy, it still is important for a clinician to be aware of and respectful toward the religious and spiritual perspectives of clients. This heightened sensitivity can prevent harmful behaviors such as ignoring, minimizing, belittling, or undermining religious or spiritual views.

Rationale for Use

Throughout the twentieth century, a compartmentalized view of human beings often created sharp distinctions in the physical and psychological treatment of persons. From this viewpoint, religion or spirituality generally were perceived as irrelevant or even harmful to the treatment process. In contrast, a holistic perspective of human beings asserts that religion and spirituality can have a strong relationship to health and well-being. This holistic view of health, which has received impressive support from recent clinical research (Koenig, 1997; Larson, 1993), provides one rationale for the integration of religion and spirituality into the healing process of therapy.

In a number of research studies and national polls, a very high percentage of Americans describe themselves as religious or spiritual (Pargament, 1997; Walsh, 1999). The majority of clients entering therapy, then, are likely to have some level of spiritual interest. Heavily influenced by the compartmentalized viewpoint of the twentieth century, clients often are uncertain how to connect their faith or spirituality to their lives. Many religious or spiritual clients enter therapy hoping to discern a spiritual perspective about their situation and wanting to respond in a faithful manner. From a Christian perspective, for instance, human beings are perceived as benefiting both individually and collectively when their faith is lived out in an authentic manner by discerning, developing, and acting out cherished beliefs.

Through spiritual dialogues, the therapist helps thes clients to discern how spiritual or religious perspective speaks to their situation. This process endeavors to tap the spiritual resources that contribute to physical, emotional, and relational health. Furthermore, a spiritual dialogue strives to provide a client with the opportunity to opt for living in a manner consistent with his or her religious or spiritual values.

Theoretical Rationale for Spiritual Dialogues

For this model, in-depth intervention with the spiritual dimension of therapeutic issues requires the willingness and ability to enter dialogue with clients. The understanding of dialogue used for this model is grounded in the I-Thou relationship of Martin Buber in which a healing interaction can occur between two people willing to disclose honestly and who are open to considering the truths of another (Buber, 1958). The I-Thou relationship generally includes qualities such as invitation, respect, empathy, acceptance, positive regard, affirmation, and confirmation (Potts, 1994). For this context, the key point is that a therapist leaves the relative safety of conventional wisdom, pragmatic solutions, and comfortable therapeutic interventions to enter dialogue in the religious-spiritual dimension in which things may be less clear or certain and the wisdom may be intuitive rather than logical. The courage to wrestle in the spiritual dimension with clients can forge the powerfully healing relationship described by Buber.

Contextual family therapy has integrated Buber's relational notions into its theoretical foundation of relational justice and trust. One product of this integration is a family therapy intervention called *direct address,* which is defined as a willingness to risk speaking honestly in order to build trust and promote healing (Krasner & Joyce, 1995). Through direct address, therapist and client(s) confront the profound pain created and maintained by indirect address—the individual/systemic behaviors that avoid pain and conflict (Krasner & Joyce, 1991). This honest confrontation can become a transforming moment for the client(s). Direct address is an in-depth intervention rooted in the I-Thou relationship that explores painful, vulnerable areas that many clients, therapists, therapeutic approaches and systems opt not to address.

The foci of religion and spirituality are often the core values, primary beliefs, meaning and purpose of individuals and/or systems. These foci seem to reside at the very heart of human beings and relationships. Furthermore, the key foci of religion and spirituality are often subject to the individual and systemic strategies of indirect address. Consequently, the therapist needs to be sensitive to the potential vulnerability of clients in exploring these issues. Similar to direct address, a spiritual dialogue is often an in-depth intervention rooted in the trust of an I-Thou relationship. The spiritual dialogue is an open, honest, respectful, and differentiated conversation in which client(s) and therapist risk exploring the religious and spiritual dimension at a profound level to activate its healing resources for the purpose of personal and/or systemic transformation.

Instructions: The Self of the Therapist

To intervene spiritually with clients, the therapist should assess his or her own readiness to engage in spiritual dialogues. Key factors in making this decision include openness, comfort, courage, experience, and expertise with spiritual issues. These qualities enable a therapist to address religion and spirituality effectively. Therapists who do not meet this criterion should consider referring devout clients to clergy for work in conjunction with therapy or to a spiritually sensitive therapist for additional therapy. Clinicians who are emotionally reactive to or cut-off from religion are particularly vulnerable to harmful interactions with devout clients.

The Spirituality of the Therapist

From the perspective of the author, a therapist is only qualified for spiritual dialogues of depth when actively pursuing a personal spiritual path that may or may not be related to a formal religion. Since a rigorous lifelong process of education, experience, reflection, and supervision is needed for effective therapy, it follows that a parallel spiritual process with the same level of effort and commitment is needed for spiritual competence. This path often fosters spiritual growth that produces the qualities of openness, comfort, courage, experience, and expertise identified as critical to the spiritual dialogue process.

Soul Searching

William Doherty (1995) argues persuasively that therapists must "soul search" to determine personal values before engaging in moral conversations with clients. Without this reflection and grounding, the therapist is vulnerable to an uncritical acceptance of shifting cultural values. Moral conversations are understood as inviting clients to take moral responsibility by considering the impact of their decisions and actions on others (Doherty, 1995). I perceive these moral conversations as one type of spiritual dialogue.

For spiritual dialogues, the concept of soul searching is re-expanded from the specific context of moral responsibility to all facets of spirituality. The process of soul searching prepares the therapist to engage in spiritual dialogues in many ways. First, the clarification of one's own spiritual position strengthens the therapist's sense of self. Buber (1965) believed that a strong sense of self greatly enhanced the I-Thou relationship. Second, soul searching can increase differentiation with religion and spirituality for the therapist. This can reduce the vulnerability of the therapist to do harm to spiritual and religious clients. Third, soul searching can increase experience with and knowledge of spiritual and religious matters, which may nurture the critical qualities of openness, comfort, and courage. Fourth, it can facilitate integration of a religious or spiritual perspective into the life of the therapist. Finally, it can hone the therapist's ability to identify the values or religious or spiritual perspective underlying conventional wisdom, cultural trends, client attitudes or behavior, therapeutic approaches, and family belief systems.

In this conceptual framework, the therapist uses his or her spiritual path to engage in the process of soul searching. This process is seen as critical to the development of a spiritually sensitive and spiritually competent therapist. In effect, this framework parallels the integration of spirituality in therapy in which the client is invited to engage his or her spiritual path to soul search through spiritual dialogues or spiritual practices.

Clinical Training and Spiritual Path

The clinical training and spiritual path of the therapist each present a vision of health. These visions can have a complex relationship. Many times, the two perspectives may be complementary, serving to reinforce an understanding of health. Other times, they can inform each other, creating a more in-depth perception of health for human beings. Clinical techniques can provide the steps to living out a spiritual value such as forgiveness. Or, a client may draw on spiritual resources to meet a clinical goal such as setting boundaries in important relationships.

At times, the two perspectives can present conflicting visions of health that may even raise serious concerns about the other viewpoint. For example, many spiritual perspectives promote selflessness as its highest ideal in startling contrast to most, if not all, psychological viewpoints. Wrestling with this tension involves a willingness to risk examining the personal spiritual perspective of the therapist while assessing the clinical viewpoint for its underlying values. Often, the tension initiates a process of spiritual dialogue with colleagues and mentors that weighs the merits of each perspective. This dialogue may lead to strong reaffirmation, significant expansion, or serious revision of one's spiritual and clinical perspective.

The potential tension between clinical and spiritual perspectives is important to note since spiritual values are often countercultural in nature. For instance, a Christian perspective of anxiety recommends the development of a radical trust in God rather than excessive investment in security-seeking behaviors. It would be easy for a therapist who is not spiritually sensitive to dismiss this spiritual perspective as impractical. As a result, the therapist must be prepared to grapple with this tension when attempting to integrate spiritual perspectives in therapy.

Instructions: Use in Therapy

This section is comprised of spiritual assessment and engaging clients in spiritual dialogues in both the early and latter stages of therapy. The format envisions increasing depth of spiritual intervention based on client goals and the growth of a trusting therapeutic relationship.

Spiritual Assessment

It is valuable to make a spiritual assessment at the beginning of therapy. This assessment not only gathers information but also functions as an initial spiritual intervention. For a variety of reasons, therapists often take a passive stance toward spirituality in therapy waiting for their clients to raise their religious and spiritual concerns. This passivity can be a disservice to religious or spiritual clients who often interpret the silence of the therapist as disinterest in or a taboo against addressing these concerns. Making a spiritual assessment communicates clearly that the therapist is open to addressing religion and spirituality for clients who want this integration.

At the Samaritan Counseling Center, one page of the intake form is devoted to the spirituality of the client. This includes faith background, current religious involvement, spiritual concerns and the opportunity to request specific spiritual interventions. An adapted copy of this form appears at the end of the chapter. This simple assessment tool conveys the Center's openness to religion and spirituality. Furthermore, it enables the therapist to respond immediately to the client's desire—or lack of desire—to integrate their spirituality in therapy. Finally, the therapist can begin to identify the spiritual concerns of the client, which are frequently closely connected to his or her presenting problem and symptoms.

When it is established that a client is seeking integration of religion or spirituality, it is important to assess his or her spiritual support system. This assessment includes gaining an understanding of the client's worldview or faith framework. It is valuable to have a sense of how the client's worldview matches that of the therapist. In addition, it is helpful to find out the client's current spiritual practices (e.g., personal prayer) including his or her participation in a faith community. These spiritual practices can activate spiritual resources that strongly support the process of healing and change in therapy.

Engaging Clients in Spiritual Dialogues Early in Therapy

The dialogue process begins when a therapist brings the spiritual dimension into therapy. Early in therapy, this often takes the form of asking an opening question such as the following:

- How does your spiritual perspective (or faith) speak to your situation?
- Do you feel that God is with you through this difficult time?
- Are you active spiritually at this time?
- Does your faith/spirituality bring you comfort?
- How do you think that God feels or thinks about your situation?

The phrasing of these questions depends on the spiritual worldview or faith framework of the client. In some instances, the client will have a ready answer to this question. It is important for the therapist to explore this response with the client. For example, two conflicted couples report the belief that God wants them to stay together. For one couple, this belief provides the impetus to work hard in therapy to resolve their conflict. The therapist generally would respond by supporting this sense of commitment. For the other couple, this same belief may communicate despair because they feel trapped between this faith perspective and a feeling of hopelessness about their marriage. A comforting response that seeks to engender hope for their relationship is often most effective for this second couple. Early in therapy, religious or spiritual couples usually are not receptive when a therapist questions this belief. If a strong trusting relationship develops then an in-depth spiritual dialogue could address this dilemma later in therapy.

Other clients may express confusion or bafflement in response to the opening question. These clients are unclear how their religious or spiritual perspective relates to their current distress. A spiritual dialogue can seek clarification or understanding of this perspective. Furthermore, the therapist may assign the client the task of using his or her spiritual path to soul search. This soul search may be an internal examination of one's religious or spiritual values, or an external exploration to understand the perspective of one's faith tradition or spiritual perspective.

Early in therapy, some clients express specific spiritual concerns. They may perceive their symptoms as a lack of faith or as a spiritual failure. The current distress may be seriously disconcerting to their faith or seen as punishment from God. Clients may express anger toward God or believe that their faith framework or spiritual perspective has let them down. These spiritual concerns usually are addressed with increasing depth through the course of therapy. At this early stage, the client generally needs support and comfort. In addition, it is valuable to normalize these experiences, which communicates an openness to explore the negative side of religion and spirituality as well as the relationship between negative feelings such as pain or anger and one's faith framework or spiritual perspective.

In sum, spiritual dialogues early in therapy generally seek to understand, to validate, to affirm, to comfort, to support or to normalize. These interventions endeavor to build the therapeutic relationship in preparation of in-depth spiritual dialogues later in therapy. It is important to avoid presenting set spiritual formulations in response to client concerns. These formulations may be experienced as platitudes. Conversely, early spiritual dialogues often are not the time to introduce profound spiritual insights. In general, the client is unprepared to listen to these insights, which can have the impact of increasing his or her distress. For example, a Christian client entering therapy with a high level of anxiety including severe panic attacks is hardly prepared for the ideas of letting go of control and radical trust. Instead, the therapist looks for opportunities to address these issues in greater depth later in therapy.

In-Depth Spiritual Dialogues

As therapy progresses, it is envisioned that these early conversations give way to spiritual dialogues of greater precision and depth. After introducing the spiritual dimension into therapy, the key focus is on making strong connections between the crucial clinical issue(s) of the client and his or her religious or spiritual perspective. This includes discovering the resources for healing and the vision for health offered by the religious or spiritual perspective. In addition, spiritual dialogues and soul searching often generate strong reactions within clients. These reactions from new insights and spiritual experiences range from inspirational to troubling. Religious and spiritual perspectives are often very challenging to conventional wisdom or the belief system of the client and his or her family of origin. Thus, it is important that the therapist is vigilant in processing these reactions with clients throughout the course of therapy.

The process of significant personal or relational transformation often begins with a spiritual dialogue focused on discerning the message in the client's current symptoms or distress. In this context, discernment is understood as sensitivity to divine communication or spiritual insights. This dialogue seeks to relate the spiritual and religious vision of health to the present difficulties. It may begin with a question such as "What are your symptoms trying to tell you?" or "What message is God sending you through this distress?" Wrestling to discern this message may unveil deep-seated fears, distorted beliefs, poor boundaries, or maladaptive behaviors. It also may clarify attitudes, beliefs, and behaviors that betray a strong trust in values contrary to the client's religious and/or spiritual perspective. In effect, discerning the message can create a spiritual "hypothesis" that can guide the remainder of treatment. For instance, a Christian client's depressive symptoms relate to a lack of personal boundaries. The client perceives these poor boundaries as living out Christian values of selflessness and sacrifice. The process of discernment, which may include prayer, grappling with alternative perspectives, and spiritual reading, leads to a belief that God is communicating through the depressive symptoms the need for personal boundaries. The spiritual dialogue continues with the goal of *differentiating* between poor boundaries and the values of selflessness and sacrifice.

A spiritual dialogue of discernment also can be a search for meaning. Clients may seek to discover the meaning or purpose for their lives. For example, a client presents with depressive symptoms rooted in a life transitional crisis. Through the discernment process, the client determines that his or her relentless pursuit of career success and financial security has resulted in a sense of personal emptiness. This assessment initiates a spiritual dialogue that seeks to find a purposeful vocation or meaningful lifestyle. Clients also may try to make sense of the very painful times of their lives. Human beings have the capacity to find meaning in trauma, tragedy, and loss through religious and spiritual resources. When client and therapist begin the search for or making of meaning, they enter the most profound dimension of spirituality or religion.

Implicit in the process of discernment are the questions of if and how to respond to this divine message or spiritual insight. Thus, the focus of the spiritual dialogue may shift to address the issue of response. Specifically, a client may discern a call to let go of control, set firmer boundaries, adopt new perspectives, change maladaptive patterns, alter priorities, and make bold new decisions. This dialogue can lead to a serious evaluation of priorities that may discover a painful disparity between cherished values and actual lifestyle. It often raises difficult decisions that require significant strength and courage. When therapy is stuck in this decision-making process, the therapist can help by *counting the cost* of remaining static. People usually see the danger of new ways of acting very clearly while being blind to the cost of homeostasis. Counting the cost of not changing may create the energy to face the dangers of the new pathway.

A client's decision to respond to a new pathway discerned through spiritual dialogue can ignite a very challenging process. This challenge may result in paralyzing fear and other homeostatic forces that block the path to significant change or transformation. At this point, the focus of spiritual dialogue becomes addressing these fearsome barriers to change. It is often very helpful for clients to fully mobilize their spiritual support network to provide encouragement while facing these challenges. This spiritual dialogue also seeks to identify and nurture new behaviors consistent with the new pathway. With each new action, the therapist journeys with the client providing encouragement in difficult times while framing and reframing the consequences of new behaviors. It is ultimately hoped that the successful implementation of new behaviors will create greater congruity between the actual lifestyle of the client and his or her cherished beliefs.

Brief Vignettes: Two Devout Christians with Anxiety Disorders

In this section, two case presentations illustrate spiritual dialogues. The first exemplifies the dialogue process early in the therapy while the second shows the use of in-depth dialogues at a later stage of counseling. The presentations begin with the journey of the therapist to demonstrate the soul-searching process. An outline for the treatment of anxiety follows to create a therapeutic context. Finally, the use of dialogue is highlighted through each case presentation.

The clinical examples used in this chapter represent a Christian therapist working with devout Christian clients. In this context, a *devout client* is defined as a Christian from any denominational background who perceives faith as an essential component of his or her life. This specific focus enables the presentation of an in-depth illustration of the spiritual dialogue process. The use of spiritual dialogues to integrate spirituality in therapy presented in this chapter, however, is perceived as adaptable to other religious and spiritual perspectives.

In the first vignette, Paul, thirty-two, is a very successful business owner with a young family. An extreme workaholic who maintains a frenetic pace, he is disconcerted by the current financial and legal problems that threaten his business. In the second vignette, Cheryl, thirty-nine, is reentering the workforce after recently graduating from college. Since her life seems to be going well, Cheryl is baffled by her current distress. She comes to therapy reluctantly after examinations by multiple physical health professionals have not found any medical reason for her symptoms. Both Paul and Cheryl enter therapy with multiple symptoms of anxiety including frequent and serious panic attacks. Each client perceives himself or herself as a strong person who usually has his or her life under control. Paul's treatment is used to illustrate the use of spiritual dialogues early in therapy while Cheryl's vignette exemplifies spiritual dialogues of depth. Although Paul and Cheryl chose to leave therapy at different points, both scenarios are perceived as successful clinical/spiritual treatment.

The Journey of the Therapist

As mentioned previously, the spiritual dialogue model begins with the therapist's assessment of his or her own readiness to engage in spiritual dialogues. The therapist uses his or her spiritual path to soul search for a personal spiritual perspective on a clinical issue that pertains to a client, such as anxiety. For the author, this soul-searching process was an in-depth study of relevant passages from the Bible, which is a critical component of his spiritual path. The spiritual perspective presented below was guided by the work of biblical scholars, Christian theologians, and spiritual mentors drawn from the broad spectrum of Christian viewpoints. It is a sincere attempt to discern and communicate faithfully the biblical message. It is not intended to present THE Christian position on anxiety. Thus, some Christian readers and clients may have a divergent faith stance regarding anxiety.

Although clinical perspectives tend to focus on coping with anxiety, the biblical perspective speaks of a freedom from its effects. Anxiety is perceived as inexorably intertwined with a need to control, which drives human beings to invest inordinate energy in security-seeking behaviors. These behaviors are assessed to fail ultimately because it simply isn't possible to fully control life. More important, anxiety shifts primary focus from the meaningful to the mundane. There are also serious systemic implications. Seeking security creates a competitive atmosphere that produces insensitivity to others. It can reduce openness, cooperation, and mutual concern— the key qualities for an effective systemic response to anxiety. In sum, the practical drive to create security ironically has adverse effects on physical, psychological, relational, and spiritual health.

The biblical antidote to anxiety is to develop a radical trust rooted in intimate relationship with a compassionate God. An invitation is extended to find security in this relationship. Radical trust rooted in intimate relationship is perceived to produce spiritual "fruits." One spiritual fruit in response to anxiety is a profound sense of inner peace called the peace that "surpasses all understanding" (Philippians 4:7, NRSV). Another key spiritual fruit is the creation of a caring community that nurtures this radical trust both in God and in one another (Killmer, 2002).

The spiritual perspective on anxiety gained from this soul-searching process had a significant impact on me. Hard work and careful planning are my typical instruments employed to control life. Yet, these actions failed to prevent anxiety. Furthermore, these security-seeking behaviors drew time, energy, and focus away from an intimate relationship with God. Shortly after this moment of insight, I was invited to participate in a spiritual formation group, which became a significant source of support and transformation. This soul-searching experience enables me to bring significant experience and knowledge to the spiritual dialogue with anxious devout Christian clients.

Treatment Outline for Anxiety

Because clients often enter therapy in serious distress, the initial clinical goal may be the reduction of anxiety. Next, treatment often focuses on helping clients cope with anxiety including the development of an anxiety management plan. Mustering spiritual support and employing spiritual practices are often a key part of this initial treatment. The early types of spiritual dialogues described above usually are engaged in this early point in therapy.

Treatment of anxiety may reach a crossroads when clients experience a reduction in distress and an increase in their ability to cope with anxiety. Feeling strengthened, many clients choose to leave therapy at this point. For other clients, the experience of handling anxiety in a different manner has provided a glimpse of the possibility of significant change. At this crossroads, the therapist can issue an invitation to remain in therapy to seek significant change. An affirmative response to this invitation can have a considerable impact on a client's long-term health, while opting to leave therapy may result in a vulnerability to repeat cycles of anxiety. Remaining in therapy often affords the opportunity for spiritual dialogues of depth.

Paul's Treatment

Paul arrived early for the initial session to complete the intake forms including the spiritual assessment. His assessment form seemed to indicate limited spiritual involvement. When I inquired about his spirituality in the first session, Paul presented a strong sense of identity as a Catholic but a history of nominal involvement in religious activities. Since the onset of his panic attacks, however, Paul began to attend Mass daily and have regular discussions with his wife—his main connection to the church and his major source of spiritual support.

When Paul entered therapy, it was clear that it would take several months to resolve his business problems. Used to being in control, this reality created an overwhelming sense of helplessness. His behavioral pattern of hard work, planning, and hustling resulted in financial success and addressed underlying anxiety rooted in the financial poverty of his childhood. The goal of therapy was to develop an anxiety management plan in order to endure this stressful period. Clinically, it was recommended that Paul muster social support, do stress-reducing activities, adopt a "one day at a time" attitude and engage cognitive interventions to block the escalation of panic. At first, these recommendations felt like "doing nothing" for Paul. Thus, he initially chose to follow the familiar path of hard work and hustling. Unable to alter his situation, these behaviors maintained his high level of anxiety, including the panic attacks.

The key spiritual dialogue began when I suggested that Paul could include spiritual practices (e.g., prayer) in his anxiety management plan. This counsel seemed impractical to Paul. He stated that he wanted to benefit from "those," pointing to my degrees and licenses on the wall. Since Paul was uncomfortable with this intervention, I vowed to re-open a spiritual dialogue only at an appropriate time. After a couple of weeks, Paul expressed frustration at both his lack of improvement and his inability to change his business situation. I asked him to assess whether his approach to the crisis was working. He reluctantly acknowledged that his efforts were not effective. I then inquired about times when he felt less anxious. Paul reported that he felt better when talking with his wife, exercising, and attending Mass. This interaction was a turning point for Paul. The spiritual content of the discussions with his wife and his participation in Mass opened the door for further dialogue. I noted that his trust in hard work, planning, and hustling had led to his business success. His current distress, however, raised the question of whether he could put his "faith" in clinical or spiritual mechanisms to cope with a situation beyond his control. Paul developed an anxiety management plan that included spiritual interventions. His panic attacks dissipated quickly and his symptoms of generalized anxiety gradually decreased.

The spiritual dialogue was ongoing throughout therapy. I shared research on the efficacy of religious coping mechanisms (Pargament, 1997) and aspects of the biblical message about anxiety, which increased his confidence in the management plan. Paul's relationship with his wife and children improved significantly during his crisis period. In the midst of their support, Paul seemed to glimpse a "call" to maintain a better balance of work and family postcrisis. Feeling much better, Paul opted to end therapy without fully pursuing this sense of call.

Cheryl's Treatment

The referral to therapy by her doctor for help with her panic attacks challenged Cheryl's pseudo-identity as a strong, totally self-sufficient person. Her spiritual assessment found a high level of interest in that dimension although her recent practice of spirituality was limited by the foci of completing college and coping with anxiety. Her initial anxiety management plan concentrated on finding the triggers for and blocking the escalation of panic. Cheryl was very open to including individual spiritual practices in her anxiety management plan. As a result, she started practicing yoga, listened to Christian music and did daily devotional reading. In the process of identifying triggers, it emerged that Cheryl had been a parentified child, caring for younger siblings and an alcoholic stepfather while her emotionally wounded mother worked evenings. Her mother's neediness continued into adulthood. It combined with the recent declining health of her in-laws to re-create an overwhelming sense of responsibility. In effect, the panic was communicating the need for Cheryl to set boundaries in her role as caretaker. This realization opened an early spiritual dialogue on the relationship between boundaries, caretaking, and Christian values of service, selflessness, and sacrifice. This dialogue supported her sense of moral responsibility to care for aging family members. On the other hand, it differentiated between selflessness and boundarilessness as well as introduced a sense of relational justice. This dialogue motivated Cheryl to establish effective boundaries with her family that fulfilled her sense of responsibility while protecting her personal health.

Cheryl's anxiety management plan effectively eliminated her panic attacks. Thus, it was an appropriate time to terminate therapy. Since the treatment had been brief, she could leave with her pseudo-identity somewhat rumpled but essentially intact. Yet, Cheryl was intrigued by the invitation to move beyond coping with anxiety toward a freedom from its effects. Over the next three months, this led to spiritual dialogues on issues of identity, intimacy, and vocation. One key spiritual dialogue addressed the relationship between her pseudo-identity of total self-sufficiency and the Christian perspective of radical trust, which include elements of dependence and interdependence. We explored these themes in conjunction with the question "What is God trying to communicate to you through the anxiety?" The dialogue particularly wrestled with the notion of radical trust, since Cheryl perceived dependence as a weakness when contrasted to "being strong." In the midst of this dialogue, the pseudo-identity of strength and self-sufficiency was reframed as a difficulty in trusting others, including God, with her needs. Through dialogue and ongoing personal meditation, Cheryl discerned a call to break out of this pseudo-identity by trying to reach out for supportive, trusting relationships. This was a frightening step for her. One way of facing this fear was the careful selection of her pastor and a friend at church as the safest persons for this new relationship. Encouraged by the support she received from these persons, she gradually widened this circle of support, including participation with an in-depth Bible study group and increased intimacy with God through prayer. As she let go of her pseudo-identity, Cheryl described this process as a "series of life-changing epiphanies."

Suggestions for Follow-Up

Ideally, the spiritual support, practices, discernment, and responses experienced by clients in therapy will be integrated into their lifestyle following treatment. This ongoing spirituality can maintain the gains of therapy and open the door to additional spiritual growth.

Contraindications

Several important factors must be considered for the use of spiritual dialogues in therapy. The qualities of openness, comfort, courage, differentiation, spiritual experience, and expertise mentioned earlier are valuable traits for both the therapist and the client. In addition, the level of trust in the therapeutic relationship is strongly related to the potential success of spiritual dialogues. The compatibility of worldviews between therapist and client is another vital consideration. Generally speaking, strong similarities in worldview can facilitate in-depth spiritual dialogues while significant differences may require increased sensitivity and caution. It is important to note, however, that differences do not automatically preclude dialogues of depth, particularly when a high level of differentiation, trust, and openness are present. Deeply spiritual people from divergent backgrounds can build a very strong dialogical relationship.

Minuchin and Fishman (1981) present *joining* and *intensity* as key therapeutic interventions. They understand joining as a conscious decision to take a close, median, or disengaged position with clients. Intensity is defined as modulating the "volume" of the therapeutic intervention. For spiritual dialogues, the level of closeness and intensity is usually based on the presence or absence of the relational qualities described above. For instance, a significant difference in worldview may require adopting a median position that focuses solely on clarifying the values of the client with limited input from the therapist. Or, a low level of trust could be the major factor in modulating the intensity of the spiritual dialogue.

Therapists often express a concern about imposing religion or spirituality on clients. As with all abuse of power issues, this can be a legitimate concern. More often, however, this concern represents a lack of differentiation with religion or spirituality. Clinicians do not regard the introduction of new ideas or interventions as imposing their clinical theories on clients. Since clients are seeking help, these recommendations are offered respectfully in the context of being helpful. This respect exists even in confrontational interventions. Clients always retain the right to accept or reject these recommendations. This respectful, differentiated approach is used in spiritual dialogues with clients who choose to have their spirituality integrated in therapy.

References

Buber, M. (1958). *I and thou* (2nd ed.). New York: Charles Scribner's Sons.

Buber, M. (1965). *Between man and man.* New York: Macmillan.

Carlson, T., Kirkpatrick, D., Hecker, L., & Killmer, M. (2002). Religion, spirituality and family therapy: A study of family therapists' beliefs about the appropriateness of addressing religious and spiritual issues in therapy. *American Journal of Family Therapy, 30*(2), 157-172.

Doherty, W. J. (1995). *Soul searching.* New York: BasicBooks.

The Holy Bible, New Revised Standard Version (1989). Nashville, TN: Holman Bible Publishers.

Killmer, J. M. (2002). The treatment of anxiety disorders with devout Christian clients. *Journal of Family Psychotherapy, 13*(3-4), 309-327.

Killmer, J. M. (2006). The use of spiritual practices in conjunction with therapy with Christian examples. In K. B. Helmeke & C. F. Sori (Eds.), *The therapist's notebook for integrating spirituality in counseling: Homework, handouts, and activities for use in psychotherapy* (pp. 257-265). Binghamton, NY: The Haworth Press.

Koenig, H. G. (1997). *Is religion good for your health?* Binghamton, NY: The Haworth Press.

Krasner, B., & Joyce, A. J. (1991). Between truth and trust: Elements of direct address. In H. Vande Kemp (Ed.), *Family therapy: Christian perspectives* (pp. 135-174). Grand Rapids, MI: Baker Book House.

Krasner, B., & Joyce, A. J. (1995). *Truth, trust and relationships: Healing interactions in contextual therapy.* New York: Brunner/Mazel Publishers.

Larson, D. B. (1993). *The faith factor: An annotated bibliography of systemic reviews and clinical research on spiritual subjects* (Vol. 2). Washington, DC: National Institute for Healthcare Research.

Minuchin, S., & Fishman, H. C. (1981) *Family therapy techniques.* Cambridge, MA: Harvard University Press.

Pargament, K. I. (1997). *The psychology of religion and coping.* New York: Guilford Press.

Potts, K. (1994). Martin Buber's "Healing Dialogue" in marital therapy: A case study. *The Journal of Pastoral Care 48*(4), 325-338.

Walsh, F. (Ed.). (1999). *Spiritual resources in family therapy.* New York: Guilford Press.

Professional Readings and Resources

The clinician may find the following resources helpful in addition to the previous references:

Brothers, B. J. (Ed.) (1992). *Spirituality and couples.* Binghamton, NY: The Haworth Press.
Burton, L. A. (Ed.) (1992). *Religion and the family: When God helps.* Binghamton, NY: The Haworth Press.
Hart, T. (1994). *Hidden spring: The spiritual dimension of therapy.* New York: Paulist Press.
McCullough, M., Pargament, K., & Thoresen, C. (Eds.) (2000). *Forgiveness: Theory, research, practice.* New York: Guilford Press.
Vande Kemp, H. (Ed.) (1991). *Family therapy: Christian perspectives.* Grand Rapids, MI: Baker Book House.

Bibliotherapy Sources for the Client

A wealth of worthy reading material is available for devout Christian clients to use in conjunction with spiritual dialogues, including the following:

Borg, M. J. (1994). *Meeting Jesus again for the first time.* San Francisco: HarperSanFrancisco.
Buechner, F. (1992). *Listening to your life.* San Francisco: HarperSanFrancisco.
Cloud, H., & Townsend, J. (1992). *Boundaries.* Grand Rapids, MI: Zondervan.
Foster, R. J. (1998). *Streams of living water.* San Francisco: HarperSanFrancisco.
Manning, B. (2000). *Ruthless trust.* San Francisco: HarperSanFrancisco.
Miller, J. K. (1991). *A hunger for healing: The Twelve Steps as a classic model for Christian growth.* San Francisco: Harper.
Nouwen, H. (1995). *Life of the beloved: Spiritual living in a secular world.* New York: The Crossroad Publishing Company.
Nouwen, H. (1992). *The return of the prodigal son.* New York: Doubleday.
Shepherd, J. B. (1989). *A pilgrim's way.* Louisville, KY: Westminster/John Knox Press.
Smith, J. B. (1995). *Embracing the love of God.* San Francisco: HarperSanFrancisco.
Yaconelli, M. (2002). *Messy spirituality.* Grand Rapids, MI: Zondervan.

Handout: Spiritual Assessment

1. If you currently attend worship, which church/synagogue do you attend?

   Name: _Victory Christian Center_

   City, State: _Youngstown, Ohio_

2. How many years have you attended?   ☐ 0-2 years ☐ 3-5 ☑ 6-10 ☑ Over 10

3. In childhood, did you attend a church/synagogue?   ☑ Yes   ☐ No

4. Have you been a part of other denominations in the past?   ☐ Yes   ☑ No

5. Please check any faith/spiritual concerns that may apply to you:

   ☑ Spiritual hunger   ☑ Loss of faith   ☐ Faith differences with partner/family

   ☐ Moral dilemma   ☐ Guilt feelings   ☐ Inability to feel forgiveness

   ☐ Unable to forgive   ☑ Religious doubts   ☐ Confusion about values

   ☐ Anger at God   ☐ Hurt by faith   ☐ Painful religious history

   Others:_____

6. Do you actively participate in and/or receive spiritual support from any of the following?

   ☐ Personal prayer   ☐ Congregation support

   ☐ Spiritual or Bible readings   ☐ Support of clergy

   ☐ Spiritual direction   ☐ Bible study

   ☐ Spiritual disciplines   ☐ Small groups at church

7. At your request, I/we can include faith, values, and spiritual concerns in the counseling process. Please check any of the items below which you would like your counselor to provide for you:

   ☐ Pray together at the close of sessions   ☐ Discuss insights of faith in relation to current problems

   ☑ Use biblical and/or faith examples   ☐ Recommend religious and/or spiritual readings

   ☐ Recommend spiritual growth activities   ☐ Share personal faith perspectives when appropriate

---

Killmer, J. M. (2006). Conducting spiritual dialogues in therapy. In K. B. Helmeke & C. F. Sori (Eds.), *The therapist's notebook for integrating spirituality in counseling: Homework, handouts, and activities for use in psychotherapy* (pp. 55-67). Binghamton, NY: The Haworth Press.

6

Using the Strengths Assessment to Mobilize Spiritual Resources

Monika Eichler
Gene Deegan
Edward R. Canda
Sharilyn Wells

Type of Contribution: Activity, Handout

Objective

The Spiritual Strengths Assessment offers a method for identifying the spiritual strengths and resources of clients who wish to mobilize spiritual aspects of their lives to promote their mental health and overall well-being, to respond to life challenges resiliently, and to help recover from crises and mental illness. The purpose of the Spiritual Strengths Assessment is to aid clients in their personal planning to attain the goals they set for themselves. This assessment activity helps clients to bring distant, amorphous aspirations into focus on clear objectives and resources to achieve them.

Rationale for Use

For our purpose, the term spirituality refers to a universal aspect of human behavior and experience that involves the search for a sense of meaning, purpose, and morally fulfilling relationships with oneself, other people, the universe, and the ground of being, however that is understood by a person (e.g., Higher Power, God, ultimate reality, transcendence, sacredness). The term religion refers to formalized patterns of beliefs, values, and practices related to spirituality that are shared by a community and transmitted over time in traditions. People variously express their spirituality in religious and nonreligious ways, including theistic, atheistic, animistic, and other worldviews. This distinction of spirituality as a broader concept than religion has become common in social work (Canda & Furman, 1999), counseling (Faiver, Ingersoll, O'Brien, & NcNally, 2001), health fields (Koenig, McCullough, & Larson, 2001), and mental health (Fallot, 1998).

Numerous studies have shown that spirituality in both religious and nonreligious forms is associated with positive health and mental health outcomes (e.g., Fallot, 1998; Koenig et al., 2001; Levin, 2001). In particular, in recent surveys, mental health service providers and consumers have indicated that spirituality is often an important source of strength for dealing with life challenges and for promoting recovery and resilience (Canda & Furman, 1999; Sullivan, 1992). Unfortunately, until recently, mental health professionals have rarely received professional education for addressing spirituality and have often either ignored spirituality or focused on it in terms of symptoms of psychopathology. Therefore, it is important to develop an assessment method for mental health professionals to help clients to identify and mobilize spiritual strengths.

The Spiritual Strengths Assessment focuses on clients' own aspirations in the context of respect for their spiritual perspectives. It is founded on principles of spiritually sensitive social work practice (Canda & Furman, 1999) and a strengths perspective on social work and mental health (Rapp, 1998; Saleebey, 2002). These principles can be summarized as follows:

1. Respect the diverse religious and nonreligious expressions of spirituality in clients' lives.
2. Relate to clients as whole persons connected with their larger life contexts.
3. Never reduce clients to problems, pathologies, labels, pieces, or parts.
4. Proceed to explore spirituality only with the permission of the client and without proselytizing.
5. Relate with clients on the basis of rapport, empathy, and genuine interest.
6. Acquire knowledge and skills relevant to the particular spiritual perspectives and cultural frameworks of one's service consumers and the service area community.
7. Establish cooperative patterns of referral and collaboration with spiritual leaders and mentors in the community as relevant to clients' spiritual perspectives.
8. Focus on clients' talents, capacities, abilities, skills, creativity, and positive personal attributes as well as resources in the social and physical environment.
9. Help clients bring to bear their strengths and resources for resilience, recovery, and growth even when they identify a focus of concern with problems, crises, disabilities, or illnesses.
10. Work with clients through a style of collaboration, dialogue, and mutual discovery rather than expert-driven elitist control.

The Spiritual Strengths Assessment is part of a comprehensive strengths model of mental health practice that provides a structure to help clients achieve their own goals. The strengths model identifies seven interrelated life domains that form a comprehensive, holistic portrait of the individual in relationship with the environment. The life domains in the strengths model are:

1. daily living,
2. financial/insurance,
3. vocational/educational,
4. social supports,
5. health,
6. leisure/recreational supports, and
7. spirituality.

In the strengths model, personal and environmental strengths are considered, rather than pathology. Personal strengths include passions, confidence and temperament as well as talents, skills and accomplishments. Environmental strengths include social relations, formal community services, and vacant niches (opportunities for expansion in the environment). The list of potential strengths is almost endless.

Strengths assessment is a collaborative process of dialogue that explores clients' particular range of actual and potential external and internal strengths and resources in the seven life domains. Information is organized regarding the client's current circumstances, which strengths and resources have been useful in the past, which are currently employed, and which may be desired to expand or create anew. Assessment is ongoing and interwoven with engagement and formation of a therapeutic alliance. It forms a structured framework for the therapeutic relationship that leads directly to personal planning, resource acquisition and goal attainment. The strengths perspective does not deny traumatic or problematic experiences, but reframes them into "lessons learned" by examining and cultivating the seeds of how clients can grow through those experiences.

The client's goals in the spiritual domain may seem less tangible in the beginning than goals in other life domains. The task of the strengths assessment, in general, is to operationalize these goals and resources to achieve them. For example, what are the specific components of inner peace, meaning in life, or the fulfillment of a life purpose for the client? How could specific religious and nonreligious resources contribute to the client's well-being?

Each domain in the strengths assessment is explored according to present, past, and future in that order. Questions related to present strengths attempt to elicit responses that identify the person's currently used and recognized spiritual strengths. This includes learning and development that have accrued through experience. Past strengths are explored in order to remind the person of contributors to past successes that may be relevant to the present. Questions about the future attempt to focus vague aspirations into specific, operational strategies and resources that can then be incorporated into the present, day-by-day reality.

Strengths assessment should be a highly interactive, ongoing process, rather than a mechanistic, linear procedure. Rather than using rigidly predetermined steps, it relies on the establishment of a therapeutic alliance, requiring the therapist to be highly attentive to the client, forming a sense of immediate "presence." Being "present" with the client in the moment allows the therapist to formulate highly effective responses with clinical intuition and practice wisdom. Therapists often experience this as being able to "read between the lines." It is a hermeneutic exercise that draws out meaning from the context, symbolism, and whole of what is occurring—verbally, nonverbally, and even synchronistically. The Spiritual Strengths Assessment instructions that follow presume that a complete strengths assessment in the seven life domains has already occurred. If this general strengths assessment indicates that spirituality is an area of special interest to the client, then the more detailed Spiritual Strengths Assessment can be conducted.

Instructions

During the course of establishing a therapeutic alliance and rapport, a general strengths assessment is completed. The therapist should not rush into a strengths assessment in the spiritual domain. Rather he or she should attend closely to the client's communication, searching for implicit as well as explicit spiritual concerns during the engagement process and while working with the strengths assessment in other life domains. The therapist validates these spiritual interests, while attempting to identify spiritual strengths and goals. Open-ended questions facilitate this process, funneling from questions that are more implicit and general to questions that are specifically and explicitly spiritual. The therapist should always follow the client's lead, and be careful to respect the client's degree of comfort, trust, and interest.

In order to elicit detailed and specific ideas, stories, and examples from clients, the spiritual domain can be explored according to several subdomains (adapted from Canda & Furman, 1999): spiritual experiences and feelings; spiritual beliefs and symbols about self and world; spiritually based key values and morals; inner (intrapersonal) strategies for drawing on spiritual resources (e.g. prayer, meditation, self-reflection, dreamwork); and external (interpersonal) strategies for drawing on spiritual resources (e.g. participation in informal spiritual support groups or religious communities). These subdomains need not be separated artificially, but rather they can be kept in mind to open possibilities for exploration throughout the Spiritual Strengths Assessment.

The handout at the end of the chapter, Spiritual Strengths Assessment, contains a list of questions covering these subdomains that the therapist can use with a client. These questions encompass introductory comments and questions that a therapist can use to begin the conversation, as well as questions that cover past, present, and future spiritual strengths. The questions in the handout are not meant to be used verbatim, but rather they should be selected, reworded, and supplemented as appropriate to particular situations and clients.

The mental health professional should become familiar with the Spiritual Strengths Assessment prior to employing it with clients. It is advisable to complete an assessment for oneself first for practice and to deepen insight into one's own spiritual path and how it may affect one's work. Next, it would be helpful to try the assessment with a client while under supervision or peer consultation with another professional who is already familiar with Spiritual Strengths Assessment or similar spiritual assessment approaches.

Brief Vignette

Mary had been seeing a clinical social worker for several weeks. Her initial reason for seeking therapy was for grief resolution, however, on a side note she explained that lately she had not been able to be alone with herself without needing to have either a radio or television on. In silence, she reported feeling highly anxious. The therapist asked, "Is there anything that helps you to calm down when you are feeling that overwhelming anxiety?" At that point Mary initiated discussions concerning her religion and her expanded sense of her relationship to "the divine" (in her own words). The therapist thought it would be useful to engage her in a spiritual strengths assessment to facilitate her gaining a clearer sense of her belief system.

In answering questions about the past, Mary was clear that her upbringing did not include many religious activities, as her father was an atheist. Her mother's background was Protestant but she did not attend church. She was trying to sort out how to combine the influences of both her atheist father and Christian mother while finding her own spiritual way. Questions posed about the present unveiled an increasing dissatisfaction with organized religion together with an increasing sense of urgency for deeper personal connection with what she called "the divine." Future-oriented questions allowed Mary to be thoughtful about how she might engage herself in activities that would facilitate this blossoming need for a deeper connection. The organization of questions from past, to present, to future seemed to work very naturally in the course of the discussions.

Mary set a goal to engage in several activities. In order to tap her inner spiritual resources and become more comfortable with quiet reflection, she decided to practice meditation for twenty minutes a day and also to keep a journal about her spiritual search. To tap into outer spiritual options, she decided to explore a range of spiritual resources in the community to help her decide whether any would be valuable for long-term involvement with like-minded people. She planned to check the telephone book listing of various spiritual groups and also to visit local bookstores with postings of many ecumenical, interfaith, and nontraditional spiritual groups, retreats, and workshops. She also enjoys walking in the woods and feels close to the divine there, so she decided to walk in a nearby forest park at least once a week. She decided to explore whether any of these activities resonated with her values and interests.

Several sessions later Mary reported that she had engaged in several of these activities. She also noted that many of these activities incorporated silence as part of their practice, yet she no longer felt uncomfortable with the silence, but rather felt nourished as she experienced an expanded sense of herself. Her desire for a deeper connection with the "divine" was beginning to be fulfilled. What that meant to her was that she truly never felt alone in the world. She experienced more connection to all that existed around her in a way that she never had before. In addition, this new change led to a change in her job to one that was even more fulfilling. Finally, her new community of like-minded individuals also fostered and supported this new sense within her and she experienced more fulfilling relationships with those in her life.

Suggestions for Follow-Up

It should be noted that the Spiritual Strengths Assessment can be completed more than once a year or as often as desired. If there is an ongoing extended helping relationship, it is useful to update it twice a year, as each person's spiritual path is in a constant dynamic ever-evolving process. Also, as a client puts into action decisions for utilizing strengths identified through the assessment, these actions and shifting goals need to be assessed in an ongoing manner.

Contraindications

When exploring spiritual concerns and issues with individuals, it is imperative to remember that these issues can be very personal and may be emotionally charged based on one's past history. Such discussions should be sensitively approached, with honor and respect for the person's beliefs, comfort level, and appropriate timing. Under no circumstances should clients be forced or manipulated into discussing religious or nonreligious spiritual matters. If clients indicate that spirituality is irrelevant to them or to the issues they wish to work on, it should not be pursued. Some mental health practitioners are concerned that discussion of spirituality with clients who experience delusions or hallucinations with religious content may exacerbate symptoms of psychopathology. For practitioners who work in mental health settings, it is worthwhile to learn more about spirituality and differential diagnosis and assessment in relation to mental illness (Canda & Furman, 1999; Canda & Smith, 2001; Fallot, 1998; Nelson, 1994). Questions in the Spiritual Strengths Assessment guide should be tailored to the situation of the client, to avoid provoking or exacerbating confusing thoughts, distressing feelings, or disruptive behaviors. However, this is not to say that spirituality should be avoided in work with persons who have mental disorders. On the contrary, spirituality may be a crucial source for resilience and recovery. It simply must be pursued according to the interests and readiness of the client.

References

Canda, E. R., & Furman, L. D. (1999). *Spiritual diversity in social work practice: The heart of helping.* New York: Free Press.

Canda, E. R., & Smith, E. (Eds.) (2001). *Transpersonal perspectives on spirituality in social work.* Binghamton, NY: The Haworth Press.

Faiver, C., Ingersoll, R. E., O'Brien, E., & McNally, C. (2001). *Explorations in counseling and spirituality.* Belmont, CA: Wadsworth/Thomson Learning.

Fallot, R. D. (1998). Assessment of spirituality and implications for service planning. *New Directions In Mental Health, 80* (Winter), 13-23.

Koenig, H. G., McCullough, M. E., & Larson, D. B. (2001). *Handbook of religion and health.* New York: Oxford University Press.

Levin, J. S. (2001). *God, faith, and health: Exploring the spirituality-healing connection.* New York: John Wiley and Sons.

Nelson, J. E. (1994). *Healing the split: Integrating the spirit into our understanding of the mentally ill.* Albany, NY: State University of New York Press.

Rapp, C. (1998). *The strengths model.* New York: Oxford University Press.

Saleebey, D. (Ed.) (2002). *The strengths perspective in social work practice* (3rd ed.). Boston: Allyn and Bacon.

Sullivan, W. P. (1992). Spirituality as a social support for individuals with severe mental illness. *Spirituality and Social Work Journal, 3*(1), 7-13.

Professional Readings and Resources

Canda, E. R., & Furman, L. D. (1999). *Spiritual diversity in social work practice: The heart of helping.* New York: Free Press.

Canda, E. R., & Smith, E. (Eds.) (2001). *Transpersonal perspectives on spirituality in social work.* Binghamton, NY: The Haworth Press.

Deegan, G., & Eichler, M. (2001). Working with spiritual concerns in mental health practice. *Kansas Chapter NASW Newsletter, 26*(6), 14.

Faiver, C., Ingersoll, R. E., O'Brien, E., & McNally, C. (2001). *Explorations in counseling and spirituality.* Belmont, CA: Wadsworth/Thomson Learning.

Fallot, R. D. (1998). Assessment of spirituality and implications for service planning. *New Directions In Mental Health, 80* (Winter), 13-23.

Koenig, H. G., McCullough, M. E., & Larson, D. B. (2001). *Handbook of religion and health.* New York: Oxford University Press.

Levin, J. S. (2001). *God, faith, and health: Exploring the spirituality-healing connection.* New York: John Wiley and Sons.

Nelson, J. E. (1994). *Healing the split: Integrating the spirit into our understanding of the mentally ill.* Albany, NY: State University of New York Press.

Rapp, C. (1998). *The strengths model.* New York: Oxford University Press.

Saleebey, D. (Ed.) (2002). *The strengths perspective in social work practice* (3rd ed.). Boston: Allyn and Bacon.

Sullivan, W. P. (1992). Spirituality as a social support for individuals with severe mental illness. *Spirituality and Social Work Journal, 3*(1), 7-13.

Bibliotherapy Sources for the Client

Elam, J. (1999). *Dancing with God through the storm: Mysticism and mental illness.* Wallingford, PA: Pendle Hill.

Frankl, V. (1962) *Man's search for meaning: An introduction to logotherapy.* Boston: Beacon Press.

Kabat-Zinn, J. (1994). *Wherever you go, there you are: Mindfulness meditation in everyday life.* New York: Hyperion.

Kornfield, J. (2001). *After the ecstasy, the laundry: How the heart grows wise on the spiritual path.* New York: Bantam Doubleday Dell Publisher.

Kornfield, J. (1993). *A path with heart: A guide through the perils and promises of spiritual life.* New York: Bantam Doubleday Dell Publisher.

Moody, R. A., & Perry, P. (1994). *Reunions: Visionary encounters with departed loved ones.* New York: Random House.

Peck, M. S. (1978). *The road less traveled.* New York: Simon and Schuster.

Ridgway, P., McDiarmid, D., Davidson, L., & Bayes, J. (2002). *Pathways to recovery: A strengths recovery self-help workbook.* Published by The University of Kansas School of Social Welfare, Lawrence, KS.

Sylva, D. (1993). *Psalms and the transformation of stress: Poetic-communal interpretation and the family.* Louvain, Belgium: Peeters Press.

Weiss, B. L. (1993). *Through time into healing.* New York: Simon & Schuster. Reprint edition (September 1993).

Handout: Spiritual Strengths Assessment

Introductory Comments and Questions

- During the general strengths assessment, you mentioned that spirituality is important to you in some way and that you would like to explore further how spirituality can play a role in our work together. Before going further, I would like to be sure I understand what spirituality means to you.
- Please explain what you mean by spirituality. Please feel free to use whatever words are most comfortable to you to discuss this area of life, for example, worldview, faith, religion, or philosophy of life.
- For you, what is the relationship between spirituality, religion, faith, and any other key words you just mentioned?

Exploring Present Spiritual Strengths

- What currently brings meaning to your life?
- What helps you develop a greater awareness of yourself?
- How do you or would you explore your greater purpose in life?
- What do you draw on to get through really hard times lately? *If other resources are identified, explore for spiritual themes, but validate the experience even without spiritual themes.*

  —Follow-up: Is there anything in addition that helps with tough challenges? Do you identify yourself with any particular spiritual perspective(s) or religion(s)? Please describe.

- Are you a member of any spiritual groups or do you participate in any type of personal spiritual activities or group services (for example, meditation, prayer, ritual, ceremony, worship, nature retreats, spiritual healing, reflection on dreams, spiritual journaling)? Please explain what they are and how often you do them, if at all.
- How well and in what ways do these activities and services work for you?
- Please describe any recent experiences in which you felt a sense of transcendence or transformative new awareness, "ah-ha," spiritual exhilaration, deep peace or joy, or enlightenment.
- What inspires you?
- What is your relationship with your sources of inspiration?
- Are there any people in your life who serve as special spiritual teachers, mentors, friends, or helpers? Please describe your relationship and how they support you.
- How would you describe your basic beliefs about the purpose and source of the world and existence? How do these beliefs provide a sense of meaning for you personally? What symbols are important for you to represent these beliefs?
- What spiritual places or beings provide you with a sense of support, if any, such as beautiful places in nature, religious worship places, God, a Higher Power, angels, or spirits?
- If there are any plants, animals, or other creatures that are special to you and provide a sense of spiritual connection, please describe them and your relationship.
- What spiritual teachings, books, scriptures, symbols, or artwork currently give you a sense of inspiration and satisfaction?
- Do you have a core worldview or belief system that you rely on?
- How would you describe your basic beliefs about life?

Exploring Past Spiritual Strengths

- In general, think back to your description of present spiritual strengths and resources. When did you develop these strengths and how did they work for you in the past?
- Are there any strengths or resources that you used previously that you forgot about or have not used recently? Is there any way they could be used again or adapted in the present situation?

Eichler, M., Deegan, G., Canda, E. R., & Wells, S. (2006). Using the strengths assessment to mobilize spiritual resources. In K. B. Helmeke & C. F. Sori (Eds.), *The therapist's notebook for integrating spirituality in counseling: Homework, handouts, and activities for use in psychotherapy* (pp. 69-76). Binghamton, NY: The Haworth Press.

Handout: Spiritual Strengths Assessment *(continued)*

- What used to bring meaning to your life? What did you draw upon in the past to pull through very difficult times or experiences? *(Perhaps, phrased "before such and such happened"—that is, before the pivotal or difficult experience that brought the client into the current helping situation.)*
- Do you recall, what used to bring joy, fulfillment, and inspiration to your life? When did you last feel that?
- Tell me about your spiritual, religious, or faith community or communities growing up, if any. What do you remember about it that was helpful? If it was not helpful, how did you decide to change it, and what did you learn from that that can help you now?
- Were there any personal spiritual activities (such as prayer or meditation) you used to use that could be helpful again now?
- Please think back to the worldview you described earlier. How did that worldview develop?
- *During the previous description of worldview, if the person made a statement of an important insight pertaining to "when I do this...this happens," a follow-up question could be:* Can you think of the last time that happened? Do you remember when you first came upon this realization?
- What and who shaped this worldview? Were there things going on in your family or community that affected this? Was there a special person or a few who had a major impact on your general outlook on life?
- Did you have any special spiritual teachers, mentors, friends, or helpers who you would like to reconnect with now?

Exploring Future Spiritual Strengths and Aspirations

- If you had a magic wand, what would you make happen to bring more meaning into your life? What would be different?
- What things can you do to renew your deepest insights and inspirations from spiritual experiences and to have new spiritual experiences?
- How can you deepen your spiritual experience in your daily life?
- *With regard to the previous questions about people and things who provided inspiration:* How can these relationships and connections be recalled, restored, or improved?
- What particular spiritual activities would you like to restore and continue to help you achieve your aspirations?
- Do you envision a future involvement with any particular faith community or spiritual support groups? How would you like to continue your present involvements, improve on them, or change them?
- If you would like me to cooperate with a clergyperson or spiritual mentor, please describe who that would be (if you already know someone) or what characteristics the person should have (if you want me to help you connect with someone new).
- How would you describe your ideal self of the future? What could you do to move toward that ideal?
- *If the current helping situation involves a particular sense of problem or goal of service:* Imagine any personal, community, or natural environmental supports and resources that would support you in dealing with this issue. Let's make a list and think about how we might include them in the helping process.

Eichler, M., Deegan, G., Canda, E. R., & Wells, S. (2006). Using the strengths assessment to mobilize spiritual resources. In K. B. Helmeke & C. F. Sori (Eds.), *The therapist's notebook for integrating spirituality in counseling: Homework, handouts, and activities for use in psychotherapy* (pp. 69-76). Binghamton, NY: The Haworth Press.

7

The Spirituality-Focused Genogram: A Tool for Exploring Spirituality and the Spiritual Resources of Individuals, Couples, and Families in Context

Adriana Balaguer Dunn
Robert F. Massey

Type of Contribution: Activity, Handout

Objective

Spirituality-focused genograms allow for a multidimensional assessment and exploration of themes of spirituality in the lives of individuals and families (Massey & Dunn, 1999; Massey & Balaguer Dunn, 2000). They depict how personal experiences of spirituality emerge in the context of families, cultures, and societies over generations. Spirituality-focused genograms can be used in a variety of ways. They can be constructed as an activity by the therapist with individuals, couples, or families during therapy sessions. They can serve either as an assessment tool or as an instrument to facilitate the therapeutic process. Spirituality-focused genograms can also facilitate therapists' reflections on their own development of spirituality in the contexts of their own multigenerational families (Carter & McGoldrick, 1976; McGoldrick & Carter, 2001). The example presented here is focused on couples during therapy.

Rationale for Use

For a significant number of people spirituality or religious experiences and practices influence to varying degrees how they organize their personal lives and relationships. This is apparent for many during critical events and at transition points in the life cycle. Crises and turning points frequently evoke affirmations of or petitions to the divine. Religious rituals symbolize central personal and cultural values and mark important transitions (joining a faith community, coming of age, marriage, death, annual remembrances and celebrations). Less obvious publicly, but equally meaningful for some, are more frequent, or even daily, spiritual and religious experiences and practices.

Spirituality develops in cultural and familial contexts (Falicov, 1999; Walsh, 1999). Spirituality involves personal experiences that are both unique to each individual and that can be influenced and mediated by family and cultural processes. Spirituality emerges and grows in a variety of forms. Spirituality may or may not be associated with religion. To encompass the range of human and client experiences, we approach spirituality in this context as those ideas, experiences, or orientations held by individuals that pertain to the transcendence of the human realm.

Spirituality can be expressed as an openness to encounter the divine, to be involved with religious experiences; as a sense of interconnection with life and the cosmos; or as fundamental guiding values or principles that provide ultimate meaning in the lives of individuals. This broad definition allows for consideration of a wide range of experiences and requires an assessment tool that is both comprehensive and that enables the emergence of that which is most special and precious in the experiences of a particular client.

In response to the need to expand therapists' assessment capacities by devising ways to give voice to and to understand spiritual processes in the lives of individuals and families, the authors propose the spirituality-focused genogram. A genogram is a pictorial representation of a family and their relationships that spans at least three generations. The genogram allows the clinician to assess individual family members in the context of their historical and immediate family dynamics as well as the broader social and cultural systems with which they interact (Bowen, 1980; McGoldrick & Gerson, 1985; McGoldrick, Gerson, & Schellenberger, 1999). Consequently, the therapist is able "to evaluate the family's strengths and vulnerabilities in relation to the overall situation" (McGoldrick & Gerson, 1985, p. 3).

Several authors have proposed the use of thematic genograms to enhance the understanding of particular issues in the lives of therapists and clients (DeMaria, Weeks, & Hof, 1999). Hardy and Laszloffy (1995) and Congress (1994) have used genograms to focus on the cultural dynamics of therapists and families. White and Tyson-Rawson (1995) have used genograms as a means of assessing gender dynamics in couples and families. Friedman (1985) employed genograms with couples who belonged to religious communities to elucidate their emotional and multi-generational-transmission processes, but did not focus on their spiritual experiences. Wood and Stroup (1990) reported using genograms in premarital counseling to promote awareness of hidden dynamics as formative couples construct their relationships. Massey and Dunn (1999) presented spirituality-focused genograms as a method to portray both individual and family processes multigenerationally.

Spirituality-focused genograms, as proposed here, provide a comprehensive means of exploring religious and spiritual issues and their impact on clients' lives. The unique format of the genogram as well as its multidimensional nature enable the therapist to obtain a perspective on a client's spirituality that would be much more difficult to obtain by other means. Since it is pictorial in format, the genogram inherently promotes client engagement and self-disclosure, while facilitating subsequent observation by both client and therapist of emerging patterns and trends. It can be used to provide the therapist with a general overview of the spiritual context of the client or can be a tool for in-depth exploration of issues of spirituality, ultimate meaning or values that might be germane to a particular case. The spirituality-focused genogram allows for information to be gathered in a very unstructured, primarily client-directed format, or can provide a framework for more formalized therapist-guided assessment. Finally, the spirituality-focused genogram can accommodate both a theistic or nontheistic spiritual focus as well as both ecumenical and denominational issues. For example, a spirituality-focused genogram could be used to provide a handy framework for understanding the norms and variations within a denomination. That framework could then serve as a context for assessing how this significant facet in concert with other dynamics helps to shape the meaning and course of the lives of clients who have been involved or currently participate in a religious group (Lovinger, 1996). On the opposite end of the spectrum, the spirituality-focused genogram could be used to facilitate a general discussion of issues of ultimate meaning, core values, and transcendence irrespective of particular religious affiliation.

In working with individuals, we have found the spirituality-focused genogram to be an invaluable tool for exploring individual processes of spiritual development over time and their interconnections with other aspects of the clients' life. They can trace the transmission of values and core beliefs across generations and the tensions and agreements that result. They can depict consistency and variability in religious or spiritual practice over time. They can also address the intersection of spirituality with other emotional, behavioral, and psychological issues and show how spiritual issues may function as impasses to or resources for inspiration, reconciliation, and healing.

Furthermore, because genograms focus on the relational elements of individuals and families, they are particularly suited for exploring the relational dimensions of spirituality when working with couples and families in therapy. On a relational level, spirituality-focused genograms allow for the portrayal of individual and shared belief systems and for addressing issues of conflict or tension regarding spiritual and religious beliefs or practices. Thus they can be particularly useful in working with couples or families in which religious or spiritual conflicts are prominent. Genograms permit analyses of the processes Snyder, Cavell, Heffer, & Mangrum (1995) perceived as pertinent to dyadic assessment—communication, affect expression and experience, relationship satisfaction, commitment, acceptance/tolerance, power and influence, as well as developmental levels. In listening to and recording the dynamics articulated in constructing genograms, further light is shed on these couple dynamics, both as they pertain to spiritual or religious processes and experiences, and as they interconnect with other variables both in multigenerational relationships and with these particular partners. For example, what is the type and level of affect, communication, and acceptance/tolerance in the past and current generations in regard to couples selecting partners of the same or a different faith community?

Spirituality-focused genograms offer a means to assess how the influences of spirituality and religion impact, are shaped by, and interact with other processes in systems. Consequently, they allow for the kind of careful assessment of spirituality supported by authors who emphasize a multidimensional approach to spiritual exploration (Doherty, 1995; Prest & Keller, 1993).

Therapists who permit awareness or exploration of spirituality, when pertinent to assessment and treatment, to play a role within the domain of therapy are likely to benefit from the added advantage of understanding the spiritual processes that motivate clients. Interventions can be targeted more precisely when the array of multileveled, multisystemic dynamics is more fully visible. With a more comprehensive context and a fuller set of purposes for symptoms and growth evident, clinicians can design more effective strategies for healing on the emotional and spiritual dimensions (Madanes, 1990).

Instructions

When using the spirituality-focused genogram as a therapeutic tool, therapists need to first recognize that the exploration of religious and spiritual issues must be conducted with respect for clients' spiritual frameworks. There should be an understanding that clients' frameworks are representative of their worldviews. Therefore, therapists need to suspend their own spiritual beliefs and attend to clients' religious and spiritual frameworks, while respectfully challenging relevant issues in a manner that is consistent with clients' belief systems (Stander, Piercy, MacKinnon, & Helmeke, 1994).

Successful introduction of the genogram in clinical work requires that therapists listen for clients' needs to have the kind of information that the genogram might provide. For example, if clients come to therapy struggling with spiritual issues or ways of making meaning of their experiences, a spirituality-focused genogram would be directly relevant. In addition, therapeutic problems involving family dynamics or individual growth and development may have a spiritual or religious component that might be helpful to explore using the spirituality-focused genogram. Finally, the spirituality-focused genogram might be useful in enabling individuals or families to discover untapped spiritual or religious resources that may facilitate the resolution of problems or assist in coping with difficult circumstances.

We suggest, therefore, that therapists listen for the possibility of expanding on religious or spiritual themes in their therapeutic work with clients. The spirituality-focused genogram should be introduced to clients when it appears to be relevant to treatment. Clients should be given the option of choosing whether they wish to engage in such exploration. If clients or families are to be actively involved in the process, they need the opportunity to view and experience the genogram as it is being constructed and to become instrumental in directing its construction. Furthermore, the discoveries regarding spirituality and religion that emerge must be connected back to the presenting problem or issue of concern to clients in order to keep the treatment clinically relevant. These guidelines for use of the spirituality-focused genogram are particularly important when working with families for whom the mistiming and intrusiveness of interventions can evoke "resistance" to therapy (Balaguer Dunn & Dawes, 1999).

The handout at the end of the chapter, Questions to Consider When Constructing Spirituality-Focused Genograms, provides a list of questions to consider when engaging in a spirituality-focused genogram (Balaguer Dunn, 1998; Balaguer Dunn & Dawes, 1999). Therapists interested in using the genogram technique should obtain training and proficiency in the construction of genograms and the use of genograms for assessment and intervention. (For reviews of genogram construction and use in assessment, see McGoldrick & Gerson, 1985; McGoldrick et al., 1999.) In addition, familiarity with intergenerational family systems theory and intervention would be advisable in order to address the intersection between spiritual issues and family dynamics (Bowen, 1980; Kerr & Bowen, 1988; McGoldrick & Gerson, 1985).

Genograms centered on the theme of spirituality in a couple relationship begin with asking first one partner and then the other what spirituality, religion, the divine, transcendence, the supernatural, or ultimate meaning (or any other word or phrase along these lines that the person chooses to use as relevant) connotes to the person. Inquiry is made about the impact of spirituality on the couple's relationship. Particular attention is paid to the consequences of belief systems and practices on relationships, especially couples. The influences between other relatives are also noted (e.g., who was most important in socialization and served as guides and models—parents, grandparents, aunts, uncles, godparents, and others who are related or unrelated). The determination of which information is gathered, in which order and from whom, should flow from the process of the conversation and not be imposed by the therapist or predetermined by the structure of the genogram. Rather the therapist should guide partners in the couple to take turns articulating observations about the significance of spirituality, religion, and ultimate meaning for themselves and other members of their families in the ways that they find most meaningful or comfortable. One response provides a clue for the next remark or question as the information interweaves in patterns of meaning. Questions flow from one aspect of a person's experiences and memories to others or from one partner to the other. Circular questioning (Palazzoli, Boscolo, Cecchin, & Prata, 1980; Penn, 1982) can also be utilized to expand perspectives and highlight the relational context. The process of inquiry continues until client information and therapist curiosity seem replete with full respect for what clients are willing to disclose.

With couples who express a pervading or dominant interest in spiritual or religious phenomena, formally constructing a spirituality focused genogram may hasten the identification of impasses or resources for resolving a presenting problem. If the couple is willing, this may also advance therapeutic processes and understanding when the couple is quite devoted to spiritual or religious practice and the therapist is not as familiar with a particular spiritual approach or religious perspective. This may also prove beneficial when conflict has arisen because one spouse is quite fervent and the other antagonistic or indifferent to the consternation of the first (Rotz, Russell, & Wright, 1993). Frequently, couples do not accentuate spiritual or religious issues and concerns in therapy. Mention of some aspect of spirituality or religion may emerge, or a therapist may hear the possibility of spiritual or religious dynamics as resources for healing and development. In these more circumscribed situations, more informal notation of the remarks or observations on a genogram of the couple records the information for future reference if relevant. A clinician is probably better prepared for undertaking these tasks if the therapist has completed a personal spirituality-focused genogram, participated with colleagues in doing so, and has also sat and listened attentively to the reflections of couples not in therapy.

Brief Vignette

Many possible types and combinations of spiritual and religious dynamics can appear in a spirituality-focused genogram. Here we offer one example as illustrative of some of the intricacies and permutations that may emerge in constructing a spirituality-focused genogram with a couple. Lynn, forty-three, and Bill, forty-five, met during their college days. Lynn grew up Catholic, and Bill was raised Congregationalist by his adoptive parents. Neither family was thrilled about their growing friendship, mostly because Lynn is from a French Canadian/Irish background and Bill is African American. They braved family pressures and committed themselves as husband and wife in a nuptial Mass twenty-three years ago. They are raising three sons, James, twenty-one, Joseph, nineteen, and Paul, sixteen.

The couple entered therapy when Lynn became seriously depressed. She had been treated and given a series of medications by a psychiatrist. This regimen relieved her depression to the point of being able to continue working, but did not bring her to a personally satisfactory point. Lynn entered treatment with a systems-oriented clinician who invited her to have her husband accompany her to sessions. A picture of multiple dynamics, beyond possible biochemical processes, emerged in the assessment interview.

During the couple therapy, Lynn and Bill raised a variety of issues. They were experiencing financial difficulties that were in part compounded by the discrimination they faced as an interracial couple. Furthermore, they were struggling to integrate different approaches to the handling of finances that stemmed from family-of-origin dynamics. Each also expressed continuing tensions with their families of origin regarding their choices of partner. Finally, they discussed concerns that arose at different times regarding each of their sons.

Although the couple never explicitly raised religion or spirituality as issues in their relationship, they often alluded to religious or spiritual themes in the therapeutic work. For example, while Bill had been increasingly accepted into Lynn's extended family despite the racial differences, he remained distant from many members of his own family because of his decision to adopt Lynn's Catholic beliefs and practices. The couple often referred in therapy to their church activities (e.g., church attendance, choir), their links to the community, and the presence of a kind of religious protection in their lives. Their son Joseph had been in an automobile accident in which the other passengers had been killed and he had survived with only minor injuries. He had been wearing a medal of St. Jude. The couple mentioned this as a sign of divine intercession.

As trust developed in the therapeutic relationship, the allusions to religion and spirituality were used by the therapist to open the possibility of further exploration of such issues within the couple relationship. The couple expressed an interest in doing so, and a spirituality-focused genogram was constructed (Figure 7.1: Spirituality-Focused Genogram). The genogram revealed the intricate interconnections between the spiritual, relational, and contextual aspects of the lives of Bill and Lynn. It also provided some important insights into how spirituality had been interwoven into each family member's approach to coping with life's difficulties in general and with depression in particular.

For both Lynn and Bill their religious and spiritual beliefs emerged as central constructs in how they live their lives and in how they interrelate. Lynn described a bond of love at the core of her nuclear family that she experienced as essentially spiritual. Lynn experienced a strong Catholic faith and consciously tried to model her family life after that of the Holy Family. She often

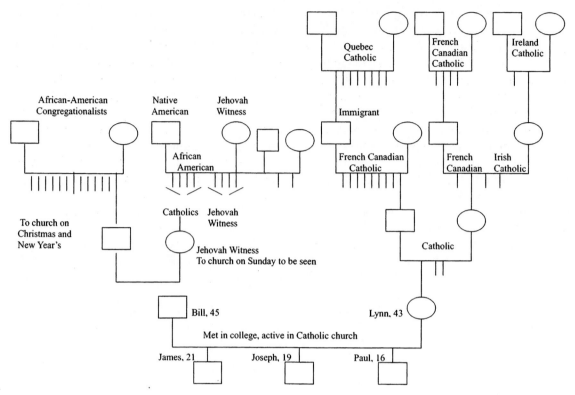

FIGURE 7.1. Spirituality-focused genogram.

prayed to Mary to help her in her role as wife and mother. Bill saw religion as a way of coming to terms with circumstances and events out of his control and as a means of remaining anchored in an often tumultuous world.

Lynn's religious conviction was modeled within her own family of origin. Her parents would pray the rosary, light candles, wear religious medals, and attend services. Their religious convictions united them despite the differences and tensions inherent in originating from different parts of Canada. They also relied on their faith to make sense of the difficulties they encountered in life. Her parents had retained a strong sense of faith in the face of the death of another daughter in childhood and her father's struggle with depression and attempted suicide. They never turned away from their faith, even when terrible events happened. They encouraged Lynn to use prayer as a support throughout her life as well, beginning when she was teased by others at school, and later when she underwent a difficult pregnancy with her first child. Lynn continues to try to integrate more spirituality into her life. Prayer has kept her going at the most difficult points in her life. She also sees marriage as a sacramental union with a spiritual dimension.

Bill came to identify religion and spirituality as a guiding force later in life, mostly through his connection with Lynn. Bill's parents were Congregationalists, and, although they attended services, they were not strongly religious or spiritual people. Bill's father was skeptical of the religious and political connections of people he encountered, partly because of experiences of discrimination. He did not see much value in religion. He was the least religious member of his family and also the only one of his siblings to go to college, both of which distanced him from the rest of his family. Bill adopted the same skepticism as his father with regard to religion. He also made an early determination to develop his own financial resources and become independent from his parents. He experienced college as a time of freedom from his parents and from church obligations.

Bill's extended family was religiously diverse, as is frequently the case in African-American families. His maternal grandmother was a Jehovah's Witness, but many of his aunts were Catholic or married Catholics. These differences often created tensions and distance among different branches of the family and also limited the possibilities for communal experiences and support at difficult times such as deaths in the family. In fact, Bill became cut off from his mother when he adopted the Catholic faith. Nevertheless, the foundation for the spiritual link between Bill and Lynn was laid within Bill's family of origin. Bill obtained his sense of spirituality from his maternal grandmother. He admired her conviction as a Jehovah's Witness, and in listening to her teachings he acquired a respect for religious principles.

Bill initially attended Catholic services with Lynn out of a desire to spend time with her. He was drawn by the sense of community and fellowship that he found there and by the comfort he derived from participation in rituals. These experiences counteracted the isolation and disconnection that had resulted from his spiritual experiences within his family of origin. Over time he found that the religious beliefs he adopted helped him to make sense of past experiences and to change his approach to life. He now tries to instill the same sense of faith in his sons by providing a spiritual context to their questions and experiences.

The experiences of Bill and Lynn exemplify Anderson and Worthen's (1997) premise that exploration of the spiritual dimension, along with the other dimensions of a couple's experience, expands the range of possibilities for therapeutic understanding and intervention. In the case of Bill and Lynn, spiritual and religious beliefs have undoubtedly influenced the structure and relationships of both extended families in contributing to both unity and disconnection. Spiritual beliefs have also intersected with and influenced individual and family responses to particular events encountered over time. The spiritual and religious realm constitutes an integral part of the stories that Bill and Lynn have developed and by which they understand themselves, those with whom they interrelate, and the world around them. Failure to take into account this dimension of human experience inherently limits the potential for individual and relational transformation within the therapeutic context. Exploration of, listening to, and providing an accepting therapeutic context for Lynn and Bill to voice their spiritual and religious experiences enhanced attunement to their personal and systemic processes. This enabled them to access a greater variety of resources for growth and healing. Understanding how they have faced discrimination with courage, dealt with losses and depression, managed the tensions of their families of origin, and summoned the strength to raise three sons became more evident when their spiritual and religious experiences were expressed openly and validated as strengths in assessment and therapy.

The unfolding of Lynn and Bill's lives as they engaged in therapy and focused on identifying and working through their problems in search of solutions and the enhancement of their strengths—including personal, marital, familial, social, and spiritual ones—exemplifies how couples may proceed through these processes. The spirituality-focused genogram encapsulates the major dynamics in their lives and in therapy (see Figure 7.1). It provides a portrait and handy reference for assessment and the design of appropriate interventions. As participants narrate their experiences, perceptions, and interpretations, the elements and themes that form the stories of their spiritual journeys-in-context emerge. These stories exemplify the intertwining of the transcendent dimension with the social-psychological dynamics that Roberts (1994) noted occur in tales and transformations in people's ongoing lives. Exploring the fourth dimension of spirituality, as proposed by Anderson and Worthen (1997), in the lives of Lynn and Bill provided a fuller range of information and experiences for assessing the structure and development of their family and relationships multigenerationally and in the present, and for understanding the emotional and moral texture of their shared lives as they voiced them. The format of a spirituality-focused genogram allowed for charting prominent meanings and values and the consequences of these for relationships and family structure.

Suggestions for Follow-Up

This activity can serve either as an initial assessment tool to provide the therapist and client with an initial overview of the presenting problem in multidimensional context, including the spiritual context, or as an ongoing intervention tool in treatment. When addressing spiritual and/or religious issues in particular, the spirituality-focused genogram can be used to track changing dynamics as an indicator of progress in therapy. The spirituality-focused genogram can also be used to address issues of differentiation and can include discussion of transgenerational patterns, reactivity, family loyalties, family roles, triangles within the family, and sequences of interaction. It can be used initially with an individual and then be expanded for use with the couple or other relevant family members or significant persons in the life of the client. In the supervisory context, the spirituality-focused genogram can be a useful tool to assess the spiritual dynamics of the therapist and how they intersect with their work in the therapeutic context with clients. Finally, the spirituality-focused genogram can be useful in nontherapeutic contexts as a vehicle for helping self-exploration into the spiritual dimensions of one's life and relationships.

Contraindications

Spirituality-focused genograms require and benefit from an atmosphere of trust. The experience of constructing a spirituality-focused genogram regularly involves a sense of encountering core meanings and experiences, of being allowed to palpably feel what is very special in perceptions and experiences to the interviewee, and to be close to the sacred for that person. The experience can be quite emotional and personal; consequently it should be pursued only when a fundamental level of trust has been established in the therapeutic relationship.

Some clients do not wish to pursue this type of a conversation, and some may express discomfort or not want to go further. Respect for client preferences must be the guiding principle of whether to proceed. Furthermore, clients in crisis may require a stabilization of the presenting problem before they may be able to engage in this activity. By responding to the immediate stress, the therapist contributes toward building the foundation of trust necessary for in-depth genogram work. Concomitantly, for some clients-in-crisis, discussion of spirituality as relevant to the client may tap into resources for resiliency and healing in a time of depletion and desperation. Conversations about spirituality at these times involve bedrock beliefs and experiences, which may be elaborated more formally during a more stable period.

To maximally draw on this resource, therapists must be aware of the values, experiences, and dynamics in their own spiritual or religious frameworks and contexts. This knowledge alerts them to their predilections and limitations of experience and comprehension, safeguards them from unconsciously or inadvertently imposing their own dynamics on clients, and opens them to the possibilities for exploring alternative forms of value systems, spirituality, and religion with clients of varying persuasions.

References

Anderson, D. A., & Worthen, D. (1997). Exploring a fourth dimension: Spirituality as a resource for the couple therapist. *Journal of Marital and Family Therapy, 23,* 3-12.

Balaguer Dunn, A. (October, 1998). Spiritual and religious contexts in therapy and supervision. Paper presented at the Student Alliance for Multicultural and Mental Health Issues Conference, South Orange, New Jersey.

Balaguer Dunn, A., & Dawes, S. J. (October, 1999). Spirituality-focused genograms: Keys to uncovering spiritual resources in African-American families. *Journal of Multicultural Counseling and Development, 27*(4), 240-254.

Bowen, M. (1980). Key to the use of the genogram. In B. Carter & M. McGoldrick (Eds.), *The family life cycle: A framework for family therapy* (p. xxiii). New York: Gardner.

Carter, E. A., & McGoldrick, M. (1976). Family therapy with one person and the therapist's own family. In P. Guerin (Ed.), *Family therapy* (pp. 193-219). New York: Gardner.

Congress, E. P. (1994). The use of culturalgrams to assess and empower culturally diverse families. *Families in Society: The Journal of Contemporary Human Services* (November), 531-540.

DeMaria, R., Weeks, G., & Hof, L. (1999). *Focused genograms: Intergenerational assessment of individuals, couples, and families.* Philadelphia: Brunner/Mazel.

Doherty, W. (1995). *Soul searching: Why psychotherapy must promote moral responsibility.* New York: Basic Books.

Falicov, C. J. (1999). Religion and spiritual folk traditions in immigrant families: Therapeutic resources with Latinos. In F. Walsh (Ed.), *Spiritual resources in family therapy* (pp. 104-120). New York: Guilford.

Friedman, E. H. (1985). *From generation to generation: Family process in church and synagogue.* New York: Guilford.

Hardy, K. V., & Laszoloffy, T. A. (1995). The cultural genogram: Key to training culturally competent family therapists. *Journal of Marital and Family Therapy, 21,* 227-237.

Kerr, M., & Bowen, M. (1988). *Family evaluation.* New York: Norton.

Lovinger, R. J. (1996). Considering the religious dimension in assessment and treatment. In E. P. Shafranske (Ed.), *Religion and the clinical practice of psychology* (pp. 327-363). Washington, DC: American Psychological Association.

Madanes, C. (1990). *Sex, love, and violence: Strategies for transformation.* New York: W. W. Norton.

Massey, R. F., & Balaguer Dunn, A. (June, 2000). *The voices of spirituality in genograms.* Oslo, Norway: World Family Therapy Congress.

Massey, R. F., & Dunn, A. B. (1999). Viewing the transactional dimensions of spirituality through family prisms. *Transactional Analysis Journal, 29,* 115-129.

McGoldrick, M., & Carter, B. (2001). Advances in coaching: Family therapy with one person. *Journal of Marital and Family Therapy, 27,* 281-300.

McGoldrick, M., & Gerson, R. L. (1985). *Genograms in family assessment.* New York: Norton.

McGoldrick, M., Gerson, R. L., & Schellenberger, S. (1999). *Genograms: Assessment and intervention.* New York: Norton.

Palazzoli, M. S., Boscolo, L., Cecchin, G., & Prata, G. (1980). Hypothesizing, circularity, neutrality: Three guidelines for the conductor of the session. *Family Process, 19,* 3-12.

Penn, P. (1982). Circular questioning. *Family Process, 21,* 267-280.

Prest, L. A., & Keller, J. F. (1993). Spirituality and family therapy: Spiritual beliefs, myths, and metaphors. *Journal of Marital and Family Therapy, 19,* 137-148.

Roberts, J. (1994). *Tales and transformations: Stories in families and family therapy.* New York: Norton.

Rotz, E., Russell, C. S., & Wright, D. W. (1993). The therapist who is perceived as "spiritually correct": Strategies for avoiding collusion with the "spiritually one-up" spouse. *Journal of Marital and Family Therapy, 19,* 369-375.

Snyder, D. K., Cavell, T. A., Heffer, R. W., & Mangrum, L. F. (1995). Marital and family assessment: A multifaceted, multilevel approach. In R. H. Mikesell, D. D. Lusterman, & McDaniel, S. H. (Eds.), *Integrating family therapy: Handbook of family psychotherapy and systems theory* (pp. 163-182). Washington, DC: American Psychological Association.

Stander, V., Piercy, F. P., MacKinnon, D., & Helmeke, K. (1994). Spirituality, religion, and family therapy: Competing or complementary worlds. *The American Journal of Family Therapy, 22,* 27-40.

Walsh, F. (Ed.) (1999). *Spiritual resources in family therapy.* New York: Guilford.

White, M. B., & Tyson-Rawson, R. J. (1995). Assessing the dynamics of gender in couples and families: The genogram. *Family Relations, 44,* 253-260.

Wood, N. S., & Stroup, H. W., Jr. (1990). Family systems in premarital counseling. *Pastoral Psychology, 39,* 111-119.

Professional Readings and Resources

Anderson, D. A., & Worthen, D. (1997). Exploring a fourth dimension: Spirituality as a resource for the couple therapist. *Journal of Marital and Family Therapy, 23,* 3-12.

Balaguer Dunn, A., & Dawes, S. J. (1999). Spirituality-focused genograms: Keys to uncovering spiritual resources in African-American families. *Journal of Multicultural Counseling and Development, 27*(4), 240-254.

Becvar, D. S. (1997). *Soul healing: A spiritual orientation in counseling and therapy.* New York: Basic Books.

Bowen, M. (1980). Key to the use of the genogram. In B. Carter & M. McGoldrick (Eds.), *The family life cycle: A framework for family therapy* (p. xxiii). New York: Gardner.

Brothers, B. J. (Ed.) (1992). *Spirituality and couples: Heart and soul in the therapy process.* Binghamton, NY: The Haworth Press.

DeMaria, R., Weeks, G., & Hof, L. (1999). *Focused genograms: Intergenerational assessment of individuals, couples, and families.* Philadelphia: Brunner/Mazel.

McGoldrick, M., Gerson, R. L., & Schellenberger, S. (1999). *Genograms: Assessment and intervention.* New York: Norton.

Bibliotherapy Resources for the Client

Moore, T. (1992). *Care of the soul: A guide for cultivating depth and sacredness in daily life.* New York: HarperCollins.

Moore, T. (1994). *Soul mates.* New York: HarperCollins.

Handout:
Questions to Consider When Constructing Spirituality-Focused Genograms

Individual Factors

1. What meaning does religion/spirituality/transcendence have for you?
2. What are the first religious or spiritual experiences you can remember?
3. What role does religion or spirituality have in your everyday life?
4. What role does religion or spirituality play during times of difficulty or crisis?
5. What defining experiences or individuals have influenced the development of your sense of spirituality or religion?
6. Where do you find yourself currently in your own spiritual growth and where would you like to go?

Family Influences

1. What was the meaning of spirituality and religion for each member of your family going back for three generations?
2. How did different family members express religious and spiritual beliefs?
3. In which ways did family members make sense of their lives and derive meaning from their experiences?
4. What was the level of involvement in organized religious institutions?
5. How were differences in religious orientations/practices or spiritual experiences negotiated among family members?
6. What role does spirituality or religion play in the everyday lives of members of the family?
7. What were significant transitions and/or critical life events in the history of your family? What impact, if any, did religion or spirituality have in making sense of or coping with those life events?
8. Who in your family most influenced your sense of spirituality and religion?

Couple Dynamics

1. What role does religion or spirituality have in your relationship as a couple?
2. How have you negotiated differences based on religious/spiritual beliefs or values?
3. How have you faced religious/spiritual/moral dilemmas as a couple?
4. What significant life events or challenges have you faced as a couple? How has religion or spirituality helped you make sense of or cope with those events?

Source: Adapted from Balaguer Dunn, 1998; Balaguer Dunn & Dawes, 1999.

Balaguer Dunn, A., & Massey, R. F. (2006). The spirituality-focused genogram: A tool for exploring spirituality and the spiritual resources of individuals, couples, and families in context. In K. B. Helmeke & C. F. Sori (Eds.), *The therapist's notebook for integrating spirituality in counseling: Homework, handouts, and activities for use in psychotherapy* (pp. 77-87). Binghamton, NY: The Haworth Press.

8

Impact of Abuse on Internalized God Images: Spiritual Assessment and Treatment Using Guided Imagery

Anita Berardi Maher

Type of Contribution: Activity, Homework, Handouts

Objective

This chapter offers a treatment protocol for working with clients who desire to address within therapy their sense of spirituality that has been impacted as a result of relational wounding. The interventions illustrated draw on concepts from attachment theory, specifically the hypothesis that one's God concept (Imago Dei) is influenced by significant early attachment relationships (Jensma, 1993; Rizzuto, 1974; White, 1984).

Rationale for Use

Relational wounding takes many forms, with the most extreme violations occurring under the rubrics of sexual, physical, emotional, and verbal abuse. The term *relational wounding* is used here to specifically emphasize that whenever abuse of any form takes place, a break in fidelity between persons has occurred. Fidelity is the hallmark characteristic of caring and loving relationships whereby people commit themselves to relating to one another with trust and mutual care (Erikson, 1964). When a child is molested, the adult has broken fidelity with that child. Likewise, when one spouse no longer invests in a marriage, whether outside sexual relationships occur or not, fidelity is broken. Without fidelity, a safe, secure, and enduring attachment relationship cannot be sustained.

Attachment theory proposes that our earliest intimate relationships form internal relational blueprints, or schemas, influencing all successive intimate relationships (Cassidy & Shaver, 1999). Most influential are attachment relationships with primary caregivers. However, attachment theory also recognizes that successive intimate relationships can strengthen, alter, or create new internalized relational schemas as well.

It is proposed that one's perceived relationship with God is not only an attachment relationship in and of itself, but is a reflection of one's internalized relational schemas (Brokaw & Edwards, 1994; Heinrichs, 1982; Jensma, 1993; Rizzuto, 1974). A client's perceived image of God will likely be, in part, a reflection of one's earliest attachments as well as significant attachment relationships experienced throughout the lifespan.

Given the nature of belief in the Divine, one's image of God will also reflect his or her idealized attachment figure. As no relationship can possibly fulfill every human need, reflecting what many refer to as a "God-shaped vacuum," one's Imago Dei will reflect the person's ultimate relational image (Heinrichs, 1982; Jensma, 1993; Rizzuto, 1974). And finally, internalized God images also reflect one's religious education, sociopolitical context, and other macrosystemic influences.

The incorporation of spirituality into the treatment process recognizes that a client's sense of spirituality both influences, and is influenced by, one's significant relationships. Since abuse, in essence, represents a relational violation, engaging in subsequent intimate connections becomes the stage in which deep relational wounds are often made manifest. Current relationships then become the crucible around which old wounds either fester or become transformed through the healing salve of mutual love and care. This chapter illustrates a method of tending to the impact of abuse on the client's sense of spirituality while also using his or her faith as an adjunct to healing.

Specifically, this treatment approach explores the relationship between a client's internal relationship schemas and internalized God images. It proposes that in order to heal distorted God images, and/or to access spirituality as a resource, new relational experiences must occur simultaneously with the client's internal cognitive reworking of relational scripts. Therefore, therapeutic techniques arise out of the therapist engaging in an I-thou relationship (Buber, 1958) with the client, a relationship informed by a co-created treatment plan contextualized according to the client's belief system.

Instructions

Due to the highly personal and subjective nature of spirituality, special consideration to its incorporation into the therapeutic process must be given. For a review of basic legal and ethical issues, consult resources such as Chappelle (2000), Miller (1999), and Richards and Bergin (1997). Effective accessing and reworking of internalized God images also requires the therapist to engage in one's own internal spiritual assessment. This issue is addressed in Maher (2006).

This section focuses on two specific elements of working with internalized God images impacted by relational wounding. First, an outline is presented for conducting a spiritual assessment of a client's relational schemas. Second, guided imagery exercises are offered as a specific intervention tool to facilitate the assessment process and the creation of new relational schemas. The chapter concludes with a series of client handouts and therapist worksheets detailing additional experiential exercises elaborating on the concepts presented here.

It is assumed that the therapist has a basic working knowledge of the impact of various forms of abuse and understands how to construct a treatment plan in response. The focus here is on an element of healing related to spirituality and its connection to internalized relational schemas.

Spiritual Assessment: Identifying Similarities Between God Images and Relational Schemas

This section provides instructions on how to compose an assessment device to identify and work with a client's God images and relational schemas. While administration instructions are suggested here, emphasis is placed on identifying the four major constructs informing this assessment process, allowing the therapist to contextualize its actual implementation according to the needs of the client. However, Handouts One to Six at the end of the chapter do offer an example of a discussion and journaling instrument based on these four themes along with instructions for its use.

The key to effective use of self-awareness assessment devices (as opposed to diagnostic instruments) is to first clearly identify the issue(s) under consideration. This allows the clinician to scan a pre-existing instrument to see if the questions match the client's objectives. The instructions provided here outline four major themes of a spiritual assessment aimed at identifying the connection between a person's God images and internalized relational schemas. Each theme is described along with the purpose it serves in the assessment process. Please note that the themes are not hierarchically arranged. You may explore the contents of each theme in whatever order matches the client's process.

The second key to effective use of a self-awareness assessment instrument is determining its best method of administration in the clinical setting. For some clients, having a form to fill out in session (depending on length) or at home works best for them. For others, offering general questions and inviting a narrative response in a journal or on a computer, which invites a more formally constructed response, is most helpful. Questions may be sent home one at a time (to pace the reflection and to not overwhelm the client with too much homework), or in logical groupings. Some assessment processes work best through client dialogue in session or a combination of in-session reflection and at-home journaling. Still others are best able to access their thoughts and feelings through artistic expression.

The final key to implementing an effective self-reflection instrument is collating the information in a manner that allows the therapist and the client to maximize understanding of the client's responses. Ultimately, the client's reflections in dialogue with the therapist is the most common and effective method in processing self-reflection instruments. Use the four themes presented below to organize client information. This will assist the therapist in exploring topics yet to be discussed or journaled.

When inviting the client to journal, you and the client decide on the client's comfort level in providing you a copy of written reflections. If the client does agree to give you a copy, it is advised that the client keep the original. Some clients may wish to engage in a reflection process by reviewing each question in session with the therapist; others will desire to speak to questions or issues of particular importance to them at that time. Still others may use the exercise as a springboard onto topics not directly related to the instrument itself. Allow the therapeutic relationship and the client's issues to be your guide.

As mentioned, an example of how these themes may be operationalized into specific questions for use with clients is detailed in Handouts Three to Six, at the end of this chapter, in which a four-part journaling/discussion program is offered. Specific instructions for its use are also provided. After reviewing each of the four themes below and the sample questions offered in Handouts Three to Six, the therapist is invited to use the instrument provided or design one's own assessment instrument. Enjoy the creative process in service to your clients!

Theme I: Questions of ultimacy. When conducting a spiritual assessment, the first series of questions invite the client to share thoughts about God, spirituality, and religion—to become a theologian, if you will. After all, theology is merely humans pondering the Divine or the spiritual nature of humanity. Supplemental questions include how the client views God's attitude and response to moral failures or wrongdoing (whatever language the client uses), and how one discerns what God desires of humanity and why. Questions also include whether and how and when the client feels a personal connection with God's presence. Another helpful device is the God Image Scales as a pencil and paper survey or as a means of initiating discussion about various ways in which God is understood and experienced (Lawrence, 1997). In Handout Three: Client Handouts: Exploring Your Spiritual History—Then, Now, and in the Future, Exercise One: Your Past and Present Spiritual History, see Exploring Life's Ultimate Meaning and Purpose for sample questions.

Theme II: Exploring early sources of spiritual and/or religious thoughts and beliefs. The second theme involves exploring significant life experiences and interactions that influence one's ideas about spirituality. This theme covers two similar subtopics: one's religious upbringing and education within the family and faith community, and one's own musings and encounter with these teachings. It is not merely enough to ask what was taught but how the client made sense of those teachings and perceive being influenced by them both then and now. These are thematic questions typically found in most spiritual genogram questions. Sample questions can be found in Handout Three: Client Handouts: Exploring Your Spiritual History—Then, Now, and in the Future, Exercise One: Your Past and Present Spiritual History, in the Family History of Spiritual and/or Religious Education and the Personal Encounter subsections.

Theme III: Reflecting on early attachment relationships. The third theme explores family-of-origin patterns of nurture and structure. A genogram or storytelling may be used to elicit this information. A helpful exercise is to invite clients to identify family-of-origin experiences using the nurture and structure parenting charts found in Clarke and Dawson (1998). Comparisons are then made between a person's conceptualizations of God and their parental introjects.

These questions are based on the hypothesis that a person's internalized images of God are reflective of one's earliest attachment figures (Brokaw & Edwards, 1994; Rizzuto, 1974; Underwood, 1986; White, 1984). As indicated earlier, the relationships we form with our earliest caregivers are often mirrored in our overt or covert image of how God relates to us, or how we mediate our spirituality. Uncovering these relational schemas helps clients identify the source of ambivalence and contradictions often hampering them. Sample questions may be found in Handout Four: Client Handouts: Exploring Your Spiritual History—Then, Now, and in the Future, Exercise Two: Exploring Significant Relationships.

Theme IV: Identifying new images of spirituality. The final theme focuses on envisioning an ideal image of God or of spirituality, and how the client would like to experience one's self as a spiritual being in relationship to that image. Its function is similar to the miracle question found in solution focused therapy (Miller, Hubble, & Duncan, 1996), and behavioral goal setting found in cognitive therapies (Beck, 1995). The process of envisioning where one wants to go begins the process of exploring ways to live "as if," of constructing new realities (Freedman & Combs, 1996).

Consistent with strategies found in Choice Theory (Glasser, 1998) and Rational Emotive Behavior Therapy (Ellis & Dryden, 1996), exploring the idealized image and path one desires after the "terrain" and roadblocks have been identified invites the person to move ahead in full awareness of strengths, hesitancies, and ambiguities. In true paradoxical form, unlike solution-focused approaches, there is no need to ignore or minimize the struggles. Rather, struggle becomes a fertile wellspring for growth. Contrary to the medical model, neither does one need to "fix" or remove the blocks. In true Jungian spirit, this process suggests that by embracing struggles, new ways of understanding or making peace may be discovered along the way (Whitemont, 1991). In theological terms, it mirrors the concept that one need not be perfect before deciding to explore a spiritual path. Rather, one looks with anticipation that deeper understanding and renewal comes while responding to the Divine within the context of struggle (Dieter, Hoekema, Horton, McQuilkin, & Walvoord, 1987).

This is perhaps the most abstract theme in that one's responses depend largely on personal reflection and insight. Handout Five: Client Handouts: Exploring Your Spiritual History—Then, Now, and in the Future, Exercise Three: Exploring the Connections, and Handout Six: Client Handouts: Exploring Your Spiritual History—Then, Now, and in the Future, Exercise Four: Envisioning Your Future, provide a sample process. You will notice that some of the questions appear redundant or have only shades of difference in intent. Alter them as needed or allow the overlap to remain as sometimes asking similar questions throughout allow deeper responses to surface.

As previously mentioned, a summary of this spiritual assessment in the form of a client handouts can be found in the Handouts Three to Six at the end of the chapter, with Handout One being additional directions to the therapist, and Handout Two being some introductory comments to the client. For additional spiritual assessment formats consult Frame (2000), Hodge (2001), and Ingersoll (2001).

Guided Imagery As an Intervention Strategy

The following instructions provide a brief overview for conducting guided imagery. However, the primary focus is on when and how guided imagery can be used to assist the client in either directly exploring spiritual meaning or accessing spirituality as an internal resource.

General guidelines. If the therapist has never experienced or been instructed in the components of guided imagery, first refer to professional resources such as Epstein (1989), Lusk (1992), and Rossman (2000). General instructions and precautions for guided imagery are also detailed in the Brief Vignette and Contraindications sections. However, the following are additional instructional elements.

Precede guided imagery with a period of relaxation, focusing on releasing tension throughout all major muscle groups while also breathing deeply. Clients are usually invited to close their eyes during the entire exercise. Therapists may opt to close their eyes or avert their gaze away from the client during the relaxation section in order to minimize client discomfort of "being watched."

Some therapists use soft instrumental music to accompany the imagery. Others find that music may distract clients from focusing on mental images and dialogues. Some imageries are more effective if the client is asked to silently envision and dialogue, while at other times verbalizing the internal dialogue is most helpful. Allow the context—the client and the issue—to dictate your approach. Finally, as with all new techniques, therapists are advised to experience guided imagery personally before using the process with clients.

Therapeutic uses of guided imagery. Once a therapist understands the power of guided imagery, its uses are only limited by one's imagination (and client fit, as not all clients enjoy or benefit from the procedure). The following details a few of the possible uses of guided imagery as it pertains to the focus of this chapter, helping clients identify and/or reconnect with their sense of spirituality that has been impacted by relational wounding. This is accomplished by assisting the client in identifying internalized God images and relational schemas in conjunction with exploring actual abusive events, here-and-now struggles, and desired futures. Additional guided imagery scripts are offered in Handout Seven: Therapist Worksheets: Guided Imagery Scripts, at the end of this chapter.

Imagery for spiritually conflicted or ambivalent clients. Many clients are deeply ambivalent about their understanding of faith yet yearn to connect with God, a sense of the spiritual, or a spiritual community. Directly incorporating specific imagery related to one's faith early in treatment may be alienating and imposing. The imagery used with Carl in the Brief Vignette section of this chapter is an example of a preliminary spiritually focused exercise. Its intent was to begin creating a "here-and-now" positive relational experience to serve as a bridge to re-imaging how God, or a sense of the spiritual, may be experienced. Observe how the imagery was based on an issue of current focus for Carl and honored his spiritual ambivalence. As a result of discovering that the client's spiritual ambivalence was directly related to relational wounding, the imagery debriefing allowed for themes of spiritual ambivalence to be directly addressed.

Another method of helping a client explore spiritual ambivalence is through a guided imagery that elicits idealized or projected images of the Divine. An example of this imagery, called Exploring Internal Images, is detailed in Handout Seven: Therapist Worksheets: Guided Imagery Scripts, at the end of this chapter.

Imagining divine presence. Perhaps the most common spiritually oriented guided imagery theme invites the client to imagine God's presence with them as either a past memory is recalled or a current situation is visualized. In the former situation, a Divine presence who looks with compassion upon past hurts and pains allows a client to be changed by that I-Thou experience with God or one's internalized parent. A detailed example of such a script, entitled Envisioning

God as Empathic Witness, can be found in Handout Seven: Therapist Worksheets: Guided Imagery Scripts, at the end of this chapter.

Similarly, inviting a client to envision God's presence with them in the here-and-now as he or she is struggling with a particular issue provides a useful method of helping a client discern one's own internal hesitancies, deeper longings, as well as internal resources the situation requires of the client. For example, a client feeling shamed and immobilized by drug addiction, an affair, or losing a job, may be invited to imagine God's presence with full knowledge of what is occurring for the client. The client would then be asked to imagine what that spiritual presence is communicating through facial expression or words. This imagery might yield internalized images of God that evoke shame and judgment or images of forgiveness and hope with or without accountability. This is where understanding a client's belief system, and maintaining clarity as to the clinical issues spiritually focused therapy is addressing is crucial. The therapist must be able to follow the lead of the client while gently prodding the client into new directions rather than dictating or prescribing how God is to be encountered.

Reenvisioning the past—envisioning the future. Another common use of spiritually oriented guided imagery exercises is to assist clients in imagining God's presence with them as they are either trying on a new and perhaps scary behavior or trying to disconnect from the pain of historical events. Although different in purpose and scope, these two themes share in common the imagery that manipulates events in the mind's eye for a particular purpose in the here and now.

Imagery that invites God or a spiritual presence to accompany a client while practicing a new behavior, for example, confronting a co-worker or taking a driver's education test, allows a client to access internal God images to sooth anxiety and bolster courage and confidence. For these clients, internal God images can be a source of new attitudes to assume in the face of stressful situations. Clients dealing with anxiety and phobic reactions, yet who have a strong faith system, often benefit most from this type of imagery.

Imagery exercises used to envision an alternate ending to past historical events most often are employed for two reasons. One function of envisioning a new sequence of events is to help a client explore alternate solutions should a similar situation arise in the future. For example, an abusive husband (deep into his treatment for domestic violence) might imagine God present with him in a past violent event and then envision an alternate response to his anger. In this scenario, the guided imagery would also help facilitate a process of true remorse and accountability.

Another use of envisioning alternate endings is to render a sense of internal justice in the aftermath of abuse. A detailed description of using guided imagery for this purpose is listed as Justice-Making, in Handout Seven: Therapist Worksheets: Guided Imagery Scripts, at the end of this chapter. The instructions for this script also include a summary regarding the role of internal justice making in the recovery process.

Brief Vignette

Carl, age fifty-two, entered therapy due to depression he soon connected to a crisis in his spiritual identity. He and his second wife, Katie, are enjoying their roles as primary parents to Carl's granddaughter, Brittany. As both pondered the role of religious education in Brittany's upbringing, Carl's distrust of organized religion surfaced in the form of a dilemma he had yet to resolve. Namely, is God loving and understanding or still waiting for him to express remorse for an affair he had during his first marriage, a relationship he credits with saving his life? While both Carl and Katie participated in the treatment process, Carl's journey is of focus here.

Spiritual Assessment

After an initial time of connecting, clarifying all of the reasons for inviting Katie to participate and co-creating treatment goals, Carl engaged in the spiritual assessment process described in the previous section. His stories reflected a family of origin that was inflexible, arbitrarily punitive, lacking in warmth and affection. This observation eventually helped Carl understand why he never told his parents that his aunt occasionally forced him to be sexual with her. Carl described his first marriage of twenty-five years as an amalgamation of his childhood, characterized by an emotionally withholding woman who disdained sex, using it to control and humiliate him. Carl contemplated suicide often during his marriage. Denouncing the God who had abandoned him, he divorced soon after the affair. Carl met Katie a few years later and described her as his soul mate and their years together as loving and affirming.

Carl easily stepped into the role of theologian when asked how he conceptualized God. It is not uncommon for individuals to have many internalized God-images; Carl is a perfect example. He viewed God as loving and accepting. This reflected his Jewish religious instruction (the "catechism response" identified by Gorsuch, 1968) as well as having been loved by his parents and significant others throughout his life. But he also viewed God as distant, demanding obedience and threatening rejection with little explanation. He believed that God condemned affairs "because when you marry you agree to sexual fidelity." Not much insight was offered regarding the reasoning underneath this moral code. These God images also reflected his family-of-origin relational schemas. Exploring Carl's responses within Fowler's (1981) model of faith development was also helpful.

The therapist sensed that Carl wanted to hear—not from the therapist but from God—that his affair was not wrong. When client issues are steeped in moral meaning, therapists must proceed with caution. For instance, if a client wants absolution to relieve guilt, it is very tempting to quickly give the desired reassurance, possibly undermining the client's faith or moral values. Or, if a client is not feeling guilty, the therapist may push the client to feel remorse before he or she is ready, inducing a shame-based application of spirituality or religious expression. See Doherty (1995; 1999) for further recommendations.

The therapist saw both sides of Carl's dilemma. No doubt his affair helped him find his way back into life again. But he grieved that he broke his promise of sexual fidelity prior to ending the legal aspects of his marriage. The therapist could understand why he felt a wrong was committed "in God's eyes."

The therapist acknowledged his gratitude and guilt. She resonated with his confusion regarding a loving God who at the same time was experienced as demanding and aloof. She chose her words carefully, imagining that the face of God he encountered within was very similar to the judgmental face of his parents or the absentee protector during moments of sexual abuse. The empathic joining allowed him to experience the therapist connecting with his pain, something he did not experience in previous relationships, and believed God could not offer due to his (Carl's) moral offenses. The relationship he shared with Katie was building new relational schemas; hopefully the therapeutic relationship would support what he was already doing.

When Carl imagined his family's response had they known he had an affair, he described disgust on his parents' faces and mocking sarcasm from his aunt. For Carl this was a powerful moment as he saw not the face of God judging or abandoning him but his own family members.

Using Guided Imagery to Create, Access, or Strengthen Relational Schemas

Carl discovered that the relational qualities of significant adults in his childhood shared much in common with the way he perceives God. Earlier he had told a story of his parents responding with anger and false accusations one night at age sixteen when he came home after curfew.

Using guided imagery, Carl agreed to explore how he wished his parents would have responded to him that night.

Before the imagery began we agreed that Carl's adult, "parental" self would interact with himself as that teenager. The therapist explained the intent of the exercise as well: in this case, to give Carl a new experience meeting the pains of his life with compassion, loosening the grip the current meaning has had on his life. This preparation gave Carl informed consent and therefore control over the exercise.

For this first imagery, the therapist avoided recommending that Carl envision the presence of God meeting him in his past, as he clearly had ambivalence regarding his religious thoughts and preferences. At a future juncture when his own spiritual interests were clarified, guided imagery was used to allow Carl to re-imagine how God may have responded to his victimization.

After Carl was lead into a relaxed state, he was asked to envision the event and himself as that teenager in its aftermath. The therapist asked him to observe what he saw on his face; what story did that image tell; what did his life at that moment feel like, look like; and what was needed most in that moment.

Carl was then asked to imagine himself as an adult approaching that young person in a manner that allowed the teen to see love and care in his adult eyes. He was encouraged to talk with the teen about what had just happened, mirroring his pain, feelings, concerns. The therapist knew Carl would understand how to do this as they were already using the Imago Therapy Couple's Dialogue (Brown, 1999; Luquet & Hannah, 1998), which teaches couples how to identify and put words to the emotional experience they observe in their partners. The therapist allowed a few minutes of quiet for Carl to focus on this internal dialogue. Finally, Carl was invited to ponder how he wished his parents would have responded to his curfew violation.

Connecting the Dots

In the early stages of therapy it became apparent to Carl that his spiritual ambivalence and depression were intimately connected to the painful experiences of both his first marriage and family-of-origin experiences. Sensing that early trauma played the pivotal role, a guided imagery exercise was intentionally chosen to assist in exploring an early memory. Its intention was to help Carl glean insight into his childhood, young adult, and current relational experiences, including his spiritual struggles. Processing of the imagery would, in fact, help Carl see the connections.

After the guided imagery concluded, Carl described the stunned face of himself as a teenager. He recalled the intense discomfort he felt that night that he now identified as shame. He felt fear that his parents might follow through with their threats should he slip up again. The presence of guilt for something he did not quite understand was strong, learned well in moments of humiliation after sexually abusive encounters with his aunt. He saw the self-disgust that permeated his young soul. But saddest of all, his parents did not even ask why he was late and Carl had learned well to remain silent. He was angry with his parents and himself.

Carl proceeded to tell the therapist more about that night. He was late leaving his grandparents' house and was speeding to get home. Visits with his grandparents were usually peaceful, but today his aunt Betty was present, treating him like a speck of dust and sending silent messages only the two of them could decipher. He could not wait to get out of there as he felt waves of anxiety seizing his gut. Suddenly he hit a deer. Unable to leave the deer there in pain, he ended its life with a hunting knife. Overwhelmed by the enormity of it all Carl contemplated ending his own life as he rested beside the dead animal. As Carl listened, he realized how desperately that child wanted to talk with someone about what had happened, not just that night but in the years prior as well. Instead, he was met with anger and judgment.

When reflecting on how to respond to that son who came home after curfew, Carl struggled for words as no one ever role-modeled nonthreatening yet mentoring responses of structure. Here, Katie helped by explaining that she would want her children home precisely because of what happened that night—she would worry about their safety. That made sense to Carl as he observed how issues of right and wrong have a caring logic.

As he told his story Carl saw how he was not violating curfew that night—he was escaping an abusive environment, crashing into his own pain and longing for relief in his encounter with the deer. If his family environment was more open and caring perhaps he would have naturally offered to tell his parents about the cause of his lateness. And perhaps Carl might have sensed greater safety to speak the unspeakable to his parents regarding Betty's abusive behavior.

Eventually the therapist asked Carl what he, as a young husband, had so desperately wanted God to understand about his first marriage. Somberly he recalled the intensity of his suicidal ideations. The therapist asked what would it be like to imagine God offering him understanding, just as he did with himself in the imagery. Giving in to that thought, he sunk into Katie's arms and cried. Carl's growing ability to verbalize deeper meaning behind moral codes also allowed him to entertain God's sorrow for his predicament, even anger that the adults in his life did not teach him to speak up in self protection. Carl always knew that his affair hurt many people. But now he could say it without feeling crippled by shame to the point of feeling unlovable. This allowed him greater freedom to acknowledge what he learned from the whole painful mess.

It is easy to see why Carl struggled with accepting responsibility for his own adult moral lapses after years of being treated unjustly; shame has a way of inducing inappropriate guilt mixed with defensiveness regarding one's true limits. Contextual theory identifies this as "destructive entitlement" (Borszormenyi-Nagy & Krasner, 1986). The first step in personal accountability often requires one's own victimization to be empathically acknowledged.

The final piece of work with Carl involved reflecting on what it was like doing individual and couple's work in the company of each other. Each shared how they were amazed at the depth of care they were able to give and receive from each other. Carl went on to say that whether or not their care for one another was a reflection of God's love, he would like to think it is. The therapist shared how she enjoyed his ability to "accept it as if" in spite of lingering doubt. A year or so later Carl wrote that he had found a place of worship. Ending with "Shalom," he told the therapist that he had reconnected with an element of his life that gave him ultimate meaning and purpose.

Final Reflections

This example illustrates the interconnectedness between people's spiritual and religious orientations and the issues that drive them into therapy. As Carl's story unfolded it became apparent that relational wounding had been a primary contributor to his spiritual ambivalence and hence depression. Successful treatment required that Carl's ambivalence about his faith and his longing for spiritual connectedness be directly addressed within therapy.

Oftentimes therapists seek to alter destructive God images through reason or sentiment. By viewing one's images as reflective of internalized relational schemas, the way to change one's Imago Dei is through a relational encounter of a different kind while also cognitively reworking internalized schemas. This too reflects a spiritual principle that it is through encounter that we experience the Divine. We typically do not abandon deeply held beliefs through a simple act of decision, but as a result of an internal shift born through experience. Carl abandoned his spiritual beliefs as a result of negative relational experiences. He found reconnection through genuine I-thou encounters.

Suggestions for Follow-Up

When conducting a spiritual assessment, recognize that clients may have deeper reflections as therapy progresses. Therefore, spiritual assessment is an ongoing process. For follow-up suggestions regarding experiential exercises such as guided imagery, refer to the following Contraindications section.

In general, when determining that one's therapeutic process can be enhanced by the participation of his or her partner, it is important to remember to invite both partners to be a part of the spiritual assessment and experiential exercises. While only Carl's experience was detailed here, Katie participated in her own process, which helped foster greater insight and trust between the couple. Finally, once a client or couple makes new and stronger spiritual connections it is recommended that the therapist assist the client(s) in exploring new relational skills and spiritual rituals to strengthen these connections. This includes exploring spiritual resources in the community of interest to them.

Contraindications

Helping clients identify the nature of their internalized relational schemas, particularly their God images, is helpful for a broad range of clients. It is a cognitive process intended to increase clients' understanding as to the source of their relational struggles in a manner that promotes greater self-empathy and relational intimacy. This process also emphasizes clients' abilities to access lesser used narratives and create new experiences in the here and now to counteract and recreate negative internalized images.

As for all forms of assessment, spiritual assessment is contraindicated for clients who do not want to discuss spirituality. Although therapists are advised to indicate in their professional disclosure statements their openness to incorporating a client's spirituality into the therapeutic process, given the subjective nature of spiritual beliefs it is unethical to impose a spiritual assessment on a client. Likewise, if a therapist cannot comfortably work within the belief structure of the client, the client's needs then extend beyond the therapist's scope of competence and a referral to an appropriate mental health practitioner is required.

Guided imagery, as one method of helping clients gain full awareness of their relational schemas and begin the process of creating new scripts, is an interactive exercise that is not necessarily effective with all clients. To increase its effectiveness the therapist is encouraged to observe the following:

1. Be clear as to the purpose and objective of the exercise.
2. Provide informed consent. Describe the activity and its purpose. Never engage in an experiential exercise without client willingness.
3. Tailor the imagery to the client's interests and issues.
4. Do not promise success. Inform the client that some individuals find this exercise helpful while others do not. This also allows the client greater freedom to evaluate the effectiveness of the exercise afterward.

In addition, highly anxious or distractible clients often have difficulty following long imagery scripts but respond well to the relaxation and focusing aspects of the exercise. For these clients short imagery scripts are recommended initially.

Some religious clients are often skeptical of interventions preceded by deep relaxation. If after exploring the client's beliefs and providing education as to how these interventions work (not through involuntary manipulation), use of the technique is contraindicated if discomfort persists. Also, guided imagery is a lengthy procedure. Therefore, adequate session time must remain before initiating the technique.

References

Beck, J. S. (1995). *Cognitive therapy: Basics and beyond.* New York: The Guilford Press.

Borszormenyi-Nagy, I., & Krasner, B. (1986). *Between give and take.* New York: Brunner/Mazel.

Brokaw, B. F., & Edwards, K. J. (1994). The relationship of God image to level of object relation's development. *Journal of Psychology and Theology, 22*(4), 352-371.

Brown, R. (1999). *Imago relationship therapy.* New York: John Wiley & Sons, Inc.

Buber, M. (1958). *I and thou* (2nd ed.). New York: Charles Scribner.

Cassidy, J., & Shaver, P. R. (1999). *Handbook of attachment.* New York: The Guilford Press.

Chappelle, W. (2000). A series of progressive legal and ethical decision-making steps for using Christian spiritual interventions in psychotherapy. *Journal of Psychology and Theology, 28*(1), 43-53.

Clarke, J. I., & Dawson, C. (1998). *Growing up again* (2nd ed.). Center City, MN: Hazelden.

Dieter, M. E., Hoekema, A. A., Horton, S. M., McQuilkin, J. R., & Walvoord, J. F. (1987). *Five views on sanctification.* Grand Rapids, MI: Zondervan.

Doherty, W. J. (1995). *Soul searching.* New York: Basic Books.

Doherty, W. J. (1999). Morality and spirituality in therapy. In F. Walsh (Ed.), *Spiritual resources in family therapy* (pp. 179-192). New York: The Guilford Press.

Ellis, A., & Dryden, W. (1996). *The practice of rational emotive behavior therapy.* New York: Springer.

Epstein, G. (1989). *Healing visualizations: Creating health through imagery.* New York: Bantam Books.

Erikson, E. H. (1964). *Insight and responsibility.* New York: W. W. Norton & Company.

Fowler, V. (1981). *Stages of faith.* New York: HarperCollins.

Frame, M. W. (2000). The spiritual genogram in family therapy. *Journal of Marital and Family Therapy, 26*(2), 211-216.

Freedman, J., & Combs, G. (1996). *Narrative therapy.* New York: Norton.

Glasser, W. (1998). *Choice theory.* New York: HarperCollins.

Gorsuch, R. (1968). The conceptualization of God as seen in adjective rating. *Journal for the Scientific Study of Religion, 7,* 56-64.

Heinrichs, D. J. (1982). Our Father which art in heaven: Parataxic distortions in the image of God. *Journal of Psychology and Theology, 10*(2), 120-129.

Hodge, D. R. (2001). Spiritual genograms: A generational approach to assessing spirituality. *Families in Society, 82*(1), 35-48.

Ingersoll, R. E. (2001). The spiritual wellness inventory. In C. Faiver, R. E. Ingersoll, E. O'Brien, & C. McNally (Eds.), *Explorations in counseling and spirituality* (pp. 185-194). Belmont, CA: Brooks/Cole/Thomson Learning.

Jensma, J. L. (1993). Kohut's tragic man in the Imago Dei. *Journal of Psychology and Theology 21*(4), 288-296.

Lawrence, R. T. (1997). Measuring the image of God: The God Image Inventory and the God Image Scales. *Journal of Psychology and Theology, 25*(2), 214-226.

Luquet, W., & Hannah, M. (1998). *Healing in the relational paradigm.* Washington, DC: Taylor & Francis.

Lusk, J. T. (Ed.) (1992). *30 scripts for relaxation imagery and inner healing.* New York: Whole Person Associates.

Maher, A. B. (2006). Incorporating spirituality into the therapeutic setting: Safeguarding the ethical use of spirituality through therapist self-reflection. In K. B. Helmeke and C. F. Sori (Eds.), *The therapist notebook for integrating spirituality in counseling: Homework, handouts, and activities for use in psychotherapy* (pp. 19-28). Binghamton, NY: The Haworth Press.

Miller, S. D., Hubble, M. A., & Duncan, B. L. (1996). *Handbook of solution-focused brief therapy.* San Francisco: Jossey-Bass Publishers.

Miller, W. R. (Ed.) (1999). *Integrating spirituality into treatment.* Washington, DC: American Psychological Association.

Richards, P. S., & Bergin, A. E. (1997). *A spiritual strategy for counseling and psychotherapy.* Washington, DC: American Psychological Association.

Rizzuto, A. M. (1974). Object relations and the formation of the image of God. *British Journal of Medical Psychology, 47*(1), 83-99.

Rossman, M. L. (2000). *Guided imagery for self-healing.* New York: H. J. Kramer.

Underwood, R. L. (1986). The presence and absence of God in object relational and theological perspectives. *Journal of Psychology and Theology, 14*(4), 298-305.

White, S. A. (1984). Imago Dei and object relations theory: Implications for a model of human development. *Journal of Psychology and Theology, 12*(4), 286-293.

Whitemont, E. C. (1991). *The symbolic quest.* New York: Putnam.

Professional Readings and Resources

Becvar, D. S. (1997). *Soul healing.* New York: Basic Books.

Brokaw, B. F., & Edwards, K. J. (1994). The relationship of God image to level of object relation's development. *Journal of Psychology and Theology, 22*(4), 352-371.

Brown, R. (1999). *Imago relationship therapy.* New York: John Wiley & Sons, Inc.

Chappelle, W. (2000). A series of progressive legal and ethical decision-making steps for using Christian spiritual interventions in psychotherapy. *Journal of Psychology and Theology, 28*(1), 43-53.

Clarke, J. I., & Dawson, C. (1998). *Growing up again* (2nd ed.). Center City, MN: Hazelden.*

Doherty, W. J. (1995). *Soul searching.* New York: Basic Books.

Doherty, W. J. (1999). Morality and spirituality in therapy. In F. Walsh (Ed.), *Spiritual resources in family therapy* (pp. 179-192). New York: The Guilford Press.

Epstein, G. (1989). *Healing visualizations: Creating health through imagery.* New York: Bantam Books.

Frame, M. W. (2000). The spiritual genogram in family therapy. *Journal of Marital and Family Therapy, 26*(2), 211-216.

Fowler, V. (1981). *Stages of faith.* New York: HarperCollins.

Hendrix, H. (1988). *Getting the love you want: A guide for couples.* New York: Holt.*

Hodge, D. R. (2001). Spiritual genograms: A generational approach to assessing spirituality. *Families in Society, 82*(1), 35-48.

Ingersoll, R. E. (2001). The spiritual wellness inventory. In C. Faiver, R. E. Ingersoll, E. O'Brien, & C. McNally (Eds.), *Explorations in counseling and spirituality* (pp. 185-194). Belmont, CA: Thomson Learning.

Lawrence, R. T. (1997). Measuring the image of God: The God Image Inventory and the God Image Scales. *Journal of Psychology and Theology, 25*(2), 214-226.

Luquet, W., & Hannah, M. (1998). *Healing in the relational paradigm.* Washington, DC: Taylor & Francis.

Lusk, J. T. (Ed.) (1992). *30 scripts for relaxation imagery and inner healing.* New York: Whole Person Associates.

Miller, W. R. (Ed.) (1999). *Integrating spirituality into treatment.* Washington, DC: American Psychological Association.

Olson, D., & Olson, A. K. (2000). *Empowering couples.* Minneapolis, MN: Life Innovations, Inc.*

Richards, P. S., & Bergin, A. E. (1997). *A spiritual strategy for counseling and psychotherapy.* Washington, DC: American Psychological Association.

Rossman, M. L. (2000). *Guided imagery for self-healing.* New York: H. J. Kramer.

Walsh, F. (Ed.) (1999). *Spiritual resources in family therapy.* New York: The Guilford Press.

Bibliotherapy Sources for the Client

Many of the spiritual genogram and God-image inventories referenced in the previous section are appropriate to use with clients. However, it is recommended that the therapist first review and contextualize the material as is appropriate for the client.

Given the diversity of spiritual and/or religious beliefs, caution is recommended when referring specific reading or video sources related to this topic. It is also recommended that the therapist help direct clients to sources within their faith perspective. However, the starred (*) resources in the Professional Readings section may be appropriate to increase personal insight and enhance I-thou relating.

Handout One:
Client Spiritual Assessment Handouts—Therapist Instructions

The following handouts (Handouts Three to Six) provide the client with a four-part take-home spiritual assessment for discussion in subsequent sessions. It elaborates on the elements of a spiritual assessment detailed in this chapter. Its purpose is to assist a client in identifying internalized God images and their connection with internalized relational scripts as part of the process of identifying the role of spirituality in the client's life now and in the future.

Only distribute one handout/exercise at a time as each exercise is lengthy and may overwhelm the client. Before sending an exercise home with the client, review the questions in session so both the therapist and client can clarify awkward and/or irrelevant questions. Mutually decide how and when the exercise is to be completed, length of each response, and how the client's finished work will be managed: narrative style in a journal or typed on the computer; completed by the next visit or longer; a paragraph, a page, or no limit specified per answer; and finally, would the client like the therapist to read the responses, obtain a copy of the responses (if not voluminous), or have the client read and/or reflect on one's responses as most comfortable when that time comes?

Maher, A. B. (2006). Impact of abuse on internalized God images: Spiritual assessment and treatment using guided imagery. In K. B. Helmeke & C. F. Sori (Eds.), *The therapist's notebook for integrating spirituality in counseling: Homework, handouts, and activities for use in psychotherapy* (pp. 89-112). Binghamton, NY: The Haworth Press.

Handout Two:
Client Handouts: Exploring Your Spiritual History—Then, Now, and in the Future
Introduction to Four Exercises

You are about to explore your thoughts and experiences related to your spiritual faith and/or understanding. Everyone has his or her own sense of the sacred. For some that means belief in a Divine, godly spiritual entity. For others, spirituality is experienced as an inner sense of well-being, of connectedness with self and other; belief in God or a spiritual presence outside of human experience may or may not be a part of their belief system. Some of us align ourselves with an organized religion; others do not. The following four exercises are intended to allow you to explore in greater depth your own understanding of spirituality as well as ponder what role it currently plays in your life and what role you want it to play in your future.

Your therapist will distribute one exercise at a time. With each exercise, the two of you will review the questions beforehand and make any adjustments according to your specific interests. For example, questions that do not pertain to your own belief system may be omitted. If a question is not worded specifically enough as it relates to your faith system, you may adjust the question accordingly. You and your therapist will also discuss how you might like to record your responses, the general length of each response, and when you would like to complete the exercise. Finally, both of you will determine how you would like to discuss your responses in therapy.

For these exercises you will need to reserve some quiet time alone to think and reflect. Work through each question at your own pace. You may find that these questions often lend themselves to different answers as time goes by and insight deepens or beliefs change. After working through all four exercises you may find interesting changes occurring in portions of your previous answers. Enjoy the process!

Maher, A. B. (2006). Impact of abuse on internalized God images: Spiritual assessment and treatment using guided imagery. In K. B. Helmeke & C. F. Sori (Eds.), *The therapist's notebook for integrating spirituality in counseling: Homework, handouts, and activities for use in psychotherapy* (pp. 89-112). Binghamton, NY: The Haworth Press.

Handout Three:
Exploring Your Spiritual History—Then, Now, and in the Future
Exercise One: Your Past and Present Spiritual History

This exercise invites you to identify the role of spirituality in your life now and in the past. Our sense of the Divine or faith is influenced not only by what we learned and how we mulled that over in our minds, but by our personal encounters with significant individuals and our faith communities. This exercise offers a way for you to begin exploring those encounters and its influence on your understanding of faith and/or spirituality.

Current Spiritual Interests

1. What is prompting you to explore your spirituality at this point in your life?
2. Later on in this exercise you will explore the growth of your spiritual beliefs over time. But for now, briefly describe your spiritual beliefs at this moment. If you believe in God or a Divine Being, how would you describe the "character" of this entity? And how do you believe this spiritual being relates to you in times of struggle, sadness, pain, fear, and happiness?
3. Many people find support in their spiritual growth by identifying with a religious faith and/or spiritual community. What are your preferences today? Are you active in a religious group? Why have you chosen this group? Or, why have you chosen to not become involved in a religious or spiritual community?

Family History of Spiritual and/or Religious Education

1. What was the religious orientation of your parents and ancestors? Did they talk about and practice their faith openly? Do you consider their faith expression to be more conservative (strict adherence to traditional interpretations and religious practices), moderate, or liberal (flexible expressions of religious belief)? How did the adults in your family speak of belief systems other than their own?
2. What were the primary sources of your religious instruction? Do you remember your first ponderings about God? What were you taught about the existence and nature of God or spirituality?
3. Prior to right now, what has been your experience in religious communities? Was participation or nonparticipation an option for you?

Exploring Life's Ultimate Meaning and Purpose

1. Religion and/or spiritual practices offer answers to the ultimate meaning and purpose of human life. Many of these answers are implied or accepted through an act of faith; some of the answers offered may be vague or specific, relative or absolute. How would you describe the purpose of your life? How have your spiritual and/or religious beliefs influenced these thoughts?
2. Religious teachings and spiritual practices suggest codes of behavior, guidelines for how and why we should relate to one another. What does your faith system teach about morality and the intent behind behavioral guidelines? How are moral failures viewed by your faith system?

Personal Encounter

1. What about your religious/spiritual background do you value? How did it serve you growing up and how does it continue to serve you now? Tell a story illustrating a meaningful event capturing these thoughts.
2. What aspects of your religious or spiritual upbringing do you now question? How are you still impacted by the limits of those teachings/experiences today? Tell a story illustrating hurtful, confusing, or empty experiences.

Maher, A. B. (2006). Impact of abuse on internalized God images: Spiritual assessment and treatment using guided imagery. In K. B. Helmeke & C. F. Sori (Eds.), *The therapist's notebook for integrating spirituality in counseling: Homework, handouts, and activities for use in psychotherapy* (pp. 89-112). Binghamton, NY: The Haworth Press.

Handout Three:
Exploring Your Spiritual History—Then, Now, and in the Future
Exercise One: Your Past and Present Spiritual History *(continued)*

3. Who in your life has served as a spiritual mentor or role model? Describe that person and how he or she has impacted your life and current spiritual beliefs and expression.
4. Describe a person whose professed faith stood in contrast to his or her behavior. How have your life and spiritual beliefs been impacted by this observation?
5. Today we are increasingly aware of spiritual and religious diversity, both conservative and liberal expressions of a variety of faith orientations. This has led to much debate—and significant disagreement—about the influence of religion in all aspects of American culture and international affairs. What voices and opinions do you resonate with? What do you see as the cause and social consequences of these often contentious debates, both positive and negative? How do you think your own faith orientation or spiritual expression has been impacted?

Maher, A. B. (2006). Impact of abuse on internalized God images: Spiritual assessment and treatment using guided imagery. In K. B. Helmeke & C. F. Sori (Eds.), *The therapist's notebook for integrating spirituality in counseling: Homework, handouts, and activities for use in psychotherapy* (pp. 89-112). Binghamton, NY: The Haworth Press.

Handout Four:
Client Handouts: Exploring Your Spiritual History—Then, Now, and in the Future
Exercise Two: Exploring Significant Relationships

This exercise explores your relationship history with significant people in your life. Ideally, this process should occur simultaneously with similar explorations in therapy. In a later exercise you will look for connections between your relationship history and your various perceptions of God, oftentimes referred to as one's image of God, or Imago Dei.

Parental Relationships

1. Who were your primary guardians? At what age did these caretakers come into your life? Also note if any are no longer in your life on a consistent basis. Describe your relationship with each person.
2. Nurture: How did your caretakers respond to your needs for emotional closeness, physical affection, encouragement, support, and empathy? Tell a story that illustrates a time when you felt truly nurtured by your parent(s) or guardian(s). Tell a story that illustrates a time when you did not feel understood or supported, or were overly cared for or "smothered."
3. Structure: How did your caretakers teach you right from wrong? How did they discipline you? Did they encourage you to learn new things and push beyond your comfort zone? Tell a story illustrating helpful structure you received and a story when structure was either absent or hurtful.
4. Communication: How was nurture and structure communicated verbally, nonverbally? How was conflict expressed? What emotions were acceptable to express; what emotions were not?
5. Describe any significant life events that occurred in your childhood not already described above. What about these events are meaningful to you?

Additional Significant Relationships

1. Describe the people beyond your immediate caretakers who have meaningfully contributed to your life. This may include siblings, extended relatives, friends, intimate others, spouses, children, etc. How have these relationships influenced who you are today?
2. Describe those relationships beyond your immediate caretakers who have hurt or strongly disappointed you. How have these relationships contributed to who you are today?

Maher, A. B. (2006). Impact of abuse on internalized God images: Spiritual assessment and treatment using guided imagery. In K. B. Helmeke & C. F. Sori (Eds.), *The therapist's notebook for integrating spirituality in counseling: Homework, handouts, and activities for use in psychotherapy* (pp. 89-112). Binghamton, NY: The Haworth Press.

Handout Five:
Client Handouts: Exploring Your Spiritual History—Then, Now, and in the Future
Exercise Three: Exploring the Connections

For many, their impression of God is like a tapestry with many variations. Our image of God is influenced by a variety of threads. Our religious education, the various communities we have participated in, our inner hopes and longings, our lifecycle stage, and our significant relationships all contribute. In this exercise you will pull all of your strands together.

1. As you have worked through the first exercise, what images of God surfaced for you? As you review your written responses, make a list of these relational qualities. Include both positive and negative images. For example, I tended to view, or I was taught, that God is loving, all present, aloof, distant, and/or nonexistent, etc.
2. What is your desired image of God? How do you wish God could be experienced if, in fact, you believe a Divine presence exists? What do you wish would be God's character? Make a list of these relational qualities. For example: I wish God were loving, caring, more real and present, etc.
3. Next, describe the relational qualities of significant people in your life who were highlighted in Exercise 2. For example: kind, warm, cold, and/or abusive, etc.
4. In the fourth list, describe what you wish were the relational qualities of those significant people. For example: kind, giving, tolerant, forgiving, more assertive, etc.
5. Observe the differences and similarities of these four lists. What connections can you make between your faith and relational history, your current and desired relational experiences and images of God?
6. Were there times in your life when you felt more attuned to your spiritual life, and times when you did not? What were the significant relational events occurring at that time, if any?
7. What images of God prevail (or how do you experience your faith) when life is least stressful? What images surface (or what role does your faith play) in times of sorrow, fear, or anger?

Maher, A. B. (2006). Impact of abuse on internalized God images: Spiritual assessment and treatment using guided imagery. In K. B. Helmeke & C. F. Sori (Eds.), *The therapist's notebook for integrating spirituality in counseling: Homework, handouts, and activities for use in psychotherapy* (pp. 89-112). Binghamton, NY: The Haworth Press.

Handout Six:
Client Handouts: Exploring Your Spiritual History—Then, Now, and in the Future
Exercise Four: Envisioning Your Future

This exercise gives you an opportunity to dream, to express thoughts and desires that you may have hesitated to verbalize in the past. Oftentimes the first step in realizing our hopes is to put them into words, to give them a voice. This exercise is intended to begin that process.

1. As you review your responses in the previous exercises, what about your current spiritual life or God image works well for you, is satisfying and meaningful? What do you wish were different?
2. In your interpersonal life, what relational hurts still exist? Which relationships are sources of strength?
3. Is there a connection between the answers to items #1 and #2?
4. How might you want to strengthen or deepen your spiritual life or faith expression? What hesitancies or roadblocks exist?
5. What spiritual resources, traditions, and/or rituals do you wish to explore and/or develop? How might you begin that process?
6. If you identified an item to explore or develop in the previous question, what are your expectations? What might be the inevitable strengths and limitations of engaging in this activity? How might acknowledging its inherent and/or unknown limits serve to maximize your experience?

Maher, A. B. (2006). Impact of abuse on internalized God images: Spiritual assessment and treatment using guided imagery. In K. B. Helmeke & C. F. Sori (Eds.), *The therapist's notebook for integrating spirituality in counseling: Homework, handouts, and activities for use in psychotherapy* (pp. 89-112). Binghamton, NY: The Haworth Press.

Handout Seven:
Therapist Worksheets: Guided Imagery Scripts

The imagery exercises detailed here are examples of how imagery might be used to further explore, utilize, and/or strengthen the client's spirituality as a resource in healing from relational wounds.

Exploring Internal Images

A common imagery with the original source unknown, this exercise often accesses actual and ideal internal God concepts.

1. After leading the client into a relaxed state, invite client to imagine one's self in the middle of a meadow on the edge of a forest. Lead the client onto the path into the forest and along a stream, traveling against the flow of water toward the stream's origins. As is common, the water is symbolic of life.
2. As you come to the stream's beginnings, invite the participant to imagine a figure who is the Source of that stream. Imagine what this figure or source looks like, its demeanor, shape, form. Avoid suggesting any anthropomorphic qualities.

   a. For clients with a strong identification with a particular faith and discomfort with the unknowns of a guided imagery, the therapist may wish to ask the client what figure best represents the embodiment of his or her belief system, i.e., Christ, Buddha, Yahweh, etc. This then becomes who is encountered at the water's source. However, using this generic, nonspecific imagery allows maximum projection and/or metaphorical imagery. It is also a recommended method in group settings in which multiple faiths or preferences are represented.

3. Then, simply ask the participant to listen to what the Source may want to communicate to him or her. Design a question relevant to the client, i.e., "as this Source looks into your eyes, what do you imagine this Source sees in your eyes, your heart, and hence wants you to know, wants to communicate to you?"
4. And finally, invite the participant to respond back to the Source in any manner desired. For example, ask the client, "What do you want to ask this Source? What do you wish this Source understood about you? What do you want to tell this Source?" Allow the conversation to finish in silence.
5. Walk the participant back down the stream to the meadow and out of the imagery.
6. Invite the client to process the content of the imagery.

   a. A powerful follow-up experiential exercise is to invite the client to draw a picture of the Source. Offer various pens, pencils, crayons, markers, and watercolors along with plain and textured papers. In a group setting clients are often inspired by the visuals of fellow participants.

Envisioning God As Empathic Witness

This exercise must be preceded by (1) knowledge of the client's belief system; (2) overt expressions on the client's part to access spirituality in the healing process, and specifically in this form; and (3) prior work with the abuse memory the two of you choose to use in this exercise. Also, it is highly recommended that the therapist have a theoretical framework from which to understand the nature of trauma as this exercise is designed to assist clients who are repeatedly being retraumatized by past memories of abuse.

Maher, A. B. (2006). Impact of abuse on internalized God images: Spiritual assessment and treatment using guided imagery. In K. B. Helmeke & C. F. Sori (Eds.), *The therapist's notebook for integrating spirituality in counseling: Homework, handouts, and activities for use in psychotherapy* (pp. 89-112). Binghamton, NY: The Haworth Press.

Handout Seven:
Therapist Worksheets: Guided Imagery Scripts *(continued)*

Preparation

1. Decide on which memory to use and the goal of the exercise as it pertains to the chosen memory.
2. Further explore with the client how his or her spiritual tradition understands God's response to innocent pain and suffering. Listen for the internal God images that may be empowering or disempowering to the client in the here and now. Explore and invite the client to embrace the more empowering narratives for this exercise. This is often easily accomplished by simply asking the client what he or she wishes was God's response in the aftermath of the specific memory of focus and then exploring how their tradition may understand God's response in that manner.

   a. For example, as Carl envisioned God's presence in his life he had many doubts about God's care due to the fact that the abuse from his aunt occurred without intervention. But he longed for a God who understood and cared about his pain, who empathized with him. He also longed for a God who would "smack her around a little bit" (as was his wording.). The themes of abandonment, and the longing for compassion and justice emerged as key elements of his God image. Likewise, he was easily able to identify how his faith tradition identifies and explores these themes as well. As he and the therapist prepared for an imagery related to a sexual abuse memory, Carl agreed to hold in suspension his anger at God's seeming abandonment (which they explored at other times) and agreed to focus on his longing for God's care and justice.

3. Ask how the client addresses the Divine and use this language throughout. Avoid using your language and phraseology.

Guided Imagery

1. The client has indicated prior to the guided imagery where and when in time the actual event began. After leading the client into a relaxed state, invite the client to imagine God, and perhaps you, safely standing side by side or perhaps holding each others' hands as together you begin to revisit the abusive event.

   a. Recognizing that the therapist is now speaking to the inner child who was abused as well as the adult client in the here and now, remind the client why the memory is being recalled, to stop the flashbacks by exploring what message the constant replaying is trying to tell the client. And part of this process means no longer reliving the abuse alone and in secret as today the client is bringing along witnesses.

2. Invite the client to begin watching the event. Ask the client to verbally tell you what is happening. During the event, offer containment of the emotional content by affirming that God and/or you, and the client's adult self are present. Offer understanding that these are painful, scary events; offer reminders that although this replay is hard, the client has survived the actual event and we are all here to help the client become free of the lingering side effects. And finally, remind the client of his or her right to take it slowly or turn back.

   a. In this imagery, the client is taking along "safe others" so another pair of eyes can stand witness along side of the client, not just hearing about the event but witnessing it as well. It is based on the premise that the traumatic event reoccurs because something about the event has not been fully understood or encountered either emotionally and/or cognitively. Inviting another to bear witness to one's story is an intimate I-thou encounter opening the client to deeper levels of understanding, comfort, and hope. (This is the premise of "confession," a spiritual discipline in which the act of sharing one's deepest thoughts with another leads to

Maher, A. B. (2006). Impact of abuse on internalized God images: Spiritual assessment and treatment using guided imagery. In K. B. Helmeke & C. F. Sori (Eds.), *The therapist's notebook for integrating spirituality in counseling: Homework, handouts, and activities for use in psychotherapy* (pp. 89-112). Binghamton, NY: The Haworth Press.

Handout Seven:
Therapist Worksheets: Guided Imagery Scripts *(continued)*

deeper healing.) Why or how a client benefits from bringing others into her or his story is different for each person. It could be the person's inner longing to simply be heard, to have one's pain validated, to have another adult acknowledge the incredulousness of the offense. Or, the person could be striving to make meaning out of the event, out of their survival. By inviting the person to imagine God present, the client has already identified a desire to experience God's healing presence in the here and now.

3. Once the event is visualized, acknowledge that the event is over. Invite the client to then turn away from watching and just focus on receiving comfort. Offer soothing words of validation and times of silence. Based on the client's belief system, invite the client to imagine God's love and care present with both of you at this moment.

4. As you continue to shift away from the memory itself, invite the client to silently recall times when comfort was received from others, times when the client felt safe, warmth, and love. Connect similarities between what she or he is imagining God providing now and moments of safe comfort experienced in the past. Suggest that in those instances of human care, the client may have experienced God's presence, just as God may be experienced in this moment. This also invites the client to bring to the forefront empowering narratives heretofore pushed into the background.

5. Invite the client and God, or the accompanying person(s) to converse by asking the client to silently or verbally express any thoughts present at the moment. The benefit of inviting the client to dialogue in silence is that it allows the client to imagine what God's dialogue in response might be, affirming the client's own inner beliefs. Verbal dialogue with the therapist communicating responses that a caring parent or God might offer allows the client to hear from an actual person what was needed most in that moment. Allow the client's issues and circumstance to guide your decision.

   a. This dialogue also identifies origins of cognitive and affective responses often unacknowledged during the original abusive event. For instance, the client may express anger, disbelief, and/or feelings of rejection as care was not offered in the form of protection. The therapist is able to acknowledge that yes, the adults and/or God did fail the client in those moments. The therapist's job is to continually mirror and validate.

6. Before the imagery ends, invite the client to hear God's voice/your voice assuring that the event is over, the client is now safe, and can no longer be hurt. In accordance with a client's belief system, end with a suggestion that God's caring presence never leaves, but may take different shapes and forms as suggested earlier (i.e., experienced through the love and care we receive from one another), while affirming that the client's anger, hurt, or doubt is logical and acceptable. Acknowledge as well the contradictions of God's love, caring, loving, yet love is not what we always expect it to look like; it does not prevent or protect us from harm.

   a. Incorporating a client's spiritual beliefs into the healing process inevitably invites the client to deal with life's polarities and incongruencies. Life is both good and bad, predictable and unpredictable, mysterious and knowable, just and unjust. The contrariness of life is acknowledged in all major religious traditions. For example, in the Jewish and Christian scriptures, goodness and hardship fall upon the just and the unjust. Healing for the client requires an acknowledgement of this, as well as a decision to choose how she or he wants to make sense of life in the face of these polarities.

7. As with all guided imageries, as you bring the client out of the imagery spend a moment once again on relaxation. If the client responds well to guided imagery as a way of managing stress, invite the client to imagine a place that represents peace, tranquility, and safety. Allow the client to "rest" in this image before ending the imagery.

8. Process the imagery.

Maher, A. B. (2006). Impact of abuse on internalized God images: Spiritual assessment and treatment using guided imagery. In K. B. Helmeke & C. F. Sori (Eds.), *The therapist's notebook for integrating spirituality in counseling: Homework, handouts, and activities for use in psychotherapy* (pp. 89-112). Binghamton, NY: The Haworth Press.

Handout Seven:
Therapist Worksheets: Guided Imagery Scripts *(continued)*

Justice Making

Adult victims of childhood abuse are vulnerable to responding to adult pressures in one of two ways, either with an over sense of entitlement leading to abusive responses, or with an undeveloped sense of entitlement leading to a passive response pattern. These individuals often find themselves vulnerable to repeated victimization. Both response sets reflect the impact of relational brokenness in which patterns of love, care, and justice were not modeled or offered sufficiently enough for the client to internalize.

Hence, addressing a client's innate need for justice is a crucial part of healing. Within the therapy process, justice making involves visualizing an alternative response to the abuse in which the client's needs are validated and the victimizer is held accountable. It often follows the imagery just described. While some therapists are concerned that this represents "revisionist history" (no justice in real life may have occurred), this exercise allows a client to internally receive justice for the abusive incident that keeps re-occurring within his or her mind's eye. Imagery in which a Divine Presence, parent, or trusted other assist the client in stopping and punishing the abuser allow the client to build stronger internal images of God as empathic responder and ultimate justicemaker leading to stronger images of self-worth and efficacy. The abusive event did not allow the client to exercise free will, to take control of the situation. Role-playing an imagined sequence of events in which the client is empowered over the abuser allows the client to experience one's power, hence minimizing the tendency of responding overaggressively or passively in future situations requiring assertiveness.

This exercise also invites discussion regarding the dilemma of why evil happens and why God does not intervene. Although this is a universal mystery with no concrete answers, invite the client to see an alternate response. We may never know why but we can often find our way through it (physically, emotionally, and/ or spiritually) within the context of caring and safe I-thou encounters with others.

1. Before the imagery begins, invite the client to discuss what was needed most at the time of the incident. What might need to be said now? This allows the therapist to go in the direction of the client's wishes as protection is offered and/or justice rendered.
2. Building on the previous imagery, invite the client to visualize a caring presence entering the abuse scene and stopping the abuse. Speaking for that caring voice (a longed-for parent, a God-image, or you), verbalize that she or he is now safe; that the other person was wrong, not the client.
3. Incorporating the client's wishes, directly address the abuser and enact the justice as the client directed. You or the client may direct the sequence of events as determined between the two of you.
   a. This is also the time for the client to hear the therapist voicing appropriate responses of justice as the therapist directly addresses the abuser. For example, statements such as "you were wrong for hurting (client's name); no one should ever treat another person in that manner," etc. Add statements of relevance to the roadblocks the client has identified.
4. After you have put those thoughts into words, so the client can hear a caring person offering such support, invite the client to silently or verbally speak any remaining thoughts to the abuser.
5. As you begin to walk the client away from the memory, invite the client to visualize a safe and peaceful place, representative of the life he or she now has and/or is seeking to build within. Affirm the client's courage.
6. Lead the client out of the imagery and process.

Maher, A. B. (2006). Impact of abuse on internalized God images: Spiritual assessment and treatment using guided imagery. In K. B. Helmeke & C. F. Sori (Eds.), *The therapist's notebook for integrating spirituality in counseling: Homework, handouts, and activities for use in psychotherapy* (pp. 89-112). Binghamton, NY: The Haworth Press.

9

Developing Forgiveness

Terry D. Hargrave
Gwendolyn J. Williams

Type of Contribution: Handouts, Activity

Objective

Many clients have issues of past pain caused by relationships. Many of these clients feel a spiritual obligation to forgive. This chapter is intended to help clients recognize that emotional reactions they consistently have in interactions may be related to past trauma or destructive relational cycles. It is also intended to help clients recognize pain resulting from relational violations and move toward relational forgiveness.

Rationale for Use

Learning to forgive requires an effort to restore love and trustworthiness to relationships so that the client and the victimizer can put an end to destructive entitlement (Boszormenyi-Nagy & Krasner, 1986). The basic principles of forgiveness have been used since ancient times in religious communities to heal and restore relationships between people. Forgiveness is the release of resentment and anger toward an offender or victimizer, and the restoration of as much love and trust as possible in the relationship. Recently clinicians have begun to examine the use of forgiveness as an intervention to help clients seek new beginnings in previously harmful relationships, resolve long-standing relational problems, and to release anger and bitterness.

Many clients are unaware of the rage and depression that often stem from resentment and anger toward those who cause injury in relationships and commit various violations such as sexual abuse, breaking marital vows, abusing drugs and alcohol, and engaging in other desecrations of trust and victimization. The resulting lack of trust drives individuals to seek what they consider to be just entitlement. It is this entitlement, which is destructive by nature, which results in family pain and hurt. This chapter illustrates how many individuals transform past relational violations into feelings concerning themselves and actions in future relationships. This chapter also presents a framework for the development of forgiveness.

As Figure 9.1 (Hargrave's Model of Violations of Love and Trust, see handout at the end of the chapter) illustrates, when individuals are violated they are likely to feel (1) rage, as they experience uncontrolled anger toward their victimizer or (2) shame, as they accuse themselves of being unlovable and not deserving of a trustworthy relationship. Further, individuals are likely to act in future relationships in ways that are (1) overcontrolling, as they try to minimize their risk of hurt or (2) chaotic, because they believe that little can be done to form trusting relationships and that they will eventually be hurt again. Many individuals alternate in shame/rage, control/chaotic cycles (Hargrave & Sells, 1997). Victims of relational injustice are likely to become victimizers themselves within other relationships. The release of blame and reconciliation are therapeutic opportunities to deal with destructive entitlement and to heal family relationships.

Figure 9.2 (The Four Stations of Forgiveness, see handout) illustrates the four stations of forgiveness that provide the foundation for the work of forgiveness. Forgiveness has often been described as letting go of transgressions and wrongs. Although the authors believe this is partly true, the authors feel that much of forgiveness is about "putting back" rather than "letting go." Putting back simply means that the transgressor and victim work to put back as much love and trust to the relationship as possible. Along these lines, we conceptualize the work of forgiveness as having two broad categories of salvage and restoration.

Salvage deals with the internal processing of the victim and his or her ability to discover how the pain was perpetrated and to establish some form of identification with the victimizer. Simply stated, salvage is the victim learning how he or she was hurt so he or she can learn to refrain from being destructive in future relationships. Further, it also involves learning that the action taken by the victimizer does not necessarily degrade that person's value as a human being, nor should it serve as a basis of shame for the victim. However, salvaging does not require the victim to engage in future relationship with the victimizer. In several circumstances the victim would not engage in interactions with the victimizer, such as when the victimizer is dead or unavailable or the victimizer is still not loving or trustworthy.

Restoration involves the internal work of salvaging, but also includes actually building the relationship by engaging once again in loving and trustworthy actions with the victimizer. Salvage includes two stations in the work of forgiveness: insight and understanding. Insight is when the victim clearly understands the past interactions that have resulted in being harmed by the victimizer and gains the power necessary to intervene in order to be safe. Understanding is making identification with the victimizer's past developmental history, and learning to sympathize and empathize with possible reasons the victimizer engaged in harmful actions. Restoration also includes two stations: giving the opportunity for compensation and overt forgiving. Giving the opportunity for compensation is when the victimizer slowly rebuilds trustworthiness with the victim by demonstrating loving and trustworthy actions over a long period of time. Finally, overt forgiving is when victim and victimizer meet together in therapy for the purposes of confronting the violation, assigning responsibility for the violation, and engaging in a promise to act differently in the future (Hargrave, 1994).

One additional clarification of the four stations of forgiveness needs to be added. These four stations of forgiveness should not be interpreted as stages. People oscillate between the four stations many times in an effort to forgive and to re-establish relational trust.

Instructions

Once the therapist believes the client has emotional reactions of rage, shame, control, or chaos, or cycles within rage/shame and control/ chaos, he or she should request that the client complete the Interpersonal Relationship Resolution Scale (IRRS) (Hargrave & Sells, 1997) as a pre-test activity (see Figure 9.3). Instructions for scoring this scale are included in a separate handout (see Figure 9.4). The scale should be repeated later for follow-up purposes.

After the IRRS has been completed, scored, and discussed, it is appropriate for the therapist to go over the scale with the client. The therapist should explain the Definitions of the Key Concepts of Hargrave's Model of Violations of Love and Trust found in Figure 9.5 (see handout) and The Four Stations of Forgiveness (see Figure 9.2) to the client. As an alternative, the therapist can draw both Figure 9.1 and Figure 9.2 on the board and describe the concepts verbally to the client.

A good approach is to describe the cycles of rage/shame and control/chaos to the client without personalizing it, and then ask the client where he or she is operating in relation to the cycle.

After the client describes his or her point of operation, the therapist can then introduce the idea of the work that is to be done in order to reach forgiveness.

Suggested activities include having the client identify the mechanisms and transactions that caused pain, describe how the pain was perpetrated, and develop a plan to establish some form of identification with the victimizer. Specific activities should be designed to address each of the concepts in the four stations of forgiveness. In addition, the client and therapist could role-play concepts and plans.

Brief Vignette

Elaine and Julie were adult sisters who were sexually molested by their brother, Joe, when they were children. Both Elaine and Julie married, but found they acted out destructive entitlement with their husbands. Julie would often berate her husband for being undependable and uncaring even though her husband made significant efforts to be both dependable and caring. She used rage and control to deal with her pain that resulted from the sexual abuse but played these characteristics out with her husband instead of her brother. Elaine, on the other hand, dealt with her victimization with deeply embedded shame and chaos. She would slip into significant times of depression when she would engage in little intimacy with her husband. When her depression became severe, she would destructively try to cover her distress by drinking and using drugs.

Elaine and Julie came to therapy because both realized the past was interfering with their present relationships. The therapist first helped them identify how the pain of molestation victimized each, and how each developed very different methods in coping. The pain scale of the IRRS was administered to both. Julie became rigid, raged at people when her boundaries were violated, and tried to control most aspects of her relationships. Elaine retreated to shame, often blaming herself for the abuse. She would also cover the anxiety and depression of the shame through using alcohol. Both began to realize that they were using destructive tactics in present relationships to deal with the old victimization.

The therapist then began to focus on the possibility of working through the pain by utilizing forgiveness. He administered the forgiveness scale of the IRRS and then proceeded to explain different options in forgiving. Using Figure 9.1, the therapist traced how violations in love and trust prompt feelings about how a person views oneself and how he or she interacts in relationships. In order to cope, victims use rage, shame, control, and chaos in order to compensate for the intense feelings or actions that they feel are necessary in relationships. Both Julie and Elaine could easily identify with the ways they had coped with the sexual abuse. The therapist then used Figure 9.2 to help the sisters understand the different perspectives of forgiveness. It was emphasized that both the work of salvage and restoration were the work of forgiveness, but the two divisions were appropriate for different types of relationships. Each station of forgiveness was explained and the therapist answered the sisters' questions regarding the process of forgiveness and how forgiveness could be applied to their situations. Julie was firmly against confronting her brother face to face. Instead, the therapist helped her realize how she could focus on setting firm boundaries with Joe and protecting herself from any feelings of victimization. In addition, she worked to understand Joe's background to gain some knowledge of why Joe did such a thing. This work was not intended to lift responsibility for the transgression, but rather to understand that Joe was a human being that made a mistake in his behavior. Julie found comfort through the work of *salvage*.

Elaine believed that she needed to have a face-to-face confrontation with Joe. She arranged with the therapist to meet with Joe. The session was complex, but basically focused on Joe and Elaine agreeing on the transgression of the molestation, Joe taking responsibility for the transgression, and then Joe asking for and receiving forgiveness. Although Joe had to continue to prove to Elaine he was trustworthy in his current behavior, Elaine experienced much less depression and was successful in confronting her own alcohol problem. Elaine found comfort through the work of *restoration.*

Suggestions for Follow-Up

Presenting the model and stations of forgiveness either verbally or through the handouts is generally an effective beginning for helping clients to develop forgiveness and break destructive patterns. The therapist may spot the need for forgiveness when he or she observes extreme behavior out of the norm, for instance, when a person becomes enraged when frustration is more appropriate. Another example would be when a person feels shameful about someone else's behavior. It is not necessary for the client to exhibit cyclical behavior, but rapidly shifting patterns of shame and rage, or control and chaos, should be noted. Still, the therapist may need to teach important skills in being forgiving. For example, clients may need help in identifying with the victimizer's position, limitations, development, efforts, and intent. This identification and understanding results in the victim acknowledging the fallibility of the victimizer. This does not remove the victimizer's responsibility for the destructive action; however, it allows the client to feel a reduction in condemnation and blame toward the victimizer.

Contraindications

The therapist needs to be careful in assessing whether the cycle is indeed present and in determining where in the cycle the client is operating. The activities discussed here would be contraindicated in cases in which physical aggression or battering was the source of the received pain. It is also important for the therapist to remember not to push clients to forgive untrustworthy or harmful people.

References

Boszormenyi-Nagy, I., & Krasner, B. (1986). *Between give and take: A clinical guide to contextual therapy.* New York: Brunner/Mazel.

Hargrave, T. D. (1994). *Families and forgiveness: Healing wounds in the intergenerational family.* New York: Brunner/Mazel.

Hargrave, T. D., & Sells, J. N. (1997). The development of a forgiveness scale. *Journal of Marital and Family Therapy, 23*(1), 41-63.

Professional Readings and Resources

Boszormenyi-Nagy, I., & Krasner, B. (1986). *Between give and take: A clinical guide to contextual therapy.* New York: Brunner/Mazel.

Enright, R. D. (2001). *Forgiveness is a choice: A step-by-step process for resolving anger and restoring hope.* Washington, DC: American Psychological Association.

Hargrave, T. D. (1994). *Families and forgiveness: Healing wounds in the intergenerational family.* New York: Brunner/Mazel.

Hargrave, T. D. (2001). *Forgiving the devil: Coming to terms with damaged relationships.* Phoenix: Zeig, Tucker, and Theisen.

Hargrave, T. D., & Sells, J. N. (1997). The development of a forgiveness scale. *Journal of Marital and Family Therapy, 23*(1), 41-63.

Bibliography Sources for the Client

Boszormenyi-Nagy, I., & Krasner, B. (1986). *Between give and take: A clinical guide to contextual therapy.* New York: Brunner/Mazel.

Enright, R. D. (2001). *Forgiveness is a choice: A step-by-step process for resolving anger and restoring hope.* Washington, DC: American Psychological Association.

Hargrave, T. D. (1994). *Families and forgiveness: Healing wounds in the intergenerational family.* New York: Brunner/Mazel.

Hargrave, T. D. (2001). *Forgiving the devil: Coming to terms with damaged relationships.* Phoenix: Zeig, Tucker, and Theisen.

Hargrave, T. D., & Sells, J. N. (1997). The development of a forgiveness scale. *Journal of Marital and Family Therapy, 23*(1), 41-63.

FIGURE 9.1. Hargrave's Model of Violations of Love and Trust

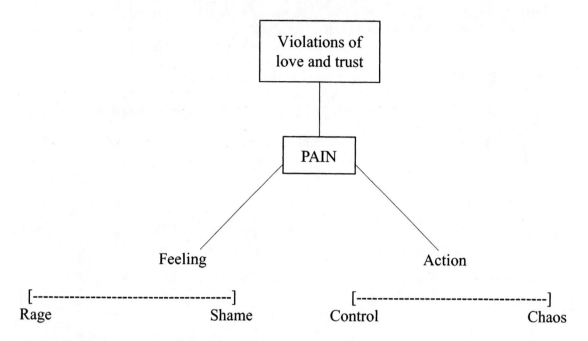

Source: Hargrave, T. D., & Sells, J. N. (1997). The development of a forgiveness scale. *Journal of Marital and Family Therapy, 23*(1): 43. Used with permission.

Hargrave, T. D., & Williams, G. J. (2006). Developing forgiveness. In K. B. Helmeke & C. F. Sori (Eds.), *The therapist's notebook for integrating spirituality in counseling: Homework, handouts, and activities for use in psychotherapy* (pp. 113-126). Binghamton, NY: The Haworth Press.

FIGURE 9.2. The Four Stations of Forgiveness

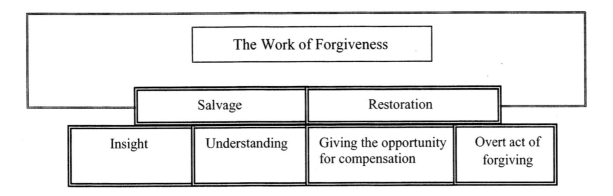

Source: Modified from Hargrave, T. D., & Sells, J. N. (1997). The development of a forgiveness scale. *Journal of Marital and Family Therapy, 23*(1): 44. Used with permission.

Hargrave, T. D., & Williams, G. J. (2006). Developing forgiveness. In K. B. Helmeke & C. F. Sori (Eds.), *The therapist's notebook for integrating spirituality in counseling: Homework, handouts, and activities for use in psychotherapy* (pp. 113-126). Binghamton, NY: The Haworth Press.

FIGURE 9.3. Interpersonal Relationship Resolution Scale

Name _____ I.D. # _____ Sex: ____ Male ____ Female

Age ____ Race: ____ Black ____ Hispanic ____ White ____ Asian ____ Native American

Marital status ____ Married ____ Never married ____ Divorced ____ Widowed ____ Remarried

Are you adopted? ____ Yes ____ No ____ Birth order: I am the ____ of ____ total children.

Directions: In any relationship, it is possible for people to experience hurts that can lead to emotional pain. In some cases, these hurts can be severe and long lasting. This scale is designed to measure

- some of the emotions and behaviors that you feel and exhibit toward the person who caused you hurt;
- some of the feelings you have about yourself;
- some of the ways you act in other situations and relationships.

Since each person is unique, there are no right or wrong answers. Just try to respond as honestly as you can. Please respond to every statement.

Rate the following statements as they apply to you and the person who hurt you in such a way that causes you distress. Even though many people may have caused you hurt, keep just this one particular person in mind when answering the statements. If you do not have a current relationship with the person who caused you hurt, answer the statements as you remember when you were involved with the person.

---

1. This person has apologized to me for the pain he or she has caused in my life.
   ____ Yes, I believe this is true.   ____ No, I believe this is false.
2. I believe we are on the road to restoring our relationship.
   ____ Yes, I believe this much of the time.   ____ No, I seldom feel this way.
3. I have a current relationship with this person and feel little need to talk about the past hurt.
   ____ Yes, this is mostly true.   ____ No, this is mostly false.
4. I believe this person would not intentionally hurt me again because he or she is now trustworthy in our relationship.
   ____ Yes, this is true much of the time.   ____ No, this is hardly ever true.
5. The only way I can deal with this relationship is to keep my distance from this person.
   ____ Yes, this is mostly true.   ____ No, this is mostly false.
6. My relationship with this person has improved gradually over time by just being together and having mostly good times.
   ____ Yes, this is mostly true.   ____ No, this is mostly false.
7. I feel powerless over circumstances of our relationship when I'm with this person.
   ____ Yes, I feel this way most of the time.   ____ No, I do not feel this way often.
8. I have difficulty in stopping this person from causing me hurt.
   ____ Yes, I have this difficulty often.   ____ No, this is mostly not the case.
9. This person has pain that has nothing to do with me.
   ____ Yes, I am fairly sure this is true.   ____ No, I do not believe this is true.
10. Things are not completely resolved in our relationship, but it is getting better.
   ____ Yes, this is mostly true.   ____ No, this is mostly false.

Hargrave, T. D., & Williams, G. J. (2006). Developing forgiveness. In K. B. Helmeke & C. F. Sori (Eds.), *The therapist's notebook for integrating spirituality in counseling: Homework, handouts, and activities for use in psychotherapy* (pp. 113-126). Binghamton, NY: The Haworth Press.

FIGURE 9.3. Interpersonal Relationship Resolution Scale *(continued)*

11. I have trouble sorting out my emotions with regard to this person.
    ____ Yes, I have this trouble often.   ____ No, I am fairly clear about my feelings.
12. This person acknowledges that he or she has done things wrong in the past concerning our relationship.
    ____ Yes, this is mostly true.   ____ No, this is mostly false.
13. I never seem to "win" when it comes to relating to this person.
    ____ Yes, this is mostly true.   ____ No, this is mostly untrue.
14. When this person is cruel to me, it has more to do with his or her problems than it does with me.
    ____ Yes, I believe this most of the time.   ____ No, I have difficulty believing this.
15. For the most part, I deserve the things that have happened to me.
    ____ Yes, most of the time.   ____ No, I hardly ever believe this.
16. I know how to effectively stop this person from causing me pain.
    ____ Yes, most of the time.   ____ No, almost never.
17. This person has taken responsibility for causing me pain.
    ____ Yes, I believe this much of the time.   ____ No, I hardly ever believe this.
18. I understand why I feel pain from this person.
    ____ Yes, it is fairly clear to me.   ____ No, I am fairly confused.
19. Our relationship is improving a little each time we are together.
    ____ Yes, I find this mostly true.   ____ No, this is mostly false.
20. If I had come from this person's background, I might do some harmful things to people.
    ____ Yes, I may have made the same mistakes.   ____ No, I think I would have done better.
21. When I talked to this person about the damage he or she caused, he or she accepted responsibility.
    ____ Yes, for the most part.   ____ No, he or she mostly did not.
22. I believe that our relationship is making progress and someday may be totally healed.
    ____ Yes, I believe this much of the time.   ____ No, I seldom feel this way.
23. People don't ask my advice or opinion.
    ____ Yes, I believe this is mostly true.   ____ No, this is mostly false.
24. Nobody knows how I really feel.
    ____ Yes, I believe this mostly true.   ____ No, I believe this is mostly false.
25. I easily misplace things.
    ____ Yes, I do this much of the time.   ____ No, this is hardly ever the case.
26. I am ashamed of what has happened to me.
    ____ Yes, I feel this way much of the time.   ____ No, I seldom feel this way.
27. I hit things when I am really angry.
    ____ Yes, this happens often.   ____ No, this hardly ever happens.
28. Winning is very important to me.
    ____ Yes, I believe this is mostly true.   ____ No, I hardly ever feel this way.
29. I can stay with tasks until they are compete.
    ____ Yes, I do this much of the time.   ____ No, this is hardly ever the case.
30. I need to cover up how I really feel.
    ____ Yes, I feel this way most of the time.   ____ No, I seldom feel this way.
31. I feel like smashing things.
    ____ Yes, I feel this way often.   ____ No, I hardly ever feel this way.
32. I swear a lot when I am mad.
    ____ Yes, I do this much of the time.   ____ No, this hardly ever happens.

Hargrave, T. D., & Williams, G. J. (2006). Developing forgiveness. In K. B. Helmeke & C. F. Sori (Eds.), *The therapist's notebook for integrating spirituality in counseling: Homework, handouts, and activities for use in psychotherapy* (pp. 113-126). Binghamton, NY: The Haworth Press.

FIGURE 9.3.
Interpersonal Relationship Resolution Scale *(continued)*

33. I don't want people to know what happened to me.
____ Yes, this is mostly true.   ____ No, this is mostly false.
34. I have difficulty compromising with other people.
____ Yes, I believe this is mostly true.   ____ No, this is seldom true.
35. I feel hopeless and alone.
____ Yes, this is mostly true.   ____ No, this is mostly false.
36. It is often better to cover up your feelings.
____ Yes, I believe this is mostly true.   ____ No, I hardly ever feel this way.
37. This person causes me to feel so angry, I cannot think.
____ Yes, this happens often.   ____ No, this seldom happens.
38. I feel responsible for what this person did to me.
____ Yes, I feel this way much of the time.   ____ No, I seldom feel this way.
39. When in an argument, I have been known to throw things.
____ Yes, this happens often.   ____ No, this hardly ever happens.
40. People say that I'm co-dependent.
____ Yes, I believe this is mostly true.   ____ No, I hardly ever feel this way.
41. After work or school, I have no motivation to get anything accomplished.
____ Yes, I believe this is mostly true.   ____ No, I hardly ever feel this way.
42. Life feels organized.
____ Yes, I believe this is mostly true.   ____ No, I hardly ever feel this way.
43. I feel enraged often.
____ Yes, this happens much of the time.   ____ No, this hardly ever happens.
44. People say that I am a person who has to have my way.
____ Yes, I believe this is mostly true.   ____ No, this is mostly false.

Source: Hargrave, T. D., & Sells, J. N. (1997). The development of a forgiveness scale. *Journal of Marital and Family Therapy, 23*(1): 59-63. Used with permission.

Hargrave, T. D., & Williams, G. J. (2006). Developing forgiveness. In K. B. Helmeke & C. F. Sori (Eds.), *The therapist's notebook for integrating spirituality in counseling: Homework, handouts, and activities for use in psychotherapy* (pp. 113-126). Binghamton, NY: The Haworth Press.

FIGURE 9.4.
Scoring of the IRRS

The Forgiveness Scale of the IRRS gives an idea of where a person is in the work of forgiveness using Hargrave's model (1994). The subscales are Insight, Understanding, Giving the Opportunity for Compensation, and Overt Act of Forgiveness.

Insight

Insight is the ability to recognize transactional patterns and mechanisms by which relational damage was perpetrated and interrupt or intervene in the patterns to prevent relational damage in the future. High scores (8 or above) may indicate that a person would experience confusion concerning emotional pain and would be unable to make specific statements regarding painful interactions or how to avoid them. Low scores (6 or below) may indicate that a person experiences clarity in identifying pain and knows how to avoid painful interactions.

Understanding

Understanding is the ability to make personal identification with the position, limitations, development, efforts, and intent with the person who caused relational damage. High scores (8 or above) may indicate that the person either blames themselves or the perpetrator to an unreasonable degree without consideration of context or circumstances. Low scores (6 or below) may indicate that a person clearly understands the circumstances which must be considered in determining responsibility for relational deterioration.

Giving the Opportunity for Compensation

Giving the Opportunity for Compensation is the ability to engage in interactions and relationship with the former perpetrator in such a way that is perceived by the victim as non-threatening and builds emotional bonding. High scores (13 or above) may indicate that a person views a continued relationship with the perpetrator as non-trustworthy and that interactions are marked with communications that cause pain. Low scores (10 or below) may indicate that a person perceives that he or she is able to engage in a relationship with the perpetrator that promotes reasonable care and desires to continue the relationship in the future.

Overt Act of Forgiving

Overt Act of Forgiving is the perceived ability of a person to discuss past relational damage with the perpetrator and resolve issues of responsibility for specific violations to the point where the relationship can be secure and trustworthy. High scores (9 or above) may indicate that a person perceives himself or herself as unable or unsuccessful in discussing and resolving the relational damage. Low scores (7 or below) may indicate that a person perceives him or herself as being successful in overtly discussing the relational damage with the perpetrator and that a greater sense of trust resulted from the discussion.

Add the following together:

Insight *score*	Understanding *score*
7. 2 for Yes, 1 for No	9. 1 for Yes, 2 for No
8. 2 for Yes, 1 for No	13. 2 for Yes, 1 for No
11. 2 for Yes, 1 for No	14. 1 for Yes, 2 for No
16. 1 for Yes, 2 for No	15. 2 for Yes, 1 for No
18. 1 for Yes, 2 for No	20. 1 for Yes, 2 for No
Total:	Total:

Hargrave, T. D., & Williams, G. J. (2006). Developing forgiveness. In K. B. Helmeke & C. F. Sori (Eds.), *The therapist's notebook for integrating spirituality in counseling: Homework, handouts, and activities for use in psychotherapy* (pp. 113-126). Binghamton, NY: The Haworth Press.

FIGURE 9.4.
Scoring of the IRRS *(continued)*

Giving the opportunity for compensation *score*	Overt act of forgiveness *score*
2. 1 for Yes, 2 for No	1. 1 for Yes, 2 for No
3. 1 for Yes, 2 for No	4. 1 for Yes, 2 for No
5. 2 for Yes, 1 for No	12. 1 for Yes, 2 for No
6. 1 for Yes, 2 for No	17. 1 for Yes, 2 for No
10. 1 for Yes, 2 for No	21. 1 for Yes, 2 for No
19. 1 for Yes, 2 for No	Total:
22. 1 for Yes, 2 for No	
Total:	

Scoring of the IRRS

The *Pain Scale* of the IRRS gives an idea of where a person is in the work of forgiveness using Hargrave's model (1994). The subscales are *Shame, Rage, Control, and Chaos.*

Shame

Shame is the degree to which an individual internalizes painful or undesirable experiences. Shame is a global measure that assesses the overall manifestation of personal guilt. High scores (10 or above) may mean the individual is comfortable with mild levels of confrontation and is secure with self. Low scores (8 or below) may indicate that individuals experience excessive guilt and internalize emotions, which indicate self is unacceptable.

Rage

Rage is the degree to which an individual externalizes painful or undesirable experiences. Rage is a global measure that assesses internal feelings of anger and actions, which are manifestations of anger. High scores (10 or above) may indicate that the individual does not express anger in an overt manner. Low scores (9 or below) may indicate that the individual expresses anger and resentment in external ways.

Control

Control is the degree to which an individual seeks to administer life to avoid or deal with situations. Control is a global measure that assesses overall effort in managing life. High scores (7 or above) may reflect a relaxed style of conducting activities and relationships. Low scores (6 or below) may reflect an authoritarian style of dealing with life goals or relationships.

Chaos

Chaos is the degree to which an individual seeks to avoid organization or responsibility in dealing with situations. Chaos is a global measure that assesses overall failure to manage life successfully. High scores (11 or above) may reflect a balanced effort in organizing life goals and being considered responsible. Low scores (9 or below) may reflect an inability to organize and manage life goals and relationships.

Hargrave, T. D., & Williams, G. J. (2006). Developing forgiveness. In K. B. Helmeke & C. F. Sori (Eds.), *The therapist's notebook for integrating spirituality in counseling: Homework, handouts, and activities for use in psychotherapy* (pp. 113-126). Binghamton, NY: The Haworth Press.

FIGURE 9.4.
Scoring of the IRRS *(continued)*

Add the following together:

Shame *score*
24. 1 for Yes, 2 for No
26. 1 for Yes, 2 for No
30. 1 for Yes, 2 for No
33. 1 for Yes, 2 for No
35. 1 for Yes, 2 for No
38. 1 for Yes, 2 for No
Total:

Rage *score*
27. 1 for Yes, 2 for No
31. 1 for Yes, 2 for No
32. 1 for Yes, 2 for No
37. 1 for Yes, 2 for No
39. 1 for Yes, 2 for No
43. 1 for Yes, 2 for No
Total:

Control *score*
28. 1 for Yes, 2 for No
34. 1 for Yes, 2 for No
36. 1 for Yes, 2 for No
44. 1 for Yes, 2 for No
Total:

Chaos *score*
23. 1 for Yes, 2 for No
25. 1 for Yes, 2 for No
29. 2 for Yes, 1 for No
40. 1 for Yes, 2 for No
41. 1 for Yes, 2 for No
42. 2 for Yes, 1 for No
Total:

Hargrave, T. D., & Williams, G. J. (2006). Developing forgiveness. In K. B. Helmeke & C. F. Sori (Eds.), *The therapist's notebook for integrating spirituality in counseling: Homework, handouts, and activities for use in psychotherapy* (pp. 113-126). Binghamton, NY: The Haworth Press.

FIGURE 9.5.
Definitions of the Key Concepts in Hargrave's
Model of Violations of Love and Trust

The following definitions of the concepts from Hargrave's model of violations of love and trust are provided to assist the therapist and client:

Insight: Every damaging violation in relationships is based in a relational transaction. Insight is the ability to recognize transactional patterns that preceded the victimizer violating the victim and giving the victim the power to interrupt or intervene in the patterns or mechanisms to prevent relational damage in the future.

Understanding: Understanding is the ability to identify with the position, limitations, development, efforts, and intent of the person who caused relational damage.

Giving the opportunity for compensation: Giving the opportunity for compensation is the ability to engage in interactions and relationships with the former perpetrator in a way that is perceived by the victim as nonthreatening and builds emotional bonding.

Overt act of forgiving: An overt act of forgiving is the perceived ability of a person to discuss past relational damage with the perpetrator and resolve issues of responsibility for specific violations to the point where the relationship can become secure and trustworthy.

Shame: Shame is the degree to which an individual internalizes painful or undesirable experiences. Shame is a global measure, which assesses the overall manifestation of personal guilt.

Rage: Rage is the degree to which an individual externalizes painful or undesirable experiences. Rage is a global measure, which assesses internal feelings of anger and actions, which are manifestations of anger.

Control: Control is the degree to which an individual seeks to administer life to avoid or deal with situations. Control is a global measure, which assess overall effort in managing life.

Chaos: Chaos is the degree to which an individual seeks to avoid organization or responsibility in dealing with situations. Chaos is a global measure, which assesses overall failure to manage successfully.

Source: Hargrave, T. D., & Sells, J. N. (1997). The development of a forgiveness scale. *Journal of Marital and Family Therapy, 23*(1): 45-46. Used with permission.

Hargrave, T. D., & Williams, G. J. (2006). Developing forgiveness. In K. B. Helmeke & C. F. Sori (Eds.), *The therapist's notebook for integrating spirituality in counseling: Homework, handouts, and activities for use in psychotherapy* (pp. 113-126). Binghamton, NY: The Haworth Press.

SECTION III:
INTEGRATING SPIRITUALITY
IN COUPLES THERAPY

10

Empathic Attunement in Marital Therapy As a Spiritual State: Some Thoughts and Strategies for Its Development

Bernard J. Baca
Shermie L. Schafer
Karen B. Helmeke

Type of Contribution: Activity

Objective

This chapter discusses three empathy-generating skills designed to increase a couple's empathic attunement with each other in therapy, using adaptations from the Imago Relationship Therapy (IRT) Model (Hendrix, 1988). Empathic attunement serves as a major dimension of spiritual connection with another person. We begin by defining empathy, and showing how it differs from compassion and sympathy, as these are often used interchangeably.

Rationale for Use

The Imago Model was developed by Dr. Harville Hendrix in his best-selling book, *Getting the Love You Want: A Guide for Couples* (1988). Hendrix proposes that couples fall in love to heal their childhood wounds, an assertion that is far different from the cultural notion of marriage as "happily ever after." He states that one picks a partner who resembles in both conscious and unconscious ways the psychological characteristics of one's childhood caretakers. Initially, this attraction is positive, but during the couple's power struggle, the positive characteristics are replaced with the more negative characteristics. During this power struggle, the fight to prove who is better or worse is activated by each dyad member. However, neither member of the dyad is viewed as psychologically, emotionally, or intellectually healthier than his or her partner. Through splitting, projection, and introjection, the couple begins to heal their respective childhood woundedness that is activated in their intimate relationship.

Hendrix (H. Hendrix, personal communication, 1992) has suggested that in many respects marriage is essentially a developmental process that mirrors the developmental process that each member of the couple is experiencing. This means that neither member of the dyad is essentially more mature or more infantile than his or her partner. Furthermore, he suggests that marital stress and conflict is a developmental arrest for each partner rooted in their respective childhoods and is a repetition of the childhood developmental arrest. Each adjustment to the arrest, though, is complementary to the adjustments being made to the partner. He also maintains that these developmental arrests are built around defenses to childhood injuries and that in adulthood they are seen as character defenses. Although character defenses are quite immune to change, each member of the couple must change his or her respective character defenses for the relationship to blossom and for childhood injuries to be healed. Hendrix maintains that each member of the couple must provide to the partner the missing nurturing that the partner did not receive. To do so must require each member to extend himself or herself and behave in ways that are not only contradictory to his or her character style or defenses, but they both must do so if the relationship is to work in a healthy fashion. Furthermore, by extending oneself to the other and growing past the character defenses, both partners are changed in the interaction. Finally he suggests that the therapist's role in this process is to facilitate this structural change for each member of the couple.

In IRT (Hendrix, 1988), the therapist uses the dialogue process, or couple's dialogue, as the container (Winnicott, 1986) for the couples to hold each other psychologically to ensure safety and healing within the context of the marital or couple relationship. True dialogue requires the suspension of each partner's projection of the other in an effort to see his or her partner's true self. The original attraction between the couple was based on negative and positive projections that must be replaced with more accurate views of who the actual person is. Couples who are in an emotionally committed exclusive relationship are seeking and longing for this authenticity. The capacity to love and hold the other for no other reason than that the other deserves such treatment is the essence of empathy.

According to IRT (Hendrix, 1988), empathy is the crucial skill that therapists use in working with couples. The purpose of couples therapy is to teach each member how to empathize, to accept and love the other for who he or she is, not who one wants the other to be. The focus of this chapter is on facilitating the development of empathy between a couple through dialogue work. This process of increasing the level of empathy within a couple also serves to increase the spiritual intimacy a couple experiences, as they develop greater empathic communication and connection.

According to H. Hendrix (personal communication, 1996), the existence of a committed exclusive couples relationship is the most significant structure in healing and wholeness. The very process of engaging our partners and experiencing them as the people they are, and not a projection of how we want them to be is, in fact, a spiritual journey of the highest order. It requires incredible levels of self-control, self-awareness, and consciousness of the other. It demands the utmost in understanding, knowledge, and commitment, and it requires constant vigilance by the respective partners. It is exhausting and spiritually challenging work because it requires the suspension of preconceptions of the partner in order to finally see and love the partner as a unique individual and not a carbon copy of ourselves. This is called unconditional love and it is at the heart of spiritual development. It is the "I-Thou process" in action (Buber, 1958). One of the ways that this spiritual process of engaging the other can occur in couples therapy is through deepening the ability of each partner to empathize with the other.

For the purpose of this exercise, it is necessary to be clear about the distinction between empathy on the one hand, and compassion and sympathy on the other. Empathy is "a special mode of perceiving the psychological state or experience of another person. It is an 'emotional knowing' of another human being rather than intellectual understanding" (Berger, 1987, p. 6). When we empathize with someone, we share and experience, at least temporarily, the feelings of the other person, perhaps not to the degree experienced by the other person, but the kind or quality of feelings (Berger, 1987). "Empathy denotes the capacity to know emotionally what another is experiencing from within the frame of reference of that other person" (Berger, 1987, p. 6).

This requires that the person empathizing must suspend his or her judgments and own self-reference in order to begin to be with the experience of the other. Ironically, the attempt of such connection requires the acknowledgment of separation, which is the most basic terror of the infant, who continues to reside, developmentally, in every adult (H. Hendrix, personal communication, 1996). Adults, separated from their caregivers as infants often chronically carry the pain involved in separation anxiety. The consequences of early abandonment may manifest in such ways as giving up (the basis for suicide), avoiding others in an attempt to keep pain at bay (schizoid defense), and/or suffering from anaclitic (chronic, pervasive, and deep) depression (Horner, 1984).

On the other hand, compassion is "a feeling of deep sympathy and sorrow for another who is stricken by misfortune, accompanied by a strong desire to alleviate the suffering" (*Webster's New Universal Unabridged Dictionary,* 1996, p. 416). Sympathy is defined as "harmony of or agreement in feeling, as between persons or on the part of one person with respect to another" (*Webster's New Universal Unabridged Dictionary,* 1996, p. 1926). Although sympathy and compassion both connote a sense of connection with the other, as does empathy, they also appear to include the notion of having to ameliorate the circumstance.

Therein lies the "rub" between empathy and compassion or sympathy. Empathy acknowledges both separation and the capacity to connect. It does not involve the need to change the experience of the other. Although it allows the observer to connect with the other in light of the separation between them, empathy does not require an attempt by one to fix the other person's circumstances. To feel what another feels and to be so deeply heard is often described by people as a profound spiritual experience (as is sometimes stated by clients in IRT who experience empathy).

The significance of the difference between empathy and compassion or sympathy is that the former is an attempt at pure sharing, while the latter suggests some attempt at alleviation of the feeling. In this latter case, attempts at alleviation may ironically exacerbate negative feelings triggered in the experiencing person. That is, if one attempts to alleviate pain in another, that action may only cause the one experiencing the pain to have further pain. For instance, if one's spouse dies, and others attempt to share in the pain by compassion rather than empathy, the following interchange may occur. "I'm so sorry to hear about your husband's death; I know that you will get over it soon." This sympathetic or compassionate connection can be interpreted by the widow in a variety of ways. One is that, despite its superficially benign quality, it is an attempt at denigrating the deceased husband's importance in the widow's life. Another interpretation is that the sender wishes to stifle the widow's heartfelt sadness as a means of alleviating the sender's own pain associated with personal loss. Finally, it can be an indication of the insensitivity of the person who is sympathizing with the widow. Any of these courses cause injury to the receiver. The sender may not intend this, but it is one of the outcomes of such a process. One can readily observe that all these attempts at connection are only a partial approximation of the connection that can be established through intimacy. This can be interpreted as attempts to connect by ameliorating the pain of the situation. In this situation, compassion is devoid of the capacity to "sit with" the pain of the other without having to repair it for oneself. Having to repair someone else's pain for one's own self-satisfaction is an act of true self-absorption. In summary, sympathy and compassion try to "fix the problem"; empathy seeks only to experience the pain without changing it.

Differences between the partners make it more difficult for couples to empathize with each other. Couples tend to form polarities based on their personalities. Each partner attempts to complete the self through the other. Individuals look to find someone who represents both similar and different aspects of one's self (Baca, 1997). It is as though each of us is a half and becomes involved with an "other" to make a whole. Over time, the differences between partners are accentuated simply because their characteristics are not ours, and as a result, polarization and envy occur. As Baca (1997) says,

> When partners in a committed exclusive relationship are in the midst of the power struggle, the basis of their conflict is envy. One partner, due to the denied, lost, and disowned aspects

of the self, perceives the other as inherently better (or worse) than the self. The projection of one partner's own lack onto the other is envy. (p. 16)

Hendrix (1988) uses the terms *maximizer* or *pursuer* to refer to the partner who expands the energy in the relationship, and the terms *minimizer* or *distancer* to refer to the partner who withholds the energy in a relationship.

In the evolution of marriage based on mutual attraction, each partner carries the denied and disowned parts of the self that are split-off, projected, then introjected (through projective and introjective identification) by the other. This usually occurs at an unconscious level and repeats the process that occurred at the hands of each partner's childhood caregivers. As Mason (1997, p. 34) states:

> The potential power of the committed relationship is dramatically and qualitatively different from that of other relationships. Especially when the interaction between two individuals generates romance, individual functioning becomes as much a function of the relationship as the relationship becomes a function of the individuals who are in it.

According to Mason (1997), this mutuality and interdependency is the height of intersubjective experience. Furthermore, the quality of the relationship when it is positive actually energizes the individuals in the relationship, and when it is negative, the individuals de-energize. Mason continues, "empathic breaks and disconnection lead to the self's enfeeblement and fragmentation" (p. 38).

The degree of empathic ability is dependent upon the degree of empathic connection the adult experienced as a child between the child and his or her childhood caregivers. This means that the more an infant, toddler, or child is mirrored by his or her caregivers, the greater the degree of empathic attunement this child achieves, which results in true empathic connection with others as an adult. The reverse is also true and is the basis of character defenses, which are developed to protect the wounded self (H. Hendrix, personal communication, 1996). Consequently, the less empathic attunement the child experienced at the hands of his or her childhood caregiver, the more self-absorbed he or she will become. The power struggle in adult relationships mirrors this self-absorption. The relationship problems (dependent on the amount or lack of childhood empathy) actually trigger the emotional wounds received by each partner in their respective childhoods.

The solution to this power struggle is quite simple. To be heard by one's partner, one must extend oneself in an empathic way to hear the other—to the very person that appears to the self to be the cause of the pain in the first place! That is why marital or couples therapy is so difficult. As therapists, we are asking the partner who firmly believes that his or her partner is the very source of his or her pain to forgo this perception. Simultaneously, we are asking that same partner the almost impossible: to empathize with the other, the perceived source of the pain! As if this was not enough of a challenge, we expect the same of the other partner. To suggest that this is a monumental task is an understatement (H. Hendrix, personal communication, 1996).

This mix of human relational needs and desires is the inherent and paradoxical dilemma for human beings. The paradox is whether one risks the pain of relationship or settles for the pain of loneliness. As Berger (1987, p. 12) states, "Paradox is inherent in the infant's first steps away from the mother: the tension between the drive towards autonomy and change on the one hand and the yearning for repetition and sameness on the other."

What makes the empathic moment viable is that both partners share the same "woundedness" from childhood; they differ only in their coping with the injury. Ironically, it is this sameness of woundedness that triggers the fear of empathic attunement between partners. Through splitting, projection and projective identification (and the subsequent introjection), the partner fears exactly that which is mirrored through the other. Despite their fears, however, when both partners are able to risk the pain of relationship, they find a connection in being able to empathize with each other. The actual process of empathizing with each other in itself is spiritual intimacy, because in so doing, one is nurturing the other as much as one nurtures the self. The therapist has the privilege of joining this sacred process by facilitating such spiritual intimacy and connectedness.

Instructions

Although we believe that creating empathy by using IRT (Hendrix, 1988), is itself a way of living, rather than a set of therapeutic techniques, a number of empathy-generating skills can enhance the empathic connection between two partners and bring about healing and wholeness in the relationship. Thus healing and wholeness experienced by giving and receiving empathy in turn deepens the spiritual development of the couple. Three particular empathy-generating skills, which are adapted from similar skills found in IRT (Hendrix), are discussed in the following text: blocking projections of the sender, asking probing questions of the sender and the receiver, and predicting future failures.

Blocking Projections of the Sender

In the beginning of couples therapy, the therapist's focus is on helping the clients by reducing and eliminating their personal projections toward each other that interfere with empathic connection with their partner. The first technique of blocking projections begins at any point the speaker (referred to as the sender or sending partner) makes some comment about his or her partner (referred to as the receiver or receiving partner). This is usually expressed in a pejorative or negative fashion, such as a wife exclaiming, "Every time I come home, the house is a complete mess. He was home all day and was just too lazy to clean anything up. I have to do all of it, even though I have worked all day long." The therapist first has the receiver mirror what the sender just said (Hendrix, 1988), and then asks the sender to wonder aloud how the other partner is likely to have experienced what the sending partner just said. The sender is encouraged to view the receiver's reactions using the sender's knowledge of the receiver's childhood history. The therapist helps the sending partner to take into consideration the receiving partner's childhood wounds that might be activated by the sender's comments, coaching the sender if need be. Sometimes it is necessary, when the sender is unable to do this, for the therapist to rehearse out loud the receiver's childhood history (based on data from the intake and information gathered in previous sessions), and then ask the sender to extrapolate from this information to see how the receiver might be re-injured by the sender's message as he or she was in childhood. Next, the therapist asks the sender to imagine his or her partner as a young child, say between four to six years old, what he or she looked like at that age, and what he or she might feel with this same hurt. This exercise enagles the sender to imagine the child within his or her partner, which in turn can help the sender to access his or her own similar childhood wounding. Next, the therapist asks the sender what it was like to think of his or her partner as a small child. The sender usually verbalizes having feelings of sadness, pain, love, or some other emotionally charged, but softer, response toward this partner when viewing the partner as a child. This exercise enables the sender to block his or her projections, and to remain more open to experiencing the receiver as he or she is. This process itself helps the sender to access his or her own disowned, lost parts.

Using Probing Questions of the Sender and Receiver

In conjunction with blocking projections, another technique, which is also adapted from the skill of couples dialogue used in IRT (Hendrix, 1988), is used to generate empathy between a couple. The point of this technique is to move both partners away from self-absorption and to begin to hold the other, to connect emotionally with the other person. In this technique, the therapist asks the sender and the receiver probing questions that evoke greater details about an issue brought up by the sender, in an effort to allow the receiving partner to have greater understanding and empathy for the sender. This technique is the counterpart to the technique of blocking projections of the sender.

First, the therapist asks the receiver to mirror the sender's message (Hendrix, 1988). After the receiver mirrors the statement and asks the sender, "Is there more?" the therapist asks the sender to provide more details about the issue to the receiver, who can then begin to understand in greater depth what the sender is saying. So, for example, in response to the sender talking about being angry at coming home to an unkempt house, and feeling overwhelmed at all of the responsibility, the therapist could ask the sender such questions as "Has there been another time in your life, before your partner, in which your requests or needs were either ignored or deemed unimportant from your perspective?" The purpose of this question is to stimulate the sender's memories of childhood and to reflect on how the current hurt simulates the hurt felt as a child. Similar questions can be posed to the receiver to see if the receiver can make connections to the sender's past and thus account for why the sender might feel a certain way. Both the questions to the sender and to the receiver serve to help the receiving partner feel more empathy to the little child who was hurt (both in the partner and in self). If the sender or receiver needs prompting, the therapist can follow up with a question to either the sender, such as "What about in childhood, with your parents, either your mother or your father or both?" or to the receiver, such as "Can you think of some time in your partner's childhood when she might have had her needs ignored?" In response to this question, the sender will often say something like, "Yes, when I was twelve years old, I remember having to ask my sister to help, but she would ignore me and Mother would get mad at me if it wasn't done. So I always felt that it was on my shoulders to do what had to be done, and I couldn't rely on anyone else to help."

The result of this interaction is that the sender, the woman in this case, began to understand the source of her frustration and that it had little to do with her husband. She understood that she was projecting her "younger and lazier" sister onto her husband's "person" and moreover, she became the scolding mother. This realization that she was more like her mother than she ever realized had some profound implications for her relationship with her husband. On that same note, her husband began to understand that he was not the source of her pain, so the defensiveness that was based on his childhood psychosocial injuries diminished. He did not have to feel blamed and attacked, nor blaming or attacking, but could begin to accept his wife for who she is, not for who he wanted her to be.

As just alluded to, the result of this process of asking probing questions also produces several effects on the receiver: a greater empathic understanding of the injury sustained by the receiver's partner in childhood, increased recognition of how the receiver's own behavior may "trigger" that pain in the sender, an understanding of how the receiver himself or herself was injured in similar ways, and a deepened spiritual love of the "other." Empathic development heightens spiritual intimacy because the other begins to love and accepts one's partner as much as oneself.

Predicting Future Failures

After the first two empathy-generating techniques are used, partners begin to recognize some of their own self-destructive behaviors and have begun to soften toward the partner. At this point, when therapy is progressing well, a third skill is used, that of predicting future failures on the part of both partners. When things are going well, the therapist asks how the couple might sabotage their relationship in the future. Such a paradoxical question hints at the dual terror faced by most clients, the fear of not changing and the fear of changing, the terror at the thought that their relationships will not change, and the terror of the unknown if their relationships do change. By using such a paradoxical question, the therapist allows the couple to explore the dynamics that might keep them from maintaining their newfound spiritual intimacy. The therapist invites both partners to think about what each might do that would undercut their progress as a couple by asking a question such as, "Things are going so well. You have both worked so hard to understand each other and yourself. But sometimes, even when it is a change that a couple desperately wants, it can be terrifying to have this new kind of relationship, one that you are not used to. As a result, some couples find ways to mess things up. I'm curious. If that were to happen to you, how are each of you most likely to mess up your part?" Such questions help to reveal and normalize each partner's very human fallibility, with the goal being for partners to grant themselves greater self-acceptance, even of their mistakes. Increasing empathic attunement is not just about empathizing and understanding the other; it is about giving that same empathy and acceptance to oneself as well. It is about becoming tender to oneself, even in the face of one's shortcomings. Once more, this work takes a couple into the realm of spirituality and learning to love others and self.

Brief Vignette

The following case history exemplifies the three intervention strategies of enhancing empathy to create true love or "real love," as Hendrix (1988) would name it. Robert, age fifty-two, has been married to Mary, age fifty-one, for twenty years. Each had been married previously; Robert has a son, age thirty, and Mary has no children from her first marriage. Robert's first marriage ended after his first wife had a number of affairs, which left him some doubts about his son's paternity. Mary was married when she was eighteen, but divorced at twenty when she discovered her ex-husband's infidelity with her best friend from high school. The couple has a seventeen-year-old son and a ten-year-old daughter.

In the first session, Robert described how Mary was making him feel inadequate when he did things around the house. He felt that whenever he did any tasks that she requested, she either redid them or told him that he needed to do something else in addition. Mary's response to him triggered intense feelings of shame in Robert. The therapist asked the sending partner, Robert, to imagine why his wife would react in such a way. He began his explanation by projecting the reasons why he would do such a thing if he was in his wife's position. At this point, the therapist asked Robert to explore any other reasons why this could occur for his wife, given her situation and background. When he was unable to do so, the therapist suggested that perhaps the reason for this behavior had something to do with Mary's background. The therapist asked him to reflect upon her childhood and how she felt when her brother seemed to be her parents' favorite and was treated as a prince, and how she felt that she was always a distant second, at best. No matter what she did or what she accomplished, she never felt recognized in her family. Indeed she felt that she "gave up in high school" and married her first boyfriend after getting pregnant with him immediately after high school graduation. He then asked Robert to picture Mary as a five-year-old, and to picture what she looked like. Next he instructed Robert to think about what it would be like for this five-year-old to feel so overlooked and ignored.

At this point, Robert, the husband, began to understand what might account for Mary's behavior and further realized that it had nothing to do with him or his negative attribution of her motivation. Robert began to understand that his wife was "triggered" by her childhood experiences that she projected onto her current relationship with her husband. This exchange was the beginning of the empathic connection between the two.

Next, the therapist used a series of probing questions to both Robert and Mary. First, the therapist focused on Mary, the receiver, and her reactions to Robert's claims that she was never content with what he did. He first asked Mary to mirror what she heard Robert say. Then he asked her a number of probing questions to try to increase her empathic understanding of Robert. The therapist asked Mary why this might be such an important issue for Robert, given what Mary knew of his background. He asked her, "Without blaming Robert, can you think of a reason that Robert would send his message to you in the way he did?" The therapist then asked Robert if he had ever had these same feelings when he was growing up in his family. After some additional probing, Robert reported feeling that, no matter what he did, his father often belittled him. Slowly, after a number of sessions of similar work, both Robert and Mary realized that the other was not a projection of self, and they began to hear and see each other for whom he or she really is, and to understand how he or she had selected this person who so complemented his or her own woundedness.

Before termination, the therapist asked the couple to think about what each had learned about self and each other, and how good it felt for them to feel so connected to each other. The therapist also discussed the ironic juxtaposition of two separate sets of feelings that many couples experience at this stage of therapy. The therapist talked about the terror of not changing, which they had begun to overcome, and the terror of changing, which they might experience in the coming months. The therapist explained how some couples, in dealing with this latter terror, sometimes did things to sabotage their progress. He asked the following question, "Robert and Mary, if you wanted to really mess up your relationship, what would each of you need to be sure to do?" Although they laughed at such a question, they each listed a number of behaviors. This effort to predict what might cause future failures between them helped to cement the growth they had experienced, and to underline what each of them would need to do and not do in order to develop even greater intimacy and empathy.

Suggestions for Follow-Up

Since this work of helping couples to achieve empathic attunement is not something that is meant to be accomplished in one session, but is work that will continue throughout therapy and the couple's future, no specific guidelines are presented for follow-up. Rather, the therapist is encouraged to remember that learning empathy toward others and self is a way of living in which each partner constantly strives to extend self through unconditional acceptance and giving.

Contraindications

Any counselor attempting to use the techniques described in this chapter is advised to become familiar with the IRT model before proceeding. Training to become a certified Imago Relationship Therapist is available and this training is also recommended. Please see www. imagorelationships.org for these training opportunities.

References

Baca, B. J. (1997). Envy's manifestation in individuals and couples: Implications for Imago Therapy. *Journal of Imago Relationship Therapy, 2*(2), 13-22.

Buber, M. (1958). *I and thou* (2nd ed.). New York: Charles Scribner's Sons.

Berger, D. M. (1987). *Clinical empathy.* Northvale, NJ: Jason Aronson.

Hendrix, H. (1988). *Getting the love you want: A guide for couples.* New York: Harper Perennial.
Horner, A. (1984). *Object relations and the developing ego in therapy.* New York: Jason Aronson.
Mason, R. (1997). Imago: A theory and therapy of connectivity. *Journal of Imago Relationship Therapy, 2*(1), 33-45.
Webster's new universal unabridged dictionary (1996). New York: Random House Value Publishing, Inc.
Winnicott, D. W. (1986). *Holding and interpretation.* New York: Grove Press.
www.imagorelationships.org.

Professional Readings and Resources

Hendrix, H. (1988). *Getting the love you want: The guide for couples.* New York: Harper Perennial.
Luquet, W. (1996). *Short-term couples therapy: The Imago Model in action.* New York: Brunner-Routledge.
Luquet, W., & Hannah, M. (1998). *Healing in the relational paradigm: The Imago Relationship Therapy casebook.* Philadelphia: Taylor and Francis.
www.imagorelationships.org.

Bibliotherapy Sources for the Client

Hendrix, H. (1988). *Getting the love you want: A guide for couples.* New York: Harper Perennial.
Hendrix, H., & Hunt, H. L. (2003). *Getting the love you want workbook: The new couples' study guide.* New York: Pocket Books.
www.imagorelationships.org.

11

Developing a Couples Mission Statement: A Resource for Couples Facing Career Decisions/Transitions

Rand Michael

Type of Contribution: Homework, Handouts

Objective

This chapter describes homework activities for enhancing marital and family life cycle transitions, and/or exploring faith and faith resources in situational crises or transitions. The purpose of this activity is to facilitate a principle-centered and mission-driven orientation to decision-making for couples faced with career decisions. (Note: This intervention is applicable in many situations, not just when being faced with a career decision.)

Rationale for Use

It is assumed that for decisions to be effective, they need to be purpose- or mission-driven and not just expedient and/or reactionary. One's work, occupation, or career significantly engages a person's time, energy, gifts, and abilities. It is assumed that one's work, occupation, or career has a profound impact on significant others in one's life. Thus, it is argued that one's work, career, or occupation is inextricably related to spirituality—to the understanding and carrying out of one's purpose in life. It is argued that career or work decisions and transitions are made most wisely and effectively when those decisions are rooted in and grow out of a person's life mission.

When in the course of therapy it becomes evident that a client is faced with a career decision, some type of intervention is indicated that is relevant to the situation being faced by the client. Sometimes a client will present for counseling with the express purpose of addressing a career issue. At other times, the career decision emerges in the course of therapy. The client already may have been faced with the career decision but presented for counseling to address another issue, without realizing that the career decision had relevance. At other times, it may be that during the course of therapy, a client is faced with a career decision that had not previously presented itself.

It is not unusual for couples to be faced with difficult career choices in which the desires and needs of the partners are in conflict—one partner being faced with whether to accept a promotion and/or relocation that will significantly impact both partners, perhaps even adversely. Although such opportunities are typically presented to only one partner, because of the nature of relationships, both partners are significantly and sometimes profoundly affected. Thus, rather than deal with only the partner whose organization is presenting the opportunity, it is recommended that the couple be engaged conjointly. It is also recommended that rather than begin with a decision-making tool, the couple begin with writing a mission statement so that the decision-making process is undertaken in light of, grounded in, and guided by the mission statement. If the couple has already written a mission statement, then that statement can be revisited, explored, and, if need be, revised. It is assumed that purpose and meaning are core values for the partners and the relationship and that purpose and meaning are inescapably spiritual. Further, it is assumed that career transitions and changes are significant times of transition and change for both partners and their relationship and that spiritually grounded interventions are particularly germane.

Does a person or couple need to be consciously spiritual in order for this mission-statement intervention to be used? The simple answer: no. It is assumed that whatever a person's spiritual awareness and orientation or even if a person declares himself or herself not to be spiritual, all persons are meaning-makers and dealing with meaning is a central task of the therapeutic process (Carlsen, 1988).

Instructions

The therapist needs to familiarize himself or herself with the basic literature and resources on developing personal and family mission statements as well as therapeutic literature on purpose, meaning, and coping. Of particular use are the resources by Stephen R. Covey. The resources come in two forms, all titled "How to Develop a Family Mission Statement": (1) in Covey's book titled *The 7 Habits of Highly Effective Families* (1997, pp. 70-112); (2) in a resource packet that combines two audio cassettes package and a learning guide (Covey, 1996). The book and the audio cassette with the learning guide are available from FranklinCovey.

When in the clinician's judgment a decision-making process is indicated due to the client or clients' being faced with a career choice, she or he can introduce not only a decision-making model but also raise the question about life purpose and meaning. The idea is to "begin with the end in mind" (Covey, 1997, p. 71). If a therapist is working with an individual client who is in a marriage or a serious relationship, then it is assumed that the partner will be significantly affected by the decision. Thus, the client is to be approached regarding what the partner has been told, what conversation has occurred between them about the decision, and what is the client's understanding about the partner's thoughts, feelings, and wants regarding the decision. It is recommended that the partner joins the counseling process in order to explore conjointly the decision and its implications.

The therapist helps the clients see the connection between life purpose and one's career, including the many decisions that comprise the pursuit of one's career. The counselor explains the nature and purpose of mission statements and how any decision is better made by grounding that decision not just in immediate pragmatics and preferences but in one's long-term life-purpose— mission. Unless a client is single, it is recommended that the therapist facilitate a process in which each person considers his or her own mission as well as the couple's considering their joint mission. Mission statements act as both vision of life's destination as well as a compass to keep the individuals and the couple on course (Covey, 1997).

Help the clients understand that whether they have articulated their mission or purpose, they live it each day. The purpose of a mission statement is to carefully consider one's purpose and to clearly articulate it so that decisions and actions are considered and made in light of the mission rather than the immediacy of the moment.

The therapist then explains that writing a mission statement is a process that takes time, and that it will be done outside of session with the work being brought back into session for discussion, clarification, and modification as needed or warranted. If the couple agrees that the process would be useful and germane, then the therapist can recommend a resource for guiding the process—either the section from Covey's *The 7 Habits of Highly Effective Families* or the audio cassette and booklet package is recommended.

According to Covey (1996), three steps are involved in developing a couple/family mission statement, as follows:

1. Exploring what your couple unit/marriage is all about in terms of vision and purpose
2. Writing the Couples Mission Statement
3. Periodically reviewing and readjusting the mission statement

The instructions for the three steps are as follows:

Step 1: Explore What Your Couple Unit/Marriage Is All About in Terms of Vision and Purpose

The couple explores vision and purpose by discussing key questions. In addition to the many useful questions to be found in the Covey resources, additional questions listed in the handout at the end of the chapter are very useful as well. Both this list of questions and a sample couple mission statement may be found at the end of the chapter and used as handouts. In addition, the couple may generate some questions of their own. Ground rules for this process are useful and can help the couple work collaboratively. The therapist can ask the couple to generate a set of basic ground rules for the process such as listening respectively and restating the partner's ideas (rather than reacting to them). The couple should write down all information generated. It can be useful to tape record as well.

- What is our purpose as a couple?
- What are we as a couple about in life?
- What is our identity as a couple?
- What kind of couple life do we want?
- To what kind of home do we want to invite friends?
- What is embarrassing for each partner?
- What makes each partner feel comfortable at home?
- What makes each partner feel uncomfortable?
- What things are truly important to us as a couple?
- What are our values?
- What are our highest priority goals?
- What are the gifts, talents, interests, and abilities of each partner? Of us as a couple?
- What legacy do we want to leave? What do we want others to remember us for?

Step 2: Write the Couple's Mission Statement

It is helpful to have the couple envision a particularly significant wedding anniversary in the future, e.g., twenty-fifth, thirtieth, fortieth, fiftieth. The mission statement itself has four parts, an articulation of

- the desired characteristics of the marriage,
- the impact the couple hopes to have on others,
- the couple's life purpose, and
- the couple's source for life and living and fulfilling their mission.

A good family mission statement:

1. is written as if it is timeless;
2. considers both ends and means;
3. deals with the four basic needs: to live, to love, to learn, to leave a legacy; and
4. addresses roles and relationship dynamics (Covey, 1996).

Step 3: Periodically Reviewing and Readjusting

From time to time, it is important for the couple to review their mission statement and how they are or are not fulfilling it so they can affirm their embodiment of the statement and adjust areas of their lives that need to be brought into line with the statement. It is also possible that the mission statement itself might need to be modified as the couple encounters the challenges of life and continue to mature.

Brief Vignette

Travis and Shelley Miller presented as a couple who were at an impasse in regard to their careers. Since their wedding, they had been working on growing and developing their relationship, emphasizing their communication and conflict management skills. However, being faced with the impasse they decided to see the counselor with whom they had done pre- and neomarital counseling.

The situation: both loved their jobs and were supportive of each other's careers. Travis worked for a national company; advancement meant periodic geographical moves around the United States. Shelley worked for a small private college in student development and leadership. Although it might be possible for her to find equivalent employment in the city to which Travis was asked to transfer, it was not likely since such jobs are not plentiful. In addition, Shelley especially appreciated the atmosphere, culture, and community of persons with whom she currently worked. Part of the dilemma was that Travis's income was more than double that of Shelley's. In addition, Shelley was thirty; she and Travis were considering starting their family but Shelley wanted to continue her employment that allowed some flexibility.

As part of the premarital counseling process, the role and significance of spirituality and religion in their lives was discussed at some length. Travis and Shelley's individual as well as couple approaches to life were characterized by what Anderson and Worthen (1997) call spirituality—"a fourth dimension of human experience"—the other three being time, space, and story. Each traditional approach to therapy tends to focus on one of the three, yet in order to consider the whole person, spirituality needs attention as well. Human beings have "an innate yearning for connection with this Divine Being" (Anderson & Worthen, 1997, p. 4) and it is this fourth dimension that orients the other three. Spirituality is the engagement in the quest to love one another more freely and maturely and to live life with a purpose that transcends time and space. Time and space become the dimensions through which transcendence is expressed concretely and temporally, adding depth, purpose, and greater vitality (Anderson & Worthen, 1997).

What Travis and Shelley presented did not fit the American Psychiatric Association's *Diagnostic and Statistical Manual of Mental Disorders* Fourth Edition, Text Revision (2000) V62.89 Religious or Spiritual Problem category. Rather, due to Travis and Shelley's life orientation and value system, their presenting concern fit into either one of two of Kelly's (1995, pp. 142-153) typology of presenting problems and spirituality: either (1) a nonspiritual/nonreligious issue or problem with *a significant spiritual/religious component* or (2) such a problem with *a potential connection* with the spiritual or religious. Although it was possible that it could be an issue with little or no spiritual or religious connection, the therapist doubted that from the prior sessions with the couple. In addition, it did not seem to fit Kelly's fourth typology, which is an issue or problem that is predominantly spiritual or religious.

The therapist inquired about the relationship between the decision and their spiritual life and values. The couple spoke at length. As a result of that dialogue, the counselor suggested for the couple's consideration that if they had not developed a couple mission statement then that might be the place to begin so that the decision could be purpose-centered and driven and not just expedient. The couple agreed that this strategy made sense to them. The therapist requested they secure a copy of Stephen R. Covey's (1996) audiotape and workbook resource titled *How to Develop a Family Mission Statement.*

Shelley and Travis brought the initial draft of their couple mission statement to the next session. They seemed both positively energized and also more relaxed. This second session consisted of their sharing their initial statement with the therapist and an exploration of how their "fourth dimension"—their spirituality—was a resource for them, both in terms of the content of the statement as well as the manner in which they engaged in developing the statement. They reported their growing awareness of their incongruency at times between what they profess as their mission and what they actually practice. The therapist explored that incongruency and how they might take steps to modify it so their actual manner of communicating and relating was congruent with their affirmation of the spiritual basis of life and of their mission as individuals and as a couple.

The next step was twofold: They were to begin to put their mission statement in a more finished, polished form and were to be thinking about the career decision they would soon need to make. They returned to the third appointment with an articulation of their mission statement. Travis and Shelley's mission statement reflects their own intentional grounding in the Christian faith. However, the process of developing a mission statement and the utilization of it in times of decision making are applicable to persons and couples of all faith orientations and, as indicated earlier, even with persons who are not interested in spirituality per se. Their statement follows.

Miller Mission Statement

Our mission is to establish a close-knit family where we love and honor each other in all things and at all times. Our highest goal is to individually pursue Christ through a growing personal relationship with Him. As a family we will read scripture, share with each other, and pray together. We will pursue deep, meaningful friendships with other family members and friends where we are giving and receiving love and support.

We will be part of a local church body, serving where we can and using the gifts God has given each of us.

Our desire is to strive for excellence in all that we choose to give ourselves to: family, relationships, work, and education.

We want to create a home where others feel welcome and comfortable. Our home is a safe haven and retreat from our daily activities where we can share openly and experience unconditional love and acceptance.

We recognize and appreciate each other's strengths and abilities. We protect each other's growing edges by supporting, honoring, and safeguarding each other. As individuals, we will guard against envy and jealousy of others and be content with who we are while making the most of our strengths, gifts, and talents.

Our desired outcome for living out this mission day to day is to leave a legacy of honor and integrity and service, so that all who really know us will see us as a good, loving, and caring family.

Their signatures appeared at the end of the statement.

The therapist affirmed their work and asked them if they were ready to move on to the decision-making process. They indicated they were. The counselor shared a basic decision-making tool with them and described how it could be used now with its roots and reference point being the mission statement. The couple not only indicated they understood but were relieved to have the mission statement as the point of reference and grounding.

After the explanation of the process, the between-sessions assignment was given: to work through the decision-making process, grounding it in the mission statement. They returned having completed the assignment in detail and having talked much, especially in light of their mission statement. Travis had decided that although electing not to move would keep his income from increasing other than cost-of-living raises, he saw more clearly how turning down the move and staying where he was was a way to clearly, intentionally, and pragmatically live out their mission statement. Shelley had come to the place that she was willing to resign her job and move, if that would be in concert with their mission statement, although she still had concerns about her own career and how much more demanding and time-consuming Travis's job would be if they accepted the move. The latter part of the session focused on what they would actually do; they decided Travis would elect not to move but to stay at his current location and rate of pay. They both looked relieved and satisfied although they were also realistic that their decision had significant implications, ones that would require ongoing conversation between them and possible consultation with the therapist from time to time. In light of their mission statement, grounded in their spirituality as the fourth dimension, they embraced as an adventure their decision and where it would lead them.

Within two weeks of their work on the career impasse, the offer was made to Travis for advancement and with it the move to another city. He turned it down. His colleagues did not understand. The company culture was not punitive; it was acceptable that he turned it down. His decision was just not comprehensible to the company and his colleagues. In the process of discussion, he shared his mission statement, with extended discussion around excellence—with family, relationships, work, and education.

Suggestions for Follow-Up

Although Shelley and Travis seemed to come to a clear decision and with definite resolve, because of the nature of the decision and its implications, it seems it would be useful to have at least one follow-up session, if not a series of them over a period of time, for further guidance, encouragement, refocusing, and renegotiating. Life, careers, hopes, expectations, and situations are not static but dynamic and need to be revisited periodically. The therapist needs to be careful not to present follow-up as a message about the couple's competency or to create a dependency. Rather, it would probably be wiser and more useful to present it as a checkup and maintenance and/or further coaching session.

Contraindications

The strategy of developing a mission statement has few contraindications. Such an intervention is useful for all persons, couples, and families regardless of race, creed, gender, or culture. However, the form, timing, and use need to be carefully considered and adapted. Although this intervention cannot be used with all clients, it is an intervention that could be productively used with many or most clients.

References

American Psychiatric Association. (2000). *Diagnostic and statistical manual of mental disorders* (4th ed.), Text revision. Washington, DC: Author.

Anderson, D. A., & Worthen, D. (1997). Exploring a fourth dimension: Spirituality as a resource for the couple therapist. *Journal of Marriage & Family Therapy, 23,* 3-12.

Carlsen, M. B. (1988). *Meaning-making: Therapeutic processes in adult development.* New York: W.W. Norton.

Covey, S. R. (1996). *How to develop a family mission statement.* (Audio cassette and learning guide). Provo, UT: FranklinCovey.

Covey, S. R. (1997). *The 7 habits of highly effective families.* New York: FranklinCovey.

Kelly, Eugene W. (1995) *Spirituality and religion in counseling and psychotherapy: Diversity in theory and practice.* Alexandria, VA: ACA (pp. 142-153).

Professional Readings & Resources

Anderson, D. A., & Worthen, D. (1997). Exploring a fourth dimension: Spirituality as a resource for the couple therapist. *Journal of Marriage & Family Therapy, 23,* 3-12.

Carlsen, M. B. (1988). *Meaning-making: Therapeutic processes in adult development.* New York: W.W. Norton.

Covey, S. R. (1996). *How to develop a family mission statement.* (Audio cassette and learning guide). Provo, UT: FranklinCovey.

Covey, S. R. (1997). *The 7 habits of highly effective families.* New York: FranklinCovey.

Covey, S. R. (1989). *The 7 habits of highly effective people: Restoring the character ethic.* New York: Simon and Schuster.

Emmons, R. A. (1999). *The psychology of ultimate concerns: Motivation and spirituality in personality.* New York: Guilford Press.

Jones, L. B. (1996). *The path: Creating your mission statement for work and for life.* New York: Hyperion.

Kelly, Eugene W. (1995) *Spirituality and religion in counseling and psychotherapy: Diversity in theory and practice.* Alexandria, VA: ACA (pp. 142-153).

Pargament, K. I. (1997). *The psychology of religion and coping: Theory, research, practice.* New York: Guilford Press.

Bibliotherapy Sources for the Client

Covey, S. R. (1996). *How to develop a family mission statement.* (Audio cassette and learning guide). Provo, UT: FranklinCovey.

Covey, S. R. (1997). *The 7 habits of highly effective families.* New York: FranklinCovey.

Jones, L. B. (1996). *The path: Creating your mission statement for work and for life.* New York: Hyperion.

Handout One:
Questions to Help Couples Develop a Vision and Mission Statement

- What is our purpose as a couple?
- What are we as a couple about in life?
- What is our identity as a couple?
- What kind of couple life do we want?
- To what kind of home do we want to invite friends?
- What is embarrassing for each partner?
- What makes each partner feel comfortable at home?
- What makes each partner feel uncomfortable?
- What things are truly important to us as a couple?
- What are our values?
- What are our highest priority goals?
- What are the gifts, talents, interests, and abilities of each partner? Of us as a couple?
- What legacy do we want to leave? What do we want others to remember us for?

Rand, M. (2006). Developing a couples mission statement: A resource for couples facing career decisions/transitions. In K. B. Helmeke & C. F. Sori (Eds.), *The therapist's notebook for integrating spirituality in counseling: Homework, handouts, and activities for use in psychotherapy* (pp. 139-147). Binghamton, NY: The Haworth Press.

Handout Two:
Sample Couples Mission Statement

Our mission is to establish a close-knit family where we love and honor each other in all things and at all times. Our highest goal is to individually pursue Christ through a growing personal relationship with Him. As a family we will read scripture, share with each other, and pray together. We will pursue deep, meaningful friendships with other family members and friends where we are giving and receiving love and support.

We will be part of a local church body, serving where we can and using the gifts God has given each of us.

Our desire is to strive for excellence in all that we choose to give ourselves to: family, relationships, work, and education.

We want to create a home where others feel welcome and comfortable. Our home is a safe haven and retreat from our daily activities where we can share openly and experience unconditional love and acceptance.

We recognize and appreciate each other's strengths and abilities. We protect each other's growing edges by supporting, and honoring and safe guarding one another. As individuals, we will guard against envy and jealousy of others and be content with who we are while making the most of our strengths, gifts, and talents.

Our desired outcome for living out this mission day to day is to leave a legacy of honor and integrity and service, so that all who really know us will see us as a good, loving, and caring family.

Rand, M. (2006). Developing a couples mission statement: A resource for couples facing career decisions/transitions. In K. B. Helmeke & C. F. Sori (Eds.), *The therapist's notebook for integrating spirituality in counseling: Homework, handouts, and activities for use in psychotherapy* (pp.139-147). Binghamton, NY: The Haworth Press.

12

WWJD: Using a Couple's Faith to Fall Back in Love

Philip M. Mamalakis

Type of Contribution: Activity

Objective

Many, if not all, of the couples who come to therapy share that they have fallen out of love with each other. Their absence of love is often accompanied by a sense of hopelessness and is fueled by their contempt for each other and the critical nature of their interactions. If the therapist helps the couple to communicate clearly and effectively, the therapist can be left with two individuals who clearly communicate how much they do not love each other anymore. This chapter presents an activity, or question, to use with couples who identify that they struggle with how to respond to the annoying or challenging characteristics of the other person. The objectives to asking clients, "What would Jesus do (WWJD)?" are as follows:

> To shift the pattern of interaction of a couple from attacking each other to cooperating and coping together
> To shift the emotional state of a couple from defensiveness and emotional distance to mutual vulnerability and intimacy
> To shift the focus of therapy toward taking responsibility for negative interactions and affect
> To situate couples therapy within a couple's marital vows
> To access a couple's faith as a resource in resolving marital disputes or destructive marital interactions
> To deconstruct and redefine a couple's understanding of marital love

Rationale for Use

Couples who finally make use of couples therapy are typically stuck in negative patterns of interacting, negative perceptions of each other, and strong negative affect. All too often, after the therapist has helped a couple to identify their negative communication patterns and their areas of conflict, what becomes apparent is that they have very little respect for each other. They are annoyed by each other or have little tolerance for some characteristics or behaviors in the other person. This can be particularly challenging when one person is annoyed at some permanent personality trait or tendency in the other person. Although a therapist can reduce the hostility between two people by interrupting negative communication patterns, this does not, in itself, build intimacy or offer a path toward intimacy. Clients can feel stuck in negative affect toward each other and often do their best to convince the therapist that the solution is to change the other person. Learning to communicate can exacerbate this sense of "stuckness." In fact, effective communication can enhance a couple's ability to communicate just how much they dislike things about the other. Learning to communicate cannot change what annoys us about our spouse. The directive to accept the other's shortcomings or habits can feel simplistic when the difficulties are numerous and deep.

Most couples in Western culture exchange marital vows in their wedding ceremony. Typically included within these vows is the commitment to love the other person. For couples that accept the biblical record and ascribe to the historical Christian understanding of Jesus, he is the model of love. In fact, those who uphold the divine nature of Christ and who believe that God is love would acknowledge that all Jesus' actions are executed out of love, never self-interest. Considering how Jesus might respond to the characteristics or personality traits of the other is an invitation to consider what the appropriate loving response might be to the annoying, challenging characteristics in a spouse. It is, thus, an invitation to articulate how a couple can live out their wedding vows.

In recent years, largely among Protestant and Catholic circles, the catch phrase "What Would Jesus Do" has became popular. The phrase is an attempt to call people to consider how Jesus Christ might respond to personal situations in daily life. While the idea of thinking about how Jesus Christ might respond in a given situation is not new, the popularity of the catch-phrase "What Would Jesus Do?" or WWJD, has increased. Bracelets, keychains, T-shirts, bumper stickers, and other items initialized with WWJD have become commonplace. Although the notion of becoming Christ-like through our own efforts is a simplistic understanding of a biblical principal, at best, considering how Jesus might respond in a particular situation provides several dramatic benefits for couples stuck on how they feel about each other.

When an individual compares how he or she is behaving to what we imagine perfect love to be, it is typically easy to identify how a person has fallen short of that marital commitment to love. Instead of blaming the other for his or her shortcomings, each person is challenged to consider the commitment made to love the other, including his or her shortcomings. Rather than explaining away the shortcoming of the spouse, or minimizing how annoying the behavior is, comparing an individual's actions to perfect love brings into clear relief an individual's own need for growth in the marital union.

In addition, this question dramatically shifts the tone of therapy from attacking and criticizing the other, to mutual admissions of how each person has failed his or her commitment to love. It is difficult to maintain a position of blaming the spouse while taking responsibility for personal failure. This results, in the best case, in a couple's mutual support of each other as each person learns to love. If this shift occurs, a number of solutions to the initial "stuckness" becomes apparent.

This activity has components of acceptance of the other person, consistent with other existing theoretical approaches, but this activity is also designed to highlight a potential course of action for an individual. Beyond simply identifying emotions, explaining origins of behavior, or even accepting behavior, this question of "What Jesus Would Do?" suggests a possible way to resolve the crisis. That is, the intent of this activity is to highlight a way to interact, a model of relating that both parties believe is appropriate for a marriage.

The intent of this activity is not to simplify marital therapy into behaving according to some spiritual principles of conduct. Falling into this type of "try harder" therapy misses the deep personal issues that this activity is intended to bring into relief. This question is intended to couch the marital conflict in terms of the couple's wedding day commitment to love each other and to access spiritual resources to resolve this type of marital impasse. Couples counseling, then, becomes a process of working together with a focus on each person's challenge to love rather than on the other's personality difficulties. Subsequent sessions can focus on the barriers to loving the other as Christ would love him or her. This can lead the way into family-of-origin issues, gender issues, unresolved marital issues, development of coping strategies, issues of power, domination, control, finances, sex, intimacy, etc. These future explorations will occur in the context of each person's acceptance of responsibility for pursuing the common goal of attaining Christ-like love for each other.

Again, this activity is designed to go beyond simply communicating with, or accepting, someone and toward a mutual self-recognition of personal imperfections: a kind of mutual confession of sorts. Confession, by its very nature, implies that an individual believes that a possible way of being exists and that the individual has not chosen that way of being.

Finally, this activity is intended to deconstruct a couple's understanding of love. In the most extreme cases, love can be misunderstood as an emotional experience of warmth. This exercise is intended to assist couples in constructing a definition of love that includes, yet transcends, feelings, and is dynamic, reflecting the dynamic nature of love. This approach is particularly effective with individuals inclined to dominate, oppress, subjugate, ignore, disrespect, or otherwise minimize the other person.

Instructions

This activity is used after the therapist has adequately joined with each member of the couple and worked with a couple to identify the marital history and interaction patterns. Once a therapist has helped a couple to identify the patterns of communicating and interacting, and the couple identifies that the problem is the annoying, difficult characteristics of the other, this activity can be used.

Once the therapist has worked with each person sufficiently to identify the affect concerning the difficult characteristics, or traits of the other, the therapist asks each person how he or she decides to respond to the other person's negative behaviors or habits. The therapist empathizes with each person, identifying the difficulty in responding appropriately to the other person's annoying, difficult qualities. In the context of appropriate empathy, the therapist can wonder out loud or ask directly, "How do you think Christ would respond to your husband in that instance?" Or, similarly, "What would Jesus do in this case if he were married to your wife?"

For couples who identify that religion or spirituality is not a part of their relationship, asking questions about the marriage ceremony, its location, who married them, and if vows were exchanged, can provide the basic information necessary for this activity. For couples who identify that they exchanged vows, one of which was to love the other, additional questions are appropriate, including what they understand that commitment to mean. Specifically, the therapist should clarify that the commitment to love meant not only a commitment to love the parts of the other that we like, agree with, admire, or respect, but also the parts of the other that are annoying, challenging, or hard to understand. In identifying the dynamics of the relationship, the therapist can ask if loving the other means criticizing, minimizing, ignoring, belittling, ridiculing, or judging the other.

If one makes the assumption that Christ was perfect, then one can safely say that he had perfect boundaries, always reacted appropriately to others and clearly spoke assertively in love. In addition, within a process of working and growing together, Jesus would continue to treat the other person with kindness, love, and mercy. It does not imply a tolerance of inappropriate behavior, but does imply a response consistent with the timeless virtues of patience, kindness, respect, and love. The focus of subsequent sessions, then, becomes identifying and coping with each person's own difficulties in pursuing these virtues rather than changing the other person. The annoying behaviors do not change, but the individual's responses to them do. This creates opportunities for change and action, essentially empowering clients to move forward together.

Brief Vignette

Debbie brought Rob to therapy as a gift to him for Valentine's Day. Rob is a successful business owner and Debbie is a stay-at-home mom for their two, school-age children. After a few sessions it became apparent that the two regularly locked horns in power struggles about every issue from the kids' bedtimes, and visiting family, to when to go to the lake. They went round and round about the same issues, and they seemed to disagree about everything. Much of their positive feelings for each other had disappeared. They spent most of the first few sessions in the therapist's office criticizing, mocking, and ridiculing each other, sometimes amid smiles and nervous laughter, all the while inviting the therapist to take sides and affirm how ridiculous or annoying the other was. They had developed a peculiar, painful intimacy from their years of dancing together emotionally in this way. They were hurting and they were stuck.

Debbie summarized the problem as Rob's unwillingness to communicate with her on anything. She claimed he was incapable of talking about his feelings, and he did not deny it. "He does not include me in decisions and then expects me to go along with his way." He did not deny her criticisms. She wondered out loud if he even wanted to be married to her. She also complained that Rob is always going 110 percent, incapable of slowing down. She described a seven-day family ski trip during which Rob insisted on skiing at a different resort each day. She could not contain her laughter as she described how odd Rob was, getting up at 7 a.m. on vacation so he could keep going. She shared that she was more normal because she had balance in her life and she fought to protect the balance in her children's lives. Rob, slightly self-conscious, simply offered his opinion that he did not see anything wrong with trying to get the most out of a day, or a ski trip.

Rob argued, with some prodding, that Debbie is lazy and complains a lot. She sleeps in until after 8 a.m. on weekdays, which creates chaos in the morning. She wanted to sleep in on Saturdays, making it hard to get to the ski slopes before noon, even though everyone else wanted to go early. Debbie defended that she has never missed making the lunches on school days and there is nothing wrong with sleeping in on weekends. He reported that she is always late, takes too long to make decisions about everything, and always spoils the fun that he wants to have with the kids. He acknowledged that it was easier for him to make decisions about the family and kids without involving Debbie. Naturally, their behaviors had become increasingly polarized through the conflict. Debbie complained that she tried hard to live up to Rob's expectations, but she never could, so she had given up trying to change for him. His overachievement was the problem. The criticisms of each other flavored more than a few sessions as the therapist explored interaction patterns, argument processes, emotions, misunderstandings, and inappropriate communication. Both Rob and Debbie were locked in battle with each other, stuck in defensive positions and, consequently, emotionally distant from each other. Both were stuck in this cycle of blaming and hurting each other.

In the midst of these early sessions, Rob revealed with much effort and discomfort that he had come to therapy because he found himself contemplating divorce more frequently, but feared that outcome. He reported after a few sessions that he no longer felt like he loved Debbie or wanted to be married to her. He shared, hesitantly for fear of her response, that he did not like being around her. Naturally, she cried when he said this, justifying his fears. On the tails of this revelation, the conflict between them subsided as did Rob's negative feelings toward Debbie. What did not leave was Rob's disrespect for Debbie's way of doing things and Debbie's lack of tolerance for Rob's style. Both parties struggled in articulating their emotions about these difficult areas. When both were asked how they felt about the other person's behaviors, they both offered frustration, but nothing more.

One of their classic disputes concerned the dinner hour. They agreed that dinner was her responsibility, and she was committed to it. However, Rob was a punctual person who expected things to be done on time. This was not a big priority for Debbie. They regularly described evenings in which Rob came home and dinner was not prepared for any number of reasons. Rob would be visibly frustrated and Debbie would feel criticized.

In the initial sessions they indicated that they occasionally attended the Catholic church where they were married. When asked, they identified that they exchanged vows in their marriage to love each other. The therapist asked Debbie that if Jesus were responsible for making dinner for Rob and Rob came home upset because dinner was late, how would Jesus respond. Without much effort, Debbie responded that Jesus would probably be patient and calm. From this she quickly identified that she took his anxiety very personally, feeling that she could never live up to her husband's expectations. Without much effort she identified a similar pattern in her relationship with her father who never respected her abilities.

For Rob's part, the therapist asked the same question. What would Jesus do if he came home and dinner was not ready? He easily identified that Jesus would likely be calm and patient. This left open the exploration of what was driving him to do things such that he would treat his wife in ways that are inconsistent with his beliefs about loving his wife. He shared his feelings of being overwhelmed with his work schedule, as well as generally disappointed in his wife. This led to a discussion of how rudely his father treated his mother, at least until she died, and his anger and sadness about that. In addition, Rob shared about his anxiety when he is not in control of situations. Once Rob identified that Jesus would not harass his wife if she needed more time to make a decision, he admitted that he tended to be impatient. As he identified to his wife his own struggles with patience, she joined him and shared her commitment to support his struggle through giving him space to struggle and doing what she can to change her behavior. As Rob took responsibility for allowing Debbie to have a different way of doing things, the interactions between them moved toward mutual vulnerability. Debbie became more willing to cooperate with Rob on how things were done while Rob remained focused on his responsibility to allow Debbie to be who she was. For Debbie's part, after our discussion about what Jesus would do, she spent several weeks focusing on her own angry outbursts with her husband and her children.

From that point on we continued to work on the marital disputes from the context of each person's own responsibilities for being a mature member of the relationship. Rob remained committed to being more respectful of Debbie, who worked to express herself and her concerns more maturely. Rather than making either party feel guilty, considering how Jesus might respond challenged them to explore their own roles as husband and wife in a relationship of mutual love. This did not eliminate any of the marital issues, but created a much more productive context for communication and negotiation. Therapy continued as they explored barriers to loving, including family-of-origin ideas about the role of women for Rob and self-esteem and competency issues for Debbie.

Suggestions for Follow-Up

Follow-up with this activity can include any number of activities or discussions about each person's unique barriers to love. Couples work together in articulating what it means for them to love each other. If it is not to judge, criticize, or evaluate the other, then what is it? What does love mean? In addition, follow-up typically involves teaching coping skills as each party learns how difficult it can be to allow the other, in love, to be who he or she is.

Follow-up discussions can easily incorporate a deconstruction of gender beliefs and roles, the power dynamics of the couple, boundaries, and any other issues that might be obstructing marital love. Couples might develop a statement on how they understand their roles as husband and wife. How do we distinguish between allowing the other to be upset and not tolerating angry talk or inappropriate treatment? How will we work together when one of us has a difficulty with the other person?

Clients might claim that they are not perfect like Jesus, and when they do become perfect, they will love perfectly. Although this is certainly the reality in all marital cases, a follow-up question might be how they would like to handle each other's inability to love in the marriage. Couples can work together to decide how they would like to handle their own and the other's annoying characteristics in their marriage. Would they like a marriage where the annoying qualities are mocked, judged, or criticized or where they are loved? How then, do they want to handle themselves if they are not prepared to respond in love? Naturally, no marriage has perfect love, and the intent of the activity is to shift the focus of the marital interaction from attacking the other toward supporting each other in the process of developing this love.

While therapists are obligated to fight for a couple's marriage, we are not obligated to fight for a dead marriage to the point of stepping on a person's right to choose his or her own life. If a person has chosen to end a marriage, it is a boundary violation for a therapist to disrespect that choice. A person might choose to end a marriage verbally or nonverbally and the therapist's job might be simply to identify verbally what one party is choosing nonverbally. WWJD might mean honoring someone's right to leave a marriage, rather than keeping a marriage together under any and all circumstances. Jesus always honored individuals' rights to choose for themselves, even if it meant that they rejected him.

Contraindications

With this activity, the therapist runs the risk of performing "try harder" therapy. That is, if used inappropriately, this activity can increase the sense of guilt, failure, or inadequacy an individual might feel, rather than empowering a client through taking responsibility for personal actions. This activity is intended to provide a path for couples to work through even the most difficult impasses by focusing on what makes it difficult to learn to love.

Some clients might maintain destructive ideas about Jesus Christ. If the therapist does not have any information about how Jesus interacted, it is better for them not to use him as the model. Rather, consider choosing a model of love familiar to the therapist and the clients.

This question is not recommended for victims of domestic violence, already prone to unhealthy boundaries and guilt about setting appropriate limits. Although redefining love is an essential element of working with victims to maintain healthy boundaries, using this activity in those incidences runs the risk of reinforcing inappropriate emotional boundaries. There is a risk that clients will assume that the most loving response is to tolerate inappropriate, abusive, condescending behavior. However, this approach is particularly effective with aggressive or oppressive individuals who claim to be practitioners of the Christian faith or adherents to the Christian scriptures. For this population, is it particularly salient to identify the nonaggressive, nondomineering stance taken by Jesus toward all people.

This activity is not recommended in cases in which someone has already decided to divorce, because the nature of imagining how a long-suffering God might respond might preclude seeing clear signs of a dead marriage or disinterested partner.

Finally, this activity is not intended to instruct clients what to do, but rather is a useful activity in helping clients to articulate what they believe and to identify the barriers toward acting accordingly. Simplistic activities run the risk of encouraging simplistic therapy. Simply identifying that one is failing to live up to some abstract principle of love does nothing, in and of itself, to further therapeutic process.

Professional Reading and Resource

Jenkins, A. (1990). *Invitations to responsibility.* Adelaide South Australia: Dulwiche Center Publications.

Bibliotherapy Sources for the Client

Holy Bible, New International Version (1990). Grand Rapids MI: Zondervan.
Thomas, G. (2000). *Sacred marriage.* Grand Rapids, MI: Zondervan.

Web Sites of Interest

www.retrouvaille.org: The word *Retrouvaille* means "rediscovery," and this Web site introduces a program geared toward marriages on the brink of failure. It is a compelling program run primarily by couples who have restored their marriages through the program. It is not counseling, and the Web site gives more information about this resource. Check out the list of links at the bottom of the page, too.

www.smartmarriages.com: This Web site is a remarkable resource for marriage, marriage support, and marriage information. Although it targets professionals, there is plenty of information on resources for couples interested in strengthening or saving their marriage.

– 13 –

I Reject That Shame

Richard S. Shaw

Type of Contribution: Activity, Handout

Objective

The purpose of this activity is for people to make the connection between the irrational beliefs they hold regarding shame and then be able to connect those beliefs to their everyday experiences. Once the connection is made, clients will be better able to understand why at times they react to people or events inappropriately. Coming to this understanding assists people in having more power over their reactions and relationships and the ability to connect more intimately with others.

Rationale for Use

There is a connection between the beliefs of shame that a person holds and the way they engage with others and the world. As a result, the more the shame, the less one has the ability to genuinely and fully engage in intimate relationships. Shame is also a major issue for people who have had negative experiences in the church. Often those negative experiences with people are intertwined with their beliefs about God. Consequently, an individual is produced that not only consciously has difficulties with other people but also has unconscious irrational beliefs about God. These clients need to be educated about shame and the role it plays in their lives. Without this understanding, shame may control their thoughts and behaviors.

From a survey of current literature, shame is a feeling of worthlessness or a complete sense of inadequacy as a person. It is an inner voice that says the individual is not good enough, worthy enough, or competent enough. These shame messages are given to the individual by families, friends, pastors, teachers or other sources from outside oneself. Shame can also arise from church teachings about the unworthiness and inadequacy of the individual before God. The messages from the church underscore the feelings of shame received elsewhere. Finally, shame robs persons of their genuineness with themselves and others causing difficulty in forming healthy relationships.

In many cases, people feel shame because their feelings, motives, and actions are not perfect. Others happenings that cannot be controlled or prevented—illegitimacy, physical handicaps, sexual abuse—may cause feelings of deficiency and shame (Wharton, 1990, p. 287). When too much shame is transmitted to people it becomes deeply accepted, internalized, and difficult to dislodge. Kaufman (1992) refers to these individuals as shame-bound and labels the harmful effects of shame as toxic.

The book of Genesis details the events in the Garden of Eden that led to the first instance of shame and describes the characteristics of shame in human history. Genesis 3:6-10 tells that

Adam and Eve, after having eaten from the forbidden tree, felt their nakedness for the first time. So ashamed were they, that they sewed leaves together to form coverings for their bodies. When God sought them they hid from him, saying that they were afraid because they were naked.

The characteristics of shame can be seen in Adam and Eve's reaction to God. The pair's first reaction was to hide themselves from God by hiding their bodies with fig leaves. The impulse to cover and hide always accompanies shame. According to Goldman (1988), overwhelming shame was the immediate result of the Fall. With this first experience of humiliation, shame became part of the makeup of human emotions.

Yet, though shame exists and the characteristic is to hide from it, God's reaction is also described in the story of Adam and Eve. In this first recorded instance of the experience of shame, God addressed the problem with love, shedding the blood of animals to cover their sin, and sewing their skins to replace the fig leaf coverings. However, at times, Christian doctrine on sin can carry with it shaming and legalistic responses to wrongdoing. Through its misinterpretation and misapplication, Christianity can lead to rigid ways of thinking, legalistic codes of behavior, strict interpretations of biblical passages, and patriarchal authority in the home.

Unhealthy, shame-based beliefs are often present in families and individuals who experience shame (Arterburn & Felton, 1991). These beliefs become incorporated into the family system and are passed on to subsequent generations. For instance:

1. Love is never free but instead is earned.
2. Unconditional love is a myth.
3. Authority is not to be questioned, and complete submission to authority is to be expected and praised.
4. One's role or position matters more than one's personhood.
5. If anything goes wrong, someone is to blame. This means judging is the responsibility of the family, not of God.
6. Performance and perfection are what matter most. Any sign of personal struggle is seen as a weakness. Events such as abortion, suicide, or divorce indicate that someone is not measuring up.
7. God will treat me the way authority figures in my life have treated me. If authority figures have been fearsome and punishing, rather than loving and understanding, then surely God must be the same way.
8. Grace is a mystery, not a personal experience. Certainly we must do more to receive God's grace than to accept it as a gift that God has freely given.

Fossum and Mason (1986) describe behavioral traits that are passed down in shame-based families. These beliefs are control, perfectionism, blame, denial, disqualification, and addictions. For instance, it is essential for a shame-based family to *control* everything. This is because a lack of control causes fear and chaos in a shame-based family. As a result, complete submission is expected. An additional trait is *perfection,* which is impossible to attain, but is nonetheless required for love and acceptance in the shame-based family. Further, *blame* is cast in all situations and every act is seen as a deliberate attempt to injure. In addition, *denial of feelings, problems,* and *addictions* are also characteristics of shame-based families. For instance, real feelings and problems are denied making relational dynamics inconsistent and untrustworthy. Furthermore, *problems are disqualified* and discounted. In addition, *addictions* such as alcohol, drugs, or pornography may underlie shame issues, which are often hidden, sometimes showing up in times of crisis. Finally, in a shame-based family, tempers may rage out of control causing fear and a lack of trust. As a result, the shame-based family lives in a constant state of chaos and confusion. In such a frightening system, rigid adherence to structures becomes more important than people.

Through dysfunctional relationships, shame is developed, creating distorted concepts of God and serious misunderstandings of grace.

Van Vonderen (1989) explains how the cycle of shame originates, grows, and is internalized and manifested in one's life. The cycle begins when shame is interjected into a child's life, usually by parents or other significant people, through insults, negative comparisons to others, favoritism, perfectionism, rejection, abuse, etc., or from external events in which the victim is not at fault, such as in the case of muggings, rapes, and accidents.

Shame is also manifested through a cycle. For instance, when people receive shaming messages, they may internalize them, believing that they are bad, inadequate, or worthless. Although erroneous, these messages are believed and incorporated into a filter through which all future messages must pass. The next logical step in the cycle is to punish the self for the bad and shameful thoughts, feelings, and actions. This is done by acting out in ways congruent with the internal messages, which result in the fulfillment of the original beliefs about their unworthiness.

Consequently, efforts to break this cycle are marked by repeated failures at trying to be perfect by force of will and even the conversion of positive messages from external sources into shaming messages. Individuals trapped in the cycle can only continue trying harder and failing until ultimately they give up. In Van Vonderen's (1989) model, the cycle begins when an outside source introduces shaming messages about behaviors or events. These repeated messages become the basis for a person's belief that he or she cannot achieve perfection. After receiving multiple shaming messages the person either continues in the rut of negative beliefs and behaviors or gives up. At some point, one must consciously stop trying harder. To do this, he or she must experience an understanding of God's unconditional love and grace. The fight changes from trying harder to accepting good messages from a God who loves intimately, a love confirmed when Jesus, on the cross, took away the shameful badness. Finally, the cycle is broken, making it possible for humankind to achieve consistently good behavior with new messages from the new source, God. Acceptance of this love obliterates all messages of inadequacy and worthlessness. Through graceful messages and graceful people, the shame filter is exposed and dismantled. Grace is the answer to shame.

Jack and Judith Balswick (1991) discuss some of the effects of gracelessness within the family system. In this system, people are self-centered and love is conditional. Performance is the criterion for love and members try vainly to measure up. However, since failure is certain, shame is inevitable. Attempting to avoid shame, family members control everything and everyone in an effort to maintain the standard of perfection. This control makes relationships unreliable and unpredictable. As a result, family members cease to communicate and shrink from intimacy.

The Balswicks (1991, Balswick, 2006) have developed a theological model for healthy family relationships in four stages: *covenant, grace, empowerment,* and *intimacy.* The first stage, covenant, refers to God's unconditional unilateral commitment to his people. God bound himself to keep His commitment whether or not His people kept it. Applying this to the family, the Balswicks identify two types of relationships: (1) the contractual relationship that depends on both sides keeping the terms of the contact and (2) the covenant relationship that is based on one's decision to keep the commitment, regardless of the other's actions. This is the nature of the relationship God has with his people. It is also the nature of the parent-child relationship; the parent commits to the child who at the beginning of life is unable to commit back to the parent.

The second stage of the Balswicks' (1991, 2006) model is grace. Grace too fits closely with the concept of covenant. Grace is receiving benefits one does not deserve and cannot earn. Covenant relationships are designed by God to be lived out in an environment of grace and forgiveness. Otherwise, they are contractual—governed by law, not by grace.

The third stage is empowerment. Generally the power of influence is used to promote oneself. By contrast, an empowering influence is used to promote others and make them stronger. Without controlling or enforcing, empowering encourages others to grow, learn, change, and take appropriate action.

The fourth stage, intimacy, is an idea that runs throughout biblical history and is still true today. Fear of intimacy leads to shame. Through the grace of God, people can build relationships without shame. The presence of covenant, grace, empowerment, and intimacy creates potential for the best relationships possible. Lack of these concepts contributes to contractual covenants, legalistic perfection, controlling power, and shame. (See Chapter 20 in this book for further elaboration on the application of these four principles in therapy.)

According to Reisner and Lawson (1992), there is adequate opportunity within Judeo-Christian religions for the development of shame. Whether they benefit or hinder emotional health seems to have more to do with whether the belief system encourages self-acceptance, or self-alienation. Many religious teachings can unintentionally engender feelings of shame and guilt. Damage is bound to occur unless grace, hope, and forgiveness are also taught. Psychotherapy and correct spiritual teaching can be combined to create a healing process for shame.

In addition, guilt is often wrongly used as a synonym for shame. Guilt is about behavior, which can be corrected. Shame is about character and personhood. Correcting behavior can alleviate guilt, but not necessarily shame. God must address shame, at the core of the self. Healing for shame does not come through new behaviors, but from dealing directly with one's core sense of self. One might describe it as a heart issue. The necessary change comes only with the understanding of, and the acknowledgment of a new, vibrant identity in Christ.

Many Christians live their whole lives alternating between giving up and trying harder. Fortunately, with healing, they can break through the shame filter and into God's rest cycle, where persons are accepted for their position in Christ through his grace, rather than for good behavior. To break free of the shame cycle and to enter the cycle of grace, something new must happen; people must experience grace, the notion that God really does love them unconditionally and that He can succeed where they cannot. The motivating experience of the shame cycle is replaced by the awakening of the grace experience. This can occur through events such as a sermon, an accurate teaching about grace, or the development of a relationship with a grace-filled person. This frees the person from the shame cycle into a new relationship of love.

The follow-up work for the recipients of this grace awakening is to keep rejecting the old, shaming messages and to believe the new grace-filled messages about themselves. Behavior will not always be perfect but, for perhaps the first time, failures do not carry a core-damning blow. With the assurance of God's acceptance, they will experience a sort of soul defense as they choose to exist within the new grace-filled paradigm.

The responsibility rests on persons to challenge shaming organizations and structures, and to heal those who have been wounded by shame whether inside or outside the church. Church leaders and helpers can begin a redirection toward healing. Pastors and church leaders can encourage believers to see their Christianity as an intimate relationship with a loving Father. These individuals can work to turn church customs into opportunities that allow people to accept sin as forgivable, and to experience holiness based on relationship rather than on behavior. They can dispense God's grace and love to build a community of faith that supports wounded people and facilitates their restoration.

Counselors and therapists also have an important role to play in the fight against shame. They can offer grace to their clients by seeing them as deserving and capable of receiving God's gift of love to them. They can view clients nonjudgmentally and can love them as they allow them to grow and change into grace-filled people. They can be especially helpful to believers by developing awareness and empathy for the particular concerns of their clients' faith and by bestowing an understanding of the impact of distorted spiritual and religious traditions.

Shame is everywhere. It can no more be eradicated than can any of the other trials that confront us daily. Although we will surely encounter it, our task is to prevent the perpetration of shame and offer grace instead.

Instructions

Before the therapist uses this activity, he or she should have evidence that the client(s) is struggling with shame issues. Ideal candidates will be struggling with perfectionism, performance issues, extremes of either openness to or defiance of authority, and difficulty in experiencing grace and acceptance.

After the therapist has decided that shame might be an issue for this client(s), the therapist proceeds to read the client(s) the nine statements connected to shame found in the handout at the end of the chapter, titled Assessing Shame Questions. In session, the therapist asks the client(s) to respond to each of the nine items, and to rate individual responses on a scale from 1 to 10, with one being not at all or never and ten being nearly all or all the time. Any answer of seven or above on an item suggests the need to address shame issues. The client can either respond to these questions verbally or in writing. After the client has finished responding to the questions, the therapist then will follow up with each question scored at seven or above and looks to incorporate this material into the ongoing work of therapy.

This exercise can be used with either an individual client or with couples. When this procedure is used with couples, it is important to use the same questions from the handout, allowing each partner to answer and reflect on the questions in session on their own. Do not assume that each knows what the other writes and talks about in regard to the questions. After one states his or her reaction to each question, ask the other if that is old or new material to them about their partner. If it is new, ask what about it is new and ask how he or she feels and responds to this new material. If it is old material, then help the partner show appropriate care and empathy for the partner's pain concerning this area of shame. This procedure provides yet another opportunity for shame to be addressed and cared for by a loving partner. As the therapist you are modeling and assisting partners to care for each another.

Sometimes, the levels of shame will be quite similar in each partner, although each may identify different questions from the handout that are hot buttons for them. At other times, one partner may have high shame reactions and the other has relatively low shame reactions. In these cases, help the partner with low shame show even more care and acceptance for the one with high shame. Help the low shame partner communicate that he or she can still relate to shame. Use their strength as a couple. Also, you can help the high shame partner celebrate that the low shame partner does not have that shame to deal with. Always look to build on the bond and attachment of the two. Help them think "team" or partnership. It is them working together against the shame that impacts their relationship.

Another option for intervening with the high/low shame partners is to recommend one or two individual counseling sessions along with the couples sessions. This allows each to have individual time in which to address the level of shame he or she feels and struggles with, without the partner being there the first time this is discussed, as he or she is to let the partner into those places of personal depth and exposure concerning the shame. Remember, when you are doing couples therapy, and you choose to see the individuals during the therapy, anything that is shared in any session is open to both. You do not want to set up an expectation of individual confidentiality outside of the partner confidentiality already established. The reason for this is that the *relationship* is your client, not either individual. This is classic systems thinking and it will serve you as you serve the couple.

Brief Vignette

Joan came to counseling due to problems with low self-esteem and not having confidence to stand up for herself. She recently had an interchange with someone at church in which she felt a man in leadership violated her boundaries and ability to say no. This current experience reminded her of her past church involvement.

JOAN: I come from a church background that was very bad . . . lots of guilt.

THERAPIST: Joan, I am wondering what you mean by your statement that your church background was very bad . . . with lots of guilt. Can you tell me more?

JOAN: Sure, I don't like church because they always make me feel so guilty. It is kind of weird, but I can't stand it. I just don't understand. It's like my skin crawls when I just think about it.

THERAPIST: Joan, I have an exercise that might help you understand your reaction to church. Would you be open for us now to talk about that?

JOAN: I would be, if it will help me understand what is going on with this guilt-church thing and me.

THERAPIST: Okay, great. I am going to ask you nine questions, and I want you to respond to each of them by giving me a score of one to ten on each. One suggests that this is no problem, or not present. Ten suggests this is always or almost always a concern or problem. Make sense?

JOAN: Okay.

At this point, the therapist proceeds to ask Joan each of the nine questions listed in the handout. Since she scored above a score of seven on questions 2 and 4, the therapist returned to those questions and talked further.

As interaction happens with each question, the therapist can use the person of the therapist to convey acceptance, grace, and care. Showing empathy, respect, acceptance, and unconditional care for the client can convey grace. Appropriately acknowledging one's own struggles with shame can also communicate your personal awareness and humanity regarding these types of issues. This use of self-disclosure allows the client to know that the therapist can relate deeply with the feeling and struggles of shame. This communicates that the client is not alone in his or her struggles.

Suggestions for Follow-Up

After the client has responded to the questions concerning shame, the therapist can go into more detail, explaining more about the concept of shame, how unhealthy it is and how to manage it better with specific interventions such as positive self-talk, and identifying negative thinking patterns (e.g., Sori & McKinney, 2006).

Contraindications for Use

This activity can be helpful for most clients, but more so particularly for those who relate to a specific faith background. For those clients who have had negative community of faith experiences, this exercise may be more difficult or painful to process. For those clients with less community of faith background, the "power" of the exercise may be lessened.

References

Arterburn, S., & Felton, J. (1991). *Toxic faith: Understanding and overcoming religious addiction.* Nashville, TN: Oliver Nelson.

Balswick, J. (2006). Biblical means to therapeutic healing. In K. B. Helmeke & C. F. Sori (Eds.), *The therapist's notebook for integrating spirituality in counseling: Homework, handouts, and activities for use in psychotherapy.* (pp. 235-239). Binghamton, NY: The Haworth Press.

Balswick, J., & Balswick, J. (1991). *The family: A Christian perspective on the contemporary home.* Grand Rapids, MI: Baker Book House.

Fossum, M., & Mason, M. (1986). *Facing shame.* New York: W. W. Norton and Company.

Goldman, H. (1988). Paradise destroyed: The crime of being born. *Contemporary Psychoanalysis, 24,* 420-450.

Kaufman, G. (1992). *Shame: The power of caring.* Rochester, VT: Schenkman Books.

Reisner, A., & Lawson, P. (1992). Psychotherapy, sin, and mental health. *Pastoral Psychology, 40,* 303-311.

Sori, C. F., & McKinney, L. (2006). Free at last! Using scriptural affirmations to replace self-defeating thoughts. In K. B. Helmeke & C. F. Sori (Eds.), *The therapist's notebook for integrating spirituality in counseling: Homework, handouts, and activities for use in psychotherapy* (pp. 223-234). Binghamton, NY: The Haworth Press.

Wharton, B. (1990). The hidden face of shame: The shadow, shame, and separation. *Journal of Analytical Psychology, 35,* 279-299.

Van Vonderen, J. (1989). *Tired of trying to measure up.* Minneapolis, MN: Bethany House Publishers.

Professional Readings and Resources

Arterburn, S., & Felton, J. (1991). *Toxic faith: Understanding and overcoming religious addiction.* Nashville, TN: Oliver Nelson.

Fossum, M., & Mason, M. (1986). *Facing shame.* New York: W. W. Norton and Company.

Van Vonderen, J. (1989). *Tired of trying to measure up.* Minneapolis, MN: Bethany House Publishers.

Bibliotherapy Source for the Client

Van Vonderen, J. (1989). *Tired of trying to measure up.* Minneapolis, MN: Bethany House Publishers.

Handout: Assessing Shame Questions

In the following activity, read each of the nine statements below to a client. Ask the client to rate his or her response to each question, either verbally or in writing, on a scale from 1 to 10, with one being not at all or never and ten being nearly all or all the time. Any answer of seven or above on an item suggests the need to address shame issues.

1. How would you rate your need for control?
2. How would you rate your need for perfection?
3. How would you rate the amount you blame others?
4. How would you rate your level of denial about difficult things in your life?
5. How would you rate your level of reliability?
6. How would you rate your need to disqualify others' truths when you disagree with them?
7. How would you rate your present level of addiction?
8. How would you rate your propensity to become angry?
9. How would you rate your level of predictability?

Shaw, R. S. (2006). I reject that shame. In K. B. Helmeke & C. F. Sori (Eds.), *The therapist's notebook for integrating spirituality in counseling: Homework, handouts, and activities for use in psychotherapy* (pp. 157-164). Binghamton, NY: The Haworth Press.

SECTION IV:
SPECIFIC TECHNIQUES AND/OR TOPICS
USED IN INTEGRATING SPIRITUALITY

14

I Am Not Worthy: Shame and Spirituality

Joseph J. Horak

Type of Contribution: Activity, Handout

Objective

Clients who experience large amounts of internalized shame present many challenges to clinicians. They are often extremely self-negative, self-deprecating and even self-loathing. Spiritually these clients may often be very religious, but frequently feel as if they are a continual disappointment to God. They feel unworthy, unacceptable, flawed, weak, and continual failures in God's eyes. Sometimes, they may consider their inability to change these feelings and feel any spiritual consolation proof of their lack of faith or spiritual adequacy. This chapter will address the concept of shame and its detrimental influence on development and spirituality. An exercise is developed to help clients struggling with internalized shame to begin to see themselves differently in relationship with God.

Rationale for Use

Prior to the late 1980s very little had been written about shame. However, more recently this construct has received considerable attention. Nathanson (1987) argued that shame plays a central role in many interactions and is the "master" emotion. Kaufman (1988) described the experience of shame as

> To feel shame is to feel seen in a painfully diminished sense. The self feels exposed to itself and to anyone else present. Shame is an impotence-making experience because it feels as though there is no way to relieve the matter. . . . The binding affect of shame involves the whole self. (p. 8)

Kaufman and Nathanson relied on Tomkin's (1963, 1987) affect theory as they developed their phenomenological shame theory models. Tomkins (1987) postulated the existence of nine innate affects that are biologically based and programmed to produce a characteristic set of expressions on the face and create other physiological reactions (e.g., blushing, increased pulse rate, perspiration, etc.). Tomkins developed his model as a young father when he observed his newborn infant and determined the existence of each innate affect by the presence of a corresponding facial expression. In the case of shame, characteristics exhibited on the face are the eyes and head cast downward with the gaze averted, with an overall slumping of the body posture.

Tomkins (1987) and Nathanson (1987) contend these innate affects are "hard wired" and universal to all humans. Cook (2001) contends that as a person develops the capacity for language and cognitions, the innate shame response becomes co-assembled with other cognitions and behaviors into the complex emotion of shame. He considers shame to be an ubiquitous emotion necessary in varying degrees to shape behavior. Shame is used by society and religions to shape behavior congruent with its norms (Cook, 2001). Without the use of shame to shape culturally acceptable behaviors, it is unlikely that civilization could have progressed in any meaningful manner.

However, shame can also become toxic and have strong negative effects upon development. Nathanson contends shame's capacity to damage one's sense of self increases with the frequency as well as how early shame is experienced. He states,

> Very little in the life experience of the child calls attention to the nature of the self as powerfully as does [the] shame affect. . . . [He suspects] that shame produces a *sense of an incompetent self,* [sic] that there is a part of the self created by shame. (Nathanson, 1987, p. 210)

An example of a shaming experience would occur when a latency-age son becomes distressed and cries in public, which results in his father feeling embarrassed by his son's show of "weakness." The father reacts by shaming his son and his crying, by telling him to stop being a sissy and to knock it off, because men do not cry. The son feels shame in response to his pain and expression of this pain by crying. Over time, if this type of shaming interaction continues to occur, it is "internalized" and becomes intricately tied to one's sense of self. As this boy matures into manhood, he will experience considerable shame in expressing vulnerability in response to emotional and physical pain. In the case of severe trauma in childhood, the result is an overwhelming and potentially intolerable feeling of shame within the child that has a dramatic impact upon the child's evolving sense of self.

Tomkins (1987) contends that shame experiences become magnified as they are embedded in the memory of associations to various scenes in which shame was originally triggered. Subsequently, when they may be experiencing a similar emotion (e.g., physical pain in public), children will remember the original scene and the intense feelings of shame, and alter their behavior to avoid the possibility of further shame. When shame becomes internalized no input from the external world is needed to activate further shame responses. Nathanson (1987) states that

> the innate affect shame-humiliation at all ages and in all stages of human development, is a powerful mechanism for the elaboration of the sense of self. . . . Through shame we are forced to know and remember our failures. While it is clear that shame affect is triggered by experiences that have nothing at all to do with competence, shame produces awareness of an incompetent self. (p. 211)

According to Kaufman (1989), once shame becomes internalized it forms a major aspect of one's identity. He describes shame as

> the affect of inferiority. No other affect is more central to the development of identity. None is closer to the experienced self, nor more disturbing. Shame is felt as an inner torment. . . . Shame is a wound made from the inside, dividing us from both ourselves and others. (p. 17)

Cook (1996) asserts all forms of psychopathology are basically emotional disorders with shame as a common component in each. Empirical studies have shown that shame is positively correlated with individual psychological symptoms. In addition, shame may play a role in relationship problems (for a review see Cook, 2001; Horak 2002).

While not cited in the shame literature, developmental theorist Harry Stack Sullivan (1953) came close to understanding shame and its relation to development and psychopathology. Central to Sullivan's model is the affect he labeled "anxiety." Sullivan used the term "anxiety" to refer to the wide range of negative feelings that would include anxiousness, shame, dread, loathing and feelings of personal worthlessness (Chapman, 1976). Sullivan also understood the central role of shame (anxiety) that cultures use to "train people in becoming people" (Sullivan, p. 8). The term Sullivan labeled anxiety is actually much closer to a contemporary definition of shame.

Sullivan (1953) understood "anxiety" to be always interpersonal in nature, resulting from things going wrong in one's relationships with others. However, when one experiences a significant amount of these strong emotional reactions, psychological problems occur, and a person's ability to improve interpersonal relationships becomes hindered. Sullivan, the founder of the Relational School of Therapy, contended that anxiety (shame) had a tendency to bind a person in whatever unhealthy relationship patterns one has previously experienced (Chapman, 1976; Sullivan, 1953). Subsequently, Sullivan developed an approach that understands the importance of current relationships (including the therapeutic relationship) in healing and resolving these difficult relational patterns and the underlying shame.

Shame is able to have a major detrimental impact upon development due to two reasons. First, because every culture uses shame in moderation to deter undesirable behavior, the child is unable to determine if the degree or use of shame is appropriate. The second reason has to do with how shame is experienced. Unlike other emotions, when one experiences a shame response, it is impossible to distinguish between "having" this response and "being" this response. This lack of awareness contributes to the quick activation of shame defenses, which may explain how someone who appears to be functioning fairly maturely becomes reactive, and acts relationally immature.

For those who experience strong amounts of internalized shame, often the spiritual overlay is one where they feel as if they are a constant disappointment or failure and are unworthy in the eyes of God. This state is not experienced as transitory, such as appropriate guilt for harmful behavior, but is experienced as an existential irrefutable fact.

In response to excessive shaming by parents and authority figures (or self-shaming in response to neglect), the child does not develop the capacity to see both good and bad aspects of self and other (including God). Subsequently a split occurs, where the parental authority figure is seen as all good and powerful, while the self is seen as all bad and powerless. People with large amounts of internalized shame often believe that there is one set of rules for how God sees them, which differs from the rules for how God sees the rest of humanity. The resulting relational style makes it extremely difficult to experience any comfort or soothing in their relationship to their God, which is sadly ironic given the fact that many in this group are very religious. Healing is complicated further by the tendency to not want to expose and discuss the shame for fear that exposing it will confirm the irrefutable "reality" of their worthlessness.

Healing shame requires the development of relationships where enough safety is established to allow these more painful feelings to be discussed over time. Eventually, the healing requires developing the capacity to tolerate the ambivalence in experiencing both good and bad aspects of self and others. The blurring of parental and authority figures (including God) is finally able to be separated. The previously (parentally) tainted lenses through which they have experienced God become clearer. As the powerful grip that shame has on one's sense of self can be lessened and healed, a new self is reconstructed as the "threads" of shame become separated from the "cloth" of self. This allows the deconstructing of the perception of God to occur, which results in a much less restrictive and rigid manner in how they experience their spirituality.

Instructions

This exercise helps clients to confront some of the negative conclusions that they have come to in regard to how they define themselves. It needs to occur after a strong therapeutic alliance has been established. Initially, the clients should be invited to participate in an exercise where they will address issues in their relationship to God. The clients should always have permission to decline the invitation or engage in this exercise only when they feel ready. If the clients agree, ask them to describe how they see themselves in relation to God (see Shame and Spirituality Handout). Ask follow-up questions such as "How do you think God sees you? How do you think God feels about you? What is God proud of in relation to you? What is God disappointed in with you?" Write down the responses in the clients' words on a dry erase board. When the clients have finished, place the dry erase board in front of the clients and ask them to be silent for a few moments, and when they are ready, read the dry erase board to God. After they have read these statements, again ask them to be silent for a period of time and listen to see if a response occurs, giving permission that it is very acceptable if nothing happens at all in the session. At the end of the session, send the clients home with these statements written on a piece of paper and ask them to pray for the next week, beginning by describing how they feel in relation to God. The goal of the exercise is to increase the awareness of how the clients see themselves in their relationship to God. Often the contradictions surface between what they believe about God and what they believe about themselves. Addressing these conflicts directly can help the clients rework their views of themselves and begin to find more consolation in their spiritual life.

Brief Vignette

Mary is a thirty-nine-year-old Caucasian female who is married to Donald. Mary is a professor at a local college, and works full time as a mother. Mary's mother could be nice and pleasant one moment and then instantly become cruel and attacking. At times her mother would adamantly deny parts of reality (i.e., "I never said that. How could you ever think that?"). Subsequently, Mary has had a difficult time trusting her view of reality. Her mother blurred the boundary at times between herself and her daughter and would make comments such as, "Why are you eating that now? I am not hungry." Mary had a more positive relationship with her father, yet he would leave for extended periods when he was in the military. Mary has experienced episodes of major depression and currently is experiencing another bout of depression. Mary describes her relationship with God as somewhat like her relationship with her father. At times she has felt God's presence in her life in a powerful way, yet at other times she is unable to feel any consolation in her relationship with God and feels acutely alone. While very spiritual and religious, Mary sees herself as a disappointment to God.

After recording the statements Mary used to describe her relationship with God, the therapist placed the dry erase board in front of her and as she read these statements she reported her thoughts as follows:

> I'm not worth the air I breathe. I feel like there is something black inside me, something evil. . . . Something rotten and ruined that can't be fixed. It's so awful that I can't get near God with it. . . . I am so tainted that I might somehow ruin God. I have to run, and hide. . . . I have to disappear.

Mary later reported feeling an overwhelming sense of emptiness. She was instructed to close her eyes and quiet herself and simply listen for God without any expectations. Having been a practicing Quaker at one point in her life, Mary settled into what she described as a Quaker-like silence and felt considerable relief. Then she had the following experience:

I was startled to hear the words "MY CHILD." Okay, I thought, I'll go with it. "My" felt cozy. . . . I am God's child, his creation. . . . Then I began to see line drawings appearing dancing across the upper corners of my line of sight, reminiscent of a Baroque wall decoration I had once seen during a concert in a palace when I was in Europe. The music I heard then seemed to fit perfectly the path my eyes followed along the curved contours of the decorations. It was one of those art moments when one feels suspended in time. But these were different. I was enthralled, like a child, happy. Then there were musical notes and beautiful, unearthly sounds, and suddenly a rainbow burst over the whole thing. . . . I felt sure that God drew me a rainbow simply to delight me. My adult self liked it because of Goethe's color theory, and the idea that light can be separated into colors. I always think of God as the white light and the colors are his way of making himself accessible to us. I still haven't figured out what the prism is—maybe Christ. . . . "SEEK ME THROUGH ART," the voice said. I wondered if it was God. Could it be? I knew to seek him through art, but I forget sometimes. Music especially is how I reach Him. Playing the oboe is pure prayer. He is always there. I get depressed and I forget music. . . . The whole vision dispelled into clouds, and the clouds became denser in the middle, forming a horizontal line. The line became the wings of a small airplane, flying away from me. Now the vision really had my attention and my guard up. This had been a recurring nightmare in my childhood years, because of my father leaving. We often stood on the runway and waved until the plane disappeared. But this time it was incredibly peaceful. As I wondered what was going on, I heard the words, quite distinctly, "I AM GOING TO TAKE YOUR FATHER." Just like that. He is sick with cancer and no one knows how long he will live. I don't know when it will be, but I felt at peace, even oddly joyful because he said, "your father," affirming that relationship and that reality, after just having said "my child," letting me know that I can have a full real relationship with both. So in effect, after I hid and couldn't say but thought I was toxic scum, God said, "You are my child, and you can find me through art and creation, and be happy doing it and I am personally going to take your father and it's okay and I am in complete control, alpha and omega, God, child, father, child, father, God, so be at peace."

Mary reported that after this session, whenever she began to feel like "I'm just scum," (shame) she would remind herself, "Remember 'my child.' What about that?" She also reported after this session,

At the very seat of my depression I know from experience is the question, "God, do you love me?" Not just am I okay, or acceptable, or worthy, or pass muster, or a good kid, or worth saving, but does He *actually* love me? Unfortunately that sits right under the question of whether my mother loves me.

Mary reported feeling hope for the first time since she began therapy, and that maybe she would not be saddled with the depression forever. The exercise appears to have helped her feel less shame and to view herself very differently in her relationship with God. She felt the exercise was a very powerful and positive experience.

Contraindications

Clients who have a history of psychosis or hallucinations should not participate in this exercise. Furthermore, clients who have disassociated should not participate in this exercise. This exercise should only be used with clients who have a belief system and are struggling with shame and spirituality. This exercise (and any therapeutic intervention) should never be used to evangelize clients whose beliefs or nonbeliefs must be respected.

Suggestions for Follow-Up

An alternate version of this exercise would be to conduct a two-chair Gestalt Therapy exercise in which the client pictures God in an empty chair. Then, begin with the previous questions. Next the client would move to the empty chair and "become" God and respond back. This variation on the exercise can also be used as a follow-up to the original exercise as well, and could also be adapted for use in couples' therapy.

References

Chapman, A. H. (1976). *Harry Stack Sullivan: The man and his work.* New York: G. P. Putnam's Sons.

Cook, D. R. (1996). Empirical studies of shame and guilt: The internalized shame scale. In D. L. Nathanson (Ed.), *Knowing feeling: Affect, script and psychotherapy* (pp. 132-165). New York: W. W. Norton and Company.

Cook, D. R. (2001). *Internalized shame scale: Professional manual.* Toronto: Multi-health Systems.

Horak, J. J. (2002). Factors predicting distress at marital therapy onset. *UMI:Dissertation Services,* 3065402.

Kaufman, G. (1988). *Shame: The power of caring.* Cambridge, MA: ShenkmanPublishing.

Kaufman, G. (1989). *The psychology of shame: Theory and treatment of shame based syndromes.* New York: Springer Publishing.

Nathanson, D. L. (1987). A timetable for shame. In D. L. Nathanson (Ed.), *The many faces of shame* (pp. 1-63). New York: Guilford.

Sullivan, H. S. (1953). The meaning of the developmental approach. In H. S. Perry & M. L. Gawel (Eds.), *The collected works of Harry Stack Sullivan:* Vol. 1, *The interpersonal theory of psychiatry* (pp. 3-12). New York: W. W. Norton and Co.

Tomkins, S. S. (1963). *Affect, imagery, consciousness: The negative affects.* New York: Springer.

Tomkins, S. S. (1987). Shame. In D. L. Nathanson (Ed.), *The many faces of shame* (pp. 133-161). New York: Guilford.

Professional Readings and Resources

Kaufman, G. (1988). *Shame: The power of caring.* Cambridge, MA: ShenkmanPublishing.

Nathanson, D. L. (1987). A timetable for shame. In D. L. Nathanson (Ed.), *The many faces of shame* (pp. 1-63). New York: Guilford.

Handout: Shame and Spirituality

The purpose of this exercise is to increase clients' awareness of how they see themselves in relationship to God. Ask clients to respond to the following questions:

- Can you describe how you see yourself in relation to God?
- How do you think God sees you?
- How do you think God feels about you?
- What is God proud of in relation to you?
- What is God disappointed in with you?

Write down clients' responses on a dry erase board. After clients are done responding, place the board in front of them. Ask them to silently ponder their responses and, when they feel ready, to read their comments to God.

After clients read their statements, ask them to be silent and listen to see if they hear a response, explaining that it is perfectly acceptable if nothing happens in the session.

Finally, write the clients' statements down on paper and send them home with them at the end of the session. Suggest that they pray during the next week, starting with how they feel in relation to God. Follow-up discussions might address contradictions between what clients believe about God and what they believe about themselves.

Horak, J. J. (2006). I am not worthy: Shame and spirituality. In K. B. Helmeke & C. F. Sori (Eds.), *The therapist's notebook for integrating spirituality in counseling: Homework, handouts, and activities for use in psychotherapy* (pp. 167-173). Binghamton, NY: The Haworth Press.

15

Reconnection: The Spiritual Journey in Recovery

Julie A. States

Type of Contribution: Activity, Handout

Objective

Each of the following imagery exercises are designed to help clients explore and understand aspects of spirituality related to their recovery process. The first imagery will focus on connectedness with a Higher Power since reconnection with a spiritual self (or higher power) is central to the ideology expressed in 12-step programs such as Alcoholics Anonymous (AA). The second imagery will focus on spirituality related to a connectedness with others and the world. These exercises are useful for assessing spiritual issues in therapy, facilitating client awareness, and identifying sources of spiritual connection or isolation.

Rationale for Use

Although spirituality is viewed as a critical component in recovery from addiction, there is a lack of research and treatment focus in this area. Even though journal articles address some spiritual components in the recovery process, they remain largely phenomenological in nature. Spiritual components address issues such as isolation, personal sense of connectedness, and internal control (Carroll, 1993; Chapman, 1996). In addition, studies have been conducted exploring spirituality in recovery related to contentment with life (Corrington, 1989), purpose in life (Carroll, 1993), and quality of life (Spalding & Metz, 1997).

For the purposes of this activity, it is important to understand the dualistic nature of spirituality as it relates to the journey of recovery from addiction. In addiction and recovery literature, spirituality is understood as the relationship or connection with self, others, and a transcendent being/higher power (Brown, Peterson, & Cunningham, 1988; Carroll, 1997; Prezioso, 1987). Prezioso defined spirituality as "our ability to stand outside of ourselves and consider the meaning of our actions, the complexity of our motives and the impact we have on the world around us. Spirituality is a process of becoming, not an achievement" (p. 233). Recovery from addiction is also a process, defined by the journey, not the destination. As part of this journey, recovering addicts are challenged to develop relationships with themselves, others, and a Higher Power.

Reconnection with a spiritual self (or Higher Power) is central to the ideology expressed in 12-step programs such as Alcoholics Anonymous (AA). By equating spirituality with a Higher Power, we tend to overlook the important spiritual process of connecting with others and the world. Although isolation from family and friends is a common sequel of addiction, it is typically not explored within a spiritual context. However, recovery through the spiritual process involves repairing relationships with self and others, as well as connecting with a Higher Power (Brown et al., 1988).

Instructions

The activity in this chapter is divided into three parts: a breathing exercise, a body relaxation exercise, and a guided imagery exercise. The first two parts (breathing and body relaxation) will help the client to relax and to prepare for the guided imagery. The therapist can choose to use breathing or relaxation alone, use both, or use neither and proceed directly to the guided imagery exercise. The third activity, a guided imagery exercise, allows the therapist to choose to explore two different dimensions of spirituality: communication with a Higher Power, or connection to others and the world. For specific instructions, please see the handout at the end of the chapter.

Brief Vignette

Joy is a thirty-seven-year-old married female who was self-referred to an agency for counseling. She has been in recovery for eight months and has remained abstinent from both alcohol and cocaine (her drug of choice). Joy is the mother of two children; Bob, fourteen, and Sam, eleven. Joy began using alcohol when she was fifteen following her parents' divorce. At age twenty-two, she began experimenting with cocaine, which quickly escalated to daily use. She has experienced brief periods of abstinence, but has been unable to sustain her recovery for more than two to three months. She was proud of herself for staying clean for eight months, but felt that "something was missing." When the therapist asked about her previous relapses, Joy said, "Being clean wasn't that great. Life seemed boring and I felt empty inside."

During her recent period of recovery, Joy became involved in Alcoholics Anonymous and Narcotics Anonymous. Although she liked the 12-step approach, she struggled with the concept of a Higher Power. "I pray because my sponsor said I should, but I don't really know what God means to me." After taking several sessions to understand Joy's spiritual background, the therapist suggested the use of guided imagery to more fully explore her concept of a Higher Power (using the handout at the end of the chapter).

Following the exercise, the therapist asked Joy to draw her experience. She drew a green field with a purple/white "light" in the middle. She explains that she was able to imagine her Higher Power as a symbol of light, rather than as a human form. Joy shares that she asked her Higher Power, "How do I find you?" and her answer was "I am always with you." Joy realized that she had not allowed herself the freedom to explore her spiritual self in any context because she was taught that "God was a big man in the sky." She shared her excitement in trying to find a sense of spirit in everyday things and life events. Joy was more open to talking about her spirituality in recovery, which was addressed regularly throughout her treatment.

Suggestions for Follow-Up

There are three primary ways to process guided imagery exercises: talking, writing, and drawing. Many times, it is best to have the client complete a drawing of the imagery first, as this avoids the tendency to move into an intellectual examination of the experience. Supply paper, colored pencils, markers, chalk, etc., and ask the client to express his or her experience on paper. Be sure to inform the client that this is not an "art exercise," and that she or he is free to draw images or simply use splashes of color to represent the experience. After the client completes the drawing, invite him or her to describe the experience (including emotional aspects) in as much detail as possible. This can also be accomplished through writing. The goal is to "ground the client in the experience" by developing a tangible representation of his or her spirituality, which can be used in subsequent counseling sessions.

In addition to processing the guided imagery, clinicians may wish to utilize the Spiritual Well-Being Scale (Ellison, 1983) in order to assess the vertical (connection with Higher Power) and horizontal (relation to the world about us) dimensions of spirituality. The Spiritual Well-Being Scale is designed to indicate the perceived spiritual quality of life or the quality of one's spiritual health. It is known as the most commonly used instrument for spiritual inquiry (Hatch, Burg, Naberhaus, & Hellmich, 1998).

Contraindications

This activity should be used once a therapeutic alliance has been established, as it requires some level of trust between the therapist and the client. It should be used as an adjunct to therapy, and as part of the client's treatment plan. Therapy should address presenting concerns before progressing to guided imagery work. There are several client populations that present special concerns for this activity:

1. Clients diagnosed with anxiety or panic disorders: Some research has shown that focusing on breathing may exacerbate symptoms of anxiety (such as shortness of breath).
2. Survivors of trauma: Relaxation and meditation may create an opportunity for disturbing images to surface.
3. Clients diagnosed with personality disorders: Boundary issues common to Axis II pathology should be considered before embarking on alternative counseling approaches such as guided imagery.

References

Brown, H., Peterson, J., & Cunningham, O. (1988). Rationale and theoretical basis for a behavioral/cognitive approach to spirituality. *Alcoholism Treatment Quarterly, 5*(1/2), 47-59.

Carroll, M. (1997). Spirituality, alcoholism, and recovery: An exploratory study. *Alcoholism Treatment Quarterly, 15*(4), 89-100.

Carroll, S. (September, 1993). Spirituality and purpose in life in alcoholism recovery. *Journal of Studies of Alcohol,* 297-301.

Chapman, R. (1996). Spirituality in the treatment of alcoholism: A worldview approach. *Counseling and Values, 41,* 39-50.

Corrington, J. (1989). Spirituality and recovery: Relationships between levels of spirituality, contentment and stress during recovery from alcoholism in AA. *Alcoholism Treatment Quarterly, 6*(3/4), 151-165.

Ellison, C. W. (1983). Spiritual well-being: Conceptualization and measurement. *Journal of Psychology and Theology, 11,* 330-340.

Hatch, R., Burg, M., Naberhaus, D., & Hellmich, L. (1998). The spiritual involvement and beliefs scale: Development and testing of a new instrument. *The Journal of Family Practice, 46*(6), 476-486.

Prezioso, F. (1987). Spirituality in the recovery process. *Journal of Substance Abuse Treatment, 4,* 233-238.

Spalding, A., & Metz, G. (1997). Spirituality and quality of life in Alcoholics Anonymous. *Alcoholism Treatment Quarterly, 15*(1), 1-14.

Professional Readings and Resources

Ellison, C. W. (1983). Spiritual well-being: Conceptualization and measurement. *Journal of Psychology and Theology, 11,* 330-340.

Hatch, R., Burg, M., Naberhaus, D., & Hellmich, L. (1998). The spiritual involvement and beliefs scale: Development and testing of a new instrument. *The Journal of Family Practice, 46*(6), 476-486.

Morgan, O., & Jordan, M. (Eds.) (1999). *Addiction and spirituality: A multidisciplinary approach.* St. Louis, MO: Chalice Press.

Ringwald, C. (2002). *The soul of recovery: Uncovering the spiritual dimension in the treatment of addictions.* New York: Oxford University Press.

Bibliotherapy Sources for the Client

Casey, K. (1991). *In God's care: Daily meditations on spirituality in recovery: As we understand God.* Center City, MN: Hazelden Publishing and Educational Services.

Small, J. (1991). *Awakening in time: The journey from codependence to co-creation.* New York: Bantam Books.

Handout:
Guidelines for Breathing, Body Relaxation, and Guided Imagery Exercises

Therapist instructions: The following exercise is divided into three parts and is designed to prepare the client for the guided imagery by first using a breathing exercise followed by a relaxation exercise. After the client has completed the breathing and relaxation exercises, you will begin reading the guided imagery. You and your client will decide whether your client wants to focus on a connection with a Higher Power (choose Box 1) or a connection with others and the world (choose Box 2). Once you have finished Box 1 or Box 2, continue with the guided imagery text after Box 2.

1. *Breathing:* Prior to the imagery exercise, lead the client in deep breathing exercises. (The reader may want to use peaceful music to enhance the experience.) Begin by slowing the breath to a three to four count inhalation, pausing, then exhaling to a count of three to four. The breath should be "pulled into" the body through expanding and contracting the diaphragm, not just the chest muscles. The following is an example of what a clinician might say to a client.

   Find a comfortable position, close your eyes, and begin by concentrating on your breath.... Notice the pace of your breathing and the depth of each breath. Concentrate on slowing and deepening your breath.... Breathe in to a count of 3 or 4, pause for a moment, and now exhale to a count of three or four.... Each time you inhale, breathe in peace and tranquility, and exhale any tension or worries that you brought with you today. ... Allow your breath to deepen until you feel your abdomen expanding and contracting with each breath.... Allow your body to find its own slow breathing rhythm.... If you find your mind thinking of other things, simply return your focus to your breath.... Breathe in.... Breathe out.... Breathing in peace and tranquility ... exhaling and letting go of tension and worries.... Notice your body becoming more relaxed, more at peace....

2. *Body relaxation:* Lead the client through a deep muscle relaxation or a progressive relaxation exercise. The following is one example; however the reader may wish to incorporate another relaxation exercise (such as progressive muscle relaxation) with which he or she is familiar.

   As your body continues to relax, allow yourself to sink into the floor (chair, couch, etc.). Feel yourself being fully supported ... feeling heavier ... more relaxed ... more at peace. Take a slow deep breath ... pause ... and exhale. Feel a warm wave of relaxation begin to flow over your body beginning at your feet.... It as if the sun is shining on your feet ... warming and relaxing them.... Feel the warmth and heaviness slowly move over your calves and thighs.... Allow your legs to become heavy and relaxed.... The warm energy continues to move up your spine, relaxing and releasing all the tension you may be holding in your back and shoulders.... Feel it move over your abdomen and chest ... feeling more relaxed and more at ease.... And now, the warmth and relaxation moves through your neck ... down your arms ... and out your fingertips ... carrying with it all of the tension you may have been holding.... Allow your body to sink into the floor (or chair) ... feeling relaxed and peaceful ... and now, allow the warmth to continue up the back of your neck ... over your head ... relaxing and releasing all the muscles around your eyes, your face, and your jaw.... Letting go ... Sinking into this peaceful place ...

3. *Imagery:* Prior to beginning the guided imagery below, you and your client should decide if your client wants to focus on a connection with a Higher Power or God (Box 1), or connections with others and the world (Box 2). When you come to the boxed text, *read only one of the boxes,* and then continue with the imagery as written. Read the imagery slowly, in a soft, even voice, pausing after each phrase (indicated by ellipses). Feel free to add your own words, thoughts, and ideas to personalize the imagery for your client.

States, J. A. (2006). Reconnection: The spiritual journey in recovery. In K. B. Helmeke & C. F. Sori (Eds.), *The therapist's notebook for integrating spirituality in counseling: Homework, handouts, and activities for use in psychotherapy* (pp. 175-181). Binghamton, NY: The Haworth Press.

Handout:
Guidelines for Breathing, Body Relaxation, and Guided Imagery Exercises *(continued)*

Picture before you a staircase that will lead you down to a forest path to begin your journey. . . . Slowly approach the staircase and take one step down . . . leaving your worries behind. . . . Take another step to the second step . . . becoming more relaxed and peaceful . . . slowly taking a third step . . . beginning to notice the forest floor ahead. . . . You take a step onto the fourth stair . . . being fully relaxed, fully at ease. . . . You take the final step onto the forest floor . . . noticing the soft earth beneath your feet . . . feeling completely safe and peaceful. . . .

And now, you begin walking down this forest path. . . . Take a moment and look around. . . . Notice the sunlight streaming through the trees . . . the cool damp smell of the woods. . . . Look to your right at the small stream and see the water moving over the rocks and pebbles. . . . Continue walking down this path enjoying the peacefulness in nature. . . .

You notice a clearing on the path ahead and, as you approach the end of the path you see a beautiful, crystal clear lake. . . . Slowly step out into the clearing and feel the sun warm your entire body. . . . Allow yourself a moment to enjoy the warm sun, and the view of the shimmering lake. . . . You walk along the bank of the lake, feeling the soft green grass beneath your feet. . . . Notice how peaceful and grounded you feel in this place. . . . You are safe here. . . . Notice the stillness and tranquility around you. . . . And now, you come across a comfortable place to sit and rest. . . . Feel the earth beneath you. . . . Reach out and feel the coolness of the grass. . . . Take a moment to rest and breathe in this peaceful, tranquil place. . . .

BOX 1

And now, you slowly look to your right . . . and notice someone, or something approaching. . . . You recognize this as your spiritual self or your Higher Power. . . . What do you see? . . . What does your Higher Power look like? . . .

(Long pause here)

You notice a strong sense of power coming from this image . . . a peaceful, powerful energy. . . . Are there questions you want to ask? . . . Take some time to be with this part of yourself . . . your most spiritual self . . . your Higher Power. . . . Ask any questions you may have . . . and listen, with your ears and with your heart for the answers. . . . What is it that your Higher Power wants to say to you?

(Allow three to five minutes before continuing)

What information did you receive from your Higher Power? . . . Take a moment to think of a word or phrase that will remind you of this message. . . . And now, it is almost time to return. . . . Take a moment to offer gratitude and appreciation to this part of yourself . . . knowing that you can return here anytime you wish . . . knowing you can connect with your Higher Power anytime you need. . . .

States, J. A. (2006). Reconnection: The spiritual journey in recovery. In K. B. Helmeke & C. F. Sori (Eds.), *The therapist's notebook for integrating spirituality in counseling: Homework, handouts, and activities for use in psychotherapy* (pp. 175-181). Binghamton, NY: The Haworth Press.

Handout:
Guidelines for Breathing, Body Relaxation, and Guided Imagery Exercises *(continued)*

BOX 2

As you sit on the earth, and feel the grass beneath you, slowly lay back until you are fully reclined. . . . Notice the feeling of the soft grass beneath your head an under your body . . . allowing the earth to support you . . . giving in to the feeling of surrender . . . of connection to the world itself. . . .

(Longer pause here)

You begin to sense that there are other people who share your struggles . . . and your triumphs. . . . Who are these people in your life? . . . Invite them to sit with you at the lake . . . feel their presence and support. . . . You look around at the people here with you. . . . Some you may know, some you may not . . . but you recognize them as individuals on the road to recovery. . . . They know your pain. . . . They understand your struggles. . . . They celebrate your success. . . . They honor you. . . . Take a moment to feel your connection with others . . . with the world . . . with yourself. . . .

(Longer pause here)

And now, it is almost time to return. . . . Think of a word or phrase that can remind you of this place, of your connections. . . . Offer thanks and appreciation to the people who have joined you here today . . . knowing that you can return here anytime you need. . . .

Think again of your word or phrase that reminds you of this place . . . of your connection . . . of your spiritual self. . . . And slowly the image begins to fade and you find you are again sitting alone on the bank of the lake. . . . Notice how peaceful and connected you feel right now. . . . Feel the sun warming your body and the earth supporting you. . . . And you slowly stand up and turn toward the forest path that brought you here. . . . Walk to the edge of the woods and turn to see the lake one last time. . . .

As you step back into the forest you feel the shade from the trees . . . and once again notice the damp smell of the woods. . . . Begin walking down the path away from the lake. . . . Take a few moments to enjoy your walk in the woods. . . . You look ahead on the path and notice the staircase that brought you here. . . . Slowly approach the staircase . . . and take one step off the forest floor onto the bottom step . . . making your return slow and gentle . . . taking another step to the fourth step . . . remembering your word or phrase and the feeling of connection. . . . Take another step to the third step . . . becoming more aware of body lying on the floor (or sitting in the chair) and my presence here with you. . . . Take another step to the second stair . . . becoming more alert and awake . . . listening to my voice and the music . . . slowing moving your body and stretching . . . and finally to the first step . . . returning to a state of every day consciousness and awareness . . . feeling rested and relaxed.

States, J. A. (2006). Reconnection: The spiritual journey in recovery. In K. B. Helmeke & C. F. Sori (Eds.), *The therapist's notebook for integrating spirituality in counseling: Homework, handouts, and activities for use in psychotherapy* (pp. 175-181). Binghamton, NY: The Haworth Press.

16

Take Two and Call Me in the Morning:
Using Religious Humor in Therapy

Catherine Ford Sori
Karen B. Helmeke
Marvin L. Ford
Jessica C. Roberson

A merry heart doeth good like a medicine: but a broken spirit drieth the bones.

Proverbs 17: 22 (King James Version)

Do we laugh because we are happy, or are we happy because we laugh?

T. S. Diggs, 2004, p. 4

A man visiting a friend who lived in a small town of 300 asked, "Why does a town of this size have two churches of the same denomination?" His friend replied, "One believes there ain't no hell, and the other says, 'The hell there ain't!'"

Type of Contribution: Activity, Homework, Handouts

Objective

The purpose of this chapter is to introduce the idea of using religious humor with clients to help them see and utilize the benefits of humor in their lives. The application of humor in therapy is discussed, and several examples of religious jokes and resources are included.

Rationale for Use

A marriage and family therapist had been working for months with a couple who fought constantly and bitterly with each other. She thought she was finally making some progress with the couple, as they were beginning to listen and be attentive and nurturing to each other. She thought it would be helpful for them to learn each other's love maps (Gottman, 2001), and so she said to them, "It is essential that husbands and wives know the things that are important to each other." She turned to the husband and asked him, "Can you describe your wife's favorite flower?" The husband leaned over, touched his wife's arm gently and whispered, "Pillsbury All-Purpose, isn't it?"

Therapists and clients alike enjoy the warmth that is generated by the humorous moments that occur in therapy. Yet therapists are left to their own devices to figure out how to make use of humor in therapy. Therapists in training take courses in numerous subjects to prepare them to work effectively and competently with their clients—ethics, counseling theory and technique, process and outcome research, multicultural issues—all topics considered essential to their growth and development as a clinician. Despite our adherence to certain models or approaches in therapy, continuing research in the field of psychotherapy seems to assert that common mechanisms or factors of change, such as the therapeutic relationship, account for a great deal of the effectiveness of outcome in therapy (Hubble, Duncan, & Miller, 1999). Relationship factors account for 30 percent of change, while model or technique factors account for only 15 percent of change in therapy (Blow & Sprenkle, 2001; Miller, Duncan, & Hubble, 1997).

Yet one aspect of the therapeutic relationship and method of strengthening the therapist-client bond that is often overlooked in training is the use of humor in therapy and the various functions that humor can play in both the therapeutic relationship and in the client's life. Important aspects of the therapeutic relationship are therapeutic warmth, and therapist-client joining, both of which can be enhanced through the appropriate use of humor in therapy.

Even less frequently discussed is the application of the use of religious humor in therapy. We view the use of religious humor as a way to join with one very important aspect of many of our clients' lives. In this section, we describe the physiological benefits of humor, the use of religious humor to enhance the therapeutic relationship, the application of humor in the life of the client, and finally some general guidelines for applying humor in therapy.

Physiological Benefits of Humor

It has long been established that humor and laughter bring about positive physical changes in the body. When we laugh, our bodies release natural endorphins that result in feelings of well-being. In addition, laughter reduces the presence of stress hormones, which can help protect us from diseases. Several years ago famed author Norman Cousins was diagnosed with a debilitating and very painful disease, with little hope of recovering. Despite heavy doses of painkillers, he had difficulty sleeping. He went home from the hospital and decided to try laughter. Cousins began to watch Marx Brothers and other old comedy films, and had someone read humorous books and stories to him. He found that watching comedy produced deep *belly laughter,* which reduced his pain enough for him to sleep for a few hours. He began to improve, and eventually beat the odds to recover (Cousins, 1989, 1991; Rayl, 2000). Thus, the "laughter cure" was born. Since then, medical doctors such as Dr. Patch Adams from the Gesundheit Institute have attested to the power of humor to heal. In addition, researchers have begun to empirically study the physiological benefits of laughter (Diggs, 2004).

A hearty laugh has the benefit of exercising the heart and other muscles—and is the equivalent of an aerobic workout (but with much less sweat and hard work!). Studies attest to the benefits of laughter and humor for cardiac rehabilitation (Tan, Tan, Berk, Lukman, & Lukman, 1997), pain perception (Weisenberg, Raz, & Hener, 1998), and coping with stress (Martin & Lefcourt, 1983).

Hospitals are beginning to recognize the benefits of laughter, and some even have special "laughter rooms" in pediatric wards. Currently, a five-year study is underway by Stuber and Zeltzer, who are cancer researchers at University of California, Los Angeles, to investigate the effects of laughter and humor on the immune functioning of both healthy children, and those experiencing life-threatening diseases. This is the first study to examine the effects of humor on both sick and healthy children (Rayl, 2000). Given the impact childhood illnesses such as cancer have on family members, the authors hope future studies might examine how laughter and humor could benefit parents and siblings of seriously ill children.

Perhaps the best-known researchers on the therapeutic benefits of humor are Lee Berk and his colleagues at Loma Linda University in California. Berk and Tan (1996) found that mirthful belly laughter leads to a *eustress* state that produces positive, healthy emotions. This is the opposite of stress, which often has an unhealthy effect on the immune system. Laughter is beneficial in two ways. First, it activates the immune system, and second, it decreases stress hormones in the body. Berk, Felton, Tan, & Bittman (2001) found humor increases natural killer cell activity, immunoglobulins and other neuroimmune functioning.

When used appropriately, humor can work wonders (dare we say it is a Godsend?) in many ways and in many different situations. Whether by listening, reading, watching television or movies, or by telling jokes to others, laughter indeed "doeth good" (Proverbs 17:22, KJV). Clinicians can educate their religious or spiritual clients about ways that religious humor can help them relax and have an "aerobic exercise" at the end of a long day or week.

The Use of Religious Humor to Enhance the Therapeutic Relationship

As mentioned above, it is well established that the therapeutic relationship is a key factor in successful therapy (Miller et al., 1997). Humor can be a very useful tool in setting clients at ease and creating warmth in the therapeutic environment. Humor draws people together, and can help create a connection between the therapist and client (Sultanoff, 1992). The use of humor may also help "lighten" a session by inducing a bit of a "cognitive shift" for those who are thinking negatively or who are depressed. We cannot be sad and be laughing at the same time. Even though the effects may be temporary, humor can be a welcome relief and engender hope that positive emotions will return (Sultanoff, 1992) for clients (as well as therapists!).

Many religious clients appreciate religious humor. Some churches include church bulletin bloopers in their weekly bulletin, monthly newsletter, or national publication. Asking clients to share this type of humor can be a particularly effective means of joining with religious clients who enjoy hearing and telling such jokes. Using well-chosen religious humor can also be a way of helping clients feel that their therapist knows them well, as it communicates an understanding and valuing of their faith, as one component of their cultural background.

The use of humor is a very effective tool in working with children and adolescents. Children laugh an average of 400 times daily while adults pale in comparison, with a mere fifteen laughs per day (Diggs, 2004). Humor is a great way to join with young clients. Therapists can engage them by sharing jokes, which in turn can change their self-concept (i.e., "I am funny! I have a good sense of humor!"), alter their emotions, and most probably, increase their immune functioning. The steps to telling jokes that must be remembered and practiced also build cognitive skills. Children love to play, and tell stories and jokes, and these activities build social skills and help children make sense of their world. In a study by Sori and Sprenkle (2004), using kid's jokes and humor were reported to be effective skills to use in therapy sessions with children and families.

Application of Humor for Clients

Not only can humor be used in therapy, but clients can also be encouraged to explore different ways they can apply humor in their lives, and to observe the benefits they get from doing so. The troubled individual can dispel tension or drive away the "blues" by laughter, as can the social misfit or the person who feels threatened by new people and new situations, especially by having to talk in front of others. Clients can observe the different reactions in themselves and in their co-workers when they approach a conflict-ridden situation with humor. The new employee or student in a new school or member of an organization can lessen the stress of new social situations with humor. A stressed-out parent awakened in the middle of the night by a screaming infant can be well served by a spouse's sense of humor. Partners can make special efforts to increase the amount of laughter in their intimate relationship, and notice how their feelings for one another are affected.

General Guidelines for Using Humor

The key to using humor in an appropriate manner means to be aware of both a few "dos" and "don'ts." "Do" try to get clients to make themselves the "goat," rather than making others the target of humor (see Sultanoff, 1995). When clients learn to laugh at themselves, they receive not only the internal benefits discussed above, they also become more likeable and acceptable to others. Thus, humor should be used to help oneself and others relax or break the ice, to stress a point, to ease both inner and outer tensions, but never to belittle others. Clients will not become more successful in their relationships or careers, or become happier, by slurring others. Making oneself the butt of the joke, however, will.

As for the "don'ts," there is a danger that clients may use humor to the extent of becoming an amateur stand-up comic, turning everything into a joke, and of letting the desire to get a laugh overshadow everything they do. Timing is important, and clients need to be sensitive when to take some aspects of life seriously (e.g., relationships, worship, work). An "everything is a laugh" attitude will often repel the very people the client wishes to attract.

Another "don't" has to do with the type of humor used. Clients should be careful not to offend anyone with their choice of humor. Therapists might discuss the importance of using "clean" humor, and not using humor to put down one particular religious or ethnic group. This is important since one primary purpose in using humor is to instill social confidence in clients, who will find themselves in different situations with various groups of people. Clients should be encouraged to be sensitive to the various ages, different sexes, social backgrounds, religions, and ethnic groups who might be offended by certain types of religious or ethnic humor. Therapists should emphasize that clients will fit into a group, make their point, illustrate a message or simply amuse their friends if they are laughing *with* them.

The activities below are beneficial to clients who are depressed, stressed, anxious, or coping with illness, and they are intended to help clients feel more comfortable and confident in social situations. Although the instructions focus on using religious humor, this activity can be adapted by using general humor for clients who are not religious, or who do not find religious humor particularly amusing.

Instructions

The therapist may use humor or a few appropriate religious jokes in early sessions to join with clients and put them at ease. If clients respond well, clinicians can discuss what this experience was like for them, and how they felt in session when they laughed. Therapists may then introduce this activity with a general discussion of the physical and emotional benefits of humor, and determine if the clients are interested in incorporating spiritual humor in their treatment plans. Therapists, as part of their assessment, can also watch for evidence of humor in their clients, to see if humor is one of the strengths or resources that their clients possess, and observe to what kind of humor they respond best.

For those who have a familiarity with the Bible, the next step might be to suggest clients search for scriptures on joy. Finding verses on being joyful, having a merry heart, and how one thinks is often an important preliminary step to using humor, as these verses emphasize that God does indeed want us to have a "merry heart" (Proverbs 17:22, KJV). Some clients may find it helpful to meditate on these scriptures in order to shift their mind to more positive thoughts (see Sori & McKinney, 2006) in preparation for the humor activity. Therapists can also suggest that clients think of Bible stories that reflect a sense of humor or irony, such as Sarah's laughter at hearing from God that she would be able to have children even though she was old and barren (Genesis 18), or the Lord using a donkey to speak to Balaam to finally get his attention (Numbers 22). Clients might also reflect on times in their lives when it has felt as though God certainly must possess a sense of humor, such as looking at an armadillo, or after trying for months to find the perfect job, finally resigning oneself to stay in the same job, and then getting a promotion.

Next, as mentioned above, clinicians can explore the types of humor that appeal to clients. Humor is a very individual matter, and often what one person does not find even mildly amusing may produce mirthful belly laughs (which are found to benefit health) in others (Zinsser, 1994). Some may respond well to jokes, others to puns. Some fall off the chair when watching slapstick comedy, while others roll their eyes at such humor. Therapists may bring in a few examples to help clients clarify what types of humor they find most appealing. Clients can then begin to find and compile lists of religious jokes, humorous books, television programs or movies, and to incorporate humor into their lives on a daily basis.

Similarly, clients can assess their responses to humor as well as the role that humor plays in their lives. Do they view themselves as the center of attention, the life of the party who is always telling a funny joke or story? Are they the kind who cannot remember a punch line if their life depends upon it, but laugh louder than anyone at a really good joke? Are they only able to connect with someone if they are being funny, and use humor as a way to keep distance and limit intimacy? Are they the ones who are always serious, are too busy to read the Sunday comics, or do not really get jokes? Is theirs a subtle, wry sense of humor that only a few others notice and even fewer appreciate?

Encourage clients to bring in their favorite jokes or examples of humor to discuss in sessions. As clients experience positive interactions within the therapeutic relationship, they can be encouraged to begin to share humor, or different kinds of humor, appropriately in other social situations. Urge them to consider additional ways they could expose themselves to humor or how they might incorporate more humor in their lives. In addition, therapists should encourage clients to track the impact humor has on their mood and/or physical health and well-being and on their relationships, such as when they can take a frustrating moment with a child and turn it into a playful one.

Brief Vignette

Pastor Rob initiated counseling because he had been feeling increasingly depressed about his work. He also wanted help in deciding whether he should seek a position in another congregation. He had been at his current church for two years, and questioned his fit with the church body. It was difficult for him to connect with his parishioners, and he was frustrated and depressed about his inability to engage them. These feelings were especially strong on Sunday mornings, as he gave his weekly sermons. When questioned, Rob described a somewhat vicious cycle, in which he worked hard to prepare a sermon and practiced his delivery, but felt that on Sunday morning everything fell flat. The harder he tried to engage the congregation, the more his attempts seemed to fail. The result was that he was becoming increasingly more tense, discouraged, and depressed. At the point he entered therapy, he felt like a failure, was considering applying to different congregations, and was even praying about his calling.

After listening to Pastor Rob describe his problem, the therapist empathized with his plight. Then he mentioned that it seemed as if the harder Rob worked at his sermons and delivery, the more frustrated he became. Next, he wondered if his attempted solution was part of what was maintaining the problem. When Rob gave him a puzzled look, the therapist wondered what might happen if he stopped working so hard, and instead started enjoying his work more. After all, he did not have much to lose since his present attempts to improve things were not working. Since negative expectations tend to come true, perhaps Rob could switch his focus a bit. He asked what might happen if he enjoyed his sermons more. Rob replied, "So would my congregation. Maybe you are on to something! But how do I do that?"

The therapist and Rob then discussed the proven benefits of humor in combating depression and illness, in connecting with others, and in easing difficult social situations. Rob thought this might be something that could help him. To begin, the therapist suggested that he search the scriptures for verses on joy, merry hearts, stories that reflected something humorous, and ways that showed him that God has a sense of humor.

The following week Rob returned with several scriptures and stories that he had found that seemed to speak to him:

- A merry heart maketh a cheerful countenance: but by sorrow of the heart the spirit is broken. (Proverbs 15:13, KJV)
- Do not grieve, for the joy of the Lord is your strength. (Nehemiah 8:10, NIV)
- The thief cometh not, but for to steal, and to kill, and to destroy: I am come that they might have life, and that they might have it more abundantly. (John 10:10, KJV)
- He loved the story of the mustard seed, and the irony that Jesus would select one of the tiniest seeds in the world for his object lesson on the possibilities of faith. (see Matthew 13:31-32)

Rob was encouraged by these scriptures and parables, and decided to meditate on them daily (see Jankowski, 2006; Sori & McKinney, 2006). He was planning a two-week retreat at the end of the month so he could pray and seek God's direction in his life. In preparation for this retreat, the therapist introduced the second part of this activity. He suggested that Rob begin compiling lists of religious jokes and humor for four purposes: First, to use as "God's medicine" to help shift his thoughts to become more positive. Second, to exercise a part of Rob that God had created, but that he had neglected—his sense of humor. Third, he was to use laughter to elevate his mood and produce positive emotions. Rob was encouraged to read his jokes or use humor whenever he felt down. Fourth, doing this activity would prepare him to incorporate humor in his work, and help him feel more at ease in social situations. This activity would result in a list of jokes Rob could draw on in future sermons. The therapist also suggested that he spend a half-hour each day during his retreat searching the Internet for religious humor. He was asked to bring in his favorite jokes when he returned for his next session following his retreat.

When Rob returned he described his experience in forcing himself to find, read, and compile religious jokes. He stated that at first he dreaded the assignment, but soon found himself chuckling and at times roaring out loud at some of the hilarious jokes he had found on the Internet. He was especially amused at the funny stories of children in Sunday School. He reported that he shared many of his favorites with his wife upon his return, and that they both laughed together until they had tears in their eyes. This shared humor brought an added benefit of feeling closer to his wife. In addition, Rob said that by the end of the two weeks, he looked forward to that half hour, and returned home feeling much lighter and more positive, largely as a result of meditating daily on his scriptures and utilizing religious humor. Rather than feeling frustrated and defeated by some of the challenges he faced in his parish, he felt much more relaxed and energized. When asked which joke he had found the funniest, Rob told the following:

> There was a man who had been out sailing in the Pacific Ocean who became shipwrecked on a deserted island. It was years before a ship came by and rescued him, and he was overjoyed at being found. But before he left, he wanted to show his rescuers around the island that had been his home for so long. He took them to the beach where they saw three huts. He took them in the first one, and told them this was his house. Then he took them to the second hut, and explained that this was his church. When they asked him what the third hut was for, he said, "Oh, that is where I *used* to go to church."

The therapist then asked him to think about how he might use this or another of his favorite jokes to open a sermon. He was to practice it, and when he stood in front of his congregation, to recall how his wife had responded, and then enjoy sharing it from his heart. Rob tried this the following Sunday, and found that he felt more confident and relaxed because he knew the joke was funny, and his congregation responded with a roar of laughter. This positive experience increased his confidence, and he delivered the rest of his sermon with ease. In the weeks that followed, the "vicious cycle" was gradually transformed into a "virtuous cycle" (e.g., Freeman, Epston & Lobovits, 1997). As Rob spent time every day reading jokes, watching *America's Funniest Videos* and old slapstick movies, and reading humorous works of Mark Twain and Will Rogers, as well as meditating on God's promises, he felt less depressed and experienced more joy in his life and relationships. Whenever he felt himself begin to feel down or discouraged, he reached for his humor or lists of positive scriptures.

Rob continued to incorporate religious jokes appropriately in his sermons, and learned to relax and laugh at himself, which helped engage his congregation. As they responded with enthusiasm, he became increasingly more energetic and upbeat. Gradually, he started to add humor to sermons that poked fun at himself as a minister. One Sunday, as he noticed he had gone on longer than usual for his sermon, he told the following joke:

> There was a pastor in the church up the road who likes to preach long sermons. One Sunday, he got a little bit windier than usual, and a little girl became restless as the preacher's sermon dragged on and on. Finally, she leaned over to her mother and whispered, "Mommy, if we give him the money now, will he let us go?"

After several months he found himself actually looking forward to Sunday mornings. An added benefit was Rob felt he was living life "more abundantly" (John 10:10), and his wife and family reported that he seemed more joyful and was more fun to be around.

Suggestions for Follow-Up

Have clients keep a list of religious (and other) jokes and stories that they find particularly amusing. They could refer to this when they have a particularly bad day. Clients could search the Internet or other sources to add to their list of religious jokes. In group counseling sessions, members could be asked to take turns sharing a joke each week. Several years ago, groups of men and women began meeting in India to begin to laugh. No jokes or humor are used (as they ran out of material within a few weeks). They begin with artificial laughter that naturally progresses into giggles and eventually uproarious, mirthful belly laughs. These groups have spread across the globe, and some clients may wish to explore joining (or starting) their own chapter of Laughter Club International (see Taking Humor Seriously at www.imagotherapy.com/therapists/ Articles/TakingHumorSeriously.htm).

Contraindications

Care must be exercised that religious humor is appropriate in general for particular clients at various stages of therapy. In general, humor is probably not recommended for use in sessions with clients who are recently bereaved, abused, or traumatized. As mentioned previously, jokes should be chosen carefully to be sure that clients or clients' audiences take no offense (i.e., that they not feel that their particular religion, ethnic, or gender group is being discriminated against).

The "joke teller" experiences a warm glow when he or she hears the burst of laughter at the end of his or her story. To some, however, this can become almost addictive, and they may strive hard to get laughs, even at the risk of telling shocking, macabre or scatological "jokes." While this may bring a gasp or even some laughter from some, the bad effects outweigh this.

Similarly, the use of humor to avoid intimacy and conflict may be a problem for some clients. Although for many, humor can assist in not taking oneself so seriously and in facing some of life's most difficult moments with grace, for others it may be used to deflect, deny, or avoid deeper issues in counseling.

Humor is good for all souls. And the benefits from religious humor know no professional boundary; all people in all walks of life can find a smile, chuckle, roar of laughter and a dissipation of tension, worry and fear from hearing or telling a *good* joke. "In other words, a lighthearted outlook on life is not a joke" (J. Sori, personal communication, August 4, 2004).

References

Berk, L., & Tan, S. (1996). The laughter-immune connection. http://www.touchstarpro.com/laughbb3.html.

Berk, L. S., Felten, D. L., Tan, S. A., & Bittman, B. B. (2001). Modulation of neuroimmune parameters during the eustress of humor-associated mirthful laughter [Electronic version]. *Alternative therapies, 7*(2), 62-76. www. laughteryoga.org/uploads/pdf/13.pdf.

Blow, A. J., & Sprenkle, D. H. (2001). Common factors across theories of marriage and family therapy: A modified Delphi study. *Journal of Marital and Family Therapy, 27,* 385-402.

Cousins, N. (1989). *"The laughter connection," head first: The biology of hope.* New York: Dutton.

Cousins, N. (1991). *The anatomy of an illness.* New York: Bantam Doubleday Dell.

Diggs, T. S. (2004). Laughter: Is it healthy? Retrieved July 17, 2004, from http://fly.hiwaay.net/~garson/laughter. htm.

Freeman, J., Epston, D., & Lobovits, D. (1997). *Playful approaches to serious problems.* New York: W. W. Norton, Inc.

Gottman, J. (2001). *The relationship cure: A five-step guide to strengthening your marriage, family, and friendships.* New York: Three Rivers Press.

Holy Bible, King James Version (1816). New York: American Bible Society.

Holy Bible, New International Version (1983). Grand Rapids, MI: Zondervan Corporation.

Hubble, M. A., Duncan, B. L., & Miller, S. (1999). *The heart and soul of change: What works in therapy.* Washington, DC: The American Psychological Association.

Jankowski, P. (2006). Facilitating change through contemplative prayer. In K. B. Helmeke & C. F. Sori (Eds.), *The therapist's notebook for integrating spirituality in counseling: Homework, handouts, and activities for use in psychotherapy* (pp. 241-249). Binghamton, NY: The Haworth Press.

Martin, R. A., & Lefcourt, H. M. (1983). Sense of humor as a moderator of the relation between stressors and moods. *Journal of Personal Social Psychology, 45,* 1313-1324.

Miller, S. D., Duncan, B. L., & Hubble, M. A. (1997). *Escape from Babel: Toward a unifying language for psychotherapy practice.* New York: Norton.

Rayl, A. J. S. (2000). Humor: A mind-body connection. [Electronic version] *The Scientist, 14*(19). www.the-scientist. com/article/display/12055.

Sori, C. F., & McKinney, L. (2006). Free at last! Using scriptural affirmations to replace self-defeating thoughts. In K. B. Helmeke & C. F. Sori (Eds.), *The therapist's notebook for integrating spirituality in counseling: Homework, handouts, and activities for use in psychotherapy* (pp. 223-234). Binghamton, NY: The Haworth Press.

Sori, C. F., & Sprenkle, D. (2004). Training family therapists to work with children: A modified Delphi study. *Journal of Marital and Family Therapy, 30*(4), 113-129.

Sultanoff, S. M. (1992). The impact of humor in the counseling relationship. [Electronic version] *Laugh It Up,* July/August, 1. www.humormatters.com/articles/therapy2.htm.

Sultanoff, S. M. (1995). Levity defies gravity: Using humor in crisis situations. [Electronic version] *Therapeutic Humor, 9*(3), 1-2. www.humormatters.com/articles/crisis.htm.

Taking humor seriously. (Summer, 1999). Retrieved on July 17, 2004, from <http://www .imagotherapy.com/therapists/Articles/TakingHumorSeriously.htm>

Tan, S. A., Tan, L. G., Berk, L. S., Lukman, S. T., & Lukman, L. F. (1997). Mirthful laughter an effective adjunct in cardiac rehabilitation. *Canadian Journal of Cardiology, 13*(Supplement B), 190.

Weisenberg, M., Raz, T., & Hener, T. (1998). The influence of film mood on pain perception. *Pain, 76,* 365-375.

Zinsser, W. (1994). *On writing well.* New York: HarperPerennial.

Professional Readings and Resources

Cousins, N. (1979). *Anatomy of an illness as perceived by the patient.* New York: W. W. Norton.

Dunkelbau, E. (1987). That'll be five cents, please!: Perceptions of psychotherapy in jokes and humor. In W. Fry & W. Salameh (Eds.), *Handbook of humor and psychotherapy* (pp. 307-314). Sarasota, FL: Professional Resource Exchange.

Eberhart, E. (1993). Humor as a religious experience. In W. Fry & W. Salameh (Eds.), *Advances in humor and psychotherapy* (pp. 97-120). Sarasota, FL: Professional Resource Exchange.

Farre, F., & Lynch, M. (1987). Humor in provocative therapy. In W. Fry & W. Salameh (Eds.), *Handbook of humor and psychotherapy* (pp. 81-106). Sarasota, FL: Professional Resource Exchange.

Gelkopf, M., & Kreitler, S. (1996). Is humor only fun, an alternative cure or magic? The cognitive therapeutic potential of humor. *Journal of Cognitive Psychotherapy: An International Quarterly, 10*(4), 235-254.

Klein, A. (1989). *Healing power of humor.* Los Angeles: Tarcher.

Sultanoff, S. M. (1992). The impact of humor in the counseling relationship. [Electronic version] *Laugh It Up,* July/August, 1. www.humormatters.com/articles/therapy2.htm.

Sultanoff, S. M. (1995). Levity defies gravity: Using humor in crisis situations. [Electronic version] *Therapeutic Humor, 9*(3), 1-2. www.humormatters.com/articles/crisis.htm.

Wooten, P. (1996). Humor: An antidote for stress. *Holistic Nursing Practice, 10*(2), 49-56.

Bibliotherapy Sources for the Client

Books

Cousins, N. (1979). *Anatomy of an illness as perceived by the patient.* New York: W. W. Norton.

Cousins, N. (1989). *"The laughter connection," head first: The biology of hope.* New York: Dutton.

Cousins, N. (1991). *The anatomy of an illness.* New York: Bantam Doubleday Dell.

Seligman, M. (1998). *Learned optimism: How to change your mind and your life* (2nd ed.). New York: Pocket Books.

Movies

Barber, G., Birnbaum, R., Oedekerk, T., Bostick, M., Brubaker, J. D., Carrey, J., Koren, S., O'Keefe, M., & Shadyrac, T. (Producers), & Shadyrac, T. (Director). (2003). *Bruce Almighty* [Motion Picture]. United States: Universal Pictures.

Shadyrac, T., Williams, M. G., Farrell, M., Kemp, B., Minoff, M., & Newirth, C. J. (Producers), & Shadyrac, T. (Director). (1998). *Patch Adams* [Motion Picture]. United States: Universal Pictures.

Schwartz, T. (Producer), & Ardolino, E. (Director). (1992). *Sister Act* [Motion Picture]. United States: Buena Vista.

Kennedy, K., Marshall, F., Molen, G. R., & Molen, J. (Producers), & Spielberg, S. (Director). (1991). *Hook* [Motion Picture]. United States: Tri-Star.

Blumberg, S., Koch, H. W., Koch, Jr., H. W., & Norton, E. (Producers), & Norton, E. (Director). (2000). *Keeping the Faith* [Motion Picture]. United States: Vista Pictures.

Handout One:
Humor Resources for Religious Clients

Internet Resources for Religious Humor

To search for religious humor on the Web try using a search engine and typing in keywords such as "religious humor," "Church bloopers," or "religious jokes." The following are a few Web sites to try to get started:

www.bible-reading.com/bulletin.html
www.ouryouthgroup.com/funnybulletins.html
www.tallrite.com/lightrelief/churchbloopers.html
www.mdausa.org/publications/Quest/q34laughter.html

Movie Resources for Religious and Nonreligious Humor

Norman Cousins used many old comedy classics in his "Comedy Cure," including films by the Marx Brothers, Charlie Chaplin, and Abbot and Costello. Although not all are religious, the following are some examples of more recent movies that are also guaranteed to have most people doubled over in laughter. (Check ratings for objectionable content.)

Patch Adams
Bruce Almighty
Sister Act
Hook
Keeping the Faith

Television Comedies

Many people still enjoy old comedies from the 1950s and 1960s, such as *Candid Camera, Carol Burnett, I Love Lucy, Red Skelton,* and *Andy Griffith.* One current but long-running show that has been producing belly laughs in viewers for years is *America's Funniest Home Videos.* Although these are family shows, discretion is advised for some shows on comedy channels, as the material may be offensive to some religious clients.

Sori, C. F., Helmeke, K. B., Ford, M. L., & Roberson, J. C. (2006). Take two and call me in the morning: Using religious humor in therapy. In K. B. Helmeke & C. F. Sori (Eds.), *The therapist's notebook for integrating spirituality in counseling: Homework, handouts, and activities for use in psychotherapy* (pp. 183-199). Binghamton, NY: The Haworth Press.

Handout Two:
Samples of "Holy Humor"

Jesus and Satan Humor

Jesus and Satan were having an ongoing argument about who was better on the computer. They had been going at it for days, and God was tired of hearing all of the bickering. Finally God said, "Cool it! I am going to set up a test that will run two hours, and I will judge who does the better job."

So Satan and Jesus sat down at the keyboards and typed away. They moused. They did spreadsheets. They wrote reports. They sent faxes. They sent e-mails. They sent out e-mails with attachments. They downloaded. They did some genealogy reports. They made cards. They did every known job.

But ten minutes before their time was up, lightning suddenly flashed across the sky, thunder clapped, the rain poured, and, of course, the electricity went off.

Satan stared at his blank screen and screamed every curse word known in the underworld. Jesus just sighed.

The electricity finally flickered back on, and each of them restarted their computers. Satan started searching frantically and screamed, "It's gone! It's all gone! I lost everything when the power went off!"

Meanwhile, Jesus quietly started printing out all of his files from the past two hours of diligent work. Satan observed this and became irate.

"Wait! He cheated! How did he do it?"

God shrugged and said, "Jesus saves."

Pastor Self-Deprecating Humor

After the church service a little boy told the pastor, "When I grow up, I'm going to give you some money." "Well, thank you," the pastor replied, "but why?" "Because my daddy says you're one of the poorest preachers we've ever had."

One Sunday morning, the pastor noticed little Alex was staring up at the large plaque that hung in the foyer of the church. The plaque was covered with names, and small flags were mounted on either side of it. The seven-year-old had been staring at the plaque for some time, so the pastor walked up, stood beside the boy, and said quietly,

"Good morning, Alex."

"Good morning, Pastor," replied the young man, still focused on the plaque. "Pastor McGhee, what is this?" Alex asked.

"Well, son, it's a memorial to all the young men and women who died in the service." Soberly, they stood together, staring at the large plaque.

Little Alex's voice was barely audible when he asked, "Which service, the nine o'clock or the eleven o' clock?"

Jokes on Heaven and Hell

An Illinois man left the streets of Chicago for a vacation in Florida. His wife was on a business trip and was planning to meet him the next day. When he reached his hotel, he decided to send his wife a quick note by e-mail.

Unable to find the scrap of paper on which he had written her e-mail address, he did his best to type it in from memory. Unfortunately, he missed one letter and his note was directed instead to an elderly preacher's wife, whose husband had passed away only the day before.

When the grieving widow checked her e-mail, she took one look at the monitor, let out a piercing scream, and fell to the floor dead. At the sound, her family rushed into the room and saw this note on the screen:

Sori, C. F., Helmeke, K. B., Ford, M. L., & Roberson, J. C. (2006). Take two and call me in the morning: Using religious humor in therapy. In K. B. Helmeke & C. F. Sori (Eds.), *The therapist's notebook for integrating spirituality in counseling: Homework, handouts, and activities for use in psychotherapy* (pp. 183-199). Binghamton, NY: The Haworth Press.

**Handout Two:
Samples of "Holy Humor" *(continued)***

Dearest Wife,

Just got checked in. Everything prepared for your arrival tomorrow.

Your Loving Husband

P.S.: Sure is hot down here.

A little girl was talking to her teacher about whales. The teacher said it was physically impossible for a whale to swallow a human because even though it was a very large mammal its throat was very small.

The little girl stated that Jonah was swallowed by a whale. The teacher reiterated that a whale could not swallow a human; it was impossible.

The little girl said, "When I get to heaven I will ask Jonah."

The teacher asked, "What if Jonah went to hell?"

The little girl replied, "Then you ask him."

A college drama group presented a play in which one character would stand on a trap door and announce, "I descend into hell!" A stagehand below would then pull a rope, the trapdoor would open, and the character would plunge through. The play was well received.

When the actor playing the part became ill, another actor who was quite overweight took his place. When the new actor announced, "I descend into hell!" the stagehand pulled the rope, and the actor began his plunge, but became hopelessly stuck. No amount of tugging on the rope could make him descend. One student in the balcony jumped up and yelled: "Hallelujah! Hell is full!"

Miscellaneous Jokes

A drunk stumbles upon a baptismal service on Sunday afternoon down by the river. He proceeds to walk down into the water and stand next to the preacher. The minister turns and notices the old drunk and says, "Mister, are you ready to find Jesus?"

The drunk looks back and says, "Yes, Preacher . . . I sure am."

The minister then dunks the fellow under the water and pulls him right back up. "Have you found Jesus?" the preacher asked.

"Nooo, I didn't!" said the drunk.

The preacher then dunks him under for quite a bit longer, brings him up and says, "Now, brother, have you found Jesus?"

"Noooo, I did not, Reverend."

The preacher in disgust holds the man under for at least thirty seconds this time, brings him out of the water and says in a harsh tone, "My God, man, have you found Jesus yet?"

The old drunk wipes his eyes and says to the preacher, "Are you sure this is where he fell in?"

In a small church the recent contributions had been decreasing alarmingly. To try to reverse this trend, the minister said one Sunday, "There is a man in this congregation who tells his wife he's working late. Instead, I have found out that he's been drinking and gambling and consorting with low lives. If he doesn't put a twenty dollar bill in the collection plate this morning, next Sunday I'll reveal his name." That morning there were eleven $20 bills in the plate, and one $5 bill with a note saying, "I'll bring the next $15 on payday."

Sori, C. F., Helmeke, K. B., Ford, M. L., & Roberson, J. C. (2006). Take two and call me in the morning: Using religious humor in therapy. In K. B. Helmeke & C. F. Sori (Eds.), *The therapist's notebook for integrating spirituality in counseling: Homework, handouts, and activities for use in psychotherapy* (pp. 183-199). Binghamton, NY: The Haworth Press.

Handout Two:
Samples of "Holy Humor" *(continued)*

Kids and Church

A Sunday school teacher asked her little children, as they were on the way to church service, "And why is it necessary to be quiet in church?"
One bright little girl replied, "Because people are sleeping."

Six-year-old Angie and her four-year-old brother Joel were sitting together in church. Joel giggled, sang, and talked out loud. Finally, his big sister had had enough.
"You're not supposed to talk out loud in church."
"Why? Who's going to stop me?" Joel asked.
Angie pointed to the back of the church and said, "See those two men standing by the door? They're the *hushers.*"

My grandson was visiting one day when he asked, "Grandma, do you know how you and God are alike?"
I mentally polished my halo while I asked, "No, how are we alike?"
"You're both old," he replied.

A ten-year old, under the tutelage of her grandmother, was becoming quite knowledgeable about the Bible. Then one day she floored her grandmother by asking, "Which Virgin was the mother of Jesus? The Virgin Mary or the King James Virgin?"

A Sunday school class was studying the ten commandments. They were ready to discuss the last one. The teacher asked if anyone could tell her what it was. Susie raised her hand, stood tall, and quoted, "Thou shall not take the covers off the neighbor's wife."

And one particular four-year-old prayed, "And forgive us our trash baskets as we forgive those who put trash in our baskets."

A little boy was overheard praying: "Lord, if you can't make me a better boy, don't worry about it. I'm having a real good time like I am."

A mother was preparing pancakes for her sons, Ronnie, five, and Johnny, three. The boys began to argue over who would get the first pancake. Their mother saw the opportunity for a moral lesson. "If Jesus were sitting here, he would say 'Let my brother have the first pancake. I can wait.'"
Ronnie turned to his younger brother and said, "Johnny, you be Jesus!"

A father was at the beach with his children when the four-year-old son ran up to him, grabbed his hand, and led him to the shore, where a seagull lay dead in the sand. "Daddy, what happened to him?" the son asked.
"He died and went to heaven," the dad replied. The boy thought a moment and then said, "Did God throw him back down?"

A little boy was attending his first wedding. After the service, his cousin asked him, "How many women can a man marry?"
"Sixteen," the boy responded. His cousin was amazed that he had an answer so quickly. "How do you know that?"
"Easy," the little boy said. "All you have to do is add it up, like the Bishop said: four better, four worse, four richer, four poorer."

Sori, C. F., Helmeke, K. B., Ford, M. L., & Roberson, J. C. (2006). Take two and call me in the morning: Using religious humor in therapy. In K. B. Helmeke & C. F. Sori (Eds.), *The therapist's notebook for integrating spirituality in counseling: Homework, handouts, and activities for use in psychotherapy* (pp. 183-199). Binghamton, NY: The Haworth Press.

Handout Two:
Samples of "Holy Humor" *(continued)*

After the christening of his baby brother in church, little Johnny sobbed all the way home in the backseat of the car. His father asked him three times what was wrong. Finally, the boy replied, "That priest said he wanted us brought up in a Christian home, and I want to stay with you guys!"

Terri asked her Sunday school class to draw pictures of their favorite Bible stories. She was puzzled by Kyle's picture, which showed four people on an airplane, so she asked him which story it was meant to represent. "The flight to Egypt," said Kyle.
"I see . . . And that must be Mary, Joseph, and Baby Jesus," Ms. Terri said. "But who's the fourth person?"
Terri replied, "Oh, that's Pontius—the Pilot."

The Sunday school teacher asks, "Now, Johnny, tell me frankly, do you say prayers before eating?"
"No sir," little Johnny replies. "I don't have to. My mom is a good cook."

A child told her Sunday school teacher, "You told us that 'From dust we came, and to dust we will return.' I looked under our sofa at home this morning, and somebody's either coming or going!"

A little girl kneeled by her bed, and in a very loud voice said, "Lord, Sunday is my birthday. I want a bicycle. I need a bicycle. Please, Lord, send me a bicycle for my birthday."
Her mother said, "Honey, you don't need to scream. God isn't deaf."
The girl said, "I know, but Grandma is."

A little boy was sent to Sunday School with two quarters, one for the collection plate, the other to buy himself candy on the way home. As he was walking to church, one quarter dropped out of his hand and fell into the grate in the street. Sadly, the little boy raised his eyes to heaven and said, "Sorry, Lord. We just lost your quarter."

A little girl came home from church and told her mother, "Today we sang about animals in Sunday school."
Her surprised mother asked, "You sang about animals?"
The little girl replied, "Yes. We learned, 'Gladly, the Cross-Eyed Bear.'"

The Kindergarten Sunday school teacher asked the class what was the greatest commandment God ever gave. One little boy raised his hand, stood up and said, "The greatest commandment God ever gave was 'Thou shalt not admit adultery.'"

Church Bulletin Bloopers

From a church bulletin: "The church is forming a Young Mothers' Group. Anyone interested in becoming a Young Mother please see the pastor in his private office as soon as possible."

From a church bulletin: "The women of the church are having a fund raiser. Come on Thursday night at 7:00 p.m. to the church basement to see the women of the church cast off clothing of many kinds."

A church bulletin announced the following: "Special guest this Sunday Evening: Come hear Bertha Belch all the way from Africa!"

Sori, C. F., Helmeke, K. B., Ford, M. L., & Roberson, J. C. (2006). Take two and call me in the morning: Using religious humor in therapy. In K. B. Helmeke & C. F. Sori (Eds.), *The therapist's notebook for integrating spirituality in counseling: Homework, handouts, and activities for use in psychotherapy* (pp. 183-199). Binghamton, NY: The Haworth Press.

Handout Two:
Samples of "Holy Humor" *(continued)*

Note: Use denominational and ethnic religious humor with caution and respect, to join with clients who share your own background.

Catholic Humor

The Pope was being driven through the countryside when he asked his chauffeur to pull over and exchange places with him, saying he'd always wanted to drive the limousine, and this was his chance. The Pope got behind the wheel while the chauffeur climbed into the back of the limousine. They sped away, but soon were pulled over by a police officer for speeding. The officer took one look at the driver, and scurried back to radio his sergeant. In an anxious voice he said, "Sir, I don't know what to do. I just pulled over someone really important."
His sergeant asked, "Well who is it, the mayor?"
"No, someone more important."
"Well, was it the governor?" asked the sergeant.
The officer replied, "No—he's even more important than the governor!"
"Well," said his superior officer, "Is it the president then?"
In a hushed voice the officer replied, "No—I don't know who he is, but the Pope is his chauffeur!"

Four Catholic ladies were having coffee. The first Catholic woman tells her friends, "My son is a priest. When he walks into a room, everyone calls him 'Father.'"
The second Catholic woman chirps, "My son is a bishop. Whenever he walks into a room, the people call him 'Your Grace.'"
This third Catholic crone says, "My son is a cardinal. Whenever he walks into a room, people say 'Your Eminence.'"
Since the fourth Catholic woman sips her coffee in silence, the first three women give her this subtle "Well . . . ?"
And she said, "My son is a gorgeous, six-foot-two, hard-bodied movie star. When he walks into a room, people say, "Oh, my God. . . ."

There's this old priest who got sick of all the people in his parish who kept confessing to adultery. One Sunday, in the pulpit, he said, "If I hear one more person confess to adultery, I'll quit!"
Well, everyone liked him, so they came up with a code word. Someone who had committed adultery would say they had "fallen." This seemed to satisfy the old priest and things went well, until the priest died at a ripe old age. About a week after the new priest arrived, he visited the mayor of the town and seemed very concerned.
The priest said, "You have to do something about the sidewalks in town. When people come into the confessional, they keep talking about having fallen."
The mayor started to laugh, realizing that no one had told the new priest about the code word. Before the mayor could explain the priest shook an accusing finger at the mayor and said, "I don't know what you're laughing about; your wife fell three times this week."

A man is struck by a bus on a busy street in New York City. He lies dying on the sidewalk as a crowd of spectators gathers around.
"A priest. Somebody get me a priest!" the man gasps. A policeman checks the crowd—no priest, no minister, no man of God of any kind. *"A priest, please!"* the dying man says again.
Then out of the crowd steps a little old Jewish man of at least eighty years of age. "Mr. Policeman," says the man, "I'm not a priest. I'm not even a Catholic. But for fifty years now I'm living behind St. Elizabeth's Catholic Church on First Avenue, and every night I'm listening to the Catholic litany. Maybe I can be of some comfort to this man."
The policeman agreed and brought the octogenarian over to where the dying man lay. He kneels down, leans over the injured and says in a solemn voice: "B-4. I-19. N-38. G-54. O-72 . . ."

Sori, C. F., Helmeke, K. B., Ford, M. L., & Roberson, J. C. (2006). Take two and call me in the morning: Using religious humor in therapy. In K. B. Helmeke & C. F. Sori (Eds.), *The therapist's notebook for integrating spirituality in counseling: Homework, handouts, and activities for use in psychotherapy* (pp. 183-199). Binghamton, NY: The Haworth Press.

Handout Two:
Samples of "Holy Humor" *(continued)*

Ethnic Humor

An Irishman moves into a tiny hamlet in County Kerry, walks into the pub and promptly orders three beers. The bartender raises his eyebrows, but serves the man three beers, which he drinks quietly at a table, alone.

An hour later, the man has finished the three beers and orders three more. This happens yet again. The next evening the man again orders and drinks three beers at a time, several times. Soon the entire town is whispering about the Man Who Orders Three Beers.

Finally, a week later, the bartender broaches the subject on behalf of the town. "I don't mean to pry, but folks around here are wondering why you always order three beers?"

"'Tis odd, isn't it?" The man replies, "You see, I have two brothers, and one went to America, and the other to Australia. We promised each other that we would always order an extra two beers whenever we drank as a way of keeping up the family bond."

The bartender and the whole town was pleased with this answer, and soon the Man Who Orders Three Beers became a local celebrity and source of pride to the hamlet, even to the extent that out-of-towners would come to watch him drink.

Then, one day, the man comes in and orders only two beers. The bartender pours them with a heavy heart. This continues for the rest of the evening: he orders only two beers. The word flies around town. Prayers are offered for the soul of one of the brothers.

The next day, the bartender says to the man, "Folks around here, me first of all, want to offer condolences to you for the death of your brother. You know—the two beers and all."

The man ponders this for a moment, then replies, "You'll be happy to hear that my two brothers are alive and well. It's just that I, myself, have decided to give up drinking for Lent."

Ecumenical Humor

A minister, a priest, and a rabbi went for a hike one day. It was very hot. They were sweating and exhausted when they came upon a small lake. Since it was fairly secluded, they took off all their clothes and jumped in the water. Feeling refreshed, the trio decided to pick a few berries while enjoying their "freedom."

As they were crossing an open area, who should come along but a group of ladies from town. Unable to get to their clothes in time, the minister and the priest covered their privates and the rabbi covered his face while they ran for cover.

After the ladies left and the men got their clothes back on, the minister and the priest asked the rabbi why he covered his face rather than his privates.

The rabbi replied, "I don't know about you, but in MY congregation, it's my face they would recognize."

At an ecumenical retreat a priest, minister, and a rabbi were taking a walk in the forest. After a time, they decided each would confess their greatest struggle with sin. The priest said he sometimes nipped a bit too much of the communion wine. The minister confessed he drove to the next state each week to purchase lottery tickets. But the rabbi remained silent.

"Come on, we all shared. Now it's your turn!" they urged.

After much prodding, the rabbi confessed, "My biggest struggle is with gossip, and right now I just can't wait to get back to the lodge!"

Sori, C. F., Helmeke, K. B., Ford, M. L., & Roberson, J. C. (2006). Take two and call me in the morning: Using religious humor in therapy. In K. B. Helmeke & C. F. Sori (Eds.), *The therapist's notebook for integrating spirituality in counseling: Homework, handouts, and activities for use in psychotherapy* (pp. 183-199). Binghamton, NY: The Haworth Press.

- 17 -

Using Popular Films to Integrate Spirituality
in Counseling: *Smoke Signals*
and Forgiveness

Paul E. Priester
Aaron H. Carlstrom

Type of Contribution: Homework, Handout

Objective

This chapter will introduce clinicians to the use of popular films as a medium from which clients may explore spirituality-related issues within the psychotherapy context.

Rationale for Use

There are two main reasons for the use of popular films as a medium from which to explore spiritual or religious themes in therapy. First, metaphor can be a powerful approach to addressing spiritual or religious issues. Metaphors offer clients new perspectives on their issues and can sidestep potential defensiveness. As an aside, it is noted that Jesus relied primarily on metaphors in the form of stories to deliver his lessons.

In our current visually emphasized culture, popular films are a compelling source of metaphoric material. Popular films often have a cathartic impact on viewers. One pitfall to addressing spiritual or religious issues in psychotherapy is the danger that the clients approach the task in an overly intellectualized manner. The use of such cathartically charged material offers a way for clients to explore issues from their hearts rather than just from their heads.

The second reason for using popular films as an adjunctive therapy tool is that greater client compliance occurs with watching films compared to reading books. Traditionally, psychotherapists have made ready use of bibliotherapy as an adjunct to the therapy process. In bibliotherapy, clients are assigned books to read outside of sessions that relate to some aspect of their presenting problem. In early bibliotherapy, respected works of literature were used to inspire and motivate clients to change through the use of metaphor and story. Currently, the bibliotherapy trend among clinicians is to refer clients to use less metaphorical works of art, such as a self-help book related to one of the client's presenting problems. Not only has much of the benefit of metaphor and story been lost in current bibliotherapy practice, but clients seldom actually read the books recommended by their therapist. According to Wedding (2001), when clients are assigned books to read, approximately 30 percent of them actually follow through with this request. Alternatively, when clients are asked to rent and view a popular film, approximately 90 percent comply.

This chapter presents a model of adjunctive therapy that provides the therapeutic benefits of metaphor and story, and that clients are more likely to comply with and therefore are more likely to benefit from. This model can be applied to most presenting issues. As an example of its applicability for integrating spirituality into counseling, this chapter focuses on the use of a specific film (*Smoke Signals*) for a specific presenting problem (forgiveness).

When we are hurt by the actions (or lack of action) of another it is a natural response to want retribution, to cause harm and injury to the person who harmed us. Condoning, excusing, forgetting, and denying are other possible reactions to injury (Madison & Schmidt, 2001), which may also lead to negative consequences and adjustment over time.

Forgiveness is a powerful alternate response to harm and injury that the great religious traditions of the world have addressed. Forgiveness is associated with positive outcomes, such as having faith in others again that helps to create and maintain emotionally intimate relationships, and leads to less depression, hostility, anger, anxiety, interpersonal sensitivity, paranoid ideation, higher self-esteem, better attitudes toward parents (when forgiving fathers and mothers), and greater hope (Madison & Schmidt, 2001; McCullough & Witvliet, 2002). Over time, forgiveness helps us become more positive in our reactions toward those who injured us (Madison & Schmidt, 2001). In addition, not forgiving someone can lead to emotional distance and cutoff from self, others, and God. However, it is important to note that forgiving someone who caused us severe harm without properly taking care of ourselves and grieving our loss can lead to negative outcomes.

Instructions

The following is a description of how to use popular movies as adjuncts in counseling. There are four main phases involved in using popular films as adjuncts in counseling: selection of a film, preparation of the client for watching the film, the client's viewing of the film, and processing the client's viewing and reactions to the film. The following steps are recommended to guide the selection of a film as an adjunct in counseling (Berg-Cross, Jennings, & Baruch, 1990; Hesley & Hesley, 2001; Solomon, 1995):

1. Client and therapist should select an issue that is currently a focus of therapy. This should be an issue in which a goal is to deepen the client's understanding of the issue or to broaden the scope of the issue.
2. Select a movie that is relevant for the client's issue.
3. Select a movie based on the client's and your familiarity of movies. You can also consult one or more of the resources listed at the end of this chapter.
4. Select a movie(s) that the client has enjoyed in the past or is likely to enjoy.
5. Select movies that can increase the client's hopefulness, motivation, or confidence for addressing the issue, or that provides modeling of adaptive coping.

After a movie has been selected it is important to prepare the client to view the movie. The main goal when preparing a client to view the selected movie is to help them understand the difference between watching a movie for entertainment and escape, versus watching a movie therapeutically. Watching a movie therapeutically involves focusing on characters (versus plot), relationships (versus action), process (versus outcome), insight (versus excitement), analysis (versus suspense), and oneself (versus the actors) (Hesley & Hesley, 2001). The goal of therapeutically watching a movie is for clients to consciously view the film so they can develop awareness and insight about how the character(s), relationships, and the development and resolution of problems in the film relate to their current life situation and therapeutic goals.

The following steps are recommended to facilitate a client's therapeutic viewing of a movie (Berg-Cross et al., 1990; Hesley & Hesley, 2001; Solomon, 1995):

1. Discuss the reasons for prescribing this movie in order to address the specific issue.
2. Discuss which characters, relationships, processes, themes, etc., that the client should pay attention to in order to assess the similarities and dissimilarities to their own life and situation. Remind the client about the difference between therapeutically watching a movie, as opposed to watching a movie for entertainment or escape.
3. Discuss scenes that may cause problems for clients, e.g. violence, sexually explicit, language, etc.
4. Discuss having clients take notes while watching the movie, or journaling after viewing the movie. Also, address having clients replay scenes that they find powerful or insightful.
5. Let clients know that if their reaction to the movie is so negative that they want to stop watching it that they should turn off the movie, and that you will discuss their reaction during the next session.
6. Discuss when in the coming week the client plans to watch the movie. Determine if it is better for the client to watch the movie soon after the current session, or closer in time to the next scheduled session.
7. Discuss whether the client is going to watch the movie alone or with other people.
8. Remind the client that you will discuss viewing, reactions, and insights from the movie at the next session.

The third phase is that the client views the movie. The fourth phase is processing the client's reactions and insights to watching the film during a counseling session. It is helpful for the psychotherapist to prepare in advance some process questions related to the movie. This can help guide the exploration of the impact of the movie on the client.

Brief Vignette

Following is a brief description of the use of the movie *Smoke Signals* as an adjunct in therapy with a thirty-year-old male client, to address the spiritually relevant therapeutic theme of forgiveness.

Before describing the case example, a brief description of *Smoke Signals* is provided. *Smoke Signals* is a PG-13, comedy-drama, which runs approximately ninety minutes. It is based on Sherman Alexie's (1994) book *The Lone Ranger and Tonto Fistfight in Heaven,* and it received the Audience Award and Filmmakers' Trophy at the 1998 Sundance Film Festival.

Following is a brief plot summary of *Smoke Signals* for those readers who may not be familiar with the movie. Thomas lives with his grandmother, and Victor lives with his mother (Arlene) on the Coeur d'Alene Indian reservation in Idaho. Arnold (Victor's father) saved Thomas (when he was an infant) from a house fire that killed Thomas's parents. Arnold is an alcoholic and leaves his family and the reservation when Victor is a child. Now, as young men on the reservation the nerdy Thomas cares for his grandmother, while the stoic Victor lives with his mother. Victor receives news from Suzy Song that his father has died in Phoenix. Thomas offers to help Victor pay for the trip, but only if Victor agrees to take Thomas along. Victor begrudgingly accepts Thomas's offer, so the two very different young men set out for Phoenix to get Arnold's truck and remains from Suzy Song, a neighbor and friend of Arnold's who provides disturbing truths about Arnold that humanize Arnold to Victor. The journey to and from Phoenix and the meeting with Suzy Song help Victor come to a different understanding of his father.

As described previously, when preparing clients to view a film as part of their counseling work, it is necessary to discuss scenes from the film that may cause problems for them prior to their viewing the film. For example, the following depictions in *Smoke Signals* may cause problems for some clients: domestic violence, parental abandonment, alcoholism, adult language, a house fire, and comments made about church-based oppression of Native Americans.

The remainder of this section describes a case example in which *Smoke Signals* was used to address the spiritually relevant therapeutic theme of forgiveness.

Chad was a thirty-year-old male who had been married to his wife, Mia, for four years. Chad and Mia had a two-year-old son named Ben. Chad was an architect for a medium-sized firm located in a large midwestern city. Originally, he was referred by his primary care physician to the clinic for self-regulation training using biofeedback to address issues of stress and anger. After four weeks of self-regulation work, Chad self-referred to another counselor at the clinic in order to more deeply explore stress and anger in his life.

Chad described work as stressful, and he no longer felt the passion for architecture that he had as a student and when he first began work at the firm. He had a "shorter and shorter fuse" when things went wrong at work and at home. In addition, work demands contributed to his spending late nights and weekends at work, or working at home. Chad and Mia's relationship was strained, and Chad felt guilty that work kept him from spending time with Mia and Ben. However, he also was relieved that sometimes work kept him away from the tension at home. Chad had grown more cynical over a two-year period, starting with Ben's birth. In fact, he had a difficult time containing his contempt for optimistic people, whom he considered foolish and naïve. This was especially true of new co-workers and new parents.

Discussion about these issues during counseling sessions revealed that Chad was also very angry with his father whom he described as not knowing "when to be helpful and when to mind his own business." Chad's father and mother were married and lived approximately twenty minutes away from Chad. Chad, Mia, and Ben spoke with Chad's parents weekly, and saw them about every two to three weeks. Since childhood, Chad's father had been very critical of Chad's academic, music, and athletic performances and accomplishments. When Chad and his father talked, they usually discussed sports and work. Chad described his father as critical and emotionally distant, and he associated much of his anger as coming from his relationship with his father. With the birth of Ben, Chad noticed that he had become angrier with his father as he saw his father being emotionally engaged with Ben. In the past Chad had ignored his father's criticism and emotional distance because he thought that his father could not act differently. However, watching him interact with Ben made Chad realize that his father possessed the ability to be emotionally supportive.

While working on the issues of stress, anger, and forgiveness of his father in counseling, Chad became stuck. Rationally he wanted to forgive his father and he thought that doing so would help him manage his anger and stress better, but emotionally he did not feel like forgiving his father. In addition, he did not know where to begin to forgive his father.

Chad and his therapist decided to use the movie *Smoke Signals* to further explore these issues in Chad's life to help him become unstuck. Prior to watching the movie, the therapist and Chad discussed how Chad should pay attention to the character of Victor, and Victor's relationship to his father, his mother, and Thomas. Chad was told to think about how Victor's relationships were similar and dissimilar to his own, what led to Victor's ability to forgive his father, and how this changed his relationships with others and himself.

Chad and his therapist processed the movie in depth during the next session, and used metaphors from the movie throughout the remainder of counseling, e.g. (1) "running on the road as a child" to describe Chad's use of work as a means to avoid family tensions; and (2) "refusing to carry the father's ashes, to carrying them, to sharing them with another, to releasing the father's ashes," to describe the process of Chad gaining insight into the role of his relationship with his father in his life and how he approached the relationship differently. Chad said that the most powerful scene in the movie was when Victor released his father's ashes into the river by the waterfall, while Thomas's voice recites the poem "Forgiving Our Fathers." The line of the poem that asked when we forgive our fathers was an especially powerful metaphor for Chad, one that he repeated to himself when he found the journey of forgiveness difficult.

The therapist and Chad continued to work for six sessions after Chad had watched the movie. At the end of counseling Chad was able to manage his stress and anger better, spent more time with Mia and Ben, was beginning to change his interactions with his father, and was well into the process of forgiving his father. Viewing and discussing the movie did not directly lead to changes in Chad's life, but the movie was used as an adjunct to counseling to help deepen his understanding of a specific therapeutic issue (i.e., forgiving his father). The movie provided metaphors that he found useful in conveying to others and himself the meaning of his experiences in the process of forgiveness and change.

As stated earlier, it is helpful for a clinician to plan ahead in developing process questions to guide the client's therapeutic exploration of the themes presented in the film. The following is an example of questions that could be used to process a client's therapeutic viewing of the movie *Smoke Signals:*

- In what ways does holding onto resentments and failing to forgive hurt you spiritually?
- What does your religious or spiritual tradition have to say about forgiveness?
- Fire can purify. Thomas's last name is Builds-the-Fire. Who is the Thomas in your life?
- Thomas told positive stories about Arnold, and Victor said that he did not want to hear them. What are the stories that you do not want to hear about the person you want to forgive?
- Water, fire, and ash are symbols of the process of purification. How was Victor's experience of water, fire, and ash connected to his father's experience? How was it disconnected? Where do you experience water/fire/ash on your journey of forgiveness?
- How was Victor's running on the road as a child when his father left different from his running to find help after the car accident? How are they similar? Which of the roads are you running on now? Which one do you want to be on?
- Who did Victor forgive? Anyone else?
- Suzy Song confronted Victor with information about his father that he did not want to hear, but that helped him on his journey of forgiveness. Who is the Suzy Song in your life?
- Victor asks his mother, Arlene, if he should accept Thomas's offer to go along on the journey. Arlene states that even though she may make the best fry bread, she does not make it by herself. Who can help you on your journey of forgiveness?
- At the beginning of the movie Thomas states that there are Children of Fire, who burn everything they touch, and there are Children of Ash, who fall apart when they are touched. Which do you identify with more?
- The waterfall is the place where: (a) Arnold finds Thomas as a young boy and takes him to Denny's, (b) Victor, in a vision, sees his father extending him a hand when he has fallen while running for help after the car accident, and (c) Victor releases his father's ashes. What/where is your waterfall?
- Forgiveness changes how we think, feel, and act. "Tell me what's going to happen?", as Grandma Builds-the-Fire asks Thomas at the end of the movie.
- The poem at the end of the movie asks how we go about forgiving our fathers. How do you forgive?
- The poem at the end of the movie asks what is left, if we *do* forgive our fathers. What is left when you forgive the person that you want or need to forgive?

Suggestions for Follow-Up

If your client finds this approach helpful, suggest that he or she attempt its use in other areas of life. The resources discussed in this chapter can serve as a guide to identifying relevant movies. Suggest experimenting with the use of more metaphorical movies in contrast to those explicitly related to a presenting issue. For example, this author has used the film *Babe* (in which a pig struggles with the stress of pursuing the nontraditional career path of wanting to be a sheep herder) with clients who are grappling with career choice issues. In another situation, the film *Interview with the Vampire* was used to explore issues related to adolescence and the process of identity formation. Making such a stretch can be highly entertaining as well as leading to dramatic insights about the options that clients have in life.

Contraindications

Hesley and Hesley (2001) offer several cautions concerning clients who may not benefit or even be harmed by the use of this approach. First, obviously, if a client does not enjoy watching movies, this model may not be very helpful. Young children may lack the cognitive complexity to think metaphorically about their problems. A high level of abstract reasoning ability is required when using metaphorical movies not explicitly connected to the presenting issue.

A certain class of clients may be vulnerable to negative consequences from using this model of adjunctive therapy. Any clients who are psychotic or who are having difficulty differentiating reality from fantasy may be harmed by the use of this model. It is inappropriate to use this approach with clients who do not have sufficient coping skills to modulate cathartic responses from watching the movies. Finally, this approach should not be used if there is the possibility that the client may believe that the clinician is suggesting a similarity between the client and an unsavory character or a negative film-based outcome. While managing client interpretation of the psychotherapist's motives in assigning a task is difficult, suggesting specific films to this type of client may invite nontherapeutic misattributions.

With any clients, it is ethically mandated that one practice informed consent when using this approach. The clinician should warn the client beforehand if any explicit violence, sexuality, or other potentially disturbing material is present in the film. Clearly, psychotherapists should never suggest that a client watch a film that they have not seen themselves.

References

Alexie, S. (1994). *The Lone Ranger and Tonto fistfight in heaven.* New York: HarperPerennial.

Berg-Cross, L., Jennings, P., & Baruch, R. (1990). Cinematherapy: Theory and application. *Psychotherapy in Private Practice, 8*(1), 135-156.

Hesley, J. W., & Hesley, J. G. (2001). *Rent two films and let's talk in the morning: Using popular movies in psychotherapy* (2nd ed.). New York: John Wiley & Sons, Inc.

Madison, R., & Schmidt, C. (2001). *Talking pictures: A parents' guide to using movies to discuss, ethics, values, and everyday problems with children.* Philadelphia: Running Press.

McCullough, M. E, & Witvliet, C. V. (2002). The psychology of forgiveness. In C. R. Snyder & S. Lopez (Eds.), *Handbook of positive psychology* (pp. 446-458). London: Oxford University Press.

Solomon, G. (1995). *The motion picture prescription: Watch this movie & call me in the morning—200 movies to help you heal life's problems.* Santa Rosa, CA: Aslan Publishing.

Wedding, D. (2001). Movies and psychotherapy: Using films to facilitate rapport and enhance personal growth. In J. C. Norcross (Chair), *Incorporating self-help into psychotherapy: Autobiographies, bibliotherapy, Internet, movies, writing.* Symposium presented at the American Psychological Association Conference, San Francisco, CA.

Professional Readings & Resources

Articles

Berg-Cross, L., Jennings, P., & Baruch, R. (1990). Cinematherapy: Theory and application. *Psychotherapy in Private Practice, 8*(1), 135-156.

Karlinsky, H. (2003). Doc Hollywood north: Part I. The educational applications of movies in psychiatry. *Canadian Psychiatric Association Bulletin, 35*(1), 9-12.

Karlinsky, H. (2003). Doc Hollywood north: Part II. The clinical applications of movies in psychiatry. *Canadian Psychiatric Association Bulletin, 35*(2), 14-16.

McCullough, M. E, & Witvliet, C. V. (2002). The psychology of forgiveness. In C. R. Snyder & S. Lopez (Eds.), *Handbook of positive psychology* (pp. 446-458). London: Oxford University Press.

Wedding, D. W. (2000). Alcoholism in the Western genre: The portrayal of alcohol and alcoholism in the Western genre. *Journal of Alcohol and Drug Education, 46*(2), 3-11.

Wedding, D. W., & Niemiec, R. M. (2003). The clinical use of films in psychotherapy. *Journal of Clinical Psychology, 59*(2), 207-215.

Books

Hesley, J. W., & Hesley, J. G. (2001). *Rent two films and let's talk in the morning: Using popular movies in psychotherapy* (2nd ed.). New York: John Wiley & Sons, Inc.

Wedding, D., & Boyd, M. (1998). *Movies and mental illness.* New York: McGraw Hill.

Bibliotherapy Sources for the Client

Books

Madison, R., & Schmidt, C. (2001). *Talking pictures: A parents' guide to using movies to discuss, ethics, values, and everyday problems with children.* Philadelphia: Running Press.

Solomon, G. (1995). *The motion picture prescription: Watch this movie & call me in the morning—200 movies to help you heal life's problems.* Santa Rosa, CA: Aslan Publishing.

Solomon, G. (2000). *Reel therapy: How movies inspire you to overcome life's problems.* New York: Lebhar-Friedman Books.

Teague, R. (2000). Reel spirit: A guide to movies that inspire, explore, and empower. Unity Village, MO: Unity House.

Vaux, S. (1999). *Finding meaning at the movies.* Nashville: Abingdon Press.

Web Sites

http://members.tripod.com/cinematherapy/: Provides information about using films in psychotherapy, references, movie suggestions, and related news.

http://www.themovietherapist.com/frameset.htm: Presents a British model of the therapeutic use of films in psychotherapy.

http://www.cinematherapy.com/: Provides a model for using films in individual psychotherapy.

http://www.movietx.yourmd.com/: Presents a model for using films in the context of group psychotherapy.

http://filmtx.com/: This site offers CEU credits to Californian psychologists and counselors for watching therapeutic films.

http://members.tripod.com/cinematherapy/discussion2.html: Provides suggestions for films that are suitable for use with children and adolescents; although geared toward school counselor, the site has applicability for any clinician working with youth.

http://allmovie.com: Provides basic information about movies, such as MPAA rating, director, movie genre, who produced it, plot synopsis, cast, production credits, keywords (to use in a movie search), year, length, country, rating on a scale of 1 to 5 stars, and flags for potential problems in viewing the film (e.g., movie is "questionable for children").

http://www.blockbuster.com: This site allows you to search for movie availability at Blockbuster stores within specified distances from you.

Film References

Bahari, M, & Dacey, K. (Producers), & Bahari, M. (Director). (2002). *And along came a spider* [Motion Picture]. United States: HBO Films.

Benn, H., Cohen, R., & Marcucci, R. (Producers), & Byrum, J. (Director). (1984). *The razor's edge* [Motion Picture]. United States: Columbia Pictures.

Big Idea Productions (Producer), & Vischer, V. (Director). (1993). *Veggie Tales,* volume I: Where's God when I'm s-scared? [Videotape]. United States: Guiding Light Video.

Bressler, C. (Producer), & Eyre, C. (Director). (1998). *Smoke signals* [Motion Picture]. United States: Miramax Films.

Bruckheimer, B., & Lowry, H. (Producers), & Khouri, C. (Director). (2002). *Divine secrets of the Ya Ya Sisterhood* [Motion Picture]. United States: Warner Brothers.

Curtis, B., Kennedy, K., & Spielberg, S. (Producers), & Spielberg, S. (Director). (2001). *A. I.: Artificial intelligence* [Motion Picture]. United States: Warner Brother.

Duchow, P., & Garner, J. (Producers), & Petrie, D. (Director). (1989). *My name is Bill W.* [Made For Television Film]. United States: Warner Brothers.

Geffen, D., & Wooley, S. (Producers), & Jordan, N. (Director). (1994). *Interview with the vampire: The vampire chronicles* [Motion Picture]. United States: Geffen Pictures.

Holmes, P., Lee, S., Sander, L., & Worth, M. (Producers), & Lee, S. (Director). (1992). *Malcolm X* [Motion Picture]. United States: Warner Brothers.

Koch, K. (Producer), & Tolkin, M. (1991). *The rapture* [Motion Picture]. United States: Fine Line Features.

Marvin, N. (Producer), & Darabont, F. (Director). (1994). *The Shawshank redemption* [Motion Picture]. United States: Columbia Pictures.

Miller, B., Miller, G., & Mitchell, D. (Producers), & Noonan, C. (Director). (1995). *Babe* [Motion Picture]. United States: Universal Pictures.

Wachowski, A., & Wachowski, L. (Executive Producers and Directors). (1999). *The matrix* [Motion Picture]. United States: Warner Brothers.

Woolley, S. (Producer), & Jordan, N. (Director). (1999). *End of the affair* [Motion Picture]. United States: Sony Pictures Entertainment.

Handout:
Suggested Films and Related Subjects for Therapeutic Exploration

The following are films that you may find useful, along with potential therapeutic topics and informed consent warnings related to potentially offensive material.

Film title	Therapeutic topic	Potentially troublesome material
Divine Secrets of the Ya Ya Sisterhood (2002)	Healing family-of-origin wounds; forgiveness	Adult situations
End of the Affair (1955) or (1999)	Faith; divine intervention	Could be viewed as glamorizing extramarital affairs; brief nudity
The Rapture (1991)	End times; conversion; false pride interfering with acceptance of divine Grace; faith	Explicit graphic sexual content demonstrating hedonistic lifestyle prior to conversion; emotionally traumatic child death scene
The Shawshank Redemption (1994)	Hope; perseverance	Mild violence, language
The Razor's Edge (1946) & (1984)	Meaning of life; authenticity	Graphic violence
My Name is Bill W. (1989)	Transforming nature of faith and being of service to others	
Malcolm X (1992)	Conversion; universalizing faith	Violence, profanity
The Matrix (1999)	Physical reality as temporary illusion	Profanity; violence
And Along Came a Spider (2001)	Religion used as justification for violence against women	
A.I.: Artificial Intelligence (2001)	Overcoming maternal rejection	Very emotionally traumatic; extremely intense; violence
Veggie Tales: Where's God When I'm S-scared? (1993)	Children's use of faith to face fear; includes the contagious song, "God is Bigger Than the Boogey Man"	

Priester, P. E., & Carlstrom, A. H. (2006). Using popular films to integrate spirituality in counseling: *Smoke Signals* and forgiveness. In K. B. Helmeke & C. F. Sori (Eds.), *The therapist's notebook for integrating spirituality in counseling: Homework, handouts, and activities for use in psychotherapy* (pp. 201-209). Binghamton, NY: The Haworth Press.

18

"Any Life Can Be Fascinating": Using Spiritual Autobiography As an Adjunct to Therapy

Marsha Vaughn
Karen Swanson

Type of Contribution: Homework, Handout

Objective

The use of journaling as an adjunct to both group and individual therapy has been described in the literature (Parr, Haberstroh, & Kottler, 2000; Stone, 1998). A specific type of journaling, spiritual autobiography, can be used as a homework assignment to help clients clarify issues and find meaning in life events. The writing of one of the earliest and best-known spiritual autobiographies, Saint Augustine's *Confessions,* has been described as "an act of therapy" (Brown, 1967, as quoted in Sisemore, 2001, p. 325).

Spiritual autobiography can be used to help clients articulate a sense of purpose and meaning in their life and also infuse their lives with hope. It is a way to find "unique outcomes" (Freedman & Combs, 1996) related to clients' spiritual lives. By writing their story instead of only telling it, clients are engaged in a more in-depth reflective process. They also have a permanent record and can see how the story of their spiritual life evolves over their life course.

Rationale for Use

Narrative Therapy

The advent of narrative therapies has introduced the importance of telling (and retelling stories) in therapy. Telling our story is not so much for the listener as it is for the storyteller—"we're shaped by the stories we tell ourselves" (Griffith & Griffith, 2002, p. 83). The heart of narrative therapy is uncovering the stories people tell themselves that are contributing to the creation and maintenance of problems. Narrative therapy presents a framework for finding stories with unique outcomes—experiences, which are different from the typical "problem-saturated" stories clients often tell (Freedman & Combs, 1996). Therapy then seeks to find more unique outcomes until those become the predominant story. The new story links unique outcomes from the past and present to desired outcomes in the future.

Narrative therapy capitalizes on the human capacity to restructure experience from memory, rather than recalling it accurately. One of the founding fathers of psychology, William James, stated, "My experience is what I agree to attend to" (1981, as cited in Kurtz & Ketcham, 1992, p. 78). Narrative therapists ask questions that lead clients to attend to different aspects of their experience—positive outcomes instead of negative, empowering characteristics instead of oppressive.

Although the "stories we tell ourselves" are important, the greatest impact of storytelling occurs in community. Stories tap into common existential issues so that "the best way to help me find my story is to tell me your story" (Kurtz & Ketcham, 1992, p. 116). Kurtz and Ketcham further describe the use of storytelling in 12-step programs as tapping into ancient spiritual wisdom of passing spiritual truth through stories rather than through doctrine. In 12-step groups, the format of stories is fairly standard—describing one's past behavior and circumstances, describing a significant turning point (such as "hitting bottom"), and describing how one has changed as a result (Kurtz & Ketcham). This is similar to early American spiritual autobiographies in which conversion stories were the dominant metaphor (Payne, 1992). Conversion stories emphasized how one's world was "re-ordered" after the conversion experience (Payne, p. 37).

Judeo-Christian Tradition

The culture in which the majority of the sacred texts were written was an oral culture, therefore it is hardly surprising that many of those texts are in story form. Kellemen (2004) states that over 75 percent of the Bible is written as narrative. As important as stories in verbal form are, the Judeo-Christian tradition emphasizes writing them down to imply the permanence and importance of significant events or God's commandments. In Deuteronomy 6:9, when giving the Law, Moses instructs the Israelites to "write them on the door frames of your houses and on your gates" (NIV). On several occasions in both the Old and New Testaments, scripture/truth is described as "written on their hearts" (see Proverbs 7:3; Jeremiah 31:33; Romans 2:15; and Hebrews 8:10).

Remembering is mentioned several times in the biblical text, and it is often paired with a tangible symbol associated with God's promises or works. A rainbow marked the renewal of God's covenant with humans (Genesis 9:15), and a stone monument marked the Israelites' crossing the Jordan River into Canaan (Joshua 4:1-7). The sacrament of communion (the Lord's Supper) was accompanied by Jesus Christ's command to "do this in remembrance of me" (Luke 22:19, I Corinthians 11:24-25). Engaging in a physical activity or having something concrete to touch or look at facilitates remembering those things central to our faith, which is unseen. A written narrative of our faith story, as opposed to a simply verbal account, gives us something more concrete than memory to hold onto.

Journaling

Journaling as an adjunct to therapy has been described by Stone (1998). Writing one's story has the same benefits as telling one's story because journaling is simply "recording our own oral tradition" (Stone, p. 539). Journaling is somewhat different from storytelling in that the *process* of journaling is more important than the *content* (Stone). Journaling, while tailored for the individual client, may be used for catharsis, reflection, articulating issues to be discussed in therapy, and increasing self-awareness and personal responsibility (Stone). Journaling could also be used for religious issues, such as sin and forgiveness (Mattson, 1994). Such issues are often part of the universal human experience, even if they are not described in religious language.

Journaling in between therapy sessions allows clients to remain focused on the work of therapy. It also allows them time to reflect on the changes in their lives and to find new stories. Therapists can guide the process by giving clients specific directives to write about.

Spiritual Autobiography

Spirituality, according to Anderson (1999), is a "way of seeing life" (p. 157). Specifically, Christian spirituality is "about accepting the complicated and muddled bundle of human experience as the theater for God's creative and transforming work" (p. 157). Storytelling is pervasive when discussing spirituality. According to Kurtz and Ketcham (1992), "stories are the vehicle that moves metaphor and image into experience. Like metaphors and images, stories communicate what is generally invisible and ultimately inexpressible" (p. 17). When people discuss their spiritual lives informally, it is rarely centered on doctrine; it is, in contrast, centered on their experiences of the Divine in the mundane events of daily life and in crisis.

Spiritual autobiography is a particular form of telling one's story that emphasizes the meaning and purpose of one's life. If one purpose of narrative therapy is to find unique outcomes, then one purpose of a spiritual autobiography is to discover those unique outcomes that clients attribute to their faith. In addition, clients may use metaphors and images that are not part of the usual discourse of their religious traditions; for example, conservative Christians who are accustomed to God as "Father" describe feminine qualities (see Kidd, 1996). Therapists can instruct clients to write about parts of their experience that do not fit the dominant discourse of their faith tradition or past experiences.

In writing a spiritual autobiography, the client has the unique position of being both author and subject of the story (Frank, 2000; Payne, 1992). Autobiography, unlike other forms of literature, makes claims to a relationship with the reader; the author is not an object to be evaluated, but someone to be identified with (Frank). This implies that autobiography is a *dialogue*—the reader has an identification and connection with the author's story (Frank).

Autobiography oscillates between the internal and the external, between self-reflection and historical facts (Payne, 1992). As the author of one's own written story, clients create a "myth of self" (Griffin, 1990, p. 152). Since autobiographies cannot include all of one's experiences, clients can choose those experiences, which help them create a coherent sense of self that matches their desired identities. The process of writing a spiritual autobiography is both retrospective and prospective—who were were/are and who we wish to be (Kendrick, 1992).

Spiritual autobiography is written from the perspective of one's brokenness (Frank, 2000) or imperfection (Kurtz & Ketcham, 1992). Speaking specifically of the impact of chronic illness on one's life, Frank says that a "self that has become what it never expected to be requires repair, and telling autobiographical stories is a privileged means of repair" (p. 135). Autobiographies are clients' stories expressing attempts to maintain a coherent sense of self. In more literary terms, author Frederick Buechner describes his process of writing his spiritual autobiography out of having a "sense of my life as a plot, not just incident following incident. . . . It was trying to take me somewhere" (Kendrick, 1992, p. 901).

Recording experiences in a spiritual autobiography also allows deviation from the stage model format of Fowler's (1981) faith development interview. This may be especially relevant for women and minorities, as one criticism of stage models of spiritual development such as Fowler's and the solo journey metaphor is that they reflect the male experience more accurately (Ray & McFadden, 2001). Spiritual autobiographies allow for including other relationships and contextual influences that impact one's spiritual development. The process of writing a spiritual autobiography also allows one to reflect on events as they spontaneously remember them, not as occurring in chronological order. Writing a spiritual autobiography often takes multiple drafts—the end form may present events in order, but they are not remembered that way.

Trent (1994) describes the use of a "story-boarding" technique to map one's faith journey. This is different from spiritual autobiography in that Trent's life mapping *begins* with a statement of one's purpose. In spiritual autobiography, often the purpose is unclear at the beginning of the process and emerges as clients write and reflect on their experiences.

Another form of spiritual autobiography is using a scrapbook or photo album to track one's faith story. Often the emphasis in creating a scrapbook or album is preserving memories for children and grandchildren. Sometimes called "faithbooking," this type of record often focuses on significant religious events, such as holidays, baptisms, weddings, first communions, and bar and bat mitzvahs (www.religionwriters.com, 2003).

An advantage of writing multiple drafts of a spiritual autobiography is that clients can order significant events chronologically and look for common themes. Those themes may be related to the continuity of God's presence in their lives. A written narrative allows clients to see patterns in their lives. Clients may also see their lives more objectively by writing in a third-person format, gaining some distance from painful or traumatic events.

One of the most well-known spiritual autobiographies, Saint Augustine's *Confessions,* has been conceptualized as broken into three parts: confessions of sin, confessions of faith, and confessions of praise (Brown, 1967, as cited in Sisemore, 2001). A confession of sin may involve an expression of regret about personal actions. It may also be confessing the sins of another—stories of abuse and neglect. It could be a description of other kinds of traumatic events—terminal illness, unexpected death, etc. A confession of faith is a statement expressing awareness of God's love, wisdom, protection, or faithfulness. Clients will state a belief that there *is* a greater purpose, even if they do not quite know what that purpose is. A confession of praise is similar to the unique outcomes of narrative therapy. Praise expresses belief in an ultimate positive outcome to one's life.

Two other characteristics of effective spiritual autobiography, according to Frederick Buechner, are "concreteness" and "candor" (Kendrick, 1992, p. 900). With those two things, "any life can be fascinating" (p. 900). Concreteness is especially applicable to a written spiritual autobiography, as clients have the time and space to include vivid details of life events. Candor, or honesty, refers to expressing all of oneself, including the parts clients are ashamed of and want to hide. Kurtz and Ketcham (1992) express candor like this: "There is *something* wrong—with me, with you, with the world—but *there is nothing wrong with that,* because that is the nature of our reality" (p. 28). Clients may be more willing to share what's wrong with them in writing than verbally.

The form and direction a spiritual autobiography takes is dependent on the client. For some, it will be an extension of the journaling they already do. It may take the form of a scrapbook or storyboard, depending on clients' preferences and the length of time available. Whatever the form, spiritual autobiography can engage clients in reflecting on the meaning and purpose of their lives.

Instructions

Even if clients are not in the habit of journaling, they may agree to write their spiritual autobiography simply because they are asked. Clients who are not prone to writing for themselves may write for a therapy assignment. Since the medium is flexible, clients who are not used to reflective writing may benefit more from the "story-boarding" technique described by Trent (1994). This technique should be modified, however, to remove the emphasis on beginning with a purpose statement, so that the purpose/meaning of one's life is allowed to emerge as clients remember significant events.

These significant events have been referred to elsewhere as spiritual stepping stones (Progoff, 1992) or emotional freeze points or emotional flash points (Trent, 1994). Often clients will not remember these events in chronological order, but the events will be associated with life cycle stage transitions—births, deaths, marriages, divorces, beginning or ending school or a career, etc. (Progoff).

It may also be helpful to give clients one or more prompts to help them reflect. These are also listed in a handout at the end of this chapter.

- What were your parents' and grandparents' spiritual/religious practices? Religious affiliation?
- What early messages about God did you receive from your family? (parents, grandparents, etc.)
- What were your earliest experiences/memories about religion? God?
- How did you celebrate religious holidays?
- What were your earliest impressions about sin? Guilt/shame? Salvation?
- How have those changed?
- What were your impressions about death/the afterlife?
- How have those changed?
- What was your conversion experience or experiences? (This allows room for multiple turning points.)
- Who were the most influential people in your spiritual life?
- Were there any crises or periods of doubt? Describe them and how you resolved them (if you have).
- Were there any books, stories, scripture passages, etc., that influenced you? Why are those so important to you?

It is important to emphasize that the story is *for the client;* often writers pay attention to the prospective audience, which in this situation may lead clients to ignore certain memories that are critical to their spiritual development. When writing one's story, clients are able to set aside any concerns about the audience. In addition, since writing requires more reflection than speaking, the emotions evoked by writing may be more profound. Therapists should also emphasize resisting the tendency to self-censor—part of the process is having multiple drafts of one's story. The autobiography will become more coherent with more reflection, but clients should be encouraged to write as spontaneously as they remember. Other tangible reminders of significant events, such as pictures, may also prompt significant memories.

Writing one's spiritual story requires a great deal of emotional energy and time for reflection. Clients experiencing a great deal of emotional distress or unresolved spiritual issues may be surprised by the amount of energy required to write about their spiritual life. Clients dealing with traumatic events may choose to write their story in the third person at the beginning; they may find they can get closer to the story with each subsequent version.

As with writing for therapy in general, clients may choose a unique journal to record their story. They can leave room for pictures or choose the scrapbook format described above. Although clients will share what they have written in therapy and/or with significant others, they choose the creative medium and the context in which to write.

Brief Vignette

Cathy presented for therapy after the extended illness and death of her husband. Daniel had battled cancer since their engagement and had passed away after three rounds of chemotherapy and two surgeries. Cathy is a deeply spiritual person, having grown up in a Christian home. Cathy first told her story as a testimony at church after her pastor asked her. Cathy later reflected in therapy that she was not concerned about becoming too emotional because she had written her story down. Also, she commented that being surrounded by friends and family who had supported her and her husband through her illness made her feel more at ease.

Several times in the three to four years after her husband's death, Cathy was asked to tell her story, and each time she wrote it down. Depending on the audience, she focused on different aspects of her marriage and husband's illness. From each of those versions of her verbal story, the theme of faithfulness through trials was evident. This is an excerpt from Cathy's story after her husband's first relapse:

> James 1:2-3 were significant verses to us at that time. We were learning to welcome trials as friends so that we could become mature in our faith. The other alternative was to resent life and become bitter. We chose to welcome cancer as you would welcome a friend because we knew we were not alone—Jesus was with us and He had overcome the world!

To add to Cathy's trials, she was diagnosed with leukemia as well:

> We spent our second anniversary sharing the same hospital room (breaking the hospital policy of not having a male and female in the same room). My first night in the hospital, I remember thinking about a song I had heard in college. Some of the words were, "I'm yours, Lord, try me now and see, try me now and see if I'm completely yours." As I reflected on this, I realized that as a Christian, I proclaimed the love and faithfulness of God and now it was time to prove my faith was real.

During the last few months of her husband's life, Cathy had begun volunteering at a local jail, teaching life skills. As an extension of this work, Cathy founded a nonprofit organization dedicated to reintegrating men released from prison into the community. She experienced quite a bit of resistance from the local community, which caused another crisis of faith. This one, Cathy remarked, was different—this crisis was because of a choice she had made rather than something that happened to her. It was similar in that the meaning she ascribed was the same—both were new experiences requiring her to rely more on her faith and trust in God.

Cathy developed two versions (chapters may be more accurate) of her story based on these significant periods of her life; who she was depended on her audience. When her therapist asked her which one was "Cathy," she replied "Both." The therapist encouraged Cathy to find connections between those two periods of her life; the result was common themes of pain, yet experiencing God's peace, the trial of new and uncharted territory, and the relevance of Scripture. Both parts of Cathy's spiritual autobiography contain several Bible references. "That's what stands out to me. Significant people mentioned certain Bible verses when I was going through something particularly difficult." She also noted that one version of her story was based on something that happened *to* her, her husband's illness, as opposed to a choice she made based on her sense of God's calling.

Another theme that emerged was the connection between significant people and significant spiritual truths. "God taught me different things at different times through different people." This is consistent with the importance of including reflections about significant relationships, because faith is not a solo journey.

Probably the greatest benefit of writing a spiritual autobiography, especially in Cathy's situation, was dealing with the tremendous amount of grief.

> Grief is a phenomenon that doesn't make sense. On September 6th I wrote: "I am absolutely exhausted. It seems like I cannot get rid of this feeling of being hit by a truck and then dragged. I sleep but find no relief—the exhaustive feeling is still there when I wake up. I seem to be going through different grief stages. Sometimes I function in denial and think Daniel will be home later. Sometimes when I think he is gone, I immediately scream 'No!' in my mind and become angry and cry out loud. 'It's not right, it's just not right.' The tears hit me when I don't expect them to come."

She remarked after writing the fourth or fifth version of her story that she was surprised at the depth of emotion she still felt. Writing one's story allows clients to enter more fully into their memories and experiences since this story is the "one they tell themselves."

Suggestions for Follow-Up

Writing is a spiritual autobiography is an ongoing process; as long as we are alive, there are experiences that infuse our lives with meaning and purpose. Even after therapy has been concluded, clients can be encouraged to keep writing, if not for themselves, then for their children or other family members. Many faith traditions emphasize the importance of parents leaving a legacy for their children. Clients who have written a spiritual autobiography can share that with close friends, family members, and their faith community. The leaders of Cathy's church compiled several spiritual autobiographies into a collected work for the church members. Sharing and self-publishing spiritual stories could also be useful in a group setting as a reminder of the experience. Regardless of what is done with the finished product, clients should be encouraged to continue to write and reflect on significant events.

Contraindications

Stone (1998) suggests that journaling, except in rare cases, should not be mandated. Spiritual autobiography, therefore, is best used with clients who are already journaling or at least show an openness to such an in-depth exercise. Clients who have limited writing ability may still record a spiritual autobiography. It could be taped and transcribed. It is important, though, that there is a written document. Having a written document enables authors to step back and read their words with more objectivity; the words are not connected to the sound of a voice.

Since this is a time- and labor-intensive process, it may not be as effectively used in brief therapy contexts, unless clients have the time to devote to writing outside of session and spiritual issues are a stated reason for therapy.

It is possible that women may be more willing to engage in reflective writing such as this. It also is consistent with the nonlinear nature of spiritual development that fits women's experience more accurately (Ray & McFadden, 2001). The process can be adapted to fit men's experiences as well. If time is a concern, therapists and clients may choose to focus on one or two significant experiences to write about.

References

Anderson, H. (1999). Feet planted firmly in midair: A spirituality for family living. In F. Walsh (Ed.), *Spiritual resources in family therapy* (pp. 157-176). New York: The Guilford Press.

Augustine. (1998). *Confessions* (H. Chadwick, Trans.). Oxford: Oxford University Press. (Original work written circa 397.)

Brown, P. (1967). *Augustine of Hippo.* Berkeley: University of California Press.

Fowler, J. (1981). *Stages of faith: The psychology of human development and the quest for meaning.* San Francisco: HarperCollins.

Frank, A. W. (2000). Illness and autobiographical work: Dialogue as narrative destabilization. *Qualitative Sociology, 23,* 135-156.

Freedman, J., & Combs, G. (1996). *Narrative therapy: The social construction of preferred realities.* New York: W. W. Norton.

Griffin, C. J. G. (1990). The rhetoric of form in conversion narratives. *Quarterly Journal of Speech, 76,* 152-163.

Griffith, J. L., & Griffith, M. E. (2002). *Encountering the sacred in psychotherapy: How to talk with people about their spiritual lives.* New York: The Guilford Press.

James, W. (1981). *The principles of psychology.* Cambridge, MA: Harvard University Press. (Original work published 1890.)

Kellemen, R. W. (2004). *Soul physicians: A theology of soul care and spiritual direction.* Taneytown, MD: RPM Books.

Kendrick, S. (1992, October 14). On spiritual autobiography: An interview with Frederick Buechner. *Christian Century, 109*(29), 900-904.

Kidd, S. M. (1996). *The dance of the dissident daughter.* San Francisco: HarperCollins.

Kurtz, E., & Ketcham, K. (1992). *The spirituality of imperfection: Storytelling and the journey to wholeness.* New York: Bantam.

Mattson, D. L. (1994). Religious counseling: To be used, not feared. *Counseling and Values, 38,* 187-192. Retrieved July 24, 2004, from Academic Search Elite.

New International Version: The NIV Study Bible. (1985). Barker, K. (Ed.) Grand Rapids: MI: Zondervan.

Parr, G., Haberstroh, S., & Kottler, J. (2000). Interactive journal writing as an adjunct in group work. *Journal for Specialists in Group Work, 25,* 229-242.

Payne, R. M. (1992). Metaphors of the self and the sacred: The spiritual autobiography of Rev. Freeborn Garrettson. *Early American Literature, 27,* 31-48.

Progoff, I. (1992). *At a journal workshop: Writing to access the power of the unconscious and evoke creative ability.* New York: Tarcher/Putnam.

Ray, R. E., & McFadden, S. H. (2001). The web and the quilt: Alternatives to the heroic journey toward spiritual development. *Journal of Adult Development, 8,* 201-211.

Sisemore, T. A. (2001). Saint Augustine's *Confessions* and the use of introspection in counseling. *Journal of Psychology and Christianity, 20,* 324-331.

Stone, M. (1998). Journaling with clients. *Journal of Individual Psychology, 54,* 535-545.

Trent, J. (1994). *LifeMapping.* Colorado Springs, CO: Focus on the Family.

www.religionwriters.com (2003, March 10). *Scrapbooking as spiritual practice.* Retrieved July 28, 2004, from www.religionwriters.com.

Professional Readings and Resources

Griffith, J. L., & Griffith, M. E. (2002). *Encountering the sacred in psychotherapy: How to talk with people about their spiritual lives.* New York: The Guilford Press.

Kurtz, E., & Ketcham, K. (1992). *The spirituality of imperfection: Storytelling and the journey to wholeness.* New York: Bantam.

Peace, R. (1998). *Spiritual autobiography: Discovering and sharing your spiritual story.* Colorado Springs, CO: NavPress.

Progoff, I. (1992). *At a journal workshop: Writing to access the power of the unconscious and evoke creative ability.* New York: Tarcher/Putnam.

Stone, M. (1998). Journaling with clients. *Journal of Individual Psychology, 54,* 535-545.

Bibliotherapy Sources for the Client

Augustine. (1998). *Confessions* (H. Chadwick, Trans.). Oxford: Oxford University Press. (Original work written circa 397)

Colson, C. (1995). *Born again.* Grand Rapids, MI: Fleming H. Revell.

Kidd, S. M. (1996). *The dance of the dissident daughter.* San Francisco: HarperCollins.

Peace, R. (1998). *Spiritual autobiography: Discovering and sharing your spiritual story.* Colorado Springs, CO: NavPress.

Smedes, L. (2003). *My God and I: A spiritual memoir.* Grand Rapids, MI: Eerdmans.

Wakefield, D. (1990). *The story of your life: Writing a spiritual autobiography.* Boston: Beacon.

Handout:
Beginning Your Autobiography: Questions and Reflections for Clients

The following questions will help you reflect on the events and people that have influenced your spiritual life. Find a place, time, and format that are most comfortable for *you*. After all, this is your story. You may choose a bound journal, 3x5 index cards to jot some thoughts, or a scrapbook.

Do not be concerned with remembering things in chronological order. You may find that your memory drifts back and forth between different periods of time. This is a *process*. There will be time to reorder your thoughts in a story that makes sense to you.

- What were your parents' and grandparents' spiritual/religious practices? Religious affiliation?
- What early messages about God did you receive from your family? (parents, grandparents, etc.)
- What were your earliest experiences/memories about religion? God?
- How did you celebrate religious holidays?
- What were your earliest impressions about sin? Guilt/shame? Salvation?
- How have those changed?
- What were your impressions about death/the afterlife?
- How have those changed?
- What was your conversion experience or experiences? (this allows room for multiple turning points)
- Who were the most influential people in your spiritual life?
- Were there any crises or periods of doubt? Describe them and how you resolved them (if you have).
- Were there any books, stories, scripture passages, etc., that influenced you? Why are those so important to you?

As you think about your responses to these questions, what common themes do you see?

Vaughn, M. & Swanson, K. (2006). "Any life can be fascinating": Using spiritual autobiography as an adjunct to therapy. In K. B. Helmeke & C. F. Sori (Eds.), *The therapist's notebook for integrating spirituality in counseling: Homework, handouts, and activities for use in psychotherapy* (pp. 211-219). Binghamton, NY: The Haworth Press.

SECTION V:
USE OF SCRIPTURE, PRAYER,
AND OTHER SPIRITUAL PRACTICES

19

Free at Last!
Using Scriptural Affirmations to Replace Self-Defeating Thoughts

Catherine Ford Sori
Lori McKinney

He has sent me to bind up the brokenhearted, to proclaim freedom for the captives and release from darkness for the prisoners.

Isaiah 61:1 (New International Version)

And do not be conformed to this world, but be transformed by the renewing of your mind.

Romans 12:2 (New King James Version)

Type of Contribution: Activity, Homework, Handouts

Objective

The purpose of this chapter is to help Christian clients who are troubled by self-defeating negative thoughts to become more aware of their negative self-statements, to recognize the origins of these statements, and to replace negative thoughts with scriptural affirmations. In so doing, clients may move toward a closer relationship with God, and begin to live life more abundantly. Although this chapter is written from a Christian perspective, much of the material is applicable to Jewish clients, and the activities herein can be easily adapted to accommodate other spiritual viewpoints as well.

Rationale for Use

Biblical and modern Christian writers have advanced the notion that we have a personal adversary who attempts to undermine the glory of God in each of us (e.g., 1 Peter 5:8; Curtis & Eldredge, 1997; Eldredge, 2003). This adversary tells us lies that are aimed at killing, stealing, and destroying our hearts (John 10:10). Many Christians go through life struggling with self-doubt, fears, and negative thoughts (or introjects) about themselves. Often these accusations are rooted in familiar voices from our past—parents, teachers, family members, or peers from our childhood. Over time we become so accustomed to these voices that they "slide almost unnoticed into our consciousness" (Curtis &.Eldredge, 1997, p. 99). These accusations become the lens through which we negatively interpret events in our lives and develop our story of ourselves and of God. People can become so resigned to self-criticism that they do not recognize it, even though it robs them of much energy and of the ability to live a joyful life (Curtis & Eldredge, 1997; John 10:10).

The goal of these exercises is to help clients draw closer to God as they identify negative thoughts that have kept them in bondage, and use the truth of God's word to refute the lies they have believed. There is biblical precedent for defeating our personal enemy by engaging in what is known as "spiritual warfare" (Ephesians 6:12). For persons who hold other faith traditions, the enemy can be viewed as anything that interferes with our becoming whole, actualized persons.

The psychological literature regarding thought change is diverse. We present a smattering of viewpoints from the cognitive (e.g., Anderson, Bjork & Bjork, 1994; Bjork, 1989), and social cognitive (e.g. Wegner, Schneider, Carter, & White, 1987) perspectives.

Thoughts, or cognitions if you will, do not simply disappear in and of themselves. They must be actively inhibited by our cognitive systems. Fortunately, mechanisms exist for such a process (Bjork, 1989; Bjork & Bjork, 1991). We are able to replace our old memories for home phone numbers, parking spaces, and sweethearts' names with new ones. The literature on thought suppression shows that when we try not to think about something, whether it be as innocuous as a white bear (Wegner et al., 1987) or something as painful as a lost love (Wegner & Gold, 1995), we often experience a rebound effect. That is, we have an increase in the very thoughts we are trying to suppress. However, other research demonstrates that when we practice certain responses to the exclusion of other possible responses, the nonpracticed response becomes actively inhibited (Anderson et al., 1994). By repeatedly using the new information, it becomes the dominant response in our repertoire and the old information is inhibited. Therefore, to successfully transform one's thinking (Romans 12:2), one must be constantly rehearsing new thoughts.

McKinney (1997) delineates three criteria for successful thought replacement. First there must be a competing thought or thoughts. One must have a new thought on which to focus rather than simply trying not to think about the old thought. Solution-based approaches would be quick to point out that one cannot focus on a negative goal, but must establish positive goals in order for change to occur (Berg & Steiner, 2003). For the client working from a spiritual perspective, these replacement thoughts should be affirming statements stemming from the client's faith tradition. The second criterion is that the new thoughts must be relevant to the situations that trigger the thoughts. When confronted with fear, for example, the client may counter that, "God hath not given us the spirit of fear; but of power, and of love, and of a sound mind" (2 Timothy 1:7, KJV). Note that the three alternatives in this scripture are not arbitrary, but rather address the root of most fears: powerlessness over harmful outcomes, lack of love from important others, and anxious or tormenting thoughts. Finally, the third criterion is that the new thoughts must be practiced so that they gain ascendancy over competing potential thoughts. For the current purposes, this would mean repeatedly rehearsing the scriptural affirmations rather than the ingrained self-defeating beliefs or introjects.

The exercises below require the client and therapist to work together to identify and repudiate self-defeating thoughts. We offer several strategies, depending on the client's familiarity with the relevant scriptures. Before using the following activities, however, therapists should first carefully assess that they fit the clients' belief system, and that the clients are interested in using scriptural affirmation to help change their negative thoughts and beliefs about themselves. We also caution therapists to encourage clients not to simply pick isolated scriptural affirmations, but to read them in the context in which they were written.

Instructions

As part of the therapeutic process, the therapist will do the following:

- Have clients start noticing when they are feeling bad, and to recognize the negative thought(s) that preceded that feeling.
- Help clients recognize the negative thoughts as whispered lies that rob their hearts of peace, joy, and thankfulness.
- Recognize that these are (1) lies from Satan (for those Christians who believe in spiritual warfare), or (2) introjects (negative statements from others that were "swallowed" or internalized in childhood, e.g., "You'll never succeed!").
- Explain that with repeated thinking these negative thoughts become entrenched (or they become strongholds). Eventually the heart becomes hardened not to believe what God's word says. This practice leads to spiritual defeat, and keeps people from living the "abundant life that God has promised" (John 10:10).
- Elicit general examples of clients' negative thoughts about themselves (e.g., "You screwed up again!" "You'll never succeed!").
- Have clients then give specific examples (e.g., feeling bad that they only got the bathrooms cleaned, and did not do any laundry. "Well, so much for all you were going to get done today. You just never do half of what you say you'll do!").
- Suggest that clients begin to keep a list of these negative self-statements (whispered lies, or introjects, depending on the clients' beliefs and language).
- After spending time in prayer (and perhaps reading *Waking the Dead,* Eldredge, 2003), have clients make a list of ALL the negative self-statements they have believed.
- Suggest clients read scriptures regarding what God says about his word and its power (e.g., Joshua 1:7-9; Psalm 119; Hebrews 4:12; 2 Timothy 3:16). Emphasize that Christ used scriptures as a spiritual weapon when tempted by the devil (see Matthew 4). Other passages are helpful for clients to believe that God's plan is to give us hope and a future (e.g., Jeremiah 29:11-13). It is important for clients to understand: "This then is how we know that we belong to the truth, and how we set our hearts at rest in his presence whenever our hearts condemn us. For God is greater than our hearts . . . if our hearts do not condemn us, we have confidence before God and receive from him anything we ask" (1 John 3:19-21, NIV). Our hearts will stop condemning us when we choose to listen to another, more loving and compassionate voice.
- *Handout One:* List all the lies or attacks (or negative thoughts) on the left side of Handout One: Scriptural Affirmations Worksheet. For each lie write corresponding scriptures that refute the lie. For example: Attack: "I will probably fail again." Scripture: "I can do all things through Christ who strengthens me" (Philippians 4:13 NKJV). The therapist can discuss how each time clients find themselves entertaining one of the negative thoughts they are faced with a choice: To believe the lie, or to choose to believe what God's word says. The importance of replacing negative thoughts with the positive truths, and of rehearsing these new thoughts, should be emphasized. Some clients may want to systematically memorize some of the scriptures so they can quickly be recalled and used to fight discouragement. Clients can be encouraged to refer to this list often, and to keep adding affirming scriptures whenever they recognize negative, discouraging thoughts. They might use a concordance to search for scriptures by positive keywords, such as joy, hope, or strength.
- Clients may consider watching the movie *The Passion of the Christ,* and noticing how each lash (or stripe) Christ suffered was to heal each of their sins (see Isaiah 53:5), and that they

were bought with a price—not to live in defeat buying into lies about themselves, but in victory because of Christ's completed work on the cross, and what God's word promises.

- *Visual activity:* Clients may elect to participate in a visualized ritual led by the therapist. Clients take their negative statements and visualize nailing them one by one to the cross (see Colossians 2:14), recognizing these negative beliefs as lies, and remembering, "It is finished" (John 19:30, NIV) because of Christ's work on the cross.
- *Ritual activity:* As an alternative to the visualization above, some clients may prefer to write out each lie or negative self-statement in a list or on separate slips of paper. They can then burn each as they symbolically lay it at the foot of the cross. This ritual would mark a turning away from the condemning thoughts, and turning toward the truth of scripture.
- Clients with alternate religious or spiritual belief systems may substitute their own spiritual affirmations for the scriptural affirmations. These affirmations may be based on religious texts or prayers, or clients may generate their own lists as homework or with the help of the therapist. Therapists may vary the activities to fit these clients' beliefs.
- Handout Two: Sample Scriptural Affirmations, contains numerous verses that can be used to counteract the negative thoughts identified in Handout One, Scriptural Affirmations Worksheet.

Brief Vignette

Liz, a married thirty-five-year old who works in advertising, initiated counseling because she reported feeling anxious, overwhelmed with problems at work, and feeling inadequate. During the course of counseling it became apparent that she had many negative self-evaluations, which the counselor did not believe accurately reflected who she was. Liz had previously discussed her deep Christian faith as a source of strength.

The therapist asked Liz to verbalize one of the negative self-statements. After thinking for a moment, Liz replied that she cannot handle work stress and she is vulnerable. The therapist then asked her what God would say, or her faith would teach about that. Liz answered that she realized that this might be coming from Satan trying to keep her down, or undermine her faith. The therapist asked her how she would counteract that, and she replied that she needed to think about the things that God says about her. The therapist then asked her for examples. Without hesitation, Liz replied, "I can do all things through Christ who strengthens me" (Philippians 4:13, NKJV). The therapist asked her what it was like to think of this scripture instead of her usual negative thoughts. She replied that this was quite different, and she felt immediately more hopeful.

For homework, Liz agreed to begin to pay attention when she was feeling discouraged or stressed, and to recognize negative thoughts that might be producing those feelings. Next, she was asked to keep track of these negative self-statements, to see them as attacks, and to think of verses she could use as scriptural affirmations.

At the next session Liz brought in her list of negative thoughts and several scriptural affirmations she had found. She titled her list "Lies," and it consisted of twenty-five items, including:

- I am weak; I will be overtaken.
- I am disorganized—I can never succeed.
- I am going to fail.
- I am a failure in God's eyes.
- I will screw up.
- I can't manage things: my life, work, family, stress.
- I am not worthy of love.
- God will never hear me or help me.

When asked which of the scriptural affirmations she had found to repute these "lies," that had the most meaning to her, she read the following two:

- "But God demonstrates his own love for us in this: While we were still sinners, Christ died for us" (Romans 5:8, NIV).
- "This then is how we know that we belong to the truth, and how we set our hearts at rest in his presence whenever our hearts condemn us. For God is greater than our hearts . . . if our hearts do not condemn us, we have confidence before God and receive from him anything we ask" (1 John 3:19-21, NIV).

The first scripture touched her because she realized that Christ loved her enough to die for her, before she knew him or was even trying to lead a Christian life! The second passage opened her eyes to see that God is greater than the negative thoughts that condemn her heart, and that she can have victory through him, which will lead to greater confidence and ability to trust in God.

Liz said that at first this was a difficult activity, but she felt encouraged that she could do something to feel better so that she did not feel at the mercy of the negative thoughts. She had seen the movie *The Passion of the Christ*, and related two scenes that had deeply moved her. The first was an opening scene, where Satan is whispering discouraging lies to Jesus as he is praying in the Garden of Gethsemane. Liz realized how subtle and insidious Satan's lies could be, and the effort it took Christ to choose to believe God's word instead. She was also moved to tears of sorrow and appreciation in the crucifixion scene. Liz said she realized how much Christ suffered for her because he loved her, and that by believing Satan's lies instead of God's word she was denigrating his work on the cross. She had made her choice to learn to replace the negative thoughts with positive scriptural affirmations.

The therapist then gave Liz Handout One: Scriptural Affirmation Worksheet, and together they began to list her self-defeating thoughts in one column, and the corresponding scriptural affirmations in the other column. The therapist then led Liz in a visualization exercise. As he read each negative self-thought from her list, Liz pictured herself laying them at the foot of the cross. At the end of the session Liz commented that she felt more empowered and energized, and was excited to leave with concrete tools to work with.

These activities were a turning point in therapy for Liz. It was something she continued to work on outside of sessions, and to discuss with the therapist in sessions. As she recognized additional negative thoughts, she added those to her worksheet and searched for corresponding scriptural affirmations. The therapist noticed that as she began to regularly rehearse and meditate on these affirmations and incorporate them in her everyday life, there was a shift in how she discussed things in therapy. She was more hopeful, more empowered, and was enjoying her life more.

Suggestions for Follow-Up

Meditation

In addition to rehearsing the scriptural affirmation, clients may elect to meditate (see Psalm 1:2; Psalm 19:14; Psalm 119:15, 16; Joshua 1:8) on a particular scripture throughout the day or week. One way to deepen the meaning and personal application of scripture is to emphasize different words or phrases, as they pray and ask God to speak to them. For example, using Philippians 4:13 (New King James Version):

I can do all things through Christ who strengthens me.
I *can do* all things through Christ who strengthens me.

I can do *all things* through Christ who strengthens me.
I can do all things *through Christ* who strengthens me.
I can do all things through Christ *who strengthens me.*

When Liz meditated in this manner on this verse, she found very different meanings and implications for her life according to the words that were emphasized.

Clients who do not have facility with the scriptures may need more assistance in generating appropriate scriptural affirmations. Pastoral counselors, clergy, or others may be qualified to offer such assistance.

One follow-up or alternative activity might be for the therapist to have a stack of laminated cards with scriptural affirmations on them (see Handout Two, Sample Scriptural Affirmations). These cards could be used as a Q-sort activity, where clients may select cards to counteract specific problems or negative thoughts they are experiencing. In a Q-sort clients sort items into categories that make sense to them. The cards associated with negative thoughts could be matched with scriptural affirmations that seem to fit for the client. Having premade cards would be particularly helpful to clients who are not very knowledgeable about the scriptures, or to offer additional suggestions to those who have already generated their own lists. In addition to the scriptural affirmation cards, the therapist can have a stack of cards with common emotional issues (such as fear, sadness, and anger), and blank cards for the client to label with their idiosyncratic concerns. (Both categories of cards should be color-coded.) For example, a client might choose a blank blue card, write the word "overwhelmed," sort through the red scriptural affirmation cards, and select "but those who hope in the Lord will renew their strength. They will soar on wings like eagles; they will run and not grow weary, they will walk and not be faint" (Isaiah 40:31, NIV).

Finally, this activity could be adapted to help couples stop automatic negative thought attacks about their spouses. The above steps could be modified to help couples move from blaming to recognizing where many of their automatic negative thoughts come from, nail them to the cross, and find scriptural affirmations to replace them (e.g., "Judge not . . ." (Matthew 7:1, NKJV); "[Love] keeps no record of wrongs" (1 Corinthians 13:5, NIV)).

Contraindications

This activity would not be appropriate for clients with thought disorders, who have religious obsessions, or who do not believe in spiritual warfare. However, those who hold different religious beliefs may come up with their own list of "spiritual affirmations" that fit their belief system. We also caution therapists to encourage clients to read the scriptural affirmations in the context in which they were written, to avoid misinterpretations. It may be helpful to encourage those clients who have religious questions or are struggling with their beliefs to consult a member of the clergy.

References

Anderson, M. C., Bjork, R. A., & Bjork, E. (1994). Remembering can cause forgetting: Retrieval dynamics in long-term memory. *Journal of Experimental Psychology: Learning, Memory, and Cognition, 28*(5), 1063-1087.

Berg, I. K., & Steiner, T. (2003). *Children's solution work.* New York: W. W. Norton & Company.

Bjork, R. A. (1989). Retrieval inhibition as an adaptive mechanism in human memory. In H. L. Roediger & F. I. M. Craik (Eds.), *Varieties of memory and consciousness: Essays in honor of Endel Tulving* (pp. 309-330). Hillsdale, NJ: Lawrence Erlbaum Associates.

Bjork, R. A., & Bjork, E. L. (1991). *Dissociations in the impact of to-be-forgotten information in memory.* Symposium on recall mechanisms in directed forgetting, hypnotic amnesia, and post-hypnotic amnesia. Presented at the annual meeting of the American Psychological Association, San Francisco, CA.

Curtis, B., & Eldredge, J. (1997). *The sacred romance: Drawing closer to the heart of God.* Nashville: Thomas Nelson Publishers.

Eldredge, J. (2003). *Waking the dead.* Nashville: Thomas Nelson Publishers.

Gibson, M. (Director and Co-writer). (2003). *The passion of the Christ* [Motion picture]. United States: Icon Distribution Inc.

Holy Bible, King James Version (1985). Akron, Ohio: Rex Humbard Ministries.

Holy Bible, New King James Version (1982). Nashville, TN: Thomas Nelson, Inc.

Holy Bible, New International Version (1984). Grand Rapids, MI: The Zondervan Corporation.

McKinney, L. C. (1997). Successful and unsuccessful thought suppression: Social and cognitive perspectives. Unpublished manuscript. University of Illinois at Chicago.

Wegner, D. M., & Gold, D. B. (1995). Fanning old flames: Emotional and cognitive effects of suppressing thoughts of a past relationship. *Journal of Personality and Social Psychology, 68*(5), 782-792.

Wegner, D. M., Schneider, D. J., Carter, S. I., & White, L. (1987). Paradoxical effects of thought suppression. *Journal of Personality and Social Psychology, 53,* 5-13.

Professional Readings and Resources

Curtis, B., & Eldredge, J. (1997). *The sacred romance: Drawing closer to the heart of God.* Nashville: Thomas Nelson Publishers.

Eldredge, J. (2003). *Waking the dead.* Nashville: Thomas Nelson Publishers.

Gibson, M. (Director and Co-writer). (2003). *The passion of the Christ* [Motion picture]. United States: Icon Distribution Inc.

Holy Bible, New International Version (1984). Grand Rapids, MI: The Zondervan Corporation.

Holy Bible, New King James Version (1982). Nashville, TN: Thomas Nelson, Inc.

Bibliotherapy Sources for the Client

Curtis, B., & Eldredge, J. (1997). *The sacred romance: Drawing closer to the heart of God.* Nashville: Thomas Nelson Publishers.

Eldredge, J. (2003). *Waking the dead.* Nashville: Thomas Nelson Publishers.

Gibson, M. (Director and Co-writer). (2003). *The passion of the Christ* [Motion picture]. United States: Icon Distribution Inc.

Meyer, J. (Pastor). *Enjoying Everyday Life* [Television series]. www.joycemeyer.org.

Osteen, J. (Pastor). (2004). Your life follows your thoughts *Lakewood Church.* Houston: Lakewood Church. www.lakewood.cc.

Holy Bible, New International Version (1984). Grand Rapids, MI: The Zondervan Corporation.

Holy Bible, New King James Version (1982). Nashville, TN: Thomas Nelson, Inc.

Warren, R. (2002). *The purpose-driven life.* Grand Rapids, MI: Zondervan.

Handout One: Scriptural Affirmations Worksheet

Anxious thoughts: Scriptural affirmation:

"What if I fail again?"		1 Pet 5:7	Cast all your anxiety on him because he cares for you. (NIV)

Worrisome thoughts: Scriptural affirmation:

Fearful thoughts: Scriptural affirmation:

Sori, C. F., & McKinney, L. (2006). Free at last! Using scriptural affirmations to replace self-defeating thoughts. In K. B. Helmeke & C. F. Sori (Eds.), *The therapist's notebook for integrating spirituality in counseling: Homework, handouts, and activities for use in psychotherapy* (pp. 223-234). Binghamton, NY: The Haworth Press.

Handout One: Scriptural Affirmations Worksheet *(continued)*

Sad thoughts: Scriptural affirmation:

Discouraged/hopeless thoughts: Scriptural affirmation:

Other negative thoughts: Scriptural affirmation:

Sori, C. F., & McKinney, L. (2006). Free at last! Using scriptural affirmations to replace self-defeating thoughts. In K. B. Helmeke & C. F. Sori (Eds.), *The therapist's notebook for integrating spirituality in counseling: Homework, handouts, and activities for use in psychotherapy* (pp. 223-234). Binghamton, NY: The Haworth Press.

Handout Two: Sample Scriptural Affirmations

This handout contains numerous scriptural affirmations that may be copied, enlarged, and attached to index cards for clients to use to counteract negative thoughts that were identified in Handout One: Scriptural Affirmations Worksheet. These verses may also be used as a Q-Sort activity, where they are sorted by themes or categories.

God hath not given us the spirit of fear, but of power, and of love, and of a sound mind. (2 Timothy 1:7, KJV)	But God demonstrates his own love for us in this: While we were still sinners, Christ died for us. (Romans 5:8, NIV)
Cast all your anxiety on him because he cares for you. (1 Peter 5:7, NIV)	I can do all things through Christ who strengthens me. (Philippians 4:13, NKJV)
Who shall separate us from the love of Christ? Shall trouble or hardship or persecution or famine or nakedness or danger or sword? . . . . No, in all these things we are more than conquerors through him who loved us. (Romans 8:35, 37, NIV)	For I am convinced that neither death nor life, neither angels nor demons, neither the present nor the future, nor any powers, neither height nor depth, nor anything else in all creation, will be able to separate us from the love of God that is in Christ Jesus our Lord. (Rom 8:38, 39, NIV)
The Spirit of the Sovereign Lord is on me, because the Lord has anointed me to preach good news to the poor. He has sent me to bind up the brokenhearted, to proclaim freedom for the captives, and release from darkness for the prisoners. (Isaiah 61:1, NIV)	This then is how we know that we belong to the truth, and how we set our hearts at rest in his presence whenever our hearts condemn us. For God is greater than our hearts, . . . if our hearts do not condemn us, we have confidence before God and receive from him anything we ask. . . . (1 John 3:19- 21, NIV)
The thief does not come except to steal, and to kill, and to destroy. I have come that they may have life, and that they may have it more abundantly. (John 10:10, NKJV)	Be self-controlled and alert. Your enemy the devil prowls around like a roaring lion looking for someone to devour. Resist him, standing firm in the faith. . . . (1 Peter 5:8,9, NIV)
And by his stripes we are healed. (Isaiah 53:5, NKJV)	'Not by might nor by power, but by my Spirit,' says the Lord Almighty. (Zechariah 4:6, NIV)
So do not fear, for I am with you; do not be dismayed, for I am your God. I will strengthen you and help you; I will uphold you with my righteous right hand. (Isaiah 41:10, NIV)	. . . no weapon forged against you will prevail, and you will refute every tongue that accuses you. This is the heritage of the servants of the Lord. . . . (Isaiah 54:17, NIV)
. . . but those who hope in the Lord will renew their strength. They will soar on wings like eagles; they will run and not grow weary, they will walk and not be faint. (Isaiah 40:31, NIV)	Some trust in chariots and some in horses, but we trust in the name of the Lord our God. They are brought to their knees and fall, but we rise up and stand firm. (Psalm 20:7: NIV)
The weapons we fight with are not the weapons of the world. On the contrary, they have divine power to demolish strongholds. We demolish arguments and every pretension that sets itself up against the knowledge of God, and we take captive every thought to make it obedient to Christ. (2 Corinthians 10:4, 5, NIV)	Consider it pure joy, my brothers, whenever you face trials of many kinds, because you know that the testing of your faith develops perseverance. Perseverance must finish its work so that you may be mature and complete, not lacking anything. (James 1:2-4, NIV)

Sori, C. F., & McKinney, L. (2006). Free at last! Using scriptural affirmations to replace self-defeating thoughts. In K. B. Helmeke & C. F. Sori (Eds.), *The therapist's notebook for integrating spirituality in counseling: Homework, handouts, and activities for use in psychotherapy* (pp. 223-234). Binghamton, NY: The Haworth Press.

Handout Two: Sample Scriptural Affirmations *(continued)*

Finally, be strong in the Lord and in his mighty power. Put on the full armor of God so that you can take your stand against the devil's schemes. (Ephesians 6:10, 11, NIV)	For our struggle is not against flesh and blood, but against the rulers, against the authorities, against the powers of this dark world and against the spiritual forces of evil in the heavenly realms. (Ephesians 6:12, NIV)
He who dwells in the shelter of the Most High will rest in the shadow of the Almighty. I will say to the Lord, "He is my refuge and my fortress, my God, in whom I trust." Surely he will save you from the fowler's snare and from the deadly pestilence. He will cover you with his feathers, and under his wings you will find refuge; his faithfulness will be your shield and rampart. (Psalm 91:1-4, NIV)	Rejoice in the Lord always. I will say it again: Rejoice! Let your gentleness be evident to all. The Lord is near. Do not be anxious about anything, but in everything, by prayer and petition, with thanksgiving, present your requests to God. And the peace of God, which tran-scends all understanding, will guard your hearts and your minds in Christ Jesus. (Philippians 4:4-7, NIV)
". . . For I know the plans I have for you," declares the Lord, "plans to prosper you and not to harm you, plans to give you hope and a future. Then you will call upon me and come and pray to me, and I will listen to you. You will seek me and find me when you seek me with all your heart . . ." (Jeremiah 29:11-13, NIV)	Finally, brothers, whatever is true, whatever is noble, whatever is right, whatever is pure, whatever is lovely, whatever is admirable—if anything is excellent or praiseworthy—think about such things. (Philippians 4:8, NIV)
But seek first his kingdom and his righteousness, and all these things will be given to you as well. Therefore do not worry about tomorrow, for tomorrow will worry about itself. . . . (Matthew 6:33-34, NIV)	Do not let this Book of the Law depart from your mouth; meditate on it day and night. . . . Then you will be prosperous and successful. . . . Be strong and cou-rageous. Do not be terrified; do not be discouraged, for the Lord your God will be with you wherever you go. (Joshua 1:8, 9, NIV)
Why are you downcast, O my soul? Why so disturbed within me? Put your hope in God, for I will yet praise him, my Savior and my God. (Psalm 43:5, NIV)	Those who sow in tears will reap with songs of joy. He who goes out weeping, carrying seed to sow, will re-turn with songs of joy. . . . (Psalm 126:5,6, NIV)
. . . weeping may remain for a night, but rejoicing comes in the morning. (Psalm 30:5, NIV)	Cast your cares on the Lord and he will sustain you; he will never let the righteous fall. (Psalm 55:22, NIV)
Submit yourselves, then, to God. Resist the devil, and he will flee from you. Come near to God and he will come near to you. . . . Humble yourselves before the Lord, and he will lift you up. (James 4:7,8-10, NIV)	The Lord appeared to us in the past, saying: "I have loved you with an everlasting love; I have drawn you with loving-kindness. I will build you up again . . ." (Jer-emiah 31:3,4, NIV)
For you created my inmost being; you knit me to-gether in my mother's womb. I praise you because I am fearfully and wonderfully made. . . . (Psalm 139:13, 14, NIV)	The Lord is my strength and my shield; my heart trusts in him, and I am helped. My heart leaps for joy and I will give thanks to him in song. (Psalm 28:7, NIV)
Do not grieve, for the joy of the Lord is your strength. (Nehemiah 8:10, NIV)	Restore to me the joy of your salvation and grant me a willing spirit, to sustain me. (Psalm 51:12, NIV)
You will keep him in perfect peace, Whose mind is stayed on You, because he trusts in You. (Isaiah 26:3, NKJV)	"Be strong and courageous. Do not be afraid or terri-fied . . . for the Lord your God goes with You; he will never leave you nor forsake you." (Deuteronomy 31:6, NIV)

Sori, C. F., & McKinney, L. (2006). Free at last! Using scriptural affirmations to replace self-defeating thoughts. In K. B. Helmeke & C. F. Sori (Eds.), *The therapist's notebook for integrating spirituality in counseling: Home-work, handouts, and activities for use in psychotherapy* (pp. 223-234). Binghamton, NY: The Haworth Press.

Handout Two: Sample Scriptural Affirmations *(continued)*

Blessed is the man who does not walk in the counsel of the wicked . . . But his delight is in the law of the Lord, and on his law he meditates day and night. He is like a tree planted by streams of water . . . Whatever he does prospers. (Psalm 1:1-3, NIV)	How sweet are your promises to my taste, sweeter than honey to my mouth! I gain understanding from your precepts; . . . Your word is a lamp to my feet and a light for my path. (Psalm 119:103-105 NIV)
. . . Forgetting what is behind and straining toward what is ahead, I press on toward the goal to win the prize for which God has called me heavenward in Christ Jesus. (Philippians 3:13-14, NIV)	And my God will meet all your needs according to his glorious riches in Christ Jesus. (Philippians 4:19, NIV)
"Peace I leave with you; my peace I give you. I do not give to you as the world gives. Do not let your hearts be troubled and do not be afraid." (John 14:27, NIV)	"I have told you these things, so that in me you may have peace. In this world you will have trouble. But take heart! I have overcome the world." (John 16:33)
All Scripture is God-breathed and is useful for teaching, rebuking, correcting and training in righteousness . . . (2 Timothy 3:16, NIV)	

Sori, C. F., & McKinney, L. (2006). Free at last! Using scriptural affirmations to replace self-defeating thoughts. In K. B. Helmeke & C. F. Sori (Eds.), *The therapist's notebook for integrating spirituality in counseling: Homework, handouts, and activities for use in psychotherapy* (pp. 223-234). Binghamton, NY: The Haworth Press.

20

Biblical Means to Therapeutic Healing

Judith K. Balswick

Type of Contribution: Activity

Objective

Clients from Christian backgrounds look to the Bible for spiritual truth and healing. The Old and New Testaments present a model of the Creator God relating to the Creation through *covenant,* God's faithful, unconditional, steadfast love; *grace,* extended in acceptance and forgiveness through Jesus Christ; *empowerment* of the Holy Spirit to inspire and empower; and *intimacy* found in a relationship and communion with God. Applying these four biblical principles in therapy is mutually beneficial for therapist and clients as they collaborate from a Christian value system.

Rationale for Use

A recent direction in family therapy is to incorporate spiritual themes in therapy while being clear about the values that underlie the therapy (Doherty, 1995; Walsh, 1999). Although it is not appropriate to persuade clients about personal beliefs or even a certain interpretation of scripture, it is helpful to have conversations about biblical principles of human relating. Taking the viewpoint that we live in a broken world, Christian therapists are realistic about human failures but also hopeful about healing and change. Through faith in God, there is promise and power to live more effective lives. Therefore, it is natural to discuss how the four biblical relationship principles (covenant, grace, empowerment and intimacy) relate to the therapeutic goals.

Instructions

Ideally, the therapist models these four principles in the therapist-client relationship. Covenant (therapeutic contract) builds trust through the therapist's faithful presence and ethical/legal commitment to the "best interest" of the client. Grace is shown through providing a safe, non-judgmental atmosphere that elicits understanding and shows respect for the client's perspectives and beliefs. Empowerment involves the work stage of therapy in which the therapist affirms strengths, equips, creates connection, develops interpersonal skills, challenges faulty thinking, considers consequences of actions, opens up new possibilities and brings hope for change. Finally, intimacy involves a therapeutic connection and mutual vulnerability through which "knowing and being known" leads to spiritual healing. The brief scenarios that follow will provide an illustration of how these principles can be part of the therapeutic process.

Brief Vignettes

Covenant Example

The biblical language of covenant was useful in working with an Asian-American family who entered therapy after an angry outburst between sixteen-year-old Jonathan and his father, Tim. During the first session, Tim talked about his parental covenant in terms of providing a good home for his family and being a strict disciplinarian. The cultural perspective was honored. However, other family members shared their ideas about covenant in terms of spending time together, doing chores, being kind, nurturing and considerate, etc., and these ideas were honored as well. These expressions of covenant love expanded everyone's views. At the end of the session, the kids agreed that Mom "did a lot of nurturing while Dad did a lot of disciplining." The obvious polarization of roles indicated a lack of balance in the parental subsystem.

During the next session, Jonathan was especially withdrawn and angry. He made the comment that he did not appreciate his dad's harsh hand of discipline. The family fell silent. Finally, Tim retorted, "This is how my father parented me and so do all the Korean fathers I know." This put the family at a standstill and they left on a rather somber note. The therapist decided it would be good to meet with the parents alone for the next session to explore more about the polarized parenting styles (mother as nurturer and father as disciplinarian). It was decided bringing more balance in the leadership roles would be helpful. The mother, Pamela, said she was willing to speak out more clearly about matters of discipline, but Tim seemed to be at a loss as to how to nurture. This is when the therapist brought in their religious faith and asked how they viewed God as a parent figure. They referred to the story of the prodigal son in the New Testament. They agreed that this picture of God as a father depicted one who gave unconditional love with outstretched arms. In taking a "one-sided" view of parenting as a father who disciplines, Tim admitted he had neglected the compassionate side of being a father. At this point, the therapist made a suggestion to help him make the transition. "Each night this week after your son is asleep, go outside his door and pray a prayer of blessing with an outstretched hand of love." This hand of blessing became a significant step in changing the old image of being a father with a harsh hand of discipline.

Later on in therapy, covenant commitment became the family goal. Each member took responsibility for "putting the interest of the others" as a priority. Pamela's challenge was to be more involved in the discipline whereas Tim worked on bringing out his soft, loving side. The children kept their covenant by contributing in positive ways to the family through their household chores and abiding by the rules. The relationships between family members improved by paying attention to the principle of covenant love.

Grace Example

Therapeutic healing comes in gracing ways as a therapist listens with compassion, honors differences, understands and accepts clients "just as they are." The therapist who understands the importance of forgiveness in relationship dynamics opens up new connections for individuals and family members. In fact, God's grace cuts straight through the human predicament.

Thirty-year-old Sylvia, a Latino-American, came to the office in an obvious anxious and disturbed state of mind. She was pregnant by a boyfriend she did not love and did not want to marry. Her conservative religious background only made things worse. She felt guilty just thinking about having an abortion but at the same time was fearful that learning about her pregnancy would be devastating to her parents. Her father had a heart condition and she was sure this secret of her pregnancy would literally kill him. Her guilt, no matter what she did, was intolerable.

The therapist and Sylvia took time to unravel the feelings and beliefs behind the guilt. She asked many questions. "What about my unborn child? How will Carlos, the father of the child, react? How will this circumstance impact my extended family? What about my future and my faith?" She believed God loved her, even though she felt great shame about these matters. Eventually she made a decision to tell her mother about her deep, dark secret. She and the therapist anticipated how the session would go and prayed for God's presence.

When Mary joined her daughter that day for therapy she was anxious, talkative, and somewhat defensive. At this point, the therapist simply asked if Mary could sit back and listen because Sylvia had something important to tell her. She relaxed and listened with undivided attention as Sylvia told her story through tears and broken sentences. Mary took it with amazing grace. Upon finishing her story, Mary moved over to her daughter and literally got down on her knees to tell her how sorry she was about the pain she was going through. It was a precious moment of acceptance and forgiveness between them that affected the therapist profoundly. Mary committed herself to stand by Sylvia whatever she decided about the pregnancy, assuring her of God's unconditional love and forgiveness.

It is a privilege for a therapist to witness acts of grace and forgiveness in a therapy session. Together, Sylvia and Mary informed Miguel, the father (who did not die of a heart attack), and Carlos (who did not want to get married). With the relational resources of family and renewed confidence in God's love and strength, Sylvia made the courageous decision to take on the responsibility of becoming a single mother. The grace shown to her by her parents gave her hope that she could meet this challenge with their support. A renewed relationship with God gave her peace.

Empowerment Example

Christian clients often rely on the Holy Spirit for insight and power to overcome their problems. God is the spiritual source to help them in the most difficult times and through extraordinary circumstances. Centering their lives in Christ provides clients with the inner courage and capacity to "go the second mile," or "turn the other cheek," or practice tough love. Such actions come out of spiritual strength rather than human weakness. God becomes the stronghold in times of suffering and struggle.

In the case of Cindy and Tom, Cindy was unable to confront her verbally abusive husband after five years of marriage. In individual therapy she not only found her voice, but also learned to assert herself. Drawing on her belief that human beings are sacred to God, she was able to stand up for herself when Tom put her down. It was not God's intention that he treat her disrespectfully and neither was it good for him or the relationship, she reasoned.

She asked God for strength to set appropriate boundaries so she could simply walk away when he was verbally abusive. She did not undermine Tom in her newfound power, but kept her cool and took the necessary action to break an old pattern. Cindy's new sense of self worth certainly got attention. Tom eventually came to therapy sessions to figure out what was happening.

In couples therapy, the concept of mutual empowerment became an important topic of discussion. To illustrate the importance of this concept, the therapist asked each of them to take time the next week to think about a person who had been an empowering force in their life. They were asked to write down in specific detail what the person did to empower them and how they felt about it. The next session Tom spoke about Walter, an older man from his church, who took a special interest in him when he was a teenager. Since his own family was riddled with alcoholism and anger, Tom was hungry for attention from someone who believed in him. Walter took Tom out for a hamburger once a week, helped him with homework assignments, pointed out the potential he saw in him, etc. It brought a warm smile to Tom's face just to talk about the difference this one person had made in his life. Upon remembering this story, Tom realized how important it was for him to empower rather than berate his wife. The following sessions were used to equip this couple with communication and conflict resolution skills. They worked together on a list of concrete things they could do each day to "build the other up." The marriage grew from mutual empowerment as they both drew on God for strength to change.

Intimacy Example

"I am my secrets!" declares Frederich Buechner (1991, p. 39). When clients tell the sad and bad parts of their stories in therapy, they come to know themselves as they have never been known before. Naming the pain, grieving the losses, and acknowledging the struggle becomes a doorway to healing. The therapist can call upon the presence of God for the healing of childhood and current wounds through gentle guidance and sensitivity.

Phil was married, a father of three young children and a graduate student in seminary. He had one serious, agonizing problem. He could not seem to finish graduate school and his wife was becoming more impatient each year that went by. He blocked when taking exams and procrastinated on finishing papers. It seemed impossible that he could ever finish and he felt like a total failure. In therapy, while investigating his family of origin, he painfully spoke about his developmentally disabled older brother. As the story unraveled, he remembered the tragic day when, at age eight, he came home from school to witness his brother being taken away in a strait jacket to the mental institution. Phil wanted to scream at the top of his lungs for them to *stop,* he wanted to run to his brother's rescue, he wanted to tell his parents not to do this terrible thing, but instead he remained frozen on his bike at the top of the hill. Finally, after the ambulance pulled away, he tore off on his bike to an alley where he cried angry tears with no one to comfort him. He also recalled the time he visited his brother at the mental institution a week before he died. Once again, Phil was frozen in his tracks and not able to respond to his brother. "I should have been able to do something, but I did nothing," he said with remorse. He had kept these feelings to himself over all these years, never having shared them with anyone. Now, as an adult, he seemed to be frozen in life.

Revealing his story in the safety of therapy was a beginning point of healing. We decided to spend the next session going back to these scenes through imagery so he could relive the moments that had been buried for these many years. A deeply religious man, he trusted in God's love and compassion and asked if we could bring the image of Jesus to this experience. Phil's wife sat behind the one-way mirror to gain a better understanding of these painful memories as we went through the imagery. The therapist had him relax and led him back in time to these two events of childhood. He was able to picture the scene in his mind and to feel the helplessness, anger, and sadness of that event. As the feelings began to flow, Phil imagined Jesus comforting him as he wept openly in the alley. He also expressed his anger and asked hard "why" questions to God, which became cathartic. In the safety of the therapy relationship, he could let himself finally express what had been pent up inside for all these years.

When the session ended, Phil was emotionally spent. At that point his wife came into the therapy room and gently put her arm around him. This gentle touch was an intimate connection between them that had been missing for some time in their relationship. They continued in therapy for some months as a couple, but terminated during finals week so he could finish his papers for the term. The following June he proudly walked across the stage to claim his diploma. They both felt God used this time in therapy as a spiritual healing that helped them enormously as a couple. They felt a renewed touch from God that opened them up to each other.

These biblical relationship principles become a means to therapeutic healing. Bringing God's love, grace, power and intimate connection to clients in therapy offers hope and transformation in the context of the Christian faith.

Suggestions for Follow-Up

Therapists may want to continue to emphasize the biblical principles that played an important role in therapy throughout the course of treatment. Such reminders can serve to highlight the significant changes experienced by the client.

Contraindications

While these four principles can apply to relationships in general, the biblical basis sets a religious tone. Even though the therapist can work within various belief systems, looking to the Almighty God as a source of healing and power is central to the work. Therefore, clients who do not believe in God may not find this as helpful.

References

Buechner, F. (1991). *Telling secrets.* New York: HarperSanFrancisco.
Doherty, W. J. (1995). *Soul searching: Why psychotherapy must promote moral responsibility.* New York: Basic Books.
Walsh, F. (Ed.) (1999). *Spiritual resources in family therapy.* New York: Guilford Press.

Professional Readings and Resources

Doherty, W. J. (1995). *Soul searching: Why psychotherapy must promote moral responsibility.* New York: Basic Books.
Walsh, F. (Ed.) (1999). *Spiritual resources in family therapy.* New York: Guilford Press.

Bibliotherapy Sources for the Client

Buechner, F. (1991). *Telling secrets.* New York: HarperSanFrancisco.
Nouwen, H. (1989). *Lifesigns: Intimacy, fecundity, and ecstasy in Christian perspective.* New York: Doubleday.

– 21 –

Facilitating Change Through Contemplative Prayer

Peter J. Jankowski

Type of Contribution: Homework, Handout

Objective

Utilizing the spiritual discipline of contemplation to facilitate change is consistent with the clinical objective of a narrative theory of change. A narrative theory of change consists of fostering change through promoting a different experience of self for the client that can then become an alternative, problem-free, dominant way of thinking and talking about his or her being-in-the-world (Freedman & Combs, 1996; White & Epston, 1990). Thus, the homework assignment of contemplative prayer described in this paper is a means of generating an alternative experience of self that forms the basis for a new self-narrative.

Rationale for Use

Utilizing contemplative prayer as a means for promoting change is couched within a larger movement by some to consider how the various spiritual disciplines may be used to enhance the practice of psychotherapy (e.g., McMinn & McRay, 1997; Tan, 1996). Spiritual disciplines are time-tested practices that persons have used to increase the intimacy of their relationship to God, and consist of practices such as silence, prayer, meditation, confession, fasting, reading and studying sacred literature, experiencing community with a larger group of like-minded persons, service to others, and corporate worship (Willard, 1998, 2000). The spiritual discipline of contemplation is essentially a combination of the practices of silence and meditation and is designed to allow persons to "receive a new perspective on life" as they experience God's love for them (Huggett, 1997, p. 46). Thus, the first rationale for the use of contemplation as a clinical intervention rests in the nature of the disciplines themselves as time-tested means to experiencing change.

A second rationale for the use of contemplation, and other spiritual disciplines, as means to change, draws from models that integrate spirituality with intergenerational theories of change. Proponents of these intergenerational models conceptualize God as a member of the client's relational system and therefore suggest that when a client experiences changes in his or her relationship with God, changes in his or her other relationships can also be experienced (Butler & Harper, 1994; David, 1979; Griffith, 1986). In other words, as a person moves closer in his or her vertical relationship with God, he or she can experience the resolution of problems in his or her horizontal relationships. One way to facilitate change in a client's horizontal relationships can be through encouraging the practice of the spiritual disciplines. In fact, when contemplation has been effective in promoting change, the person gets a sense of God's "compassion for a hurting world," which results in movement within the horizontal sphere of the person's life (Huggett, 1997, p. 46).

241

A final rationale for the use of contemplation in psychotherapy is based on the meditative aspect of contemplative prayer. Meditation refers to repeating the words of God over and over again as recorded in sacred literature, and while doing so, involves pondering or reflecting upon the meaning of the words for oneself and one's life (Huggett, 1997). As Huggett suggested, "we meditate to give God's words the opportunity to penetrate, not just our minds, but our emotions—the places where we hurt—and our will—the places where we make choices and decisions" (p. 38). As a person reflects upon the written text, he or she can come to experience him or herself differently. In other words, sacred texts can be used as sources of alternative knowledge that challenge the client's dominant, problem-saturated story, thereby altering the experience of self. In addition, the client can be encouraged to consider how his or her story fits into the larger on-going narrative of God's involvement and work in the world (Green, 2002; Hart, 1995). Change can occur when a person's understanding of him or herself is written into that larger narrative, such that the person becomes a character "in the subsequent chapters of that story" (Hart, 1995, pp. 152-153). This process can provide a client with a calling upon, or missional perspective with which to see his or her life, and can therefore provide a significant source of meaning and purpose, again altering his or her experience of self.

Instructions

Contemplation, first and foremost, consists of taking "time to relax in God's presence" (Huggett, 1997, p. 44). Thus, the first instruction for use involves finding a place of solitude and structuring enough time to simply rest in God's presence. During the session in which the homework is assigned, clients can be encouraged to plan ahead as to when in the coming week they can find time for such an opportunity.

Once the client actually gets to the place of solitude, Huggett (1997) suggested preparing to encounter God by freeing oneself from distractions, primarily through giving the stressors weighing oneself down over to God. The client can be asked to visualize him or herself piling the stressors at the feet of God and/or asked to visualize him or herself simply resting at God's feet. The client can also be asked to begin this time of contemplation by asking God to meet him or her, and to help experience God's love for him or her, and then wait in silence. The basis for the practice of silence is the biblical example of the psalmist who exclaimed, "cease striving and know that I am God" (Psalm 46:10, NASB) and "My soul, wait in silence for God only" (Psalm 62:5).

Next, as the person is still and quiet before God, he or she begins to ponder and reflect upon a sacred text. The clinician can assign a particular reading for meditation, or simply have the client choose something in which he or she is interested. The former helps structure the assignment further, and can therefore increase the likelihood of compliance. Some examples of biblical texts that could be used include: 2 Kings 21 and 2 Chronicles 33 that involve a story about God's compassion, mercy, relenting, and longing to commune with persons, which can be used for persons with narratives of despair, hopelessness, isolation, and loneliness; Luke 13:31-35 that consists of Christ's longing and compassion for people through the metaphor of a hen gathering her children, which can be used for persons with narratives of loneliness, isolation, rejection, and self-doubt; or John 11 that contains a description of Christ openly and compassionately grieving with his friends over the death of a loved one, which can be used for those with narratives of loss and sadness. The handout, Narratives for Use in Contemplative Prayer, consists of a nonexhaustive and suggestive listing of biblical passages that can be used as contemplation texts to address particular client narratives.

The client can be asked to read and re-read the text, keeping track of any new understanding of God and/or him or herself gained from the repetitious reading of the passages. As a variation of the assignment presented in this paper, the reading and re-reading of a text can follow what is known as *lectio divina* (Sire, 2000, p. 152). *Lectio divina* involves alternating the reading and re-reading of a passage out loud to him or herself with times of silent reading (Sire). As a method of reading sacred literature, *lectio divina* is designed to enhance "the likelihood that readers will really hear God speak to them" (Sire, p. 153), and like the practice of contemplation outlined in this paper, *lectio divina* is not so much a technique as it is "an atmosphere or ambience within which" the practice of the discipline takes place (Sire, p. 153). Whether the person reads silently or out loud, he or she can be encouraged to write his or her reflections in a journal in order to maximize the reflection process. He or she can then be asked to bring in the written reflections for the next therapy session.

The last aspect of the assignment involves another time of silence before God, but this time with the additional focus of listening to God rather than simply resting in God's presence. This aspect follows the biblical examples of Moses who listened as God spoke with him "face to face, just as a man [*sic*] speaks to his friends" (Exodus 33:11), Samuel who exclaimed to God "speak, for thy servant is listening" (1 Samuel 3:10), Mary who listened to Christ as she rested at his feet (see Luke 10:38-42) and John who rested on Christ's chest during the last supper listening while basking in Christ's love for him (see John 13:23-25). The primary purpose of this time of listening is to clarify the impressions obtained during the time of reading and reflection. A particular word or phrase from the reading may stand out for the client, and this key word or phrase can then be used as a mantra to focus and re-focus attention following any distraction that may occur naturally while being silent before God (Williamson, 2003). The cooperative nature of God's involvement in human life is most evident during this phase of the discipline (Maddox, 1994). The person rests, reads, reflects, listens, and attends, while God conveys love, dispenses grace, and moves within the internal and experiential realm of the person's being.

Brief Vignette

A male client presented in therapy with complaints of irritability, having a "short fuse," and desiring more peace in his life. Conceptualized within a narrative framework, the client had a dominant self-narrative of worthlessness that consisted of believing that he deserved to feel bad about himself and that there was no way in which to overcome this experiential reality. Every day was a constant battle against these recurring thoughts and feelings, and one in which he "was losing."

Conversations about the formative and maintaining context of the dominant narrative uncovered several "unique outcomes" (White & Epston, 1990). For example, at times he had brief moments and glimpses of the peace and joy for which he longed. This longing was evident in his spiritual life and resulted in an urgent and earnest prayer life in which he consistently and persistently asked God to "help him." Understanding that the largest contributor to change in therapy consists of client factors such as the strengths and competencies that a client brings to the clinical relationship (Miller, Duncan, & Hubble, 1997), the client's earnest prayer life was recognized as such and formed the basis for the homework assignment of contemplation.

During a conversation about his prayer life, the client was asked if he was familiar with the concept of spiritual disciplines. After some discussion about the nature and purpose of the spiritual disciplines, including self-disclosure on the clinician's part about the role of the disciplines in his own life and others, the client was asked to consider experimenting with silence and meditation. The client was enthused and curious about adding another element to his prayer life, so he agreed to try it once during the week to see what would happen. Specific instructions for using silence and meditation were provided to the client; for example, the client was encouraged to follow his usual prayer routine, but to begin the time with a period of silence before God. Following the time of stillness, the client was instructed to read and reread Romans 7:14-25 and then to wait in silence. While doing so, he was asked to pay attention to any thoughts and/or feelings that might occur. Reading Romans 7:14-25 was suggested because of the language that the client used during sessions regarding the internal struggle he experienced over "good" and "bad urges" within himself. It seemed appropriate to offer the passage as a means for structuring the homework because of the biblical writer's own description of an internal struggle. Last, the client was told that the clinician would be curious to hear about what happened at the next session.

During that next session, the client was asked to describe what happened; more specifically, he was asked whether the reading of the passage resulted in any moments of insight and contrasting experiences to what usually took place. The client downplayed the effectiveness of reading the passage, particularly in yielding any significant experiential changes. However, the client did comment on being able to identify with the biblical writer's experience and that was somewhat comforting. It became clearer during the conversation that reading and reflecting upon the passage did have a normalizing effect on the client's experience, but the difference was not considered "a difference that makes a difference" (de Shazer, 1988, p. 10). The suggestive nature of the assignment requires that the clinician be open to the possibility that the client will modify the assignment to fit him or herself. Such was the case with this client, for he used the assignment more as an opportunity to extend the intensity and duration of his own prayer life, rather than follow the instructions as suggested in therapy in a rigid manner, once again illustrating that client factors are the largest contributor to change in therapy.

The different experience of self that made a difference to the client was an increased intimacy in his relationship to God and the sense of purpose or mission in his life with which he left the prayer time. This increased intimacy and sense of meaning produced the internal peace for which he had been longing. The previously mentioned shift in the horizontal dimension of a person's spiritual life that contemplation can bring was evident in this client's experience. In fact, he left the time of prayer with a renewed sense of calling on his life to better serve the needs of persons around him and, in doing so, better testify to God's love.

Over time, as the alternative experience of self was expanded upon during therapy conversations, the client experienced more agency over the "bad urges," which primarily had to do with lashing out in frustration and anger at others, again testifying to the shift in the horizontal dimension. These "bad urges" increasingly became less intense and less frequent. The client was also able to increasingly act upon the "good urges" by engaging in concrete acts of service that reinforced the emerging narrative of purpose and meaning.

Suggestions for Follow-Up

Follow-up of the homework assignment initially consists of being sure to ask about the homework at the beginning of the next session. The client can simply be encouraged to describe any new experiences of self that may have been generated by the practice of contemplation. Once an alternative experience of self has been identified in the therapeutic conversation, psychotherapy can follow the narrative processes of adding details to the experience, and acting upon the new experience of self so as to further construct the new dominant story (Freedman & Combs, 1996). Adding details to the new experience of self consists primarily of the therapist asking questions that bring forth a thorough description of the alternative experience. The clinician can ask questions such as, "What was it like to practice the spiritual discipline of contemplation? What new insights about yourself did you gain? How was this different from how you thought about yourself before? Tell me about other times you experienced something similar. What emotions were involved in your experience of contemplation? Who do you think would be most surprised by what you learned from the experience, and why? What difference do you think this new experience will make for how you relate to others, do your job, and/or live your life?" Freedman and Combs (1996) have categorized the aforementioned examples of questions as story development and meaning questions.

Performance of the new emerging narrative can involve any number of practices that will support the behaviors connected to the new narrative, thereby reinforcing the narrative and related experience of self (Freedman & Combs, 1996). In fact, simply sharing the experience with a therapist is a means of performing the alternative experience and helps clarify the new emerging narrative. Oftentimes having a larger supportive social context with which to share the changes can further strengthen the new narrative (Freedman & Combs). Perhaps, there is a family member, clergyperson, or group of church members that the client can be encouraged to share the experience of change with, either by having them invited to attend a session or by having the client tell them outside of therapy. Or, the client can be asked to write a "success story" letter to someone who would support the change in his or her life, or to document the change in other ways such as videotape or audiotape recordings and other creative formats of expression (White & Epston, 1990, p. 163). If a particular behavior change flows out of the new narrative and experience of self, the client can be encouraged to practice that new behavior as a homework assignment or to practice it in the context of the therapeutic relationship.

Contraindications

Since the reflecting position (Freedman & Combs, 1996; Griffith & Griffith, 1994) is so central to both contemplation and a narrative theory of change, the assignment may have to be modified for clients at different life cycle stages. For example, younger adolescents and children may find the homework as presented here to be a difficult task because they have not yet developed the cognitive ability of abstract thinking that reflection requires. Furthermore, some adults who exhibit strong concrete thinking ability may also have a difficult time with the assignment and therefore may need to have the assignment adapted. Nevertheless, the assignment could be quite beneficial in helping clients develop more abstract thinking ability, perhaps even countering the lack of opportunity they may have had for developing such a skill.

One way to modify the assignment, making it more concrete, could involve the clinician modeling the exercise of the discipline during a session with the client. Or, as is the case with all of the spiritual disciplines, since there is a community or corporate element to the practice of the discipline, rather than modeling for the client, the therapist and client could simply practice the discipline together. In fact, even the more individualistic disciplines such as contemplation are to be practiced within a supportive community of persons who can provide accountability and encouragement in the practice of the discipline (Maddox, 1994). To practice the more private disciplines apart from the more public disciplines, or to practice them in a way that neglects the horizontal dimension of spirituality, can result in an imbalance and incompleteness that has the potential to create problems (Maddox; Rolheiser, 1999). If the client lacks such a supportive community outside of therapy, then the therapist-client relationship could become that context, or persons from the community or client's family could be recruited in order to play that role in his or her life. As indicated earlier, contemplation results in horizontal movement within the client's life, and the performance of the new experience, including sharing the experience of the discipline with the therapist, highlights the communal element of the discipline.

Another means to making the assignment more concrete involves the previously mentioned component of having the client journal his or her reflections. Furthermore, rather than having the client write down his or her own reflections, the assignment could be made more concrete by providing specific questions to address while reading and re-reading the passage. For example, a question that was used during psychotherapy with the client in the case vignette consisted of asking the client to describe the biblical writer's struggle in Romans 7:14-25, and asking "In what ways can you identify with him and his struggle? And if you do identify with the writer, what does it mean to you that you and he shared a similar experience?"

A second contraindication for use involves clients who lack an interest in spirituality. Clients need not be "believers" of a particular faith tradition such as Christianity but they should at least be open to the topic of spirituality in their own lives. Furthermore, it seems important that clients view the sacred literature of their faith tradition as having some relevance for how they live, otherwise the assignment could lack meaning for them. While the focus of this paper has been on the use of contemplation with biblical passages, contemplation could be used with the sacred writings from other faith traditions. In fact, clinicians should feel as though they can use their own spirituality as a means to informing their clinical work, and therefore can tailor the assignment to fit with their own faith tradition and spiritual experiences. In fact, the clinician's own spirituality can guide the application of the assignment to particular clinical situations. The need to tailor the assignment to the self of the clinician is based on the psychotherapy outcome research and common change factors literature that indicates that it is the conviction and genuineness with which an intervention is delivered that promotes change and not the actual technique (Miller et al., 1997). For this particular homework assignment, as was illustrated in the vignette, the application of contemplation to a clinical situation must fit contextually and be consistent with the clinician's self, or who he or she is as a person.

One last contraindication further consists of the way in which the assignment is carried out in a clinical context. Consistent with a narrative approach to psychotherapy, the clinician is encouraged to relate to clients from a "not-knowing" position (Anderson, 1990; Anderson & Goolishian, 1992). A "not-knowing" position involves a desire to listen to and learn from the client about his or her experience, and to offer assignments suggestively, hesitantly and tentatively. In other words, a clinician who sees the assignment as a required task for therapy, taking a strong expert-like position with clients and dictating that the assignment must be accomplished in order for change to happen, counteracts the overall tone of the homework assignment and the invitational nature of change inherent within both contemplation and narrative psychotherapy. Contemplation is based on a view that consists of God inviting the person into relationship and inviting the person to rest and receive love. The "not-knowing" stance has a similar feel to it in that the client is invited to be an active contributor to the process of therapy, including any decisions that need to be made about homework assignments. In fact, the element of choice can help promote change through generating the alternative experience of agency that is lacking in problem-saturated stories (Durrant & Kowalski, 1993). Thus, the mere invitation to consider the practice of the spiritual discipline may be enough to generate an alternative experience of self that can then be expanded upon in therapy.

Referencess

Anderson, H. (1990). Then and now: A journey from "knowing" to "not-knowing." *Contemporary Family Therapy, 12,* 193-197.

Anderson, H., & Goolishian, H. (1992). The client is the expert. In S. McNamee & K. J. Gergen (Eds.), *Therapy as social construction* (pp. 25-39). Newbury Park, CA: Sage.

Butler, M. A., & Harper, J. M. (1994). The divine triangle: God in the marital system of religious couples. *Family Process, 33,* 277-286.

de Shazer, S. (1988). *Clues: Investigating solutions in brief therapy.* New York: W. W. Norton.

David, J. R. (1979). The theology of Murray Bowen or the marital triangle. *Journal of Psychology and Theology, 7,* 259-262.

Durrant, M., & Kowalski, K. (1993). Enhancing views of competence. In S. Friedman (Ed.), *The new language of change: Constructive collaboration in psychotherapy* (pp. 107-137). New York: Guilford Press.

Freedman, J., & Combs, G. (1996). *Narrative therapy: The social construction of preferred realities.* New York: W. W. Norton.

Green, J. (2002, March). Reforming imagination, reframing practices: A New Testament portrait of moral formation. Paper presented at the Center for Applied Christian Ethics Conference: Exploring Moral Formation, Wheaton, Illinois.

Griffith, J. L. (1986). Employing the God-family relationship in therapy with religious families. *Family Process, 25,* 609-618.

Griffith, J. L., & Griffith, M. E. (1994). *The body speaks: Therapeutic dialogues for mind-body problems.* New York: Basic Books.

Hart, T. (1995). *Faith thinking: The dynamics of Christian theology.* Downers Grove, IL: InterVarsity Press.

Huggett, J. (1997). *Learning the language of prayer.* New York: Crossroad Publishing.

Maddox, R. L. (1994). *Responsible grace.* Nashville, TN: Abingdon Press.

McMinn, M. R., & McRay, B. W. (1997). Spiritual disciplines and the practice of integration: Possibilities and challenges for Christian psychologists. *Journal of Psychology and Theology, 25,* 102-110.

Miller, S. D., Duncan, B. L., & Hubble, M. A. (1997). *Escape from Babel: Toward a unifying language for psychotherapy practice.* New York: W. W. Norton.

New American Standard Bible (1977). Nashville, TN: Holman Bible Publishers.

Rolheiser, R. (1999). *The holy longing: The search for a Christian spirituality.* New York: Doubleday.

Sire, J. W. (2000). *Habits of the mind: Intellectual life as a Christian calling.* Downers Grove, IL: InterVarsity Press.

Tan, S. (1996). Practicing the presence of God: The work of Richard J. Foster and its application to psychotherapeutic practice. *Journal of Psychology and Christianity, 15,* 17-28.

White, M., & Epston, D. (1990). *Narrative means to therapeutic ends.* New York: W. W. Norton.

Willard, D. (1998). *The divine conspiracy: Rediscovering our hidden life in God.* New York: HarperSanFrancisco.

Willard, D. (2000). Spiritual formation in Christ: A perspective on what it is and how it might be done. *Journal of Psychology and Theology, 28,* 254-258.

Williamson, B. (2003, February). God's own peace: Systems theory and spirituality. Paper presented at the Lombard Mennonite Peace Center Workshop, Wheaton, Illinois.

Professional Readings and Resources

Freedman, J., & Combs, G. (1996). *Narrative therapy: The social construction of preferred realities.* New York: W. W. Norton.

McMinn, M. R., & McRay, B. W. (1997). Spiritual disciplines and the practice of integration: Possibilities and challenges for Christian psychologists. *Journal of Psychology and Theology, 25,* 102-110.

Tan, S. (1996). Practicing the presence of God: The work of Richard J. Foster and its application to psychotherapeutic practice. *Journal of Psychology and Christianity, 15,* 17-28.

Willard, D. (1998). *The divine conspiracy: Rediscovering our hidden life in God.* New York: HarperSanFrancisco.

Bibliotherapy Sources for the Client

Foster, R. J. (1978). *Celebration of discipline.* New York: Harper & Row.

Foster, R. J., & Griffin, E. (Eds.) (2000). *Spiritual classics: Selected readings for individuals and groups on the twelve disciplines.* New York: HarperSanFrancisco.

Willard, D. (1991). *The spirit of the disciplines: Understanding how God changes lives.* New York: Harper SanFrancisco.

Willard, D. (1998). *The divine conspiracy: Rediscovering our hidden life in God.* New York: HarperSanFrancisco.

Handout: Narratives for Use in Contemplative Prayer

Text	Themes	Client narrative(s)
1 Kings 19:1-14	A story of God's comforting presence, provision for needs, intimacy, tenderness, and compassion; symbolized by the angel touching Elijah's lips on two occasions, and God's voice in the gentle blowing wind.	fear, depression, despair, loneliness, discouragement
2 Kings 21 (2 Chronicles 33)	A story about God's compassion, mercy, relenting, patience, longing for relationship with persons; and a story about possibilities and second chances.	isolation, loneliness, hopelessness, feeling unwanted
Nehemiah 9	A poetic recounting of the history of the people and their relationship to God: deliverance from captivity and alternating themes of rebelling and turning away from God despite God's goodness and provision, and God's rescue and redemption. The summary characterization of God: "Thou art a God of forgiveness, gracious and compassionate, slow to anger, and abounding in loving-kindness; and Thou dids't not forsake them" (Nehemiah 9:17, NASB).	rejection, loneliness, isolation, doubt, despair, sadness
Jonah 3	A story of hope and possibility for change embedded within God's character: "a gracious and compassionate God, slow to anger and abundant in loving-kindness, and one who relents concerning calamity" (Jonah 4:2).	doubt, loneliness, hopelessness, despair, discouragement
Luke 13:31-35	A story of Christ's longing and compassion for relationship with people through the metaphor of a "hen gathering her brood" (Luke 13:34); a conveying of tenderness, and provision.	inadequacy, doubt, loneliness, isolation
John 11	A story of Jesus' openness, genuineness, and love for his friends illustrated in his compassionate grieving with them over their loss.	grief, sadness, loss, loneliness, fear

Source: New American Standard Bible (1977). Nashville, TN: Holman Bible Publishers.

Jankowski, P. J. (2006). Facilitating change through contemplative prayer. In K. B. Helmeke & C. F. Sori (Eds.), *The therapist's notebook for integrating spirituality in counseling: Homework, handouts, and activities for use in psychotherapy* (pp. 241-249). Binghamton, NY: The Haworth Press.

22

Using Concepts of NTU Psychotherapy to Encourage the Use of Prayer: Overcoming Distress and Trauma in Christian Clients

Lonnie E. Duncan

Type of Contribution: Activity

Objective

The objective of this activity is to help devout Christians pray through painful situations, with the goal of helping them to connect with God to gain insight, liberation, and healing. During times of stress or traumatic events devout Christians may experience spiritual disconnection from God that causes them to withdraw and experience guilt and shame. This activity will allow therapists who practice from a spiritually dynamic perspective to help clients examine their current functioning while spiritually centering the client.

Rationale for Use

The need to examine client problems from a holistic perspective has been advocated by many in the helping profession. The field of counseling psychology has begun to embrace the unique role of spirituality in the lives of potential clients as well as its role in the psychotherapy process (Richards & Bergin, 2000). Many traditional counseling theories have been modified to include spiritual issues or at least have acknowledged their role in the counseling process (Jones, 1994). Several professional organizations have made explicit that religion is one type of diversity that psychotherapists and counselors are obligated to respect (Richards & Bergin). With counseling becoming more accepted by many Christian denominations, it is imperative that counselors are able to draw upon the spiritual resources that are available to potential clients.

NTU (pronounced "in-too") psychotherapy is an Afrocentric approach that recognizes the influence of spirituality on an individual's value system, and its importance in providing focus and direction to human goals and purpose. NTU psychotherapy is based on the Nguzo Saba principles, which are the seven principles of effective guidelines for healthy living (Phillips, 1990). The principles are Umoja, Kujichagulia, Ujima, Ujamaa, Nia, Kuumba, and Imani. Although these principles are not connected to any particular religion, they provide organization for working with devoutly religious clients. The word NTU is derived from the Bantu language, which according to Maniacky (2002)

> belongs to a huge language family in Africa. Bantu is spoken in Cameroon, Equatorial Guinea, Gabon, Congo-Brazzaville, Congo-Kinshasa, Central African Republic (just a

few languages are Bantu), Kenya, Uganda, Rwanda, Burundi, Tanzania, Malawi, Zambia, Zimbabwe, Mozambique, Comoro Islands, Angola, Namibia, Botswana, Swaziland, and Lesotho, South Africa. (p. 1)

NTU is a Bantu word that "describes a universal, unifying force that touches upon all aspects of existence" (Phillips, 1990, p. 56). Phillips states:

> When we are harmonious, we are "at peace" whether or not the external forces surrounding us are fragmented since being in harmony depends more on our abilities to adapt through a clear process of organizing the disparate parts into a meaningful whole. (p. 56)

This statement highlights the importance and interrelatedness between the intrinsic (psychic and material) and the extrinsic (social and material) factors that play a role in a person's ability to respond to everyday problems. According to Phillips (1990), NTU is both a spiritual force inside and a spiritual force outside. One of the goals of NTU Psychotherapy is to restore the natural order within an individual (i.e., harmony, balance, and authenticity). The prayer exercise described in this chapter will be utilized to achieve this goal. The natural order is unity between mind, body, and spirit throughout life. For the Christian client, this harmony or balance requires a personal feeling of connectedness with God through the presence of the Holy Spirit. Jesus, responding to Judas, states "But the Comforter, which is the Holy Ghost, whom the Father will send in my name, he shall teach you all things, and bring all things to your remembrance, whatsoever I have said unto you" (John 14:26, KJV). The Holy Spirit then becomes the spiritual force that allows the Christian client to have balance to deal with everyday problems. The Holy Spirit is also the spiritual force that God uses to bring things to our remembrance. For the scriptures states, "Thou knowest my downsitting and mine uprising, thou understandest my thought afar off" (Psalm 139:2). Therefore helping the Christian client to utilize this gift is an important aspect of the therapeutic process.

For Christian clients this process involves a commitment to the Lord and his word. When this bond is fractured it creates disunity between mind, body, and spirit. Psalms 37:5 states, "Commit thy way unto the Lord; trust also in him; and he shall bring it to pass." The Christian clients who can achieve this balance have purpose and direction in their life and have healthy relationships.

Instructions

The following prayer activity may serve to restore the natural order in hopes of reenergizing clients spiritually, so that they can draw from this spiritual power to improve their daily functioning.

The use of this intervention should be within the framework of those therapists who work from a spiritually dynamic perspective. Therapists who are considering this intervention should spend time becoming familiar with the tenets of NTU psychotherapy and the Christian experience. An understanding of the various tenets of Christianity and NTU psychotherapy will help the therapist determine the compatibility with their particular therapeutic approach. This activity emphasizes the Nguzo Saba principle of Umoja (Unity) between the client and God.

In line with this approach to counseling, this intervention does not require any preparatory work. It naturally comes out of the relationship between the client and the therapist. The therapist should have information from prior sessions about the client's idiosyncratic use of the Holy Spirit and a sense of how active it is in the client's level of functioning. It would be beneficial to the therapist to acquire a deeper understanding of the way that the Holy Spirit operates within the framework of those who ascribe to a life of holiness as part of their Christian experience. Information can be obtained through the Holy Bible and Richards and Bergin (2000). Asking the client to rate the level of his or her spiritual self on a scale from 1-10 would give the therapist a good idea. After establishing the client's level of spirituality, the activity can then be utilized.

With the client's permission, the therapist leads the client in a progressive prayer exercise, which is consistent with the Christian experience of entering the inner sanctuary with God through uninhibited prayer. Dobbins (2000) states that "praying through" consists of the following four steps. The believer: (1) talks honestly with God about what is hurting him or her; (2) relates emotionally to the particular problem; (3) meditates and asks God for help in finding a different and less disturbing way of interpreting the pain and hurt; and (4) spends time praising God for the new way of looking at the pain and mentally rehearsing the new interpretation. The following progressive prayer exercise is based on the aforementioned process, and includes some slight modifications.

Progressive Prayer Exercise

The first step in this prayer exercise is to allow the clients to get in a comfortable praying position. For some this may be in the traditional prayer position. For others, it may be lying prostrate on the floor, and for others it may be sitting on the couch or chair.

The second step involves helping the clients to imagine themselves standing in the presence of the Lord and worshipping and asking him to help in this present situation. Some clients may not like this image and so the therapist and the clients may have to spend time developing non-threatening images.

The third step involves leading the clients on how they are to start the prayer. During this phase the therapist's voice is calm and not disruptive to the process. The therapist wants to instruct the clients to meditate on the aforementioned image and the voice of the Holy Spirit, the issues that brought them to therapy, and their feelings and thoughts about the issue. According to Dobbins (2000), the therapist may have to reassure the clients that God wants to hear from them and will not express anger toward them just because they have expressed their pain. This part of the progressive prayer may have been discussed before the exercise and so it may just need to be reiterated.

The fourth step is a continuation of the third step in which the therapist is going to instruct the clients to pray and ask God to give guidance with their present situation. In addition, the therapist encourages the clients to ask for a healthier way of looking at their current situation and to strengthen their spiritual understanding and mental well-being. The clients should be encouraged to be honest about what they need in order to deal with their current situation.

The fifth and final stage involves helping clients to process the experience after completion of prayer. Let the clients express themselves in any way that they want. The processing of the exercise should focus on the experience of doing the exercise. The therapist may have to help clients to process emotions that may be uncomfortable or shameful. It is important to highlight any difficulties in focusing on any aspect of the activity. It is also important to discuss the how the clients feel about talking to God with sincerity and honesty about what has been going on with them. It is important to encourage the clients to talk with their minister or pastor. Issues may arise that can only be addressed with their pastor or minister, particularly if there are issues that involve restoration or repentance.

Brief Vignette

Bobby is a thirty-two-year-old single male who has struggled with feelings of inadequacies, particularly in romantic relationships. He desires a relationship that will lead to marriage but has had problems sustaining the attention of the women that he dates. He stated that they have commented on his negative attitude and unwillingness to admit to common faults. Bobby originally ignored these complaints but a recent breakup with a woman that, in his words, "he really loved" has led to him reexamining past criticisms of former girlfriends. Bobby reports having a strong faith in God but admits that he struggles at times because he feels that God is not answering his prayers to find a wife.

During one session, the therapist asked Bobby about his prayer life. Bobby revealed that he does not pray regularly because he feels that his hectic life and lack of privacy make it very hard to concentrate. The therapist introduced the possibility of doing a progressive prayer exercise in therapy with Bobby, and after describing it, Bobby agreed to do the exercise. The therapist led Bobby through the progressive prayer exercise:

> Bobby, I want you to relax, get into a comfortable position, and think about being in the presence of the Lord. Take a minute and meditate on this thought. (Pause.) I now want you to pay attention to that small voice. What is it telling you about yourself? (Pause.) I want you to continue to relax. In a moment we are going to pray together. I want you to tell me what we should pray for? (Pause.) I now want you to think about the issue that brought you here. I want you to focus on how you feel about this issue. What emotions come to mind for you? Do not verbalize them to me—just get in touch with the experience. (Pause.) What things do you need from God? How would you like him to help you in working on these things? You want to seek God and be honest and sincere about your feelings. (Pause.) We are going to ask God to guide us for the rest of this session. We are going to ask God to help us help you to become a better person. We are going to help God to help us find those things that are hindering you in your relationships.

After praying, the therapist then helped Bobby to relax and ease back into the session. The therapist asked Bobby to describe what he learned and asked Bobby for his assessment on the value of this exercise. Bobby reported that the prayer exercise helped him to clear his mind and draw closer to God. He reported that he was comforted by the fact that he felt the presence of God in his life and he was beginning to see his problem more clearly. He also did not feel that his problems were insurmountable and his hope was in the process of being restored. Bobby talked openly about needing to have a more active prayer life to combat his feelings of hopelessness. He also was interested in making prayer an integral part of his therapy. Toward the end of the session the therapist suggested to Bobby that he talk with his pastor about ways of improving his prayer life and to get feedback on his assessment of his problem.

Suggestions for Follow-Up

This exercise may encourage more discussions about spiritual issues and may require a referral or a coordinated effort with the client's pastor or spiritual leader. This exercise may also require that the therapist seek out additional supervision in order to integrate the spiritual dimension with the overall well being of the client. This activity can serve as an assessment or an intervention with a client who is working on being more aware of messages and cognitive processes that interfere with their connection to God.

Contraindications

This activity may not be effective with clients who are overly defensive or in an acute crisis. Clients who are unable to handle intimate interpersonal relationships may also have problems in completing this activity. In addition, non-Christians who do not ascribe to the Christian concept of holiness and who are uncomfortable with meditation may have some problems with this form of prayer.

References

Dobbins, R. D. (2000). Psychotherapy with Pentecostal Protestants. In P. S. Richards & A. E. Bergin (Eds.), *Handbook of psychotherapy and religious diversity* (pp. 155-184). Washington, DC: American Psychological Association.

Holy Bible, King James Version (1816). New York: American Bible Society.

Jones, S. I. (1994). A constructive relationship with the science and profession of psychology. *American Psychologist 49*(3), 184-199.

Maniacky, J. (2002). *Bantu languages and their statuses.* Retrieved December 12, 2002, http://www.bantu.ovh.org/status.html.

Phillips, F. B. (1990). NTU psychotherapy: An Afrocentric approach. *The Journal of Black Psychology, 12*(1), 55-74.

Richards, P. S., & Bergin, A. E. (2000). *Handbook of psychotherapy and religious diversity.* Washington, DC: American Psychological Association.

Professional Readings and Resources

Cox, H. (1995). *Fire from heaven: The rise of Pentecostal spirituality and the reshaping of religion in the twenty-first century.* Reading, MA: Addison-Wesley.

Griffith, E. E. H., English, T., & Mayfield, V. (1980). Possession, prayer, and testimony: Therapeutic aspects of the Wednesday night meeting in a Black church. *Psychiatry, 43,* 120-127.

MacArthur, J. F., & Mack, W.A. (1994). *Introduction to biblical counseling: A basic guide to the principles and practices of counseling.* Dallas TX: Word Publishing.

Walker, C. (1992). *Biblical counseling with African Americans: Taking a ride in the Ethiopian's chariot.* Grand Rapids, MI: Zondervan Publishing House.

Bibliotherapy Sources for the Client

Johnson, D. (2002). *A light in the darkness: Spiritual warfare strategies for the end time Christian.* Nazareth, MI: G3 Ministries Publishing.

Jones, C. (2002a). *Fasting for change.* Cincinnati, OH: Bethesda Ministries, Inc.

Jones, C. (2002b). *The prayer clinic manual.* Cincinnati, OH: Bethesda Ministries, Inc.

Jones, C. (2003). *Lord heal me from the inside.* Cincinnati, OH: Bethesda Ministries, Inc.

23

The Use of Spiritual Practices in Conjunction with Therapy with Christian Examples

J. Mark Killmer

Type of Contribution: Activities

Objective

This chapter introduces the second aspect of a model for integrating spirituality in therapy. A spiritual practice is an individual or community activity that taps spiritual or religious resources and/or nurtures spiritual growth. In this model, spiritual practices are employed by clients _in conjunction with_ therapy to activate spiritual resources that can facilitate change. The other aspect of this model consists of in-depth conversations with clients about spiritual concerns called spiritual dialogues. These dialogues occur _within_ therapy and are presented in Chapter 5.

This chapter presents a number of individual and group spiritual growth practices drawn from the wide spectrum of Christian traditions. It is anticipated that the majority of therapists and clients will be unaware of most of these practices. Thus, the chapter strives to acquaint spiritually sensitive therapists with the potential and availability of spiritual practices to augment therapy. The specific focus on Christian spiritual practices in this chapter, which reflect the experience and expertise of the author, enables an in-depth presentation of this aspect of the model. It is envisioned, however, that the spiritual activities of other faith traditions or current spiritual movements have the same potential for contributing to the growth and healing of clients.

Intentional and intensive participation in spiritual practices by an individual often leads to significant spiritual growth. These practices can be useful in conjunction with therapy for several reasons. First, they can tap internal spiritual resources and religious coping mechanisms that produce intangible healthy qualities including inner peace, courage, meaning or hope. Second, spiritual practices may create or activate a spiritual support network that provides support, encouragement, guidance or assistance for the client. This network is understood as religious/ spiritual relationships such as a faith community, spiritual friends or small groups, pastoral care providers and/or a relationship with God. Finally, these practices can be therapeutic interventions serving to block the escalation of emotions or impacting cognitive distortions. In sum, spiritual resources can contribute significantly to the process of change within therapy and may become a powerful context for sustaining or increasing this growth after therapy.

Since Christian examples are used to illustrate the use of spiritual practices, this chapter is also an opportunity to increase the effectiveness of spiritually sensitive therapists working specifically with devout Christian clients. A devout client is defined as a Christian from any denominational background who perceives faith as essential to their life. Devout Christians often enter therapy hoping to discern God's perspective about their situation and wanting to respond in a faithful manner. The use of spiritual practices can be an effective response to the spiritual agenda of these clients.

Rationale for Use

Religion and spirituality have emerged as vital factors in health and well-being from recent research into myriad physical and psychological health issues (Koenig, 1997; Larson, 1993). The research to discover how people cope with trauma, tragedy, and high levels of distress seems particularly relevant to therapy. In addition to the discovery that religion and spirituality consistently play a vital role in successful coping, this stream of research has begun to identify specific aspects of religion and spirituality that are especially helpful or detrimental to coping with high levels of pain and distress.

For the past decade, Kenneth Pargament (1997) has conducted research to determine the specific aspects of religion and spirituality that help people cope with serious distress. In addition to these projects, Pargament has made a meta-analysis of the coping research. This combined research has identified four particularly effective religious coping devices that are *not specific* to any single faith tradition. The first coping mechanism is *spiritual support* defined as "the perception of support and guidance by God in times of trouble." Strongly associated with positive outcomes, spiritual support includes intimate spiritual experiences such as feeling strengthened or reassured, receiving guidance for problems and a sense of not being alone in the midst of crisis (Pargament, p. 288).

Second, *collaborative religious coping* is a perspective that "the individual and divine work together to solve problems." This interdependent perspective to high distress is contrasted with a totally passive posture on one end of the spectrum and a totally self-reliant stance on the other end. Third, an individual's belief in "a loving God who is in control" is a religious coping mechanism termed *benevolent religious reframing.* This affirming understanding of God seems strongly implied in the two coping mechanisms previously delineated. Finally, the activation of a spiritual community to assist the individual is called *congregational support* (Pargament, 1997, pp. 288-290).

A strong relational component can be discerned from a close examination of these four positive religious coping mechanisms. Each device seems to imply a strong relationship with God, spiritual source and/or an active spiritual community. From within these relationships, the religious coping mechanisms appear to produce effective internal spiritual resources and a strong spiritual support network. Taken together, these spiritual resources result in the capacity to cope with and even thrive in the midst of the most painful events of life. For therapists committed to a systemic perspective, it is not surprising that much of the healing power of spirituality is found in relationships.

With the knowledge of the efficacy of these four religious coping mechanisms, it seems logical to encourage clients to purposely pursue the development and/or activation of spiritual resources as part of the healing process of their therapy. Consequently, spiritual practices are envisioned as intentional and intensive efforts to bring these effective religious coping mechanisms to bear on a client's current distress.

The spiritual practices described in the remainder of the article are divided into individual and community activities. Spiritually sensitive therapists who choose to recommend spiritual practices must determine how to present them to clients. A therapist with limited experience with or knowledge of spiritual practices may choose simply to make their clients aware of their availability. Interested clients may be referred to a colleague, such as a clergyperson, with the appropriate experience and knowledge. A spiritually experienced therapist, however, can effectively guide the client in the process of choosing and initiating spiritual practices. Finally, spiritually adept therapists may integrate spiritual practices *within* therapy when there is a high level of trust, comfort and differentiation in the therapeutic relationship. For instance, the therapist may engage in prayer or employ guided imagery with a client. In general, the inclusion of spiritual practices in therapy requires a strong compatibility in the worldviews between the therapist and client. This use of spiritual practices is not explored in depth in this chapter.

Instructions: Individual Spiritual Practices

This section describes a variety of individual spiritual practices accessible to devout Christian clients. It is intended to increase awareness for therapists of the availability of these spiritual practices. Integrating this aspect of the model begins when the therapist recommends the use of individual spiritual practices in conjunction with therapy to a client. In general, individual spiritual practices activate inner spiritual resources that assist the process of healing and change. For devout Christian clients, these practices often aim to deepen an individual's relationship with God. Ideally, the therapist will identify spiritual practices that are a good fit with a client's key therapeutic issues.

A sense of appropriate timing for these practices is also valuable. For instance, spiritual practices that activate support and comfort can be particularly helpful to distressed clients early in therapy. As this distress decreases, clients are more prepared for spiritual practices that promote serious personal reflection and significant change.

Personal Prayer

The daily practice of personal prayer is a primary resource in building a closer relationship with God. Prayer can serve to develop or activate the spiritual support, benevolent reframing and collaborative religious coping skills identified by Pargament. It can be a mistake to assume that all Christians pray on a regular basis. As a result, the recommendation for devout Christian clients to consider daily prayer is often an important early intervention.

Many therapists and clients have a very limited knowledge of prayer and thus are unaware of the rich diversity in the styles of prayer. Increased awareness of these varied practices can aid the therapist in finding a prayer style that is a good fit for the personality style and/or specific clinical issues of the client. For example, *centering prayer* (Keating, 1995) is an ancient Christian contemplative practice that strives to still the mind in order to listen to God. The deep state of relaxation produced by centering prayer can be helpful to anxious clients who often experience a strong sense of peace and closeness to God.

Centering prayer is recommended for approximately twenty minutes one or two times daily in a quiet time and place. It can be a very beneficial way to begin the day. Since centering prayer can create a deep state of relaxation, many participants use a quiet timer to announce the end of the session. The specific steps for centering prayer include:

1. The participant selects a word or brief phrase that is personally meaningful to them. This word/phrase serves as their "sacred word." Examples: faith, grace, peace, love of God.
2. Sitting comfortably, the participant closes their eyes and attempts to let go of what is "around and within" them. He or she might start by relaxing their body.
3. When the participant becomes aware of distracting thoughts, he or she gently says the sacred word. This serves to reinitiate the process of letting go.
4. At the close of prayer time, the participate keeps his or her eyes closed for a few moments before slowly opening them. (Keating, 1995)

In addition to creating awareness of this spiritual practice, centering prayer has been presented in some depth in order to provide a sense of the steps needed to introduce a new spiritual practice to clients. A therapist who is simply familiar with a spiritual practice may recommend it to a client. It requires some experience and/or expertise, however, to instruct the client in a new spiritual practice. In the absence of this ability, it is necessary to refer a client to resources such as books, clergy and/or retreat centers.

Spiritual Readings

A wealth of spiritual readings is readily available for use in conjunction with therapy. Spiritual readings can introduce a spiritual perspective on clinical issues, activate spiritual support, reinforce key themes in therapy or impact cognitive distortions. As a result, it is valuable for the therapist to be aware of spiritual readings that have a strong connection to the issues and goals of therapy. A few examples of spiritual readings for devout Christians are presented at the end of this chapter.

In distress, many devout Christians turn to the Bible for consolation. The Bible has a special authority in guiding the spiritual path of most devout Christians who are often interested in discovering how it speaks to their situation. It is helpful, then, when the therapist can direct clients to passages that are particularly relevant to their current distress or key clinical issue.

A wide array of daily meditation books is available for devout Christians. These resources contain one or two daily readings usually comprised of a brief reflection on a passage from scripture. The reflections are particularly helpful to clients who find the Bible difficult to read. Daily meditations can create a positive focus to start a day, help a client refocus in the midst of stress or bring a measure of comfort in the evening.

Some spiritual readings address particular issues with a strong relevance to therapy. These readings present a spiritual perspective on clinical issues such as anxiety, depression, forgiveness, self-image, and boundaries. A spiritual reading that speaks directly to the client's dilemma or distress can play a significant role in the integration of spiritual perspectives and resources in therapy. In turn, these spiritual resources often contribute to the process of change for a client.

The therapist should not underestimate the profound impact that spiritual readings can have for a client. The client may discover spiritual perspectives that are comforting, inspiring, or enlightening. On the other hand, the readings may be confusing, challenging, painful, or troubling. Thus, it is important for the therapist to process the responses that a client has to recommended readings. Strong emotional and/or cognitive reactions to spiritual readings often create the opportunity to enter in-depth dialogue with a spiritual client. As mentioned earlier, the process of spiritual dialogue with a client in therapy is delineated in a previous chapter (Killmer, 2006).

Spiritual Disciplines

In addition to prayer and spiritual readings, a vast number of spiritual disciplines or exercises are available for devout Christian clients. For instance, there is a spiritual discipline called *lectio divina* or praying the scriptures (Pennington, 1998). This meditative approach to the Bible fosters integration between scripture and the current concerns of the participant. Fasting is an ancient spiritual practice found in many religious traditions. This practice can be a very empowering experience that nurtures spiritual sensitivity. Usually associated with food, it is possible to fast from other activities such as watching television (Smith, 1999).

Spiritual exercises can be part of a therapeutic intervention. For example, a client may select a comforting spiritual phrase that is currently meaningful to him or her. Each morning, the client places a small cross in a pocket or purse. Whenever the cross is consciously or unconsciously touched during the course of a day, he or she is reminded of the comforting phrase. As a result, these meaningful words may intervene several times daily to provide comfort, refocusing and/or blocking the escalation of distress. As a person's experience with spiritual disciplines increases, these exercises can be tailored to address crucial therapeutic issues. This may dramatically increase their value in conjunction with therapy. Therapists with a strong interest in the use of spiritual practices in conjunction with therapy are encouraged to become familiar with these spiritual disciplines.

Brief Vignette: Individual Spiritual Practices

Susan is a fifty-year-old woman who entered therapy with multiple symptoms of major depression including suicidal ideation. She is very enmeshed with her mother and two older sisters. Her mother is a very angry woman who was emotionally and verbally abusive. This anger often took the form of repetitive derogatory statements about Susan's appearance and lack of intelligence. Although she is an attractive person who was an outstanding student, Susan introjected these derogatory statements creating a very poor self-image. This pseudo-identity is maintained by a loveless marriage to a pastor as well as ongoing enmeshed interactions with her mother and siblings. While she is angry with her family and husband, Susan also desires their affirmation. This underlying desire often results in a lack of boundaries in these relationships that leaves her vulnerable to hurtful interactions.

At one point of therapy, a spiritual dialogue addressed her image of God. Rooted in the stoic Calvinism of her faith tradition, she perceived God as distant, stern, and uncompromising. Susan was convinced that God is angry with her, perhaps due to her disloyal anger toward her family. During the course of the dialogue, the notion that God could be loving and compassionate was introduced. Susan struggled with this image of God; it seemed utopian to her. Eventually intrigued by the notion, she agreed to read *Meeting Jesus Again for the First Time* (Borg, 1994). In this book, New Testament scholar Marcus Borg powerfully develops the theme that the love and compassion of God was central to the message of Jesus. Interestingly, her husband, mother, and siblings were upset when she shared the image of a compassionate God with them. This spiritual reading contributed to a long-term, in-depth spiritual dialogue that slowly transformed her damaged self-image. One day, Susan reported that her damaged self-image must be getting better. Susan explained the startling realization that at some recent point in her life she had stopped saying those derogatory childhood names to herself while looking into the mirror each morning.

Instructions: The Use of Community Spiritual Practices

Community spiritual practices also may be available for devout Christian clients. Like individual spiritual activities, community practices can facilitate the progress of clients in therapy. Furthermore, a spiritual community can provide systemic resources such as support, encouragement and guidance. Relationships formed through spiritual practices and/or a faith community comprise an individual's spiritual support network. This network may include a relationship with God. Some clients can turn to a strong faith community (e.g., church) while other clients may need encouragement to strengthen or to seek spiritual community.

Congregational Support

Emotional and spiritual support from a congregation can take many forms. *Prayers* from the faith community through clergy, prayer chains or prayer partners can provide comfort and strength for hurting individuals. A number of clinical research projects have demonstrated the positive effect that community prayer can have on emotional and physical health (Dossey, 1993). Some Christians find spiritual support through participation in *worship*. Similar to personal prayer, worship can take many forms. For instance, an increasing number of congregations offer *healing services,* which usually include the opportunity to pray for the physical, emotional, and relational concerns of individuals. Another type of worship service is called *taize,* a very peaceful, meditative worship experience, which participants often find gently uplifting.

Many congregations offer *trained listeners* sometimes called Stephen's Ministers or deacons, who can provide emotional and spiritual support for individuals in distress. The caring, understanding presence of trained listeners communicates support and encourages catharsis. Finally, faith communities offer a variety of small group experiences that can offer strong spiritual support. These groups may be topical (e.g., parenting skills), educational (e.g., Bible study) or supportive (e.g., divorce recovery).

Pastoral Leadership

People in distress often receive strong spiritual and emotional support from the pastors of their faith community. Pastors can be an invaluable resource for therapists and clients in identifying individual and community spiritual practices that can facilitate spiritual growth. If necessary, a clergyperson can work in conjunction with the therapist by guiding the spiritual path of the client.

Discernment and Spiritual Decision Making

The process of therapy often creates the need to make important decisions regarding priorities, behaviors, relationships, or vocation. Devout Christian clients may want to make crucial decisions that are consistent with their spiritual values. They may seek divine guidance or want to understand what God is calling them to do. In this context, discernment is understood as sensitivity to spiritual values and/or divine communication. The ultimate goal of discernment is to make spiritually healthy decisions for the future. There are community spiritual practices that can assist this process. For instance, The Pilgrimage Project is a one evening a week program spread over several weeks. Participants help one another discern a future direction through group process and spiritual practices (Carr & Carr, 1988). Another example is a clearness committee in which an individual facing a major decision invites four to eight spiritually sensitive people to assist in discernment. During the course of a lengthy session, participants ask the individual pertinent questions that seek to clarify a spiritual perspective of the situation as well as to sense where God may be leading that individual.

Spiritual Formation Groups

A spiritual formation group is a small group experience with the intentional focus of creating intimate community that facilitates individual spiritual growth. This group is distinguished from other spiritual groups by its depth and clear focus. Ideally, a spiritual formation group becomes a primary group experience in which members take one another seriously, creating strong bonds and exerting significant influence with one another. The most common form of a primary group is a family. This realization provides a sense of profound impact that an alternative primary group can make on its members. Thus, an intimate spiritual formation group has the potential to create a nurturing spiritual environment that enables its members to make and sustain significant change.

For example, a Renovare group encourages its members to practice a rich array of spiritual growth exercises. (Renovare is an international church renewal movement founded by Richard J. Foster that encourages spiritual growth through spiritual formation groups.) This group begins when three to six individuals make the commitment to meet for eight to twelve weeks to work through together *A Spiritual Formation Workbook* (Smith, 1999). This easy-to-use resource introduces the group to the practice of spiritual disciplines. The group provides support, encouragement, insight, and accountability. After completing the workbook, the group makes a decision about whether to continue working together focused on the practice of spiritual disciplines. Renovare groups can be sustained for many years.

In *Hunger for Healing,* Keith Miller (1991) uses the 12 steps as a model for spiritual growth. As with Renovare, participants make an initial commitment to spend several weeks guided by a series of tapes introducing 12-step spirituality followed by a decision about the future of the group. In this model, group members encourage and assist one another in working through the various steps (Miller). A significant strength of both spiritual formation models is that no special leadership expertise is required to begin a group. When spiritual formation groups become primary groups, they can play an enormous role for persons seeking to make significant changes in therapy.

Spiritual Direction

Individuals seeking intensive spiritual growth may choose to work with a spiritual director. A spiritual director is a spiritually mature and sensitive individual specifically trained to guide the spiritual path of other individuals. In addition to teaching and assigning spiritual exercises, directors seek to nurture spiritual sensitivity in participants. This sensitivity is designed to see the divine and/or spiritual in every day life. Thus, participants strive to integrate spirituality into their lives in order to live out their faith in an authentic manner by discerning, developing, and acting upon cherished beliefs.

Retreats

Retreats can be a refreshing time away from stress, a spiritual growth experience, and/or a life-changing event. Retreat centers exist throughout the country where individuals can experience renewal through quiet reflection or learn spiritual skills such as centering prayer. One type of retreat is an international, inter-denominational movement known by various names including Cursillo, The Great Banquet, and The Walk to Emmaus. Led primarily by laypersons, this weekend retreat is a moving experience that can provide a powerfully intimate encounter with a compassionate God. This experience can be very effective support for the work of in-depth therapy particularly when a damaged sense of self is a key clinical issue.

Brief Vignettes: Community Spiritual Practices

In this section, two brief vignettes are presented in order to illustrate the use of a number of group spiritual practices with two different clinical issues. David entered therapy with symptoms of depression. He expressed frustration about feeling very distant from his wife and children as well as a lack of interest in his work or leisure activities. After a few sessions, his depression was linked to his family of origin, particularly the apathy of his parents toward him. As a child, he responded to this apathy by becoming "invisible." In recent years, he has begun to repeat this behavior at home. Over the course of several months, David made small gains in therapy. Yet, there remained an emptiness that therapy was unable to impact. Several months after the termination of therapy, David attended The Great Banquet where he was overwhelmed by a sense of unconditional love following a particularly powerful moment at the retreat. At first, David expressed the belief that he does not deserve this kind of positive attention. In subsequent weeks, however, he began to integrate this experience. This integration resulted in a dramatic change in his relationships and attitude. As part of this integration, he briefly returned to therapy.

From the perspective of the therapist, the spiritual experience impacted David's emptiness at a much more profound level than was feasible for individual therapy.

Cheryl entered therapy with multiple symptoms of anxiety including frequent and serious panic attacks. Since her life seems to be going well, she was baffled by her current distress. Cheryl perceived herself as a strong person whose life usually was under control. Her story is reported in greater detail in Chapter 5.

Since Cheryl entered therapy in serious distress, the initial clinical goal was the reduction of anxiety. Next, treatment focused on coping with anxiety including the development of an anxiety management plan. In these first phases of therapy, spiritual practices were able to activate spiritual support. In addition, they could play a vital role in the development of an anxiety management plan. Immediately receptive to individual spiritual practices, Cheryl engaged in yoga, took an education class at church, listened to Christian music and did daily devotional readings. Overall, these activities reduced her stress while the music and yoga often functioned to block the escalation of anxiety before it resulted in a panic attack.

The reduction in stress combined with her strong cognitive abilities to eliminate the panic attacks within a few weeks. At this point, Cheryl chose to remain in therapy to pursue more significant change. Since she saw herself as self-sufficient, Cheryl initially was reluctant to seek social and relational spiritual support. Eventually, she began to practice centering prayer on a daily basis. She found that this dramatically altered her relationship with God. In addition, Cheryl shared her situation with a spiritual friend who responded in a very supportive manner. This friendship ultimately resulted in the formation of a Renovare group. Her growing relationship with God and the creation of a primary group nurtured significant change both during and after therapy. She described this process as "a series of life-changing epiphanies."

Suggestions for Follow-Up

When a client chooses to employ spiritual practices in conjunction with therapy, it is important for the therapist to process these practices in therapy. This enables the therapist to integrate the positive effects of these practices into therapy or to assist the client with any negative effects such as confusion, sadness, or a sense of failure in performing the exercise.

Ideally, clients will choose to integrate the spiritual practices employed during therapy into their lifestyle following treatment. These ongoing practices can help clients maintain the gains made in therapy. They also may lead to a deepening sense of intimacy with God or their spiritual perspective that may open the door to additional growth.

Contraindications

The major contraindication for use of spiritual practices is discomfort for the therapist or client. Some clients may be uncomfortable with specific activities perhaps because of a poor fit with their personality style and/or their religious background.

References

Borg, M. J. (1994). *Meeting Jesus again for the first time*. San Francisco: HarperSanFrancisco.

Carr, J., & Carr, A. (1988). *The Pilgrimage project*. Nashville, TN: The Upper Room.

Dossey, L. (1993). *Healing words: The power of prayer and the practice of medicine*. San Francisco: HarperSanFrancisco.

Keating, T. (1995). *Open mind, open heart*. New York: The Continuum Publishing Company.

Killmer, J. M. (2006). Conducting spiritual dialogues in therapy. In K. B. Helmeke & C. F. Sori (Eds.), *The therapist's notebook for integrating spirituality in counseling: Homework, hand-*

outs, and activities for use in psychotherapy (pp. 55-67). Binghamton, NY: The Haworth Press.

Koenig, H. G. (1997). *Is religion good for your health?* Binghamton: The Haworth Press.

Larson, D. B. (1993). *The faith factor: An annotated bibliography of systemic reviews and clinical research on spiritual subjects* (Vol. 2). Washington, DC: National Institute for Healthcare Research.

Miller, J. K. (1991). *A hunger for healing: The Twelve Steps as a classic model for Christian growth.* San Francisco: HarperSanFrancisco.

Pargament, K. I. (1997). *The psychology of religion and coping.* New York: Guilford Press.

Pennington, M. B. (1998). *Lectio divina: Renewing the ancient practice of praying the scriptures.* New York: The Crossroad Publishing Company.

Smith, J. B. (1999). *A spiritual formation workbook.* San Francisco: HarperSanFrancisco.

Professional Readings and Resources

Brothers, B. J. (Ed.) (1992). *Spirituality and couples.* New York: The Haworth Press.

Burton, L. A. (Ed.) (1992). *Religion and the family: When God helps.* New York: The Haworth Press.

Carlson, T., & Erickson, M. (Eds.) (2002). *Spirituality and family therapy.* New York: The Haworth Press.

Doherty, W. J. (1995). *Soul searching.* New York: BasicBooks.

Hart, T. (1994). *Hidden spring: The spiritual dimension of therapy.* New York: Paulist Press.

Killmer, J. M. (2002). The treatment of anxiety disorders with devout Christian clients. *Journal of Family Psychotherapy, 13*(3-4), 309-327.

McCullough, M., Pargament, K., & Thoresen, C. (Eds.) (2001). *Forgiveness: Theory, research, practice.* New York: Guilford Press.

Michael, C. P., & Norrisey, M. C. (1991). *Prayer and temperament: Different prayer forms for different personality types.* Charlottesville, VA: The Open Door, Inc.

Vande Kemp, H. (Ed.) (1991). *Family therapy: Christian perspectives.* Grand Rapids, MI: Baker Book House.

Walsh, F. (Ed.) (1999). *Spiritual resources in family therapy.* New York: Guilford Press.

Bibliotherapy Resources for the Client

Worthy reading material for devout Christian clients includes the following:

Buechner, F. (1992). *Listening to your life.* San Francisco: HarperSanFrancisco.

Cloud, H., & Townsend, J. (1992). *Boundaries.* Grand Rapids, MI: Zondervan.

Fischer, K., & Hart, T. (1991). *Promises to keep.* New York/Mahwah, NJ: Paulist Press.

Foster, R. J. (1995). *Seeking the kingdom.* San Francisco: HarperSanFrancisco.

Foster, R. J. (1998). *Streams of living water.* San Francisco: HarperSanFrancisco.

Hart, T. (1988). *Coming down the mountain.* New York/Mahwah, NJ: Paulist Press.

Manning, B. (2000). *Ruthless trust.* San Francisco: HarperSanFrancisco.

Nouwen, H. (1995). *Life of the beloved: Spiritual living in a secular world.* New York: The Crossroad Publishing Company.

Nouwen, H. (1992). *The return of the prodigal son.* New York: Doubleday.

Patterson, R. (2002). *Writing your spiritual autobiography.* Allen, TX: Thomas More.

Shepherd, J. B. (1989). *A pilgrim's way.* Louisville, KY: Westminster/John Knox Press.

Smith, J. B. (1995). *Embracing the love of God.* San Francisco: HarperSanFrancisco.

Sweet, L. (2003). *Jesus drives me crazy.* Grand Rapids, MI: Zondervan.

Yaconelli, M. (2002). *Messy spirituality.* Grand Rapids, MI: Zondervan.

24

Embracing Emotional Pain As a Means of Spiritual Growth: Tools from the East

Karen Horneffer

Type of Contribution: Handouts, Activities, Homework

Objective

Although it is commonly acknowledged that difficult experiences bring about positive growth and change, it can be challenging as psychotherapists to offer clients the assurance and tools necessary to embrace painful emotions. Several spiritual practices from the East, including mindfulness meditation, hatha yoga, and tonglen meditation, offer conceptual ideas and concrete methods that can assist in this process. The current chapter offers in-session activities and homework assignments that can be integrated into psychotherapy with clients holding diverse religious beliefs.

Rationale for Use

The idea of *connection* is often present in descriptions and definitions of what spirituality means to people. This word can be used in reference to feeling a connection with a divine source greater than oneself, a connection with the divine within oneself, or a meaningful connection with the surrounding world and one's place in this community. The concept of connection is at the core of mystical descriptions of spirituality, which focuses on having a direct experience of the divine (e.g., Harvey, 1996). The word religion, which means to "bind together" or "to bind back" infers a similar notion of the human desire to feel a sense of union or at least an active relationship with a larger, and at times mysterious, dimension of life. As Kornfield (2000) notes, "connecting to the sacred is perhaps our deepest need and longing" (p. 3). It is interesting to consider how this quality of human yearning can be addressed and attended to within the context of traditional psychotherapy.

When individuals come into therapy they are often motivated by experiences of emotional pain, which come in a variety of forms (e.g., depression, anxiety) in relation to a multitude of difficult life events and transitions. Often this pain is accompanied by a set of judgments and opinions, such as "I don't want to feel this way" or "I shouldn't feel this way." Such judgments can create a dynamic of internal disconnection as clients push away their emotional experience. By not embracing their feelings, clients create an internal condition that is exactly the opposite from what they may be seeking outside of themselves. At one level, the human yearning for connection with the divine can also be seen as a cry within to experience unconditional acceptance from oneself.

Relational models of psychotherapy (e.g., Raskin & Rogers, 1989; Teyber, 1997) view the role of the therapist as modeling this type of acceptance, with the intention that eventually the client will internalize a compassionate stance toward him or herself. If clients are able to receive this unconditional "embrace" from the therapist, and are able to inwardly feel a similar nurturing care toward themselves, then their experience, both interpersonally and intrapersonally, mirrors what they are seeking to feel in relationship to the divine. In fact, this process of working with emotional pain can be seen as a gateway between psychological and spiritual growth. What is modeled in the therapeutic relationship and then cultivated inwardly, can serve as fertile soil for experiencing such a relationship spiritually. The experience of feeling fully accepted by another and within oneself can also be viewed as sacred, in and of itself.

The emphasis placed on acceptance in relational models of therapy is supported by considerable research that demonstrates the importance of key relationship factors, such as accurate empathy, positive regard, nonpossessive warmth, and genuineness (Asay & Lambert, 1999). These factors have been shown to be central to the establishment of therapeutic alliance (Asay & Lambert, 1999), which in turn, is central to the outcome of therapy (Bachelor & Horvath, 1999). For example, the therapeutic relationship has been shown to account for approximately 30 percent of clients' improvement in therapy, in comparison to only 15 percent that is attributable to the use of particular therapeutic techniques (Lambert, 1992). As Greenspan (2003) aptly summarizes: "By a kind of grace, good listening transforms suffering. . . . This is the secret of all successful therapy, regardless of training or theoretical orientation of the therapist" (p. 15).

Embracing Emotional Pain

The value of embracing emotional pain as a gateway between psychological and spiritual growth has been the focus of several recent books written for laypersons. Greenspan's (2003) *Healing Through the Dark Emotions* offers a series of psychological and spiritual practices that can be used to engage the emotions of grief, fear, and despair. The author explores how individual and global suffering are caused by not listening to painful emotions and adhering to the predominant message in our culture that if it hurts, we should medicate it. Instead, she suggests that by attending to, befriending, and mindfully surrendering to feelings that are most resisted, they can be alchemized to the gold of spiritual wisdom (p. 13).

In her book *Radical Acceptance,* Brach (2003) applies Buddhist teachings to the common human condition of not feeling good enough, or as she calls it, "the trance of unworthiness" (p. 5). Through guided reflections and meditations she offers suggestions for how to experience and accept the full human experience. Similarly, Weintraub (2004) focuses on the use of yoga as a tool for healing depression and as a means of deepening into one's emotional and physical experience.

Invitations Within the Field of Psychology

Along with these and other examples of popular books on the subject of embracing pain (e.g., Ford, 1998; Rutledge, 2002), a considerable amount of scholarly attention has been given to the role of emotions and healing over the past fifty years. The importance of engaging, fully experiencing, and expressing one's feelings is central to several conceptualizations of the therapeutic process. An interpersonal approach to therapy views part of the therapist's role as helping clients to "experience more fully the emotional content of what they are discussing" (Teyber, 1997, p. 130). Similarly, in Roger's (1961) classic discussion of client-centered therapy, he describes a process of clients moving toward a congruence between their emotional experience and their awareness of that experience, in hopes that clients are able to feel the fullness of emotions and own them as a part of who they are. In Gestalt therapy, avoidance and fear of painful emotions are viewed as being at the core of many presenting problems (Perls, Hefferline, & Goodman, 1951; Yontef & Simkins, 1989). Thus, in the experiential approaches to psychotherapy, clients are encouraged to become more aware of their feelings, either by therapeutic techniques involving empathic responding or by in-session experiments that heighten clients' awareness of their emotions and the processes that interrupt emotional experience (Greenberg & Safran, 1989).

The key role of affective experience in therapeutic change, apart from any one therapeutic orientation, has also been considered. In their summary article, Greenberg and Safran (1989) discuss the benefits of replacing such general terms as *catharsis* with a more thoughtful consideration of the complex forms of emotional expression and emotional interventions. For example, they discuss four categories of emotional expression: (1) adaptive primary emotion, (2) secondary emotion (e.g., defensive or reactive responses), (3) instrumental emotion (i.e., learned responses used to influence others), and (4) maladaptive emotion. Both the first and the fourth category of emotions are to be accessed in therapy, although the goal of working with each is different. Adaptive primary emotions are to be intensified and used as orienting information, whereas maladaptive emotions are to be elicited in order to be modified. These authors make a similar distinction between five types of emotionally based therapeutic interventions: (1) acknowledging previously unacknowledged emotions, (2) the evocation and intensification of emotion to motivate new behavioral responses, (3) emotional restructuring, (4) accessing state-dependent core beliefs, and (5) modifying maladaptive emotional responses.

It is also worth noting that the benefits of emotional expression outside the context of therapy has received scholarly attention. For example, research findings regarding journaling about stressful experiences (e.g., Pennebaker & Beall, 1986; Smyth, 1998) have shown that psychological and physical benefits can be derived from writing about emotionally charged events on several occasions. Thus, several bodies of research support the notion that engaging emotional content is a necessary aspect of change and healing.

Spiritual Invitations to Embrace Pain

In a society that is infused with messages about avoiding pain, it is no wonder that the act of engaging negative emotions can feel unfamiliar and undesirable to clients (as well as therapists). For some clients, a spiritual lens can provide a useful source of encouragement by suggesting that there might be some value to the presence of pain in life. The Chinese symbol for "crisis," which is comprised of the symbols for "danger" and "opportunity," captures the notion that difficult experiences may be a gateway to important life transformation. There are also images and ideas from a variety of religions, both Eastern and Western, that suggest that emotional pain can be a means of deepening one's spiritual life. As Palmer (2000) suggests, in describing his journey through depression: "The way to God is down" (p. 69).

Within the tradition of yoga, teachings offer praise for the role of pain. According to Yogi Swami Kripalu (Futuronsky, 2003), "Crying is one of the highest devotional songs. One who knows crying, knows spiritual practice. If you can cry with a pure heart, nothing else compares to such a prayer. Crying includes all the principles of yoga" (p. II).

Within Christianity, St. John of the Cross (Hazard, 1994) is often quoted in reference to his depiction of pain as being a doorway to God. More profoundly, he suggests that it is God "Himself" who inflicts pain on human beings as a means of lovingly opening their hearts to His presence:

God's purpose is to so enkindle us in love that we are full of life and full of delight

But first, in order to penetrate into our souls, it is necessary for love to wound . . .

The sense of wounding that we feel is really only the way our flesh perceives the first actions of God coming to join himself with us . . .

So I say—and now you will not think it strange—that God will wound you deeply

For in this way He continues to open all the inner chambers of your soul . . . . (pp. 33-34)

The Sufi poet, Rumi, offers a similar invitation to view painful experiences with gratitude since they are often what brings a person more deeply into relationship with God. Rumi (Barks, 1995) tells the story of preacher who prayers for thieves and muggers, and offers the following response to his congregation who asks why he does this:

Because they have done me such generous favors. Every time I turn back toward the things they want. I run into them, they beat me, and leave me nearly dead in the road, and I understand, again, that what they want is not what I want. They keep me on the spiritual path. That's why I honor them and pray for them. (p. 176)

Rumi goes on to explain:

Those that make you return, for whatever reason, to God's solitude, be grateful to them. Worry about the others, who give you delicious comforts and keep you from prayer. Friends are enemies sometimes, And enemies friends. . . . (p. 176)

Rumi's poetry also suggests a particular intimacy between God and those in pain, suggesting that one can "dig a way out through the bottom to the ocean" (Barks, 1995, p. 52). He goes on to describe a secret medicine that God offers only to those who feel hopeless.

Spiritual writing and poetry can widen the vision with which a client views emotional pain. The examples given offer encouragement to enter into these feelings, to partake in the primary definition of "embracing," which is to "clasp in the arms" (Webster, 1986). There is also a second, and equally important, definition of embracing, which is "to accept readily." This is where the therapeutic relationship is so important in modeling an acceptance of difficult emotions. It is also the point in the therapeutic process where the wisdom contained in spiritual writings can be essential.

In Kornfield's (2000) book, *After Ecstasy, the Laundry,* he includes the personal story of a Christian contemplative who experienced acceptance of his own pain as a turning point in his spiritual journey. He describes an encounter with a spiritual teacher who responded to his attempts to be something different than he was. The teacher suggested, "Why not be your own unique self. That's all God wants from you" (p. 103). As the man describes:

I wept and I danced and laughed at all I was trying to be. And now for years my life of prayer and contemplative practice has continued in its ordinary way, but I'm not depressed and I've come to love my life. No great experience ever happened, but through loving myself, everything changed. (p. 103)

Such stories offer an invitation to turn toward that which is often pushed away, and to experience and accept it. This call is at the heart of Buddhist teachings on *tonglen* meditation practice. The essence of the practice (which literally means, "sending and taking") is to reverse the tendency of running from pain and discomfort, and instead to acknowledge and own them fully (Chodron, 2001). By doing this, one comes to experience *bodhichitta,* or an awakened heart, which is defined as a heart that contains compassion, openness, and clarity. Within this teaching opening to pain is considered not only a helpful tool, but also the essential path to awakening spiritually. As Chodron (1994) describes, this *bodhichitta* is in fact "our wounded, softened heart" (p. 11).

A similar idea is conveyed in Levine and Levine's (1995) description of suffering. "The armoring around the heart is the accumulation of our everyday, ordinary grief. All of the moments we have put ourselves out of our heart. All the times we have given ourselves and others so little mercy" (p. 124). The authors go on to explain that it is this disconnection, the distance placed between ourselves and our pain, that is responsible for the distance we feel from others and the lack of connection that is felt from the Divine Beloved. A spiritual gift can be seen not only in feeling emotional pain, but also in the pain—or "broken-heartedness" itself. As poet and philosopher, Mark Nepo (2005) describes, to be willing to not fill the cracks in our heart is what allows spirit to enter, and it is what allows us to be open and honest in the world. This, as he points out, captures the meaning of the word sincere, which comes from the Latin *sin cere,* meaning "without wax." This word was originally used to describe stone sellers who did not fill their marble with wax in order to hide its flaws.

Spiritual Tools from the East

Returning from these mystical examples to the context of therapy, the first question that arises is how best to offer clients a starting point for accessing and experiencing their emotions. It is here that the introduction of several contemplative practices from the East can be a useful supplement to the process of traditional psychotherapy. An asset of these tools is that they can be used within the context of various religious faiths. In fact, the tools themselves can be used as psychological interventions, without any reference to spirituality, as is often done when simple meditation techniques are used within the context of biofeedback and behavioral medicine. Of course, for people who are interested in exploring different spiritual and religious systems, these practices may serve as a doorway to a much richer spiritual journey. When there is an openness to seeing the complementary nature of various religious backgrounds (e.g., Hahn, 1995), the practices and ideas contained in Eastern religions can be incorporated into psychotherapy with great benefit.

The emerging popularity of the field of Buddhist psychology suggests the compatibility of these two areas of study, a marriage that has been attributed to the usefulness of Buddhism's "comprehensive view of the human psyche" (Epstein, 1995, p. 9) and the utility of meditation practice as a means of loosening the grip of the ego. There is an implicit and explicit acknowledgment at the heart of Buddhism that the functions of the mind are deeply related to emotional functioning. Within the practice of yoga, which is more closely aligned with the Hindu religion, there is an inclusion of body-based practices (known as hatha yoga), that rely on the intrinsic interconnectedness between mind, body, and spirit. This relationship is aptly captured by Levine and Levine (1995) who describe how the belly hardens in response to the armored heart, and that both of these are reflections of the imprisonment of the mind (p. 113).

The practices of mindfulness meditation and yoga are quite similar in purpose, even if their outer forms appear to differ. Both emphasize the value of bringing the mind's attention into the moment and noticing what is without the typical judgments and reactions that we as humans tend to impose. This can be an important first step in helping clients to be able to fully attend to their emotional experience, since this requires a certain level of concentration as well as a willingness to not allow oneself to be immediately distracted by habitual patterns of responding, judging, and distorting.

For individuals who have a difficult time sitting still in meditation, the movement involved in yoga can be useful by providing more sensations to notice. Yoga also has the advantage of bringing the body into the therapeutic process; a process which is often guilty of becoming overly-focused on mental functioning. For clients whose difficulty in "getting out of their heads" becomes an obstacle to therapeutic progress, more body-based approaches to psychotherapy (e.g., Lee, 1997) can serve as fruitful alternatives to traditional talk-therapy. For other clients, it can be sufficient to encourage them to be present in their bodies during their contemplative time outside of therapy sessions. The included handout on hatha yoga is intended for this client population.

A third Eastern practice that is relevant to the therapeutic process is tonglen meditation. In tonglen, instead of using the breath as an object of focus, one's emotions are used. As mentioned, the intention behind this practice is to reverse the often habitual pattern of pushing away what is unwanted. Instead, individuals are asked, metaphorically, to place their head in the mouth of the dragon which they have been running away from, with the intention that this will create an open-hearted courageousness to be fully present to one's own experiences and the experiences of others.

Instructions

The chapter includes handouts on mindfulness meditation, yoga, and tonglen meditation. Each of those has handouts for both clients and therapists. The client handout for each of these three tools contains an overview of the practice and a suggested homework assignment. For both meditation practices, an in-session exercise is also provided in the handouts for the therapist. There is also a handout for the therapist (see Handout Four: Hatha Yoga (for Therapists) at the end of this chapter) also includes an in-session yoga exercise, although as explained in Handout Four, it is preferable for this exercise to be used as a homework assignment, so that clients can experiment with yoga in a space where there is adequate room for movement and where they will feel most comfortable. Handout Four offers instructions on introducing the yoga homework assignment. Therapists who are interested in also doing an in-session yoga activity can do so by following the instructions in Handout Three: Hatha Yoga (for Clients).

It is suggested that the therapist read through the handouts for the clients (see Handout One, Three, and Five) as a preliminary step in determining the appropriateness of introducing each of the tools into therapy practice. A resource list of readings can also be highly beneficial if these philosophical ideas and practices are new to the reader. The order in which these tools are presented is intentional. Each practice builds on the one before, with mindfulness meditation serving as a foundation for the latter two. The benefit of introducing all three practices is that each offers a slightly different avenue for achieving a similar result. While some clients might be drawn to the simplicity (or at least noncomplexity) of mindfulness meditation, other clients may find that by bringing in the movement of yoga, they are able to experience the essential practice of bringing their attention into the present moment. For other clients, particularly those who are willing and interested in embracing their feelings as a vehicle for growth, the specific emotional focus of tonglen meditation can be especially useful.

When all three practices are integrated into the therapeutic process, it is best to stagger their introduction in order to not overwhelm the client with too much information and homework. For some clients, it may be appropriate to use only one tool, depending on their interest, experience, and the context of the therapy process. As mentioned in the section on contraindications, for some clients and therapists these practices would not be appropriate.

With cases in which the inclusion of these practices is fitting, the integration of them into the therapeutic process involves a dance of weaving together four threads: (1) empathically exploring the content of the client's presenting concerns, (2) emphasizing the importance of embracing the emotional aspects of this experience, (3) exploring the relationship between opening to emotional pain and opening to one's spirituality, and (4) introducing one or more tools that can assist with this process. The fabric that will be woven with these four ingredients will, of course, differ with each therapist and client relationship.

Brief Vignette

Jeff is a twenty-four-year-old male who is coming in for counseling because his girlfriend of one year recently ended their relationship. He reports feeling angry with her and overwhelmed by the decision he needs to make regarding a job offer that would require relocating out of the area. A friend suggested he seek counseling because he "wasn't acting like himself" and seemed stressed and preoccupied. Jeff reports difficulty falling asleep and that he feels worst in the morning. "I force myself to get out of bed and go running in the morning in order to get my mind off of things."

In the first session, the therapist allows the client to share in detail about the relationship, the events that led up to the break-up, and his anxiety about needing to make a decision regarding his professional career. The therapist responds empathically, helping the client to feel safe in exploring the various facets of his experience. The therapist acknowledges the client's desire to "get over" this situation and to have things return to normal as quickly as possible. She also introduces the potential benefit of exploring this situation as fully as possible so that it can serve as a learning tool for future stresses that will arise in life. The therapist suggests that next week, along with continuing to explore Jeff's current concerns and history with relationships, that she demonstrate a simple meditation technique. "This tool," she explains, "could help you to feel more present during the day, and possibly help you calm your mind before going to sleep."

During the second half of the next session, the therapist discusses the philosophy behind mindfulness meditation, and leads the client through a ten-minute experience of focusing on his breath. At the end of this experience, Jeff reports feeling more calm and clear in his thinking, but also that he feels sad. The therapist encourages him to be willing to stay with this feeling, that there might be something useful in letting this sadness arise. Jeff agrees to practice meditating for five minutes in the morning (and takes a copy of the handout).

The next session, Jeff reports that he has had a difficult time staying focused when he tries to sit and pay attention to his breath. He begins to feel "antsy" and distracted. He also notices moments of feeling tears begin to come, or anger well up, and is unsure what to do with these emotions. During the first part of the session, the therapist explores Jeff's ways of coping with his feelings in various aspects of his life, as well as inquiring about previous significant relationships that he has had within his family and in other social and romantic contexts. The therapist also suggests that he continues with his contemplative time in the morning, but suggests that he might want to try focusing on his breath while doing yoga, as a way of helping him to stay more focused. This would also prepare him to transition into his morning run. The therapist reviews the handout with him in order to offer a more thorough explanation of why doing yoga might be helpful. In the next session, Jeff reports that adding movement to his meditation time was helpful.

Several weeks later, Jeff discusses that he is beginning to be aware of a life pattern of feeling let down by others and angry at life in general "because it doesn't seem to be what it should be." The therapist introduces the philosophy of tonglen meditation, and the idea that people often push away what they do not want and shut down when they do not get what they do want. This description seems to hit on something for Jeff, who then describes his religious upbringing in which he thought if he just did the right things, God would reward him.

The therapist offers some other ways of viewing the role of pain in life from various spiritual disciplines and encourages Jeff to talk with some older adults whom he respects about their experiences with pain. One aspect of the tonglen philosophy that Jeff responds to is the awareness that other people feel this way too.

"It never occurred to me," he said, "that there are other guys out there feeling like damned fools. There's something comforting in that!"

The therapist read through Handout Five: Tonglen Meditation (for Clients) and related this practice to his current emotions. By doing the in-session tonglen experience, the therapist was able to help Jeff more deeply experience his current anger and sadness. He was better able to understand why she had encouraged him to stay present with his feelings several weeks before.

Weekly counseling sessions continued over the next few months, with the focus on helping Jeff to more deeply experience and accept his emotions, to feel more present in his day-to-day life and to make decisions about what he needed to do during this time of transition. The counseling sessions also offered him an opportunity to explore some "larger" questions regarding finding meaning in life, making sense of why things do not always work out as planned, and reflecting on how this relates to his spiritual beliefs and faith.

Suggestions for Follow-Up

Taking time to follow-up on the in-session activities and homework assignments is essential for successfully integrating these practices with the more traditional aspects of counseling. Emphasis should be given to helping clients identify which of the exercises could be useful in an ongoing way, or as a future tool for embracing difficult emotions. It is also worth returning to a discussion of the advantages and disadvantages of being willing to experience one's emotions. There are many reasons why people tend to avoid emotional experiences, and often insight can be gained from processing not only the specific content of current concerns, but more generally, the client's ways of being in relationship with their emotions. When this conversation can include the relevance of emotional awareness to our relationships with others and our relationship spiritually, the therapeutic process can be particularly fruitful.

Contraindications

These practices would not be suitable for clients with conservative religious beliefs that would cause them to be closed-minded to any idea or practice originating from the East. Encouraging clients to heighten their emotional experience must also be balanced with a consideration of the optimal level of anxiety in the session, as well as the client's ego-strength and overall level of functioning. These tools should not be used with clients who have impairment in reality testing or other psychotic symptoms. This is particularly true for advanced practices of tonglen meditation. Although the exercises presented here are introductory, the traditional practice of tonglen, when done in a more involved manner, should be reserved for higher-functioning individuals. It is important to be aware if a client has experienced trauma, or is experiencing severe anxiety. In this situation, introducing even a simple meditation exercise should be done with care because for these individuals, closing their eyes and focusing on their breath may be more overwhelming than relaxing.

A final consideration is the therapist's experience and comfort with basic relaxation and meditation skills. These materials will be presented more effectively by an individual who is able to guide someone else through a relaxation exercise and who can respond, from personal experience, about the advantages and challenges of engaging in a daily contemplative practice.

References

Asay, T. P., & Lambert, M. J. (1999). The empirical case for the common factors in therapy: Quantitative findings. In M. A. Hubble, B. L. Duncan, & S. D. Miller (Eds.), *The heart and soul of change: What works in therapy*. Washington, DC: APA.

Bachelor, A., & Horvath, A. (1999). The therapeutic relationship. In M. A. Hubble, B. L. Duncan, & S. D. Miller (Eds.), *The heart and soul of change: What works in therapy* (pp. 133-178). Washington, DC: APA.

Barks, C. (1995). *The essential Rumi*. San Francisco: HarperSanFrancisco.

Brach, T. (2003). *Radical acceptance: Embracing your life with the heart of a Buddha*. New York: Bantam.

Bradley, R. A., & Montagu, A. (1996). *Husband-coached childbirth: The Bradley Method of natural childbirth* (4th ed.). New York: Bantam.

Chodron, P. (1994). *Start where you are: A guide to compassionate living*. Boston: Shambala.

Chodron, P. (2001). *Tonglen: The path of transformation*. Halifax, Nova Scotia: Vajradhatu.

Epstein, M. (1995). *Thoughts without a thinker: Psychotherapy from a Buddhist perspective*. New York: Basic.

Ford, D. (1998). *The dark side of the light chasers*. New York: Riverhead.

Futuronsky, A. N. (2003). Kripalu yoga off the mat: Choosing to be present. *Kripalu Yoga Association Yoga Bulletin, 12*(2), II. In Weintraub, A. (2004). *Yoga for depression: A compassionate guide to relieve suffering through yoga*. New York: Broadway.

Greenberg, L. S., & Safran, J. D. (1989). Emotion in psychotherapy. *American Psychologist, 44,* 19-29.

Greenspan, M. (2003). *Healing through the dark emotions: The wisdom of grief, fear, and despair*. Boston: Shambala.

Hahn, T. N. (1995). *Living Buddha, living Christ*. New York: Riverhead.

Harvey, A. (1996). *The essential mystics: Selections from the world's great wisdom traditions*. New York: HarperCollins.

Hazard, D. (1994). *You set my spirit free: A 40-day journey in the company of John of the Cross*. Minneapolis, MN: Bethany House.

Kornfield, J. (1993). *A path with heart: A guide through the perils and promises of spiritual life*. New York: Bantam.

Kornfield, J. (2000). *After the ecstasy, the laundry*. New York: Bantam.

Lambert, M. J. (1992). Implications of outcome research for psychotherapy integration. In J. C. Norcross & M. R. Goldstein (Eds.), *Handbook of psychotherapy integration* (pp. 94-129). New York: Basic Books.

Lee, M. (1997). *Phoenix rising yoga therapy: A bridge from body to soul*. Health Communications.

Levine, S., & Levine, O. (1995). *Embracing the beloved: Relationship as a path of awakening*. New York: Doubleday.

Nepo, M. (2005). *The exquisite risk*. New York: Harmony.

Palmer, P. (2000). *Let your life speak: Listening to the voice of vocation*. San Francisco: Jossey-Bass.

Pennebaker, J. W., & Beall, S. K. (1986). Confronting a traumatic event: Toward an understanding of inhibition and disease. *Journal of Abnormal Psychology, 3,* 274-281.

Perls, F., Hefferline, R., & Goodman, P. (1951). *Gestalt therapy*. New York: Dell.

Raskin, N. J., & Rogers, C. (1989). Person-centered therapy. In R. J. Corsini & D. Wedding (Eds.), *Current psychotherapies* (4th ed.). Itasca, Illinois: Peacock.

Rogers, C. (1961). *On becoming a person: A therapist's view of psychotherapy*. Boston: Houghton Mifflin.

Rutledge, T. (2002). *Embracing fear and finding the courage to live your life.* San Francisco: HarperCollins.

Smyth, J. M. (1998). Written emotional expression: Effect sizes, outcome types, and moderating variables. *Journal of Consulting and Clinical Psychology, 66*(1), 174-184.

Teyber, E. (1997). *Interpersonal process in psychotherapy: A relational approach* (3rd ed.). Pacific Groove, CA: Brooks/Cole.

Webster (1986). *New world dictionary of the American language.* New York: Prentice Hall.

Weintraub, A. (2004). *Yoga for depression: A compassionate guide to relieve suffering through yoga.* New York: Broadway.

Yontef, G. M., & Simkins, J. S. (1989). Gestalt therapy. In R. J. Corsini & D. Wedding (Eds.), *Current psychotherapies* (4th ed.). Itasca, IL: Peacock.

Professional Readings and Resources

Embracing Difficult Emotions

Brach, T. (2003). *Radical acceptance: Embracing your life with the heart of a Buddha.* New York: Bantam.

Greenspan, M. (2003). *Healing through the dark emotions: The wisdom of grief, fear, and despair.* Boston: Shambala.

Mindfulness Meditation

Austin, M. (2003). *Meditation for wimps: Finding your balance in an imperfect world.* New York: Sterling.

Hanh, T. N. (1991). *Peace is every step: The path of mindfulness in everyday life.* New York: Bantam.

Kabat-Zinn, J. (1990). *Full catastrophe living: Using the wisdom of your body and mind to face stress, pain, and illness.* New York: Delta.

Kornfield, J. (1993). *A path with heart: A guide through the perils and promises of spiritual life.* New York: Bantam.

Kornfield, J. (2000). *After the ecstasy, the laundry.* New York: Bantam.

Salzberg, S. (1997). *A heart as wide as the world: Stories on the path of lovingkindness.* Boston: Shambala.

Yoga

Fraser, T. (2001). *Total yoga: A step-by-step guide to yoga at home for everybody.* London: Thorsons.

Gates, R., & Kenison, K. (2000). *Meditations from the mat: Daily reflections on the path of yoga.* New York: Anchor.

Lidell, L. (1983). *The Sivananda companion to yoga.* New York: Fireside/Simon & Schuster.

Sivananda Yoga Vedanta Center (1996). *Yoga mind and body.* London: Dorling Kindersley.

Weintraub, A. (2004). *Yoga for depression: A compassionate guide to relieve suffering through yoga.* New York: Broadway.

Tonglen

Chodron, P. (1994). *Start where you are: A guide to compassionate living.* Boston: Shambala.
Chodron, P. (2001a). *Good medicine.* Boulder, CO: Sounds True.
Chodron, P. (2001b). *Tonglen: The path of transformation.* Halifax, Nova Scotia: Vajradhatu.
Trungpa, C. (1993). *Training the mind and cultivating loving-kindness.* Boston: Shambala.

Bibliotherapy Sources for the Client

Embracing Difficult Emotions

Brach, T. (2003). *Radical acceptance: Embracing your life with the heart of a Buddha.* New York: Bantam.
Greenspan, M. (2003). *Healing through the dark emotions: The wisdom of grief, fear, and despair.* Boston: Shambala.

Mindfulness Meditation

Austin, M. (2003). *Meditation for wimps: Finding your balance in an imperfect world.* New York: Sterling.
Hanh, T. N. (1991). *Peace is every step: The path of mindfulness in everyday life.* New York: Bantam.
Kabat-Zinn, J. (1990). *Full catastrophe living: Using the wisdom of your body and mind to face stress, pain, and illness.* New York: Delta.
Kornfield, J. (1993). *A path with heart: A guide through the perils and promises of spiritual life.* New York: Bantam.
Kornfield, J. (2000). *After the ecstasy, the laundry.* New York: Bantam.
Salzberg, S. (1997). *A heart as wide as the world: Stories on the path of lovingkindness.* Boston: Shambala.

Yoga

Fraser, T. (2001). *Total yoga: A step-by-step guide to yoga at home for everybody.* London: Thorsons.
Gates, R., & Kenison, K. (2000). *Meditations from the mat: Daily reflections on the path of yoga.* New York: Anchor.
Lidell, L. (1983). *The Sivananda companion to yoga.* New York: Fireside/Simon & Schuster.
Sivananda Yoga Vedanta Center (1996). *Yoga mind and body.* London: Dorling Kindersley.
Weintraub, A. (2004). *Yoga for depression: A compassionate guide to relieve suffering through yoga.* New York: Broadway.

Tonglen

Chodron, P. (1994). *Start where you are: A guide to compassionate living.* Boston: Shambala.
Chodron, P. (2001a). *Tonglen: The path of transformation.* Halifax, Nova Scotia: Vajradhatu.
Chodron, P. (2001b). *Good medicine.* Boulder, CO: Sounds True.
Trungpa, C. (1993). *Training the mind and cultivating loving-kindness.* Boston: Shambala.

Handout One:
Mindfulness Meditation (for Clients)

Overview

A wonderful cartoon shows a picture of a monk sweeping the floor. The bubble over his head, depicting what he is thinking, contains the same image of a monk sweeping the floor. The humor of the cartoon comes from the reality that for many of us, if we were to draw such a bubble, it would rarely depict that same scene as that which is currently happening. It would be more likely that a person sitting at his or her desk at work would be thinking about an upcoming vacation on the beach, and this same person one month later on the beach would be thinking about what awaits him or her back at work.

The idea behind mindfulness meditation is to offer a practice that helps us to be aware of the present moment, and in so doing, to better able to show up in our lives. It is quite amazing to think about all of the ways that most of us are masters in not being present, either by thinking about the past or the future, or by using an activity or a substance as a distraction or numbing device. If we are to bring a sense of richness to our lives, and bring attention to what in us needs to be healed, often this process begins with the simple (yet not so easy) act of noticing what is.

The purpose of the following activities is to help strengthen your capacity to observe or witness what is happening in the moment. If it helps, you can think of this exercise as a form of weight lifting to tone one's mind.

Suggested Homework Exercises

Sitting Meditation

Set aside five minutes a day for one week to practice focusing on your breathing. It is helpful to choose the same time each day (such as first thing in the morning, at lunch time, or just before bed). Find a quiet place where you can sit with a straight back, either in a chair or on the floor. You can set a timer if that helps to know when five minutes is up.

During the five minutes, your practice is just to notice your inbreath and your outbreath. It may help to choose a place in your body to focus on the physical aspect of your breath, such as the air entering and leaving the nostrils, the chest expanding and contracting with air, or the movement in the belly as the diaphragm lengthens and contracts.

Remember that this five minutes is about *practicing the skill* of bringing your attention into the moment. Do not expect to be able to really do it! Jack Kornfield (1993) offers a wonderful analogy of how meditation is like training a puppy:

> You put the puppy down and say, "Stay." Does the puppy listen? It gets up and it runs away. You sit the puppy back down again. "Stay." And the puppy runs away over and over again. Sometimes the puppy jumps up, runs over, and pees in the corner or makes some other mess. Our minds are much the same as the puppy, only they create even bigger messes. In training the mind, or the puppy, we have to start over and over again. (p. 59)

As thoughts arise, compassionately notice the nature of the mind to think, and gently bring your attention back to your breath.

Horneffer, K. (2006). Embracing emotional pain as a means of spiritual growth: Tools from the East. In K. B. Helmeke & C. F. Sori (Eds.), *The therapist's notebook for integrating spirituality in counseling: Homework, handouts, and activities for use in psychotherapy* (pp. 267-285). Binghamton, NY: The Haworth Press.

Handout One:
Mindfulness Meditation (for Clients) *(continued)*

Mindfulness Meditation

At least once per the day, see if you can "catch yourself" in the act of being present with what you are doing (just like the monk). In a sense, this is like practicing sitting meditation in the midst the activities of daily life, which is the essence of mindfulness. You might want to use some everyday events as reminders to bring your attention into the present moment. For example, you can use waiting at a red light, the phone ringing, brushing your teeth, or waiting for your computer to turn on as cues to bring your attention to your breath and notice what is happening in the moment.

Reference

Kornfield, J. (1993). *A path with heart: A guide through the perils and promises of spiritual life.* New York: Bantam.

Horneffer, K. (2006). Embracing emotional pain as a means of spiritual growth: Tools from the East. In K. B. Helmeke & C. F. Sori (Eds.), *The therapist's notebook for integrating spirituality in counseling: Homework, handouts, and activities for use in psychotherapy* (pp. 267-285). Binghamton, NY: The Haworth Press.

Handout Two:
Mindfulness Meditation (for Therapists)

In-Session Exercise

After introducing the client to the rationale of mindfulness meditation, either in your own words or by reading along with them the "overview" section of Handout One: Mindfulness Meditation (for Clients), the following five- to ten-minute exercise can be done during a session. You can either read through the following script verbatim, or use it as a guide:

> Either close your eyes, or bring your gaze to your lap or the floor in front of you. As you do this, just begin to notice your breath. One of the helpful aspects of focusing on our breath is that it is always with us. When we notice our breathing we bring our attention right into our bodies in this moment.
>
> You do not need to change the way in which you are breathing. Just begin to notice your breath entering your body and leaving your body. To begin, bring your attention to your nostrils, and just notice how the air feels as it enters your nose and leaves your nose. It might be helpful in your mind to mentally note, "inbreath" as your breathe in, and "outbreath" as your exhale. Just try working with this for the next minute (pause).
>
> Now try bringing your attention to your chest, and just notice how the inbreath and outbreath feel as the air enters and leaves your lungs. As you notice other thoughts or feelings pull your attention away from your breathing, see if you can gently bring your awareness back to your breathing. It might help to mentally note "ahh, a thought," or "ah, the feeling of anger" and then gently bring your mind back to the breath (pause).
>
> Now bring your attention to your abdomen, and notice how the belly expands as the diaphragm lowers with each inbreath. You can mentally note the inbreath and outbreath in the belly (pause).
>
> Now take two or three more breaths to complete the exercise. You might want to note which place in your body was the easiest for you to focus on your breath. As you feel ready, you can open your eyes. If you like, you can stretch your arms up over your head.

How was that experience for you?

Horneffer, K. (2006). Embracing emotional pain as a means of spiritual growth: Tools from the East. In K. B. Helmeke & C. F. Sori (Eds.), *The therapist's notebook for integrating spirituality in counseling: Homework, handouts, and activities for use in psychotherapy* (pp. 267-285). Binghamton, NY: The Haworth Press.

Handout Three:
Hatha Yoga (for Clients)

Overview

The practice of hatha yoga represents one aspect of a larger life philosophy which originated in India over 5,000 years ago. Hatha yoga is often thought of as a physical practice, but it also has many emotional benefits, including offering a way to experience feelings within the physical body. Although it is helpful and often necessary to talk about life events and feelings, this process can sometimes become overly-intellectual, as though we human beings are only talking heads, with nothing occurring from the neck down. Often it is in the core of the body where emotions are held, along with the wisdom of what healing needs to occur.

The word yoga, which is Sanskrit for "yoke" or "union," suggests the connection between body, mind, and spirit that can be experienced by bringing our awareness into the sensations that arise in our physical body. The downside of this interconnection can be seen when our emotions and our ways of thinking cause stress and tightness in the body. On the other hand, this mind-body-spirit connection can also be an asset when we involve one dimension to help support another. For example, sometimes it is easier to quiet the mind by using the body to help. It may be easier to learn how to meditate in the context of moving versus sitting because there are more sensations to engage the mind's attention. As a matter of fact, one of the most useful aspects of yoga is that as we bring ourselves into various posture and stretches, we can learn to be present, and even relax in the midst of a lot of sensation in the body. This can be a very useful skill to have in day-to-day life given that it is often in intense moments that we lose our capacity to be present. In a sense, yoga can teach us how to actively show up and surrender in the heat of life. It is a bit similar to the Bradley Method (Bradley & Montagu, 1996) approach to natural childbirth in which mothers are encouraged to "relax as if your life depends on it."

People's experiences while doing yoga often provide useful metaphors for understanding their reactions and responses in daily life. It is easy to see our tendency to judge ourselves for how we think our body should be different, or for how we compare to others, or even for the fact that our mind is being judgmental. We can also notice if there is a tendency to overstretch or to avoid moving fully into a posture; and if it is the mind's habit to escape into something more interesting or to decide that what is happening is boring. The intention in yoga is to notice all of this and to bring the mind back to the breath. In doing this, the mind, the heart, and the breath can be brought fully into the body with compassion and nonjudgment.

Suggested Homework Exercises

If you are unfamiliar with yoga, it would be helpful to have a book that shows pictures of different postures (several examples are listed below). It also works to follow your own sense of what type of stretch you want to do. Various postures and stretches contain different emotional qualities. For example, by opening the chest and the heart through a backbend we are invited to embrace our vulnerability and the fullness of our expression. In a forward bend, we are mirroring a posture of surrender, and when the head is brought below the chest, this can be seen as a surrendering of the intellect to the wisdom of the heart. The child's pose evokes a sense of being comforted and protected. To access our courage, we can do a standing, lunging posture such as the warrior pose. We can also do the spinal twist as a way to access our strength and flexibility.

First, take about five minutes and move into a posture, stretch, or movement that seems to match your emotional state. Pay attention to what you experience in your body and your emotions as you do this. Notice the tendency of the mind to judge, accept, stay present, or escape. As you come out of the posture, spend at least a minute in stillness. It is often said that a person truly experiences a yoga posture after it is complete.

Horneffer, K. (2006). Embracing emotional pain as a means of spiritual growth: Tools from the East. In K. B. Helmeke & C. F. Sori (Eds.), *The therapist's notebook for integrating spirituality in counseling: Homework, handouts, and activities for use in psychotherapy* (pp. 267-285). Binghamton, NY: The Haworth Press.

Handout Three:
Hatha Yoga (for Clients) *(continued)*

Next, repeat the same exercise, but this time choose a posture that represents a quality you most need, or a quality that is the opposite of what you are feeling. Again notice your experiences during and after. You may want to spend a few minutes writing down anything that strikes you about this exercise and its relevance to what is going on in your life right now.

Examples of Yoga Books with Pictures of Postures

Fraser, T. (2001). *Total yoga: A step-by-step guide to yoga at home for everybody.* London: Thorsons.
Lidell, L. (1983). *The Sivananda companion to yoga.* New York: Fireside/Simon & Schuster.
Sivananda Yoga Vedanta Center (1996). *Yoga mind and body.* London: Dorling Kindersley.

Reference

Bradley, R. A., & Montagu, A. (1996). *Husband-coached childbirth: The Bradley Method of natural childbirth* (4th ed.). New York: Bantam.

Horneffer, K. (2006). Embracing emotional pain as a means of spiritual growth: Tools from the East. In K. B. Helmeke & C. F. Sori (Eds.), *The therapist's notebook for integrating spirituality in counseling: Homework, handouts, and activities for use in psychotherapy* (pp. 267-285). Binghamton, NY: The Haworth Press.

Handout Four:
Hatha Yoga (for Therapists)

Explanation of Homework Exercise

In order to introduce the yoga homework assignment to the client, it is helpful to first provide an overview of hatha yoga and its relevance to embracing emotions. This can be done by giving the client a copy of the Handout Three: Hatha Yoga (for Clients) and reading through the first section together. You may also choose to summarize this information in your own words before giving the client the handout. Your conversation can include a discussion of why it might be preferable for the client to do the yoga exercise at home, particularly if office space does not permit adequate room for movement. If this is not the case, and adequate space exists, you and the client can decide if the exercise should be done in-session or at home.

Either way, it is useful to show the client some pictures of the yoga postures that are mentioned in the Handout Three (several example books with pictures are listed in the Handout Three). This will both clarify how these poses reflect various emotional states, and will also offer more concrete guidance for moving into the postures. In reading through the instructions for the homework exercise, you can assess the client's comfort level with this activity. You can also assist them in choosing their postures, as well as answering any questions they might have. This conversation will also provide an opportunity to help the client identify a time and place where the exercise can happen, and to plan for discussing the client's experience in the following session.

Horneffer, K. (2006). Embracing emotional pain as a means of spiritual growth: Tools from the East. In K. B. Helmeke & C. F. Sori (Eds.), *The therapist's notebook for integrating spirituality in counseling: Homework, handouts, and activities for use in psychotherapy* (pp. 267-285). Binghamton, NY: The Haworth Press.

Handout Five:
Tonglen Meditation (for Clients)

Overview

The philosophy behind tonglen practice can at first seem a bit counter intuitive, given that it involves imagining breathing in difficult emotions and exhaling to others the opposite quality—such as a sense of lightness and well-being. This ancient practice of *sending and taking* has been revitalized in recent years by Buddhist nun, Pema Chodron. The idea behind this practice is to become aware of our tendencies to push away things that we do not like and to grasp for things that we do like, and to notice that in automatically responding this way we tend to close our hearts and create unnecessary suffering. It is often this same impulse to shut down to what we do not like or do not want that causes us to run away from our own emotions, and in so doing, to abandon ourselves in the moments when we could most benefit from staying with our experience of pain.

We often move so quickly out of our experiences of anger or sadness that we do not even really know what these emotions feel like—or what messages they might hold for us. Instead, we might find ourselves automatically reacting to people and situations that trigger our feelings by blaming, running away, or telling ourselves stories in order to create a safe frame around what is occurring. We do this instead of just being present with what arises within us in order to come to know what this emotion holds. For healing to begin, we must first be willing to turn, face, and experience these uncomfortable emotions. As Pema Chodron says, we must "abide" in these experiences as opposed to "abandoning ourselves" in them. It can also be useful to recognize that in any moment, other people are feeling what we are feeling: in this way our emotional experiences are something that bring us back to the commonality of our human experience. By embracing our pain, we embrace all of who we are. When we see a connection between our experience and others' experiences we begin to cultivate an awakened heart. This is a heart that holds clarity, compassion, and openness because it is softened by pain (Chodron, 1994).

Suggested Homework Exercises

This can be a useful exercise to do when a life situation evokes a difficult emotion. If you are feeling consumed by a feeling, or if you find yourself thinking through or playing out a scenario over and over in your mind (or having a repetitive argument in your head—especially if you are always winning), this is a good opportunity to do tonglen practice!

You will want to begin by taking one or two breaths and bringing your attention to your breathing. Then begin to allow yourself to invite in the feelings that you are experiencing. It might help to imagine breathing them in, even with a visual image that matches the emotional quality. Notice if there is a tendency for your mind to push away the feelings, by talking yourself out of it, or returning to the story of the events and the people involved. Try to drop the story line and return to your experience in your body. Notice what you are feeling, whether it be sadness, anger, fear, defeat. See if you can embrace that feeling, just as you would embrace a child who was experiencing this emotion. What does it feel like to really let yourself feel what you feel?

Allow yourself to be aware of the reality that at this moment other people are feeling this same type of emotion, maybe for different reasons, but the same feelings. As Chodron (2001) summarizes, the practice of tonglen is a practice of "sharing your heart": "When anything is delightful in life, you wish other people could share it. . . . When you feel a sense of suffering, you think that many other people are also suffering and you wish that they could be free from it" (p. 10). You may want to spend a few minutes writing down your reflections from this exercise.

References

Chodron, P. (1994). *Start where you are: A guide to compassionate living.* Boston: Shambala.
Chodron, P. (2001b). *Tonglen: The path of transformation.* Halifax, Nova Scotia: Vajradhatu.

Horneffer, K. (2006). Embracing emotional pain as a means of spiritual growth: Tools from the East. In K. B. Helmeke & C. F. Sori (Eds.), *The therapist's notebook for integrating spirituality in counseling: Homework, handouts, and activities for use in psychotherapy* (pp. 267-285). Binghamton, NY: The Haworth Press.

Handout Six:
Tonglen Meditation (for Therapists)

In-Session Exercise

After introducing the client to the rationale of tonglen meditation either in your own words or by reading along with them the "overview" section of Handout Five: Tonglen Meditation (for Clients), the following ten- to twenty-minute exercise can be done during a session. It is best done at a time when the client is experiencing something with intense emotional content and is focusing on the events more so than on emotions. You can either read through the following script verbatim, or use it as a guide:

First, allow yourself to close your eyes or bring your gaze toward the ground in front of you. Take one or two inbreaths and exhalations. You have been sharing some of the details of what has happened that has caused you pain, and I want us to take some time now to explore what you are feeling. Give yourself a chance for a few minutes to let go of all of the details of what has occurred—the whole story of what has happened, and let yourself feel what you are feeling (pause).

Imagine allowing yourself to breathe in what you are feeling. Allow yourself to be present with the emotions. Sometimes we create more pain by the effort we put into avoiding our feelings. Gently allow yourself to feel what you are feeling. You can notice where in your body you feel it, and what it feels like. Sometimes we do not even really know what our sadness or fear or anger feels like (pause).

If you notice your mind starting to replay images of events that have happened, see if you can drop underneath the story of what happened. Drop into the emotions that have been evoked. What does it feel like to stay with the feeling (pause)?

You can imagine yourself embracing this emotion, like a loving parent would embrace a child, with a sense of acceptance, a willingness to notice and allow the presence of the feeling (pause).

Notice if your feelings shift at all as you do this. Do the emotions feel more intense or less intense? Are there new emotions that arise? Just be present with whatever the experience is (pause).

Taking a few more breaths, come back to just noticing your breath in your body. See if you can feel a bit of space surrounding your feelings (pause).

As you feel ready, you can open your eyes. . . . Let's talk about what that was like for you.

Horneffer, K. (2006). Embracing emotional pain as a means of spiritual growth: Tools from the East. In K. B. Helmeke & C. F. Sori (Eds.), *The therapist's notebook for integrating spirituality in counseling: Homework, handouts, and activities for use in psychotherapy* (pp. 267-285). Binghamton, NY: The Haworth Press.

25

Integrating the Discernment of Spiritual Guidance in Family and Couples Therapy: Use of the Examen

Paul E. Priester

Type of Contribution: Activity, Handout

Objective

This chapter is designed to teach families and/or couples how to use a specific prayer ritual that was developed in the context of the Ignatian spiritual exercises. The prayer is the examen (alternatively referred to as the examen of conscience). This ritual can assist individuals in discerning what God's will is for them in their daily lives. This intervention can be implemented by clergy, mental health clinicians, or by families/couples themselves as a means of exploring the direction that God would have them take and as a means of keeping current in the ebbs and flows of one another's lives.

Rationale for Use

In today's culture, people are becoming busier and more preoccupied with the high level of distraction and stimulation of daily life. Lost in this unending chase is the practice of contemplative prayer. Contemplative prayer is an attempt to quiet yourself so that you can discern the message that God has for you. Another thing that is lost to this hectic pace is the ability to stay connected, on an intimate level, with the ongoings and fluctuations of the events in the lives of one's family members and partner. Other forces such as new configurations of the family structure contribute to the challenge of really knowing what members of the family are going through each day. One such new challenge is the reality of dual career partnerships in which spouses (or partners) are both so consumed with their individual careers that they find it difficult to attend to the details of each other's or the lives of their children. Another challenge is the frequent occurrence of noncustodial parenting. Under these situations, there are immense challenges to staying connected to the daily life of a child. This chapter will introduce a contemplative practice that can facilitate both the discernment of God's will for family members as well as facilitate the cohesiveness of the family by contributing to a deeper understanding of what is occurring in each member's daily life. This prayer is called the examen.

The examen, or examination of conscience, was developed as part of the Ignatian spiritual exercises. St. Ignatius of Loyola was a Christian mystic (1491-1556) who developed an elaborate process of rituals for discerning what God's will was for an individual (Fleming, 1981). These spiritual exercises were initially employed as part of the formation process of priesthood. In more recent times, they have been employed with lay individuals as well. The examen is a daily ritual taken from the spiritual exercises that can facilitate individuals' understanding of what God's will is for them.

This "discernment of spirits" process can be understood by realizing that God has a specific plan for each individual's life. In discernment, an attempt is made to understand when individuals are being influenced by God or by "evil spirits" who wish to lead the individual away from the path that God would have them take. The examen is a tool for understanding which direction God would have them take.

Instructions

The examen is a straightforward process in itself. An individual enters a relaxed state, asks for divine guidance in prayer, and then responds to two specific questions. These questions can be stated in a number of similar forms. The first question may be expressed as one of the following:

> For what moment today am I the most grateful?
> When did I give and receive the most love today?
> When did I feel the most alive today?
> When did I have the greatest sense of belonging to myself, others, God, and the universe?
> When was I the happiest today?
> What was today's high point?

This question is seeking what is referred to as the "movement of consolation." Consolation is a direct indication from the Supreme Being that they are engaged in an activity, or heading in a direction that is according to divine will.

The second question seeks what is referred to as the "movement of desolation." This question can also take many similar forms, including:

> For what moment today am I least grateful?
> When did I give and receive the least love today?
> When did I most feel life draining out of me?
> When did I have the least sense of belonging?
> When was I saddest?
> What was my low point?

The movement of desolation can be understood in one of two ways. In its original conceptualization, St. Ignatius suggested that when an individual felt desolation, it was because the behavior or choice was being suggested or endorsed by "evil spirits," and was contrary to God's plan and will for that individual. A more recent theological interpretation of desolation is that it is God directing you away from a specific behavior or course of action (Linn, Linn, & Linn, 1995).

It is crucial that the form of the questions be developmentally appropriate and asked in a way that the individual finds appealing. In the vignette that follows, the questions were stated in a developmentally appropriate form for a six-year-old. Some individuals may feel very comfortable with a form such as, "In what circumstances did I feel the Life Energy flowing through me at the highest level today?" For others, such a question would seem awkward and silly. The questions should be stated in such a way that the individuals are comfortable with the form.

The examen ritual is completed with a prayer of gratitude for the guidance received. This discernment process, while straightforward, still requires discipline and patience. St. Ignatius instructs individuals undergoing the spiritual exercises process to be diligent.

It is important to note that this practice is meant to be integrated on a daily basis into an individual's life. Proper interpretation of the examen is arrived at by exploring patterns of consolation and desolation within the ongoing context of the individual's life. What, at first, may appear to be an inconsequential insight, when placed in the broader context of the individual's life, may lead to the realization of a larger pattern and have "divine" significance.

Some proponents suggest lighting a candle in a dark room and concentrating on the flame as way of becoming quiet and centered for the examen (Linn et al., 1995). As shown in the following vignette, it can also be used in a highly informal manner integrating the ritual into dinnertime conversation. Once again, the exact details as to how one goes about engaging in this ritual are not important but deference is made to personal comfort and regularity of use.

While the use of the examen has been described above as an individual practice, it can also be adapted to use as a family spiritual practice. Used consistently as described below in the vignette, the use of examen as a family can become a meaningful ritual within the spiritual life of the family.

Brief Vignette

This vignette will examine the impact of daily use of the examen for a family of three. This family consists of a father (Edward), a stepmother (Louise), and a six-year-old daughter (Grace). Edward and Louise are practicing Catholics and Grace belongs to a conservative Christian church that her mother attends. At the suggestion of a pastoral counselor, Edward obtained the book *Sleeping with Bread* (Linn et al., 1995) and initiated daily regular use of the examen with his family. Edward has joint custody of Grace, allowing him weekly visitation for an evening meal as well as every other weekend. Edward made the decision to implement the examen during mealtimes. This vignette will focus only on the use of the examen during meals when the entire family was present.

At the beginning of each meal that the family was present, after saying a prayer, Edward would begin the process by asking Grace, "What did you like the most today?" After she completely finished answering the question, he would then ask her, "What did you *not* like the most today?" When Grace was finished, she was then allowed to choose whom she would ask the questions. She would then choose either her father or her stepmother and ask the first question (of consolation). Family members are free to ask further questions getting the answeree to elaborate on the responses. When they had sufficiently explored the answer, Grace would then ask the second question (of desolation). When this person had finished with the second question, he or she then asked the remaining family member both questions. This ritual quickly became an integral aspect of family dining for the family. Grace particularly seemed to enjoy it and would initiate the questions, if her father failed to do so.

The regular use of the examen had two separate impacts on the family. First, it led to a deeper exploration of the daily lives of members than had occurred in the past when they may have asked each other in passing, "How was your day?" This was especially true for six-year-old Grace. She disclosed unhappy aspects of her life about which her father and stepmother would never have considered inquiring. In this way, the family was much more keenly aware of what was going on in one another's life. The second impact relates to the original purpose of the examen: discernment of God's will for the family members. Insights from this discernment process will be described for each family member.

At the time, Edward was wrestling with a career decision that potentially involved him moving a significant distance away from his daughter (who lives with her mother). This exciting career possibility would only last a year and had significant career advancing potential. When applying the examen to this aspect of his life, he came to realize that he felt great desolation

290 THE THERAPIST'S NOTEBOOK FOR INTEGRATING SPIRITUALITY IN COUNSELING

when considering being away from his daughter for a year, even allowing for long distance visits that would only exclude the midweek dinner visit. When considering what moments in his life brought consolation, these consistently revolved around being closely involved in his daughter's and wife's life. This pattern emerged over a time frame of several months of practicing the examen. In the end, he became convinced that God's will for him was to be as involved in his daughter's life as much as the joint custody agreement allowed and that an absence of weekly dinners was not worth the potential career advancement possibilities that the opportunity provided.

Louise used the examen to gain guidance and insight regarding what God's will was for her as well. She was having a very difficult time in her career as a computer programmer. Her moments of desolation consistently centered on how unhappy she was in her work. At first, she came to the conclusion that she needed to leave this field and retrain for a new career track. However, she also learned that a pattern was emerging that her moments of consolation many times centered around success that she had in specific challenging tasks in her work. Upon careful analysis and significant elaboration and discussion with her family members, she came to the conclusion that she actually enjoyed her work activities and that it was the social environment and dissatisfying interactions with her colleagues that was the cause of desolation. This prompted her to seek a new position in the same line of work but at an alternate company.

Interestingly, Grace's use of the examen also concerned career decisions. She had wanted to be a doctor since she was three years old. She enjoyed playing doctor with her dolls. When using the examen, she reported the most intense level of discomfort when her first grade class did an instructional module on the human brain and body systems. Her moments of desolation related to any discussion and particularly the visual depiction of human organs (in her words "inside body parts"). She had such a negative reaction that she instituted a list of topics that she requested would not be discussed during the meal, many of these involving any reference to "inside body parts." Through meal-based discussion, she came to the realization that she did not want to be a doctor as this would involve contact with and discussion of "inside body parts." When reflecting on her pattern of consolation, she came to the decision that what appealed to her about being a doctor was the aspect of actively helping people. She currently has the career aspiration of being a teacher, counselor, or poet. She sees these career choices as helping people but having no discussion or contact with "inside body parts."

An interesting side discussion to Grace's use of the examen is her discussion of unpleasant daily events that would probably never have surfaced without discussion of moments of desolation. One specific incident was that she was being mercilessly teased by an older child at her babysitter's house. She was able to discuss her feelings about being teased, explore options that she had for dealing with the situation, as well as engaging her father in the process of remedying the situation.

Although each person benefited individually from this family's ritualized use of the examen, the marital relationship was also strengthened, as this practice opened room for both partners to share openly about their struggles and joys. Similarly, the relationship between Louise, the stepmother, and Grace was strengthened, as Grace came to understand her stepmother as someone who had her own personal difficulties and vulnerabilities. The family as a whole developed a greater bond and unity, as all of them came to look forward to this time of sharing at mealtimes.

Suggestions for Follow-Up

Families (or couples) may choose to include more ritual-based prayer of reflective practices into their lives beyond the examen. Some excellent resources are suggested at the end of this chapter to assist you in identifying ways to incorporate spirituality into your daily lives.

Contraindications

The examen was designed to discern God's will for an individual. This is a comfortable concept for individuals from the main monotheistic religions and 12-step programs. If an individual does not embrace the concept of a *personal* Divine Being, this practice may still have some benefit in contributing to personal involvement in family member's lives. By a *personal* God, this author refers to forms of spirituality in which the individual believes in a Higher Power who is available for the development of a relationship and who may become involved in the daily life of the individual. This could be contrasted to individuals who have a "clockmaker" image of God, where, although God created the universe, He is not immediately involved in its unfolding. Some polytheistic traditions may not have this concept of a *personal* God. As stated, even if the couple/family are agnostic or atheistic, this practice still has benefit in the form of heightened awareness of the vicissitudes of each others' lives.

References

Fleming, D. L. (1981). *Notes on the spiritual exercises of St. Ignatius of Loyola.* St. Louis, MO: Review for Religious.

Linn, D., Linn, S. F., & Linn, M. (1995). *Sleeping with bread: Holding what gives you life.* New York: Paulist Press.

Professional Readings and Resources

Fleming, D. L. (1981). *Notes on the spiritual exercises of St. Ignatius of Loyola.* St. Louis, MO: Review for Religious.

Meissner, W. W. (1999). *To the greater glory: A psychological study of Ignatian spirituality (Marquette Studies in Theology, No 16).* Milwaukee, WI: Marquette University Press.

Newman, J. W. (1996). *Disciplines of attention: Buddhist insight meditation, the Ignatian spiritual exercises, and classical psychoanalysis (Asian Thought and Culture, Vol. 26).* New York: Peter Lang Publishing.

Bibliotherapy Sources for the Client

Callahan, W. R. (1994). *Noisy contemplation.* Hyattsville, MD: Quixote Center Inc.

Fossum, M., & Fossum, M. (1992). *Making time for God: Daily devotions for children and families to share.* Grand Rapids, MI: Baker Book House.

Hamma, R. M. (1995). *Let's say grace: Mealtime prayers for family occasions throughout the year.* Notre Dame, IN: Ave Maria Press.

Linn, D., Linn, S. F., & Linn, M. (1995). *Sleeping with bread: Holding what gives you life.* New York: Paulist Press.

Spohn, D. (1998). *Gift: Daily meditations for families (Hazelden Meditation Series).* Center City, MN: Hazelden Information Education.

Travnikar, R., & Luebering, C. (2002). *The blessing cup: Prayer-rituals for families and groups.* Cincinnati, OH: St. Anthony Messenger Press.

Vlaun, J., & Gaeta, F. X. (1999). *Life, love and laughter: The spirituality of the consciousness examen.* Totowa, NJ: Resurrection Press.

Handout:
The Use of the Examen: Questions About Consolation and Desolation

Instructions: To begin the use of the examen, enter a relaxed state, ask for divine guidance in prayer, and then respond to the two sets of specific questions that follow. These questions do not have to be worded or used exactly as printed below, but can be adapted to include your own language and way of expressing yourself. You might want to find a place that is peaceful or soothing to you as you reflect on the questions. You also might want to darken the room, and light a candle as you reflect.

Questions About Moments of Consolation

For what moment today am I the most grateful?
When did I give and receive the most love today?
When did I feel the most alive today?
When did I have the greatest sense of belonging to myself, others, God, and the universe?
When was I the happiest today?
What was today's high point?

Questions About Moments of Desolation

For what moment today am I least grateful?
When did I give and receive the least love today?
When did I most feel life draining out of me?
When did I have the least sense of belonging?
When was I saddest?
What was my low point?

After you have spent some time on these two questions, reflect upon how these moments of consolation and desolation might be viewed as God directing you toward or away from a specific behavior or course of action.

Priester, P. E. (2006). Integrating the discernment of spiritual guidance in family and couples therapy: Use of the examen. In K. B. Helmeke & C. F. Sori (Eds.), *The therapist's notebook for integrating spirituality in counseling: Homework, handouts, and activities for use in psychotherapy* (pp. 287-292). Binghamton, NY: The Haworth Press.

Index

Page numbers followed by the letter "f" indicate figures.